D0471096

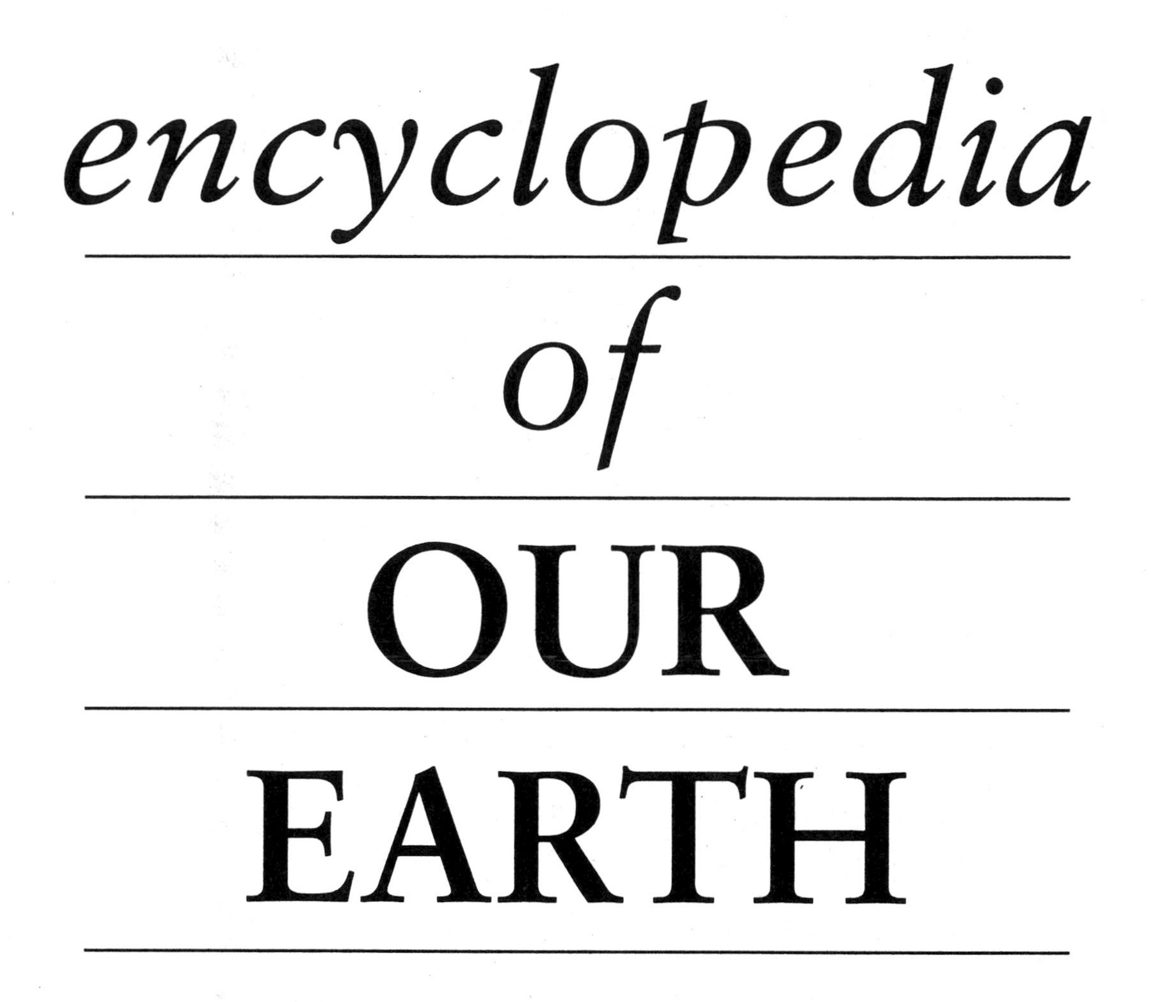
encyclopedia
of
OUR
EARTH

This edition produced in 1995 for
Shooting Star Press Inc
230 Fifth Avenue
Suite 1212
New York, NY 10001

© Aladdin Books Ltd 1995

Designed and produced by
Aladdin Books Ltd
28 Percy Street
London W1P 0LD

All rights reserved

Printed in Italy

ISBN 1-57335-146-6

Some of the material in this book was previously published in the Hands on Geography and Save our Earth series

MAIN CONTENTS

encyclopedia of OUR EARTH

Written by

John Clark, David Flint, Tony Hare, Keith Hare and Clint Twist

Illustrated by

Ron Hayward, Ian Moores, Alex Pang, Mike Saunders and Simon Tegg

SHOOTING STAR PRESS

INTRODUCTION TO ECOSYSTEMS

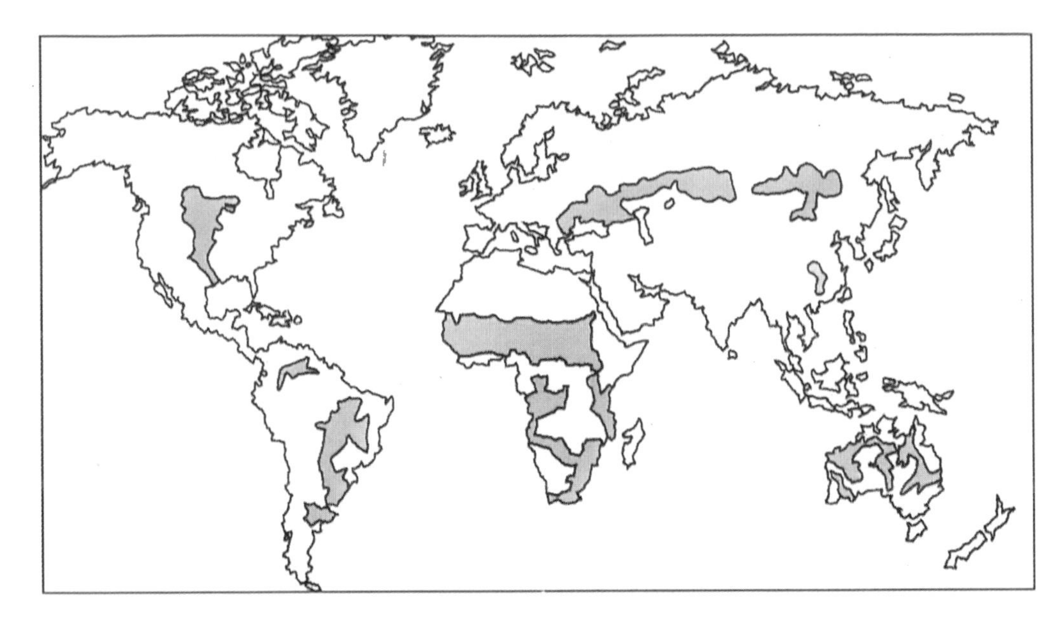

Grasslands

Our earth contains many different patterns of wildlife, or ecosystems, that are governed by various features, such as the climate and the local geographical features. Grasslands, above, occupy areas of land within the larger continents. These include the steppes of Russia, the pampas of South America and the prairies of North America.

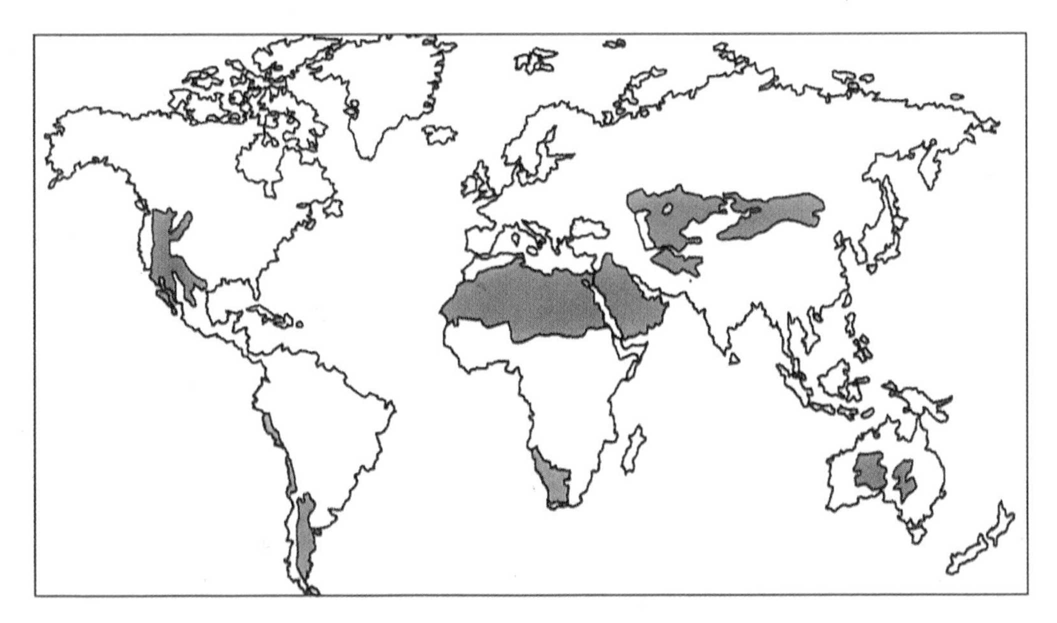

Deserts

The dry, and largely barren regions of the world are known as deserts, above. These include the Sahara in Africa, the Mojave in North America and the Gobi in northern China. Many deserts, such as the Sahara, are growing larger all the time. This is due to bad farming practices and deforestation which damages the land that surrounds them.

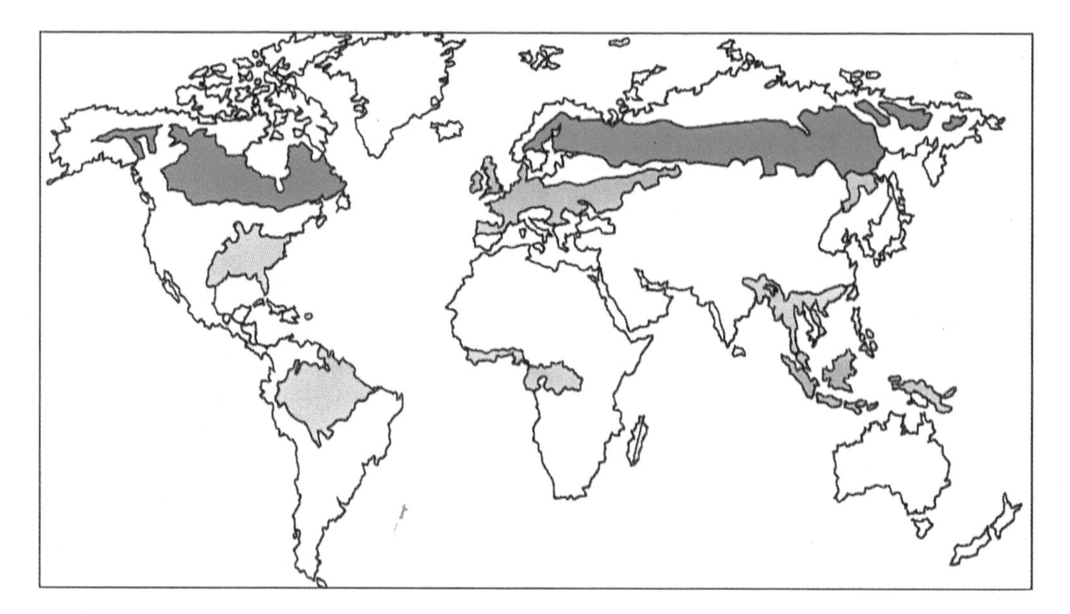

Forests

In contrast to deserts, the wetter parts of the world are covered in forests, above. These include rainforests which are situated on the equator in South America, Africa and Southeast Asia. Further away from the equator are the deciduous forests of Europe and North America. Further still are coniferous forests which occupy a harsher climate, as found in northern Russia and Canada.

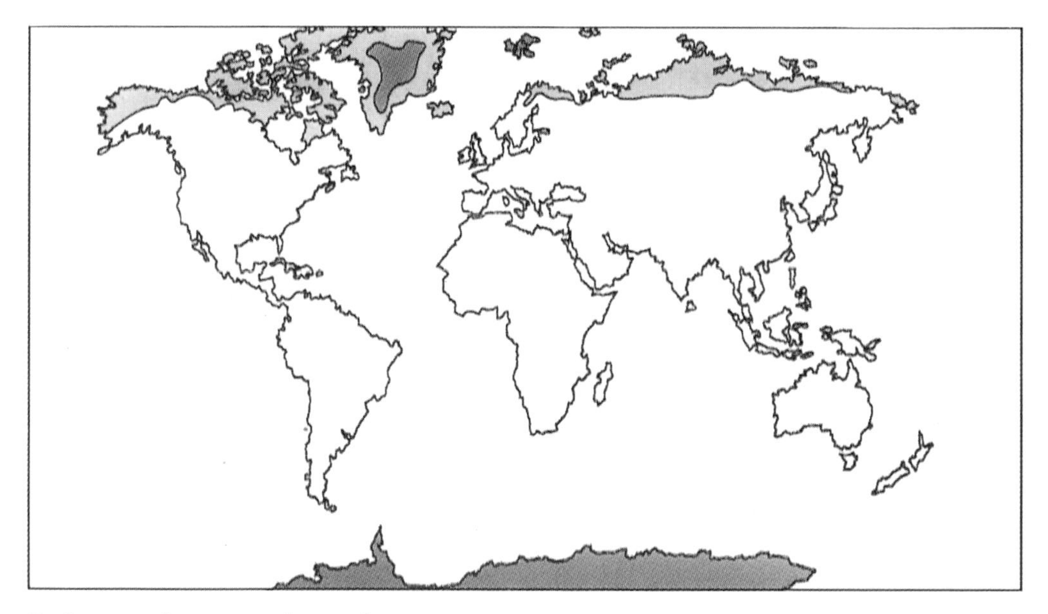

Polar regions and tundra

At the very top and bottom of our planet are found the polar regions, above. The climate here is cold and dry, and most of the land is classified as tundra, with very little plant and animal life. In the very coldest regions, such as Antarctica and Greenland, huge sheets of ice, known as ice caps, cover the ground throughout the year.

HOW TO USE THIS BOOK

This book concerns itself with our earth. The topics covered range from the atmosphere that blankets the planet to the jungles and forests. It takes you through the realms of ice and snow to the murky depths of the ocean floor. The book tells you what causes such phenomena as earthquakes and weather, while easy-to-understand photos and illustrations reveal many of the secrets that occur above, around and beneath our very feet. Special feature sections focus on the human impact in different parts of the environment, and the effects for life on earth. There are "hands on" projects for you to do which use everyday items as equipment, allowing you to experience how our earth works at first hand. There are also "did you know?" panels which supply fascinating information about the world in which you live.

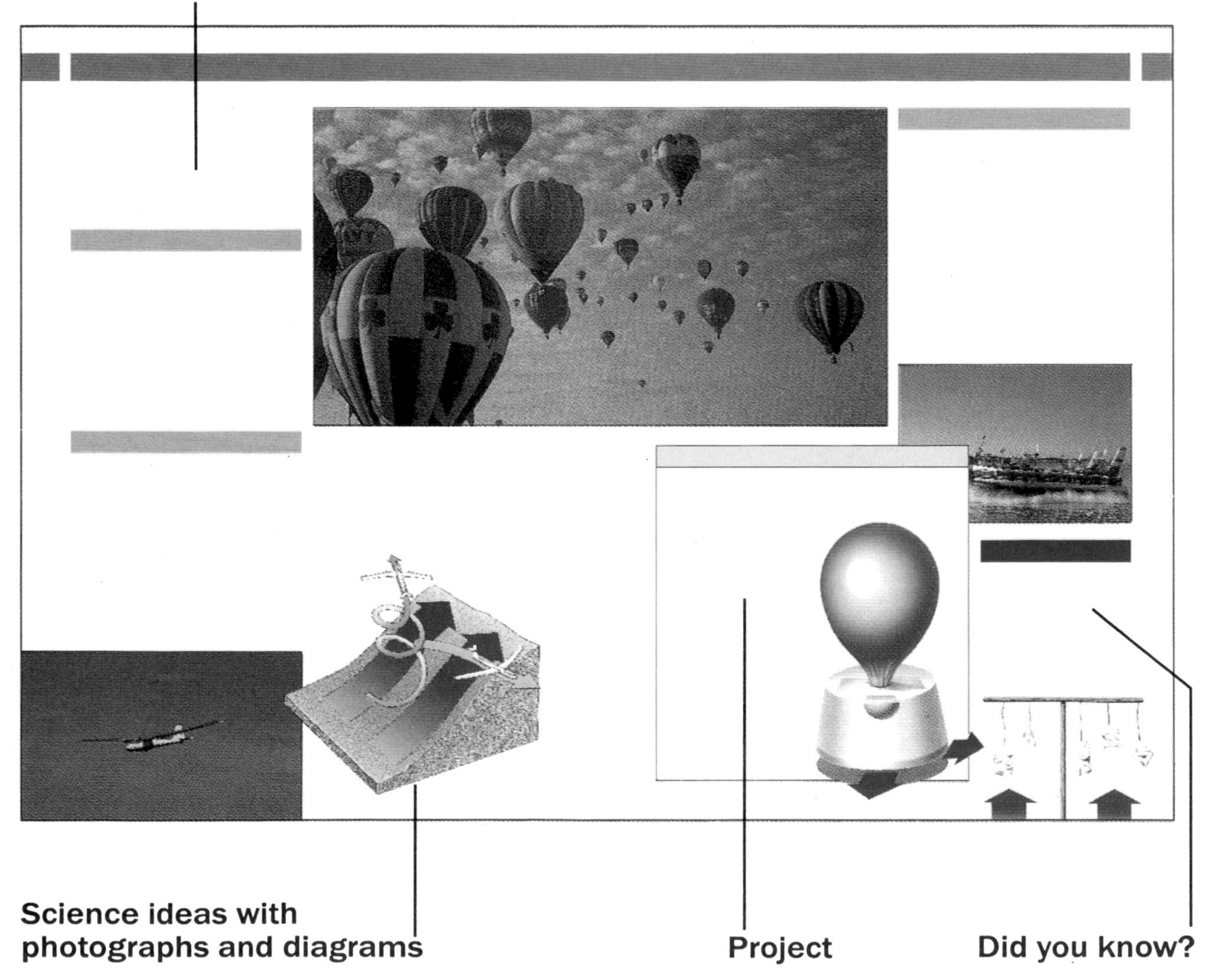

THE ATMOSPHERE

CHAPTER 1

CHAPTER ONE:
THE ATMOSPHERE

THE OZONE LAYER

INTRODUCTION

The atmosphere is the blanket of air that surrounds the earth, held there by the force of gravity. It consists of a mixture of gases, three of which (nitrogen, oxygen and carbon dioxide) play key roles in the maintenance of life on earth. Movement of the air in the lower atmosphere creates winds, which in turn are responsible for much of our weather.

The atmosphere is not the same all the way up. It is densest near the ground, but gets thinner with altitude until it fades into the nothingness of outer space. Although the atmosphere reaches several hundred miles above our heads, on a global scale proportionally it is as thin as the skin of an apple.

Unfortunately, the activities of humankind are changing the air around us, and atmospheric pollution must be stopped before some of the effects — described in this chapter — take their toll on life on earth.

Life is dependent on the envelope of air surrounding the earth.

COMPOSITION OF THE ATMOSPHERE

The atmosphere has developed in distinct stages. The early atmosphere was determined by processes involved in the formation of the earth and its early evolution. The development of life has had a great influence on the atmosphere, increasing the oxygen content dramatically over a short period.

DEVELOPMENT

The early atmosphere of the earth is believed to have consisted predominantly of nitrogen, carbon dioxide, carbon monoxide, water vapor, hydrogen and inert gases. Solar winds may have removed a lot of the primitive atmosphere in the first billion years of the earth's life.

As the earth cooled, gases escaped from the interior to form the atmosphere, predominantly through volcanoes. This volcanic activity increased water vapor, carbon dioxide, hydrogen sulfide and nitrogen in the atmosphere.

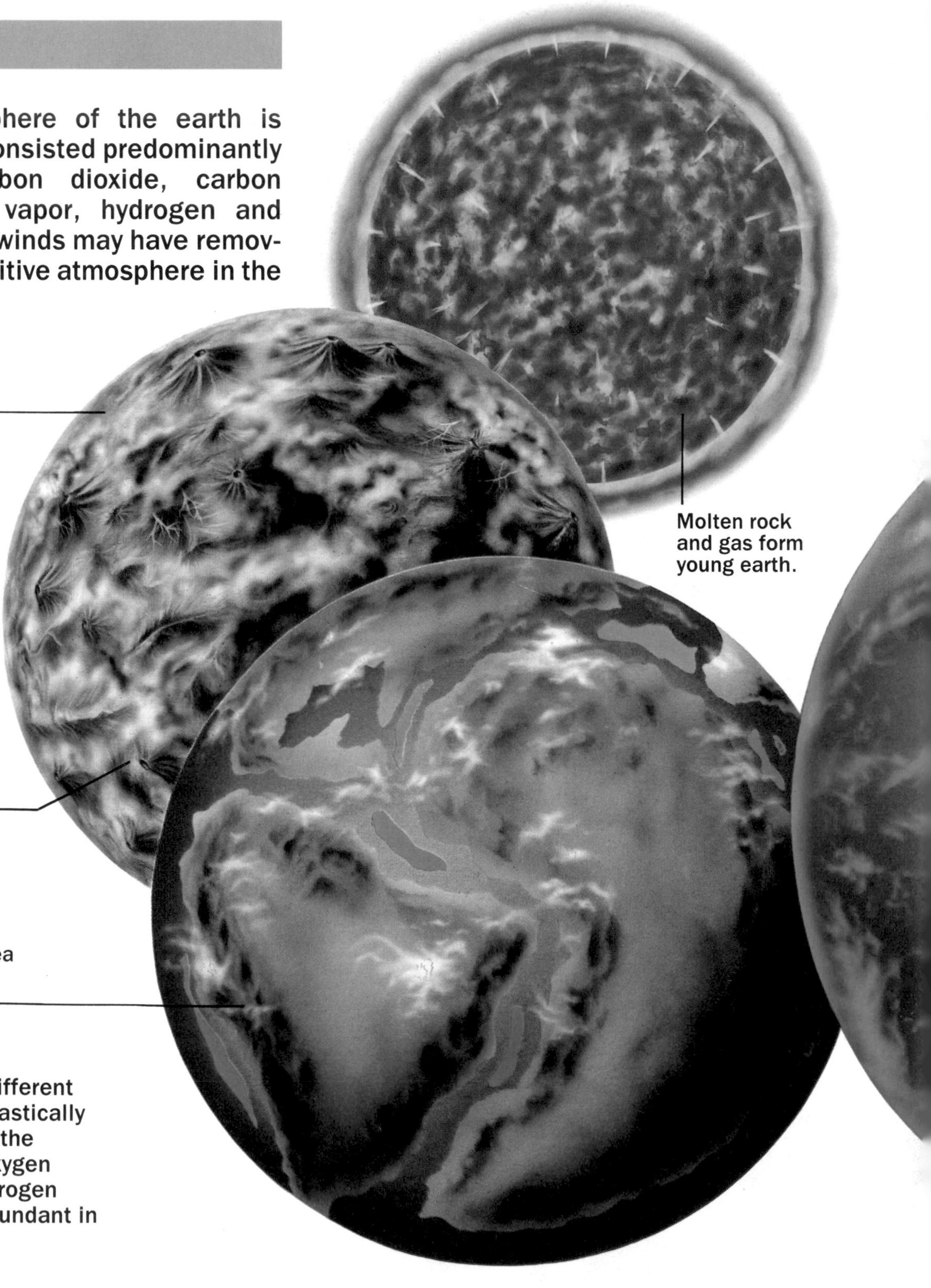

Surface cools and early crust forms.

Molten rock and gas form young earth.

Volcanoes release gases and water vapor.

Mountains and sea appear. Plant life evolves.

▷ The proportion of different gases has changed drastically since the evolution of the earth. Nitrogen and oxygen have replaced the hydrogen and carbon dioxide abundant in the early atmosphere.

As water vapor increased, the saturation point of the atmosphere was eventually reached and water started to collect to form the oceans. Carbon dioxide was absorbed into the oceans. Green plants evolved that use sunlight to make carbohydrates from CO_2 and water. Green plants also expel oxygen into the atmosphere. This process is called photosynthesis.

Today's atmosphere appears blue.

▽ The earth's atmosphere has been changing throughout its history. The advent of photosynthetic life has contributed significantly by greatly increasing the oxygen content.

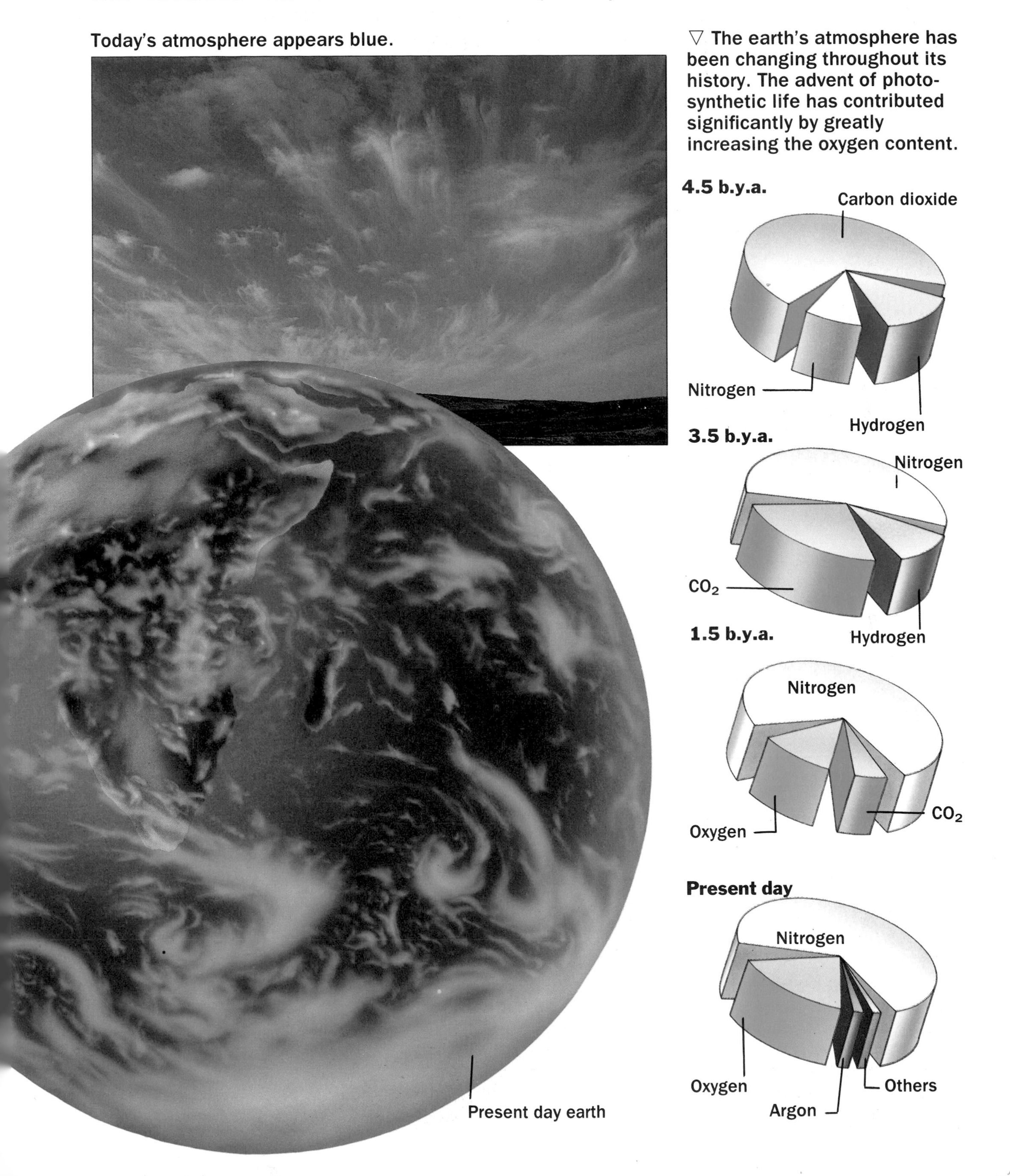

STRUCTURE OF THE ATMOSPHERE

The atmosphere can be divided into various layers. The bottom layer, the troposphere, extends about 7 miles above the earth's surface. It contains about 80 percent of atmospheric gases. Climatic variations occur in this layer.

Above this the stratosphere extends to 30 miles above the ground and includes the ozone layer which protects the surface from harmful radiation from the sun.

Then the mesosphere extends to about 50 miles above the surface. The temperature drops gradually to a minimum of −300°F.

Above this lies the thermosphere, where temperatures may rise to several thousand degrees Fahrenheit. It stretches over thousands of miles, gradually merging with space. The layer above 300 miles is the exosphere.

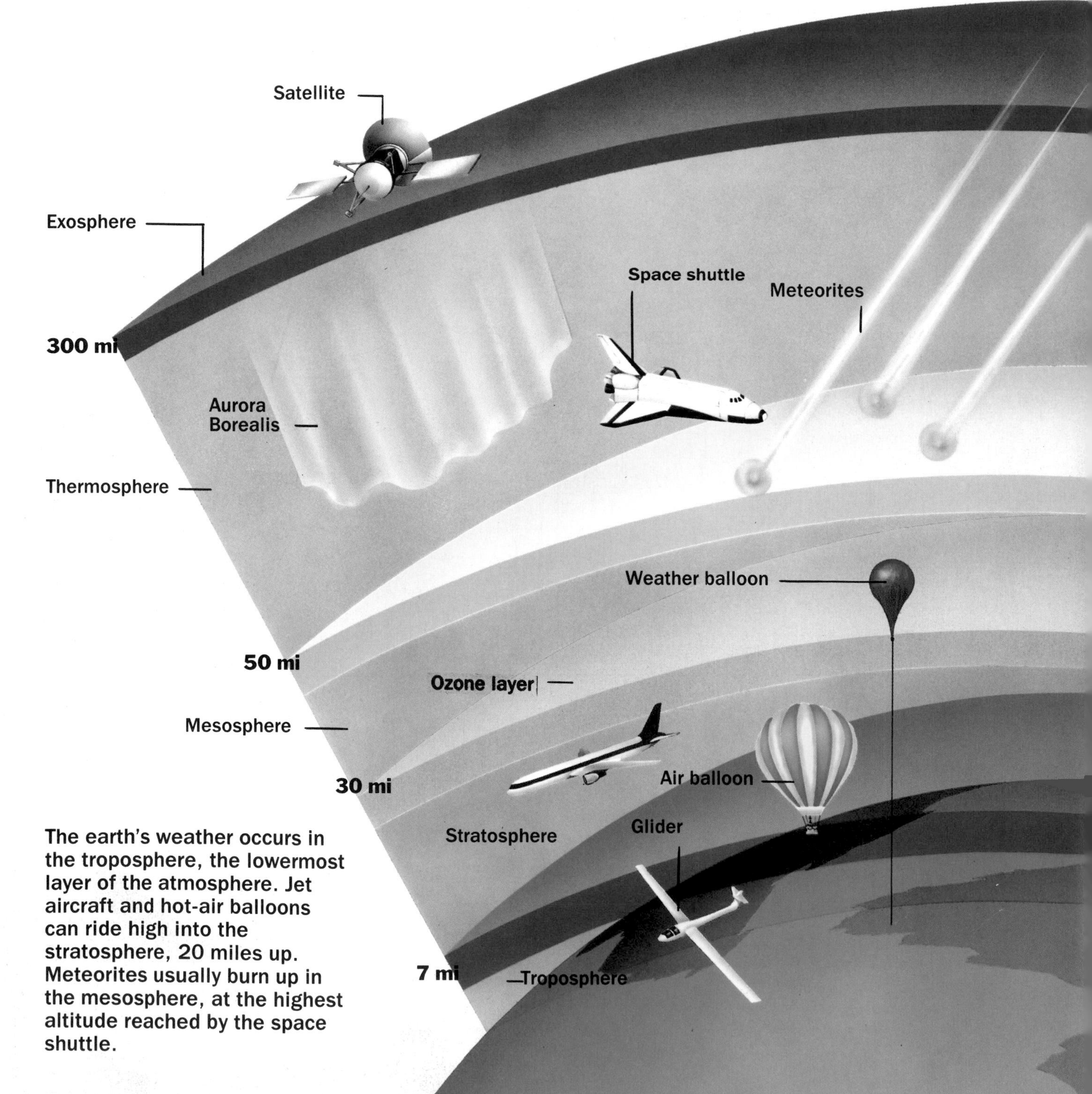

The earth's weather occurs in the troposphere, the lowermost layer of the atmosphere. Jet aircraft and hot-air balloons can ride high into the stratosphere, 20 miles up. Meteorites usually burn up in the mesosphere, at the highest altitude reached by the space shuttle.

IONOSPHERE

The ionosphere is a layer of electrically charged particles (also called D, E and F layers) between the mesosphere and thermosphere. The particles are ions, which are gas atoms stripped of their electrons. Normally radio waves can only reach places within line-of-sight of the transmitter. But if the waves travel up into the atmosphere, they bounce off the ionosphere and reach distant places.

Reflected radio (sky waves)
Ionosphere
Transmitter

▷ Long-distance radio communication is possible because radio waves bounce off the ionosphere. The ionized gases in the ionosphere also emit a faint light called an airglow, which prevents even the darkest night sky from being truly black.

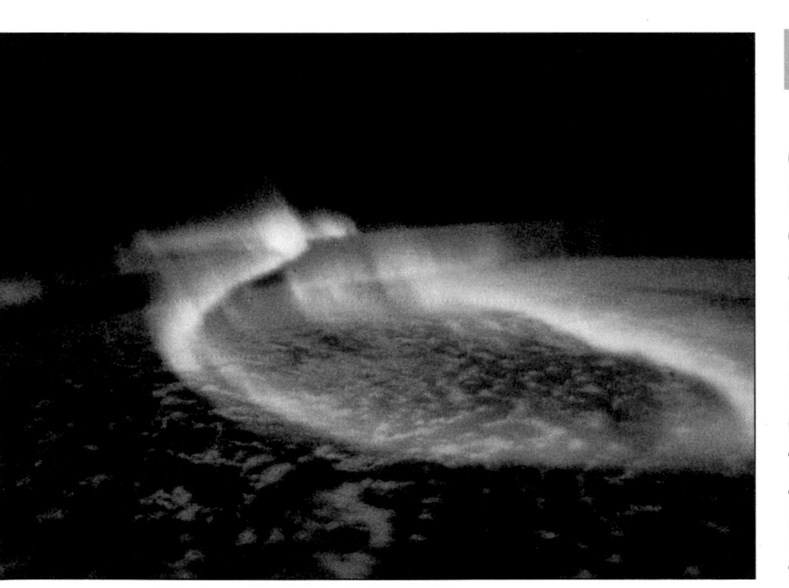

△ Solar winds, composed of charged particles streaming out of the sun, collide with the upper atmosphere over the poles resulting in colorful light displays called aurorae.

▷ The red sky of a sunset is caused by dust particles in the atmosphere scattering red light. For this to happen, the air has to be dry indicating that the following day may be fine.

COLORED SKIES

On a cloudless day, the sky looks blue. But the gases in the atmosphere are not colored. White light from the sun is actually made up of all the colors of the rainbow, which when mixed together make white. The gases and dust particles in the atmosphere scatter the blue colors, or wavelengths, of sunlight, more than the other colors so the sky appears to be blue. At sunset, dust near the horizon also scatters the light, but this time it is red that is scattered.

ATMOSPHERIC DENSITY

The gases that make up the atmosphere, although light, do have mass. Under the influence of gravity, such as that exerted by the earth, the gases of the atmosphere have weight. But because the atmosphere gets thinner with altitude, most of its mass is concentrated in the thin, lowermost layer, the troposphere.

▷ The 9-mile thick troposphere, the lowermost layer of the atmosphere, contains more than four-fifths of the atmosphere's mass. But because the atmosphere thins with altitude, the troposphere contains only 1.5 percent of the atmosphere's volume.

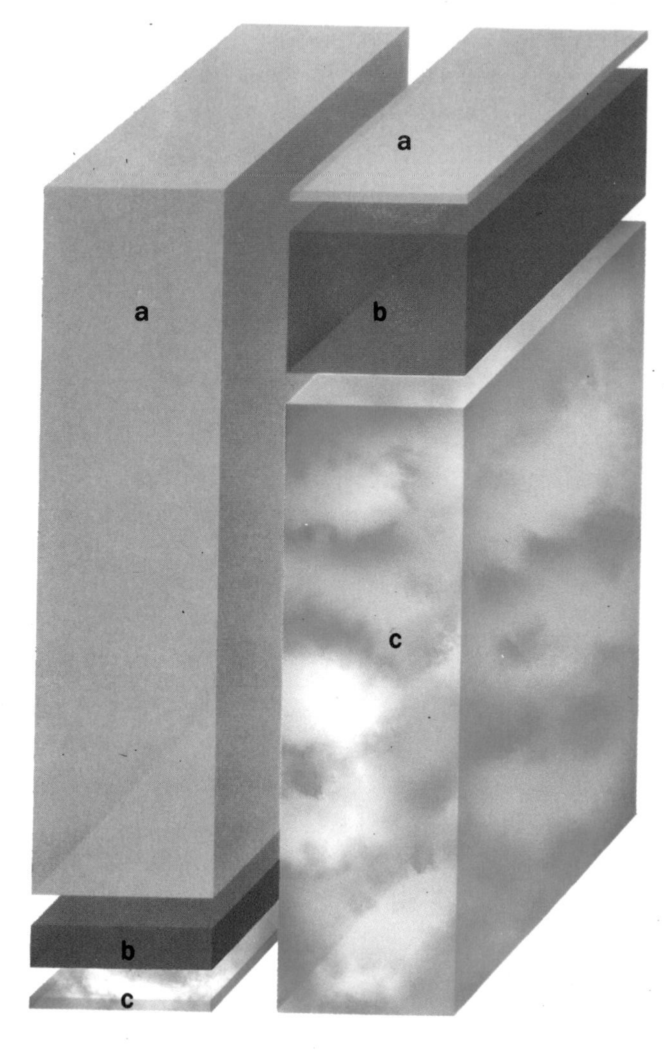

▽ Mountaineers on high peaks need oxygen masks.

ALTITUDE

The atmosphere gets less dense with altitude – the higher you go, the thinner the air becomes. As the air gets thinner, it contains less oxygen. This has two important consequences. First, high-flying passenger aircraft have to have sealed cabins containing air under pressure so that people can breathe normally. Second, by about 30 miles there is not enough oxygen to burn the fuel in an aircraft's jet engines. Above that height rocket motors have to be used. These burn fuel in the absence of an external source of oxygen.

Altimeters used in aircraft measure height above sea level. They work in the same way as barometers in measuring changes in atmospheric pressure. Pressure changes can be read from the altimeter and translated accurately into height above sea level on a dial. The altimeter contains a near-vacuum capsule which alters in size with changes in pressure. This capsule is attached to an arm which relays these movements to a rocking bar, which is in turn attached to a needle on a dial mounted on a hairspring. The dial is calibrated so that pressure changes correspond to height. This enables the pilot to keep the aircraft at the prescribed altitude.

LIGHTER THAN AIR

Because air has density, anything that is less dense than air floats in it — just as a piece of wood , which is less dense than water, floats. Some gases, such as hydrogen and helium, are less dense than air. So a balloon or blimp filled with one of these gases floats in air. Hydrogen is the lightest of all gases, but it is also very flammable and therefore dangerous to use. Helium does not burn and so is generally used for filling weather balloons and blimps. A gas expands and becomes less dense when it is heated. For this reason, it is possible to make a balloon by filling a cloth bag with hot air. Hot-air balloons are used for sport and leisure (see page 22).

A weather balloon is filled with helium.

WEIGHING AIR

Air has mass and so it can be weighed. To show this, make a sensitive balance. Tie two canes about 20 inches long to a length of string suspended as shown. Attach two balloons to the ends of the lower cane with thread and adjust them until they balance. Mark where the right-hand balloon is and then blow it up with air. Tie it and put it back in the same place. The filled balloon is heavier than the empty balloon because of the air it contains.

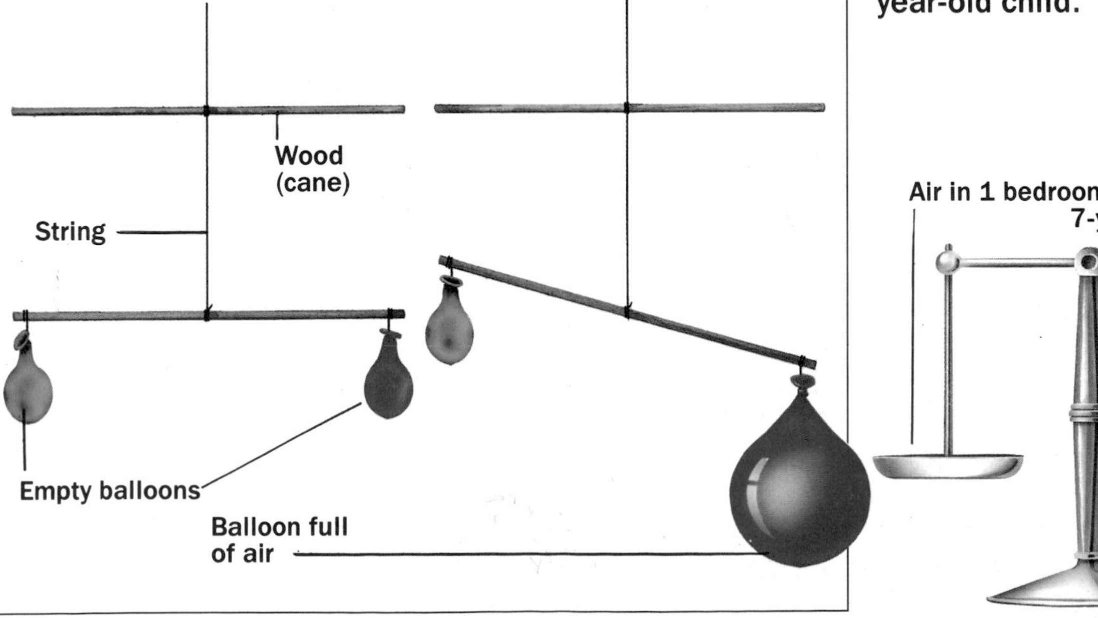

DID YOU KNOW?

The density of a substance is its mass divided by its volume. The density of air is about 1.4 ounces per cubic foot. The air in a small bedroom with a volume of 706 cubic feet weighs 62 pounds, or about the same weight as a seven-year-old child.

AIR PRESSURE

The mass of air in the atmosphere presses down on the surface of the earth and everything on it. At sea-level, this atmospheric pressure is 14.7 pounds per square foot. But at high altitudes, where the air is much thinner, the pressure decreases, until at the outer edge of the atmosphere it falls to zero.

Air pressure is lower on high peaks.

DISCOVER AIR PRESSURE

Put a sheet of paper over one end of a slim ruler. Hit the other end of the ruler as it hangs over a table. The force preventing the ruler from tipping is air pressure.

▽ The air is less dense in the upper atmosphere because there are fewer gas atoms in each cubic foot. The air is therefore at a lower pressure than it is nearer the ground.

WEIGHT OF AIR

The existence of the weight of the air pressing down on everything around us is demonstrated by the simple experiment shown on the left. This natural air pressure also presses on us, and it can be useful. For example, it forces air into our lungs so that we can breathe in the oxygen the atmosphere contains. But in order for us to breathe out again, muscles around our rib cage and diaphragm have to work to squeeze the air out of our lungs at an even higher pressure than that of the atmosphere.

BOILING POINT

When a liquid is heated, molecules leap out of the surface to form a gas or vapor. The vapor has a pressure, called the liquid's vapor pressure. When the vapor pressure equals the atmospheric pressure pushing on the surface of the liquid, the liquid boils. But we have seen that atmospheric pressure varies with altitude, being lower at high altitudes. So what happens when you try to boil a liquid at the top of a high mountain? At sea level, water boils at 212°F. But at high altitudes it boils at temperatures as low as 176°F. This is because the atmospheric pressure is lower and it takes less energy for the vapor pressure to reach the atmospheric pressure.

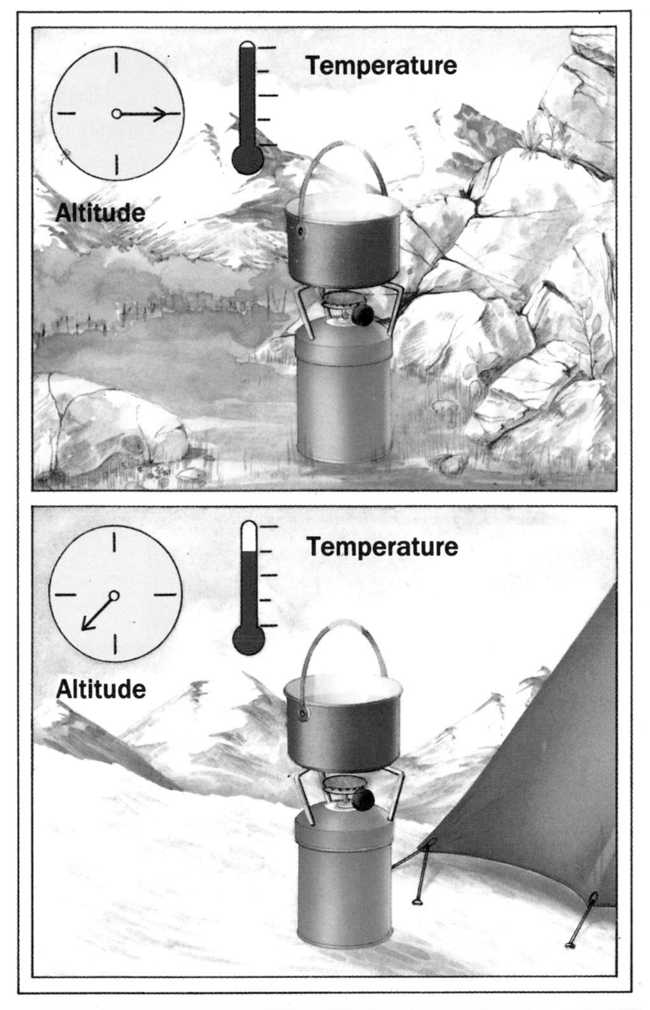

▷ At low altitudes, water boils at 212°F. At high altitudes, as at the top of a tall mountain, water still boils, but at a much lower temperature.

Spacesuits resist the vacuum of space.

AIRLESS SPACE

In outer space, beyond the earth's atmosphere, there is no air at all. Therefore, there is no atmospheric pressure, just an empty vacuum. The vacuum is more complete than any that can be produced in a laboratory. Obviously, a human being cannot breathe in space. Indeed, without atmospheric pressure, a person's blood would boil and his or her body explode. To overcome both of these problems, astronauts who enter free space wear spacesuits. These are pressurized and supplied with air or oxygen, so that the astronaut's lungs can work properly and the boiling point of his body fluids remains normal. The suit also does something else that the atmosphere normally does for us. Its silvery surface reflects back the sun's heat rays and blocks other harmful radiation.

Changes in atmospheric pressure are largely responsible for changes in the weather. The chief effects of pressure changes are winds and other air movements, which in turn control the movements of clouds and rain. For these reasons, weather forecasting relies heavily on measuring air pressure.

▽ In high-pressure areas cool air spirals downward – clockwise in the northern hemisphere. In low-pressure areas, warm air spirals upward in the opposite direction.

LOW PRESSURE

Warm air rises

Air is drawn in counterclockwise

HIGH PRESSURE

Cool air sinks to the surface

Air spirals out clockwise

HIGHS AND LOWS

When a weather forecaster writes "HIGH" on a weather map, he or she is indicating the location of a high-pressure area in which descending cool air gradually spirals outward. The cone of moving air is called an anticyclone. A "LOW," or low-pressure area, is just the opposite. It occurs when warm air rises, causing it to spiral outward as it climbs. This is called a cyclone or depression.

In the northern hemisphere, the air in an anticyclone spirals in a clockwise direction, whereas a cyclone (depression) has winds rotating counterclockwise. The directions of rotation are reversed in the southern hemisphere. This is due to the effect of the earth's rotation. Anticyclones are usually associated with fine settled weather and light winds near the ground. Cyclones tend to bring cloudy, wet weather with strong winds.

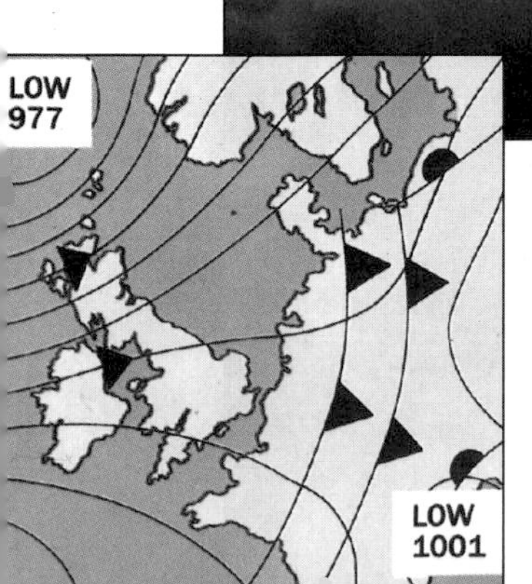

◁△ Storm clouds often form in areas of low pressure. On a weather map (left), isobars (lines) join places with the same pressure. Isobars close together indicate strong winds.

INSIDE A DEPRESSION

In meteorology – the study of weather – the boundary between a mass of warm air and a mass of cold, denser air is called a front. When a mass of cold air forces itself under a mass of warm air, a cold front forms. The warm air is forced up rapidly to create a deep depression, often with heavy rainfall. When a mass of warm air catches up with a mass of cold air, the result is a warm front. The warm air rises only slowly, creating only a shallow depression, and any rain is light or even just drizzle.

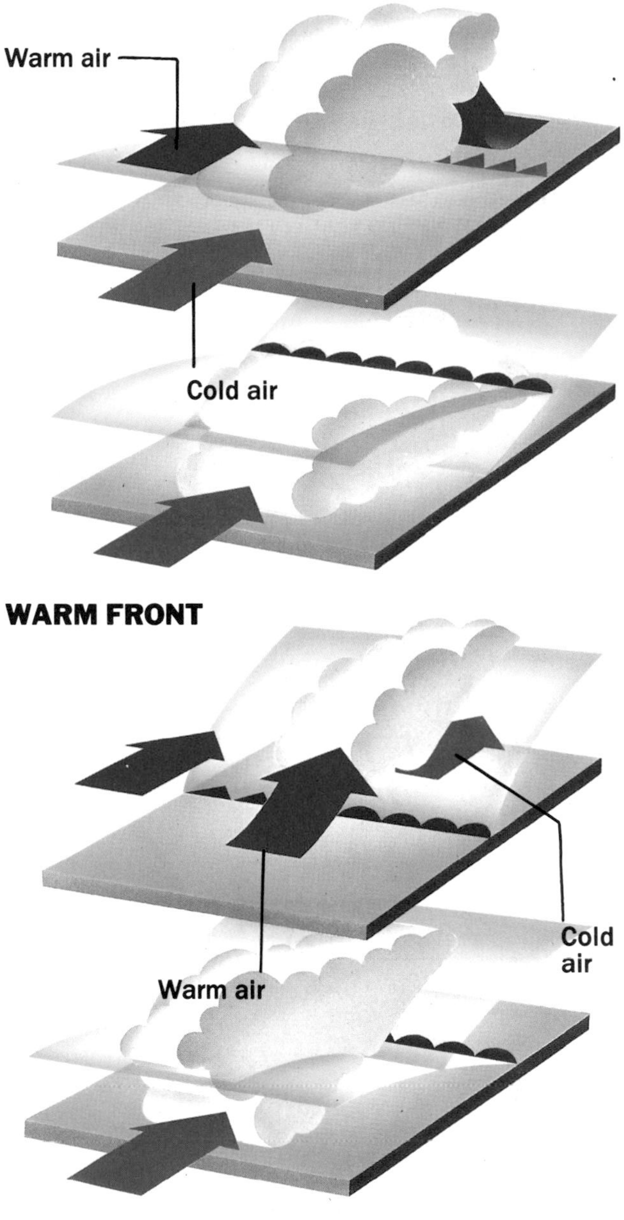

▷ On a weather map, the symbol for a cold front is a line with a series of triangles along it. A warm front is represented by a line with a series of semicircles.

MAKING A BAROMETER

Tape plastic wrap over an icecream tub. Attach a pin to one end of a straw, and glue some thread to the other end. Pivot the straw to an upright sheet of cardboard, with a pin stuck into modeling clay. Tape the thread to the plastic wrap, and draw a scale by the pointer.

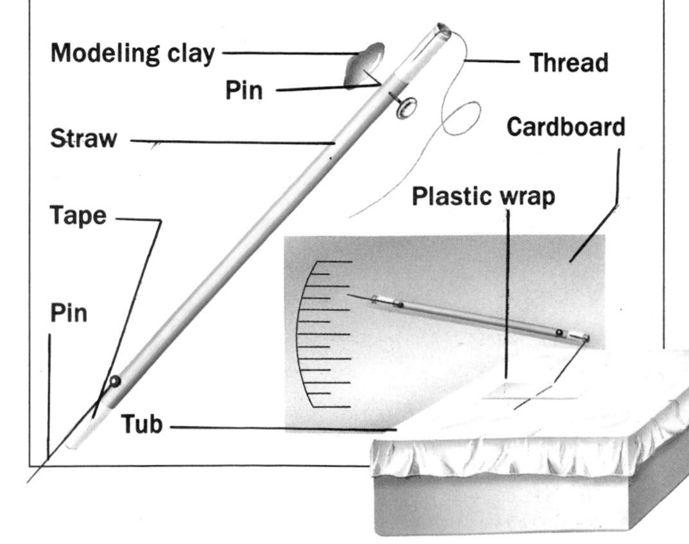

The barometer on the left works only if the icecream tub is airtight. The outside pressure varies daily, but the pressure in the tub should remain roughly the same. As the outside pressure increases, it pushes in on the plastic wrap causing the pointer to move up the scale. If the outside pressure decreases, the higher pressure in the tub pushes the plastic wrap out causing the pointer to move down across the scale. This works best if the barometer is kept at a constant temperature.

COMPRESSED AIR

Like all gases, air can be compressed – that is, it can be squeezed so that it occupies a smaller space. But because the smaller volume now contains more gas molecules than usual, the gas exerts a higher pressure. The pressure of a compressed gas can be made to work for us in many ways.

BICYCLE PUMP

The tire on a bicycle contains air at higher than atmospheric pressure. The air is forced into it using a pump, which takes air from the atmosphere and compresses it. The pump consists of a tube or barrel with a tight-fitting piston at the end of a long handle. The piston has a one-way valve that opens to let air into the pump as the handle is drawn back. But when the handle is pushed forward, the valve closes and the piston compresses the air in the tube.

On the input stroke of a bicycle pump, the piston is drawn back and air enters the barrel. On the compression stroke, the piston moves forward to compress the air.

PNEUMATIC DRILL

Drills used to dig up the road function through a pneumatic mechanism. The term “pneumatic” means that the drill is driven by compressed air. It is usually driven by a compressor run on a diesel engine. This increases the safety of the drill as it does away with the need for electrical wires trailing across public streets. The drill mechanism causes rapid hammering blows of the drill head on the road surface. This is achieved by a valve in the drill which flips up and down many times a second, rerouting the air around a piston, alternately raising and lowering the drill head.

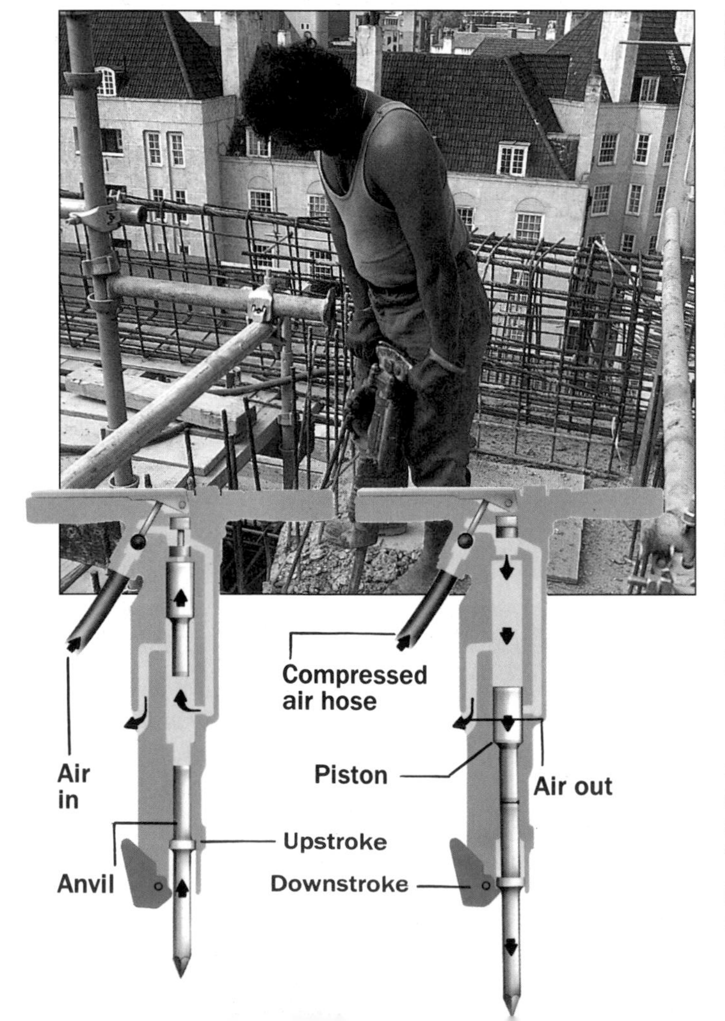

A pneumatic drill is driven by compressed air, usually from a diesel-engined compressor. The air pressure makes a piston drive the drill point downward.

FIRE EXTINGUISHER

Air is not the only gas that is useful when it is compressed. Carbon dioxide, one of the trace gases in the atmosphere, has many applications. Small cylinders of compressed carbon dioxide are used in domestic carbonated drink-makers. Carbon dioxide gas pressure works various types of fire extinguishers, such as those that spray out a white vapor for putting out electrical fires.

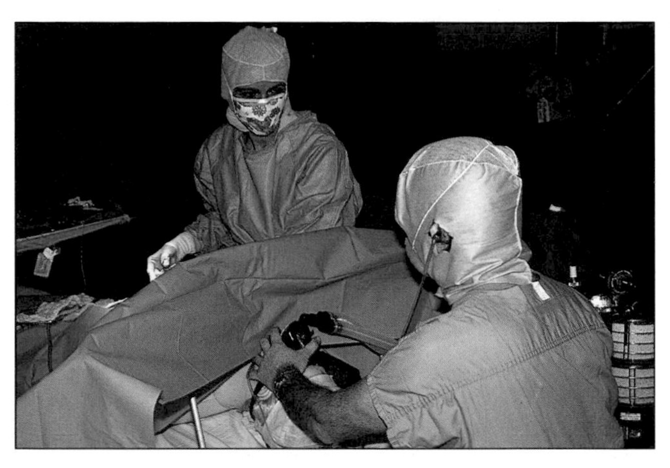

An anesthetist mixes various gases.

A carbon dioxide fire extinguisher

ANESTHETICS

An anesthetist, who is a doctor who puts a patient to sleep for surgery, uses various chemicals, all of which are supplied as compressed gases in metal cylinders. Dentists also sometimes use anesthetic gases. Chief of these are nitrous oxide, once called laughing gas, and a gas called halothane. Anesthetists usually mix these gases with oxygen, also from cylinders.

AEROSOLS

Aerosols are the familiar spray cans that we use every day. They give sprays of a wide range of liquids, from paint and insect killer to perfume and deodorant. The liquid is sold in a metal can, which also contains a propellant gas under pressure. When the button is pressed, it opens a valve so that the compressed gas pushes the liquid up the narrow tube through a jet in the form of a fine spray.

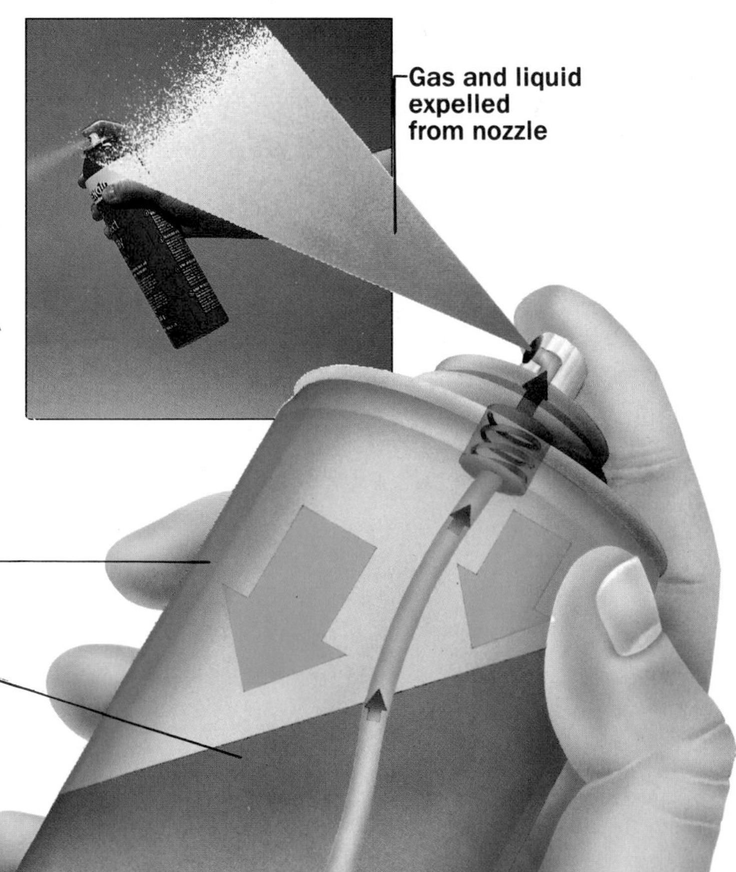

▷ Various gases have been used as propellants in aerosol sprays. Some of the gases used, called CFCs, get into the atmosphere where they damage the ozone layer.

WARM AIR FLOW

The fact that warm air rises is responsible for winds and much of our weather (see pages 14-15 and 18-19). The reason it rises is because warm air is less dense than cooler air. Several other things make use of this effect, including hot-air balloons, and birds and aircraft that glide on thermals.

HOT-AIR BALLOONS

The first hot-air balloons were made in France in 1783 by the Montgolfier brothers. The brothers were paper-makers and these early balloons were made of paper or silk. Today the balloon is made of a fabric such as nylon. A butane gas burner beneath it pumps hot air into the balloon, and a basket hanging beneath the burner carries people. Modern hot-air balloons have reached heights of more than 22 miles.

Hot-air ballooning is a popular pastime.

THERMALS

Currents of rising warm air are called thermals. They often occur near the edges of cliffs or steep hills. Near cliffs, soaring birds such as gulls and fulmars use the thermals over the sea to gain height on stationary wings. Gliders do the same thing, spiraling slowly upward on the updraft of warm air. Even when a glider loses height, a skilful pilot can usually "find" another thermal and spiral upward again.

▽ After being winched into the air or towed by a powered aircraft, a glider gains extra height by spiraling upward on a thermal of rising warm air.

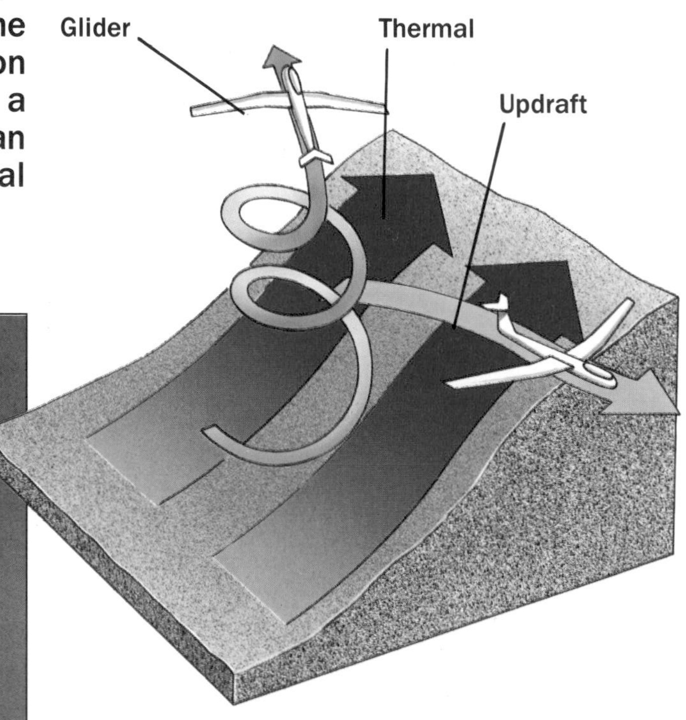

A modern glider is made of fiber-glass.

AIR CUSHIONS

A different type of air flow can also provide a machine with lift. Air can be forced downward out of the base of a vehicle so that it rides on a cushion of air. This is the principle of the hovercraft, or air-cushion vehicle. It is used mainly for boats and ferries, which often have a flexible rubber skirt around the hull to keep the air cushion in place as the vessel rides over the waves. The air is forced beneath the hull by large fans. Air-cushion vehicles are also used on swampland and even on dry land where there are no real roads.

A passenger-carrying hovercraft

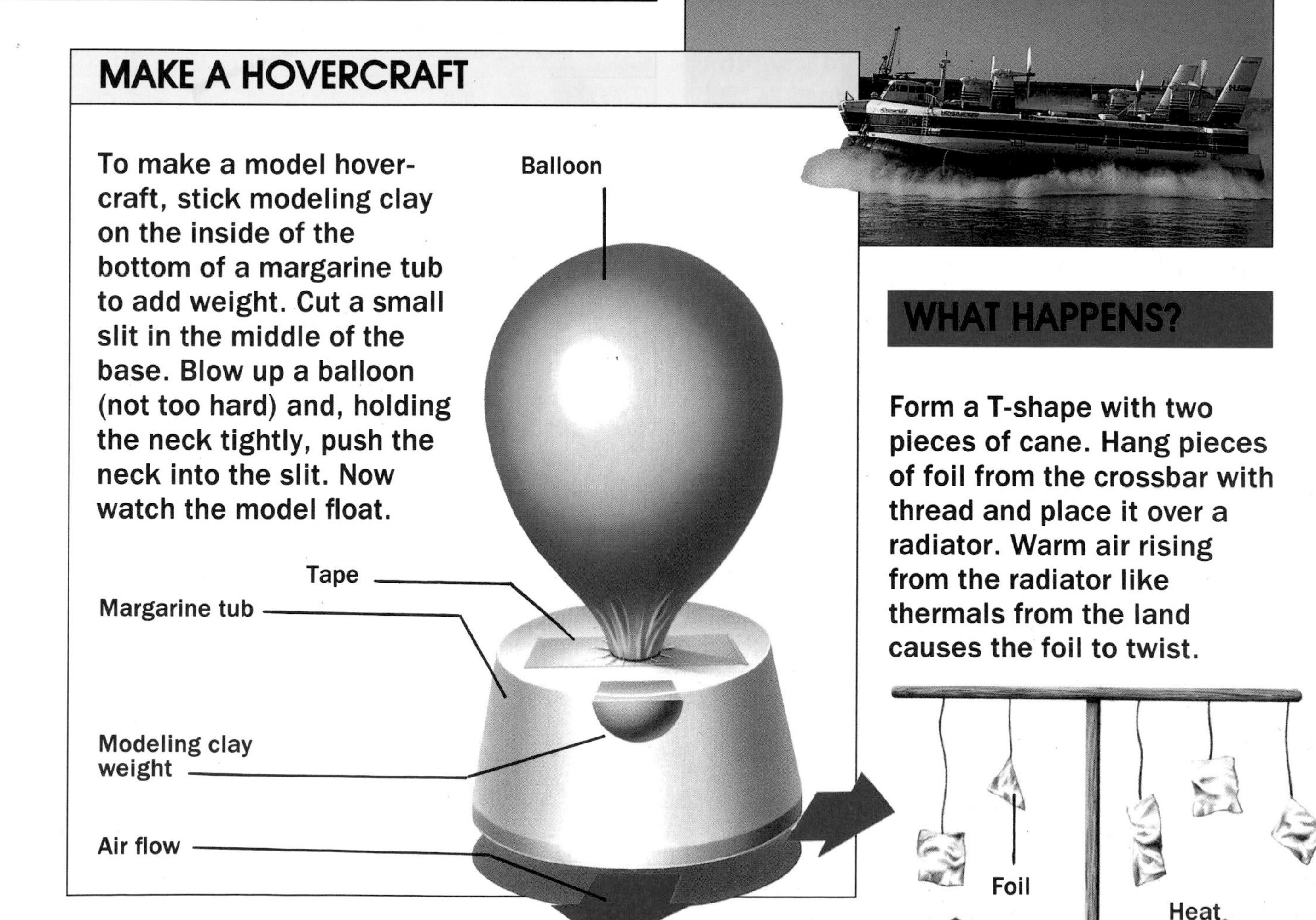

MAKE A HOVERCRAFT

To make a model hovercraft, stick modeling clay on the inside of the bottom of a margarine tub to add weight. Cut a small slit in the middle of the base. Blow up a balloon (not too hard) and, holding the neck tightly, push the neck into the slit. Now watch the model float.

WHAT HAPPENS?

Form a T-shape with two pieces of cane. Hang pieces of foil from the crossbar with thread and place it over a radiator. Warm air rising from the radiator like thermals from the land causes the foil to twist.

One of the remarkable things about air is its ability to hold moisture in the form of water vapor. Air can hold up to three percent of its volume of water in this way. But a fall in air temperature can precipitate the water as tiny droplets, forming clouds high in the sky, or mist and fog near the ground.

CLOUDS AND RAIN

The sun heats the seas and oceans causing water to evaporate from the surface. It rises on thermals (see page 22) into the air. As this water vapor rises, it may meet cooler air and condense in the form of droplets of water, forming clouds. If the clouds are blown over land and forced to rise over mountains, they get even cooler. The water droplets get bigger and fall as rain. In very cold regions they may freeze and fall as snow. Eventually, rain and melted snow find their way into rivers that carry the water back to the sea. This continual sequence is called the water cycle.

If air near the ground is saturated with water vapor it may cool during the night causing the vapor to condense as fog or form dew.

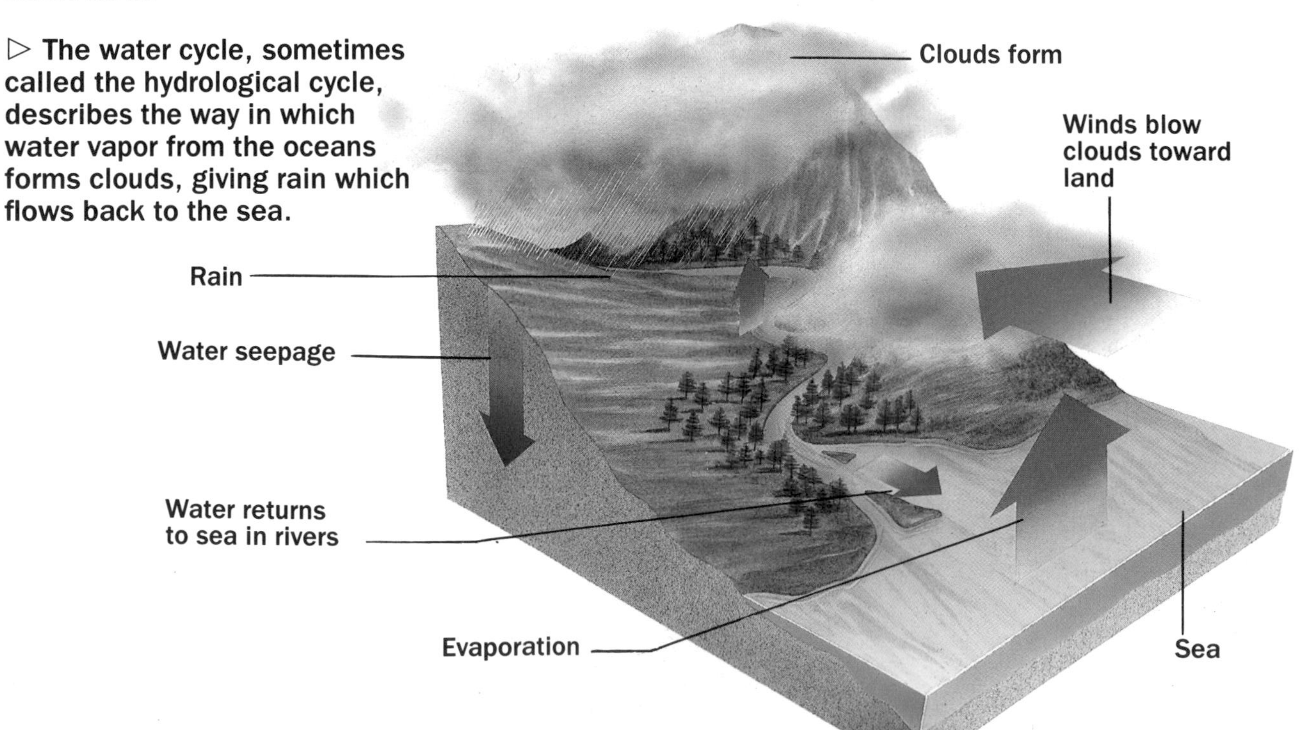

▷ The water cycle, sometimes called the hydrological cycle, describes the way in which water vapor from the oceans forms clouds, giving rain which flows back to the sea.

RAINBOWS

Invisible water droplets in the air can give rise to one of the most spectacular visible phenomena — a rainbow. It depends on the ability of water — like any other transparent substance – to bend light that passes through it. White sunlight is actually made up of many different colors, or wavelengths (see page 13), and each is bent, or refracted, by a slightly different amount as light enters a raindrop. As long as the drops are at the correct angle to the rays of the sun, we see the separated wavelengths that emerge from the droplets as a rainbow of colors arching across the sky.

△ Rainbows usually appear as low arcs of colors across the sky. If the rainbow is very bright, there may be a second rainbow outside it, with the order of colors reversed.

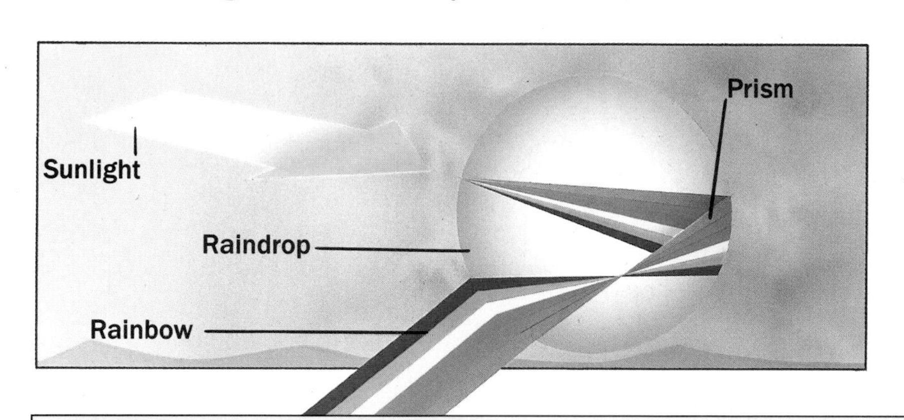

◁ Light entering a raindrop at the correct angle is split up into its colors. These are reflected from the back of the drop, and split even further as they leave the drop again.

MAKING A RAINBOW

You can make an artificial rainbow, or spectrum, by using water to split sunlight into its component colors. Put some water into a tray or shallow bowl near a window, and angle a mirror so that it reflects bright sunlight coming through the window. Now position a piece of white cardboard near the window to act as a screen to catch the spectrum that is formed.

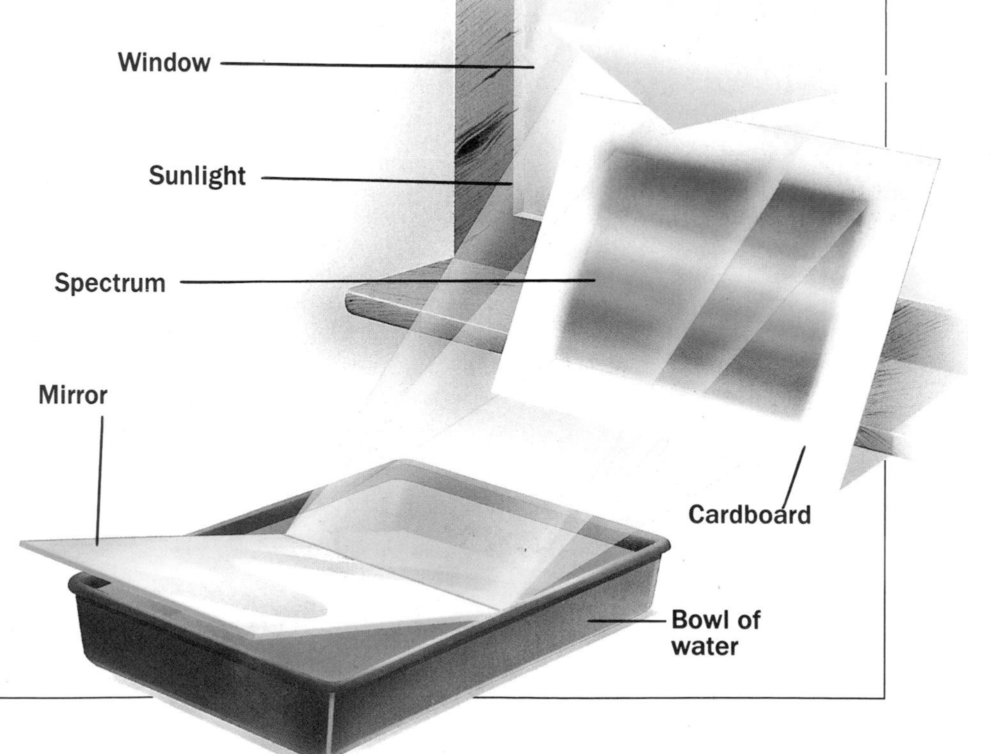

As well as holding water vapor (see page 24), air can also contain particles of dust and smoke, and a whole range of poisonous chemicals. Many forms of atmospheric pollution result from the activities of humankind, such as smoke from factory chimneys and car exhausts, and chemicals from aerosol sprays.

ACID RAIN

When a fossil fuel such as coal or oil is burned, gases such as sulfur oxides and nitrogen oxides are produced. The gases are released into the air in smoke, where they are dispersed by the wind and dissolve in airborne water droplets to form acids. When these droplets finally fall as rain, the acids are released to damage soil and water.

Acid rain can have disastrous effects on the environment. Since the 1960s, acid rain from Britain has been killing fish in lakes in the countries of Scandinavia. In Germany and elsewhere, it has destroyed millions of trees. In towns and cities, acid rain corrodes the stonework of buildings.

△▽ Acid rain forms when pollutant gases in the smoke from factories dissolve in water vapor in the air. The rain may fall hundreds of miles away, killing plants and fish.

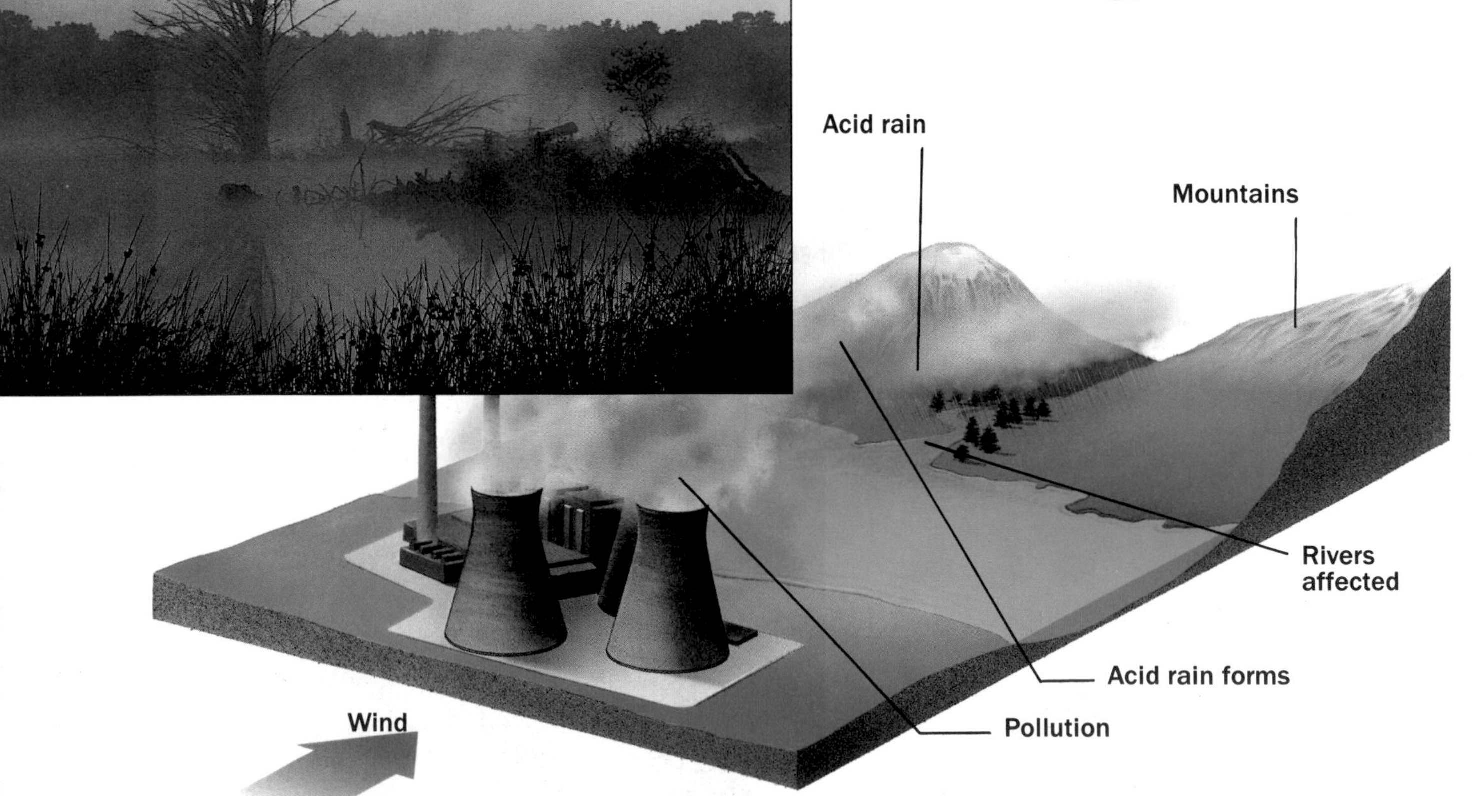

SMOG

Fog forms when air saturated with water vapor is cooled below its dew point (see page 24). If the air is over an industrial area, it probably also contains smoke which mixes with the fog to form smog, a choking, acrid mixture that makes people cough. In cities, car exhaust fumes and other pollutants containing hydrocarbons and nitrogen oxides can be converted into photochemical smog by sunlight. Ozone can form in this smog, adding another poison to the air. This smog irritates the eyes and damages lungs. Like acid rain, smog can be prevented by stopping atmospheric pollution.

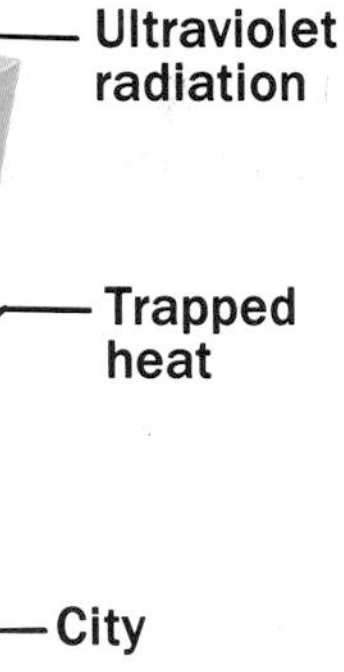

△▷ Sunlight converts urban pollution such as smoke and car exhaust fumes into a photochemical smog. The poisonous ozone this produces helps to form acid rain because it facilitates the conversion of sulfur oxides into sulfuric acid.

THE OZONE LAYER

About 10-20 miles up in the atmosphere is a diffuse layer of the gas ozone. It is a form of oxygen (with three atoms instead of two) and serves to block most of the sun's ultraviolet radiation. This is important because too much ultraviolet radiation would be harmful to life in earth. Some substances break up ozone molecules, converting them back to normal oxygen. Among such substances are CFCs, the propellant gases used in some aerosols (see page 21). Satellite photographs have shown a thinning in the ozone layer over the poles, thought to be caused by pollutants like CFCs.

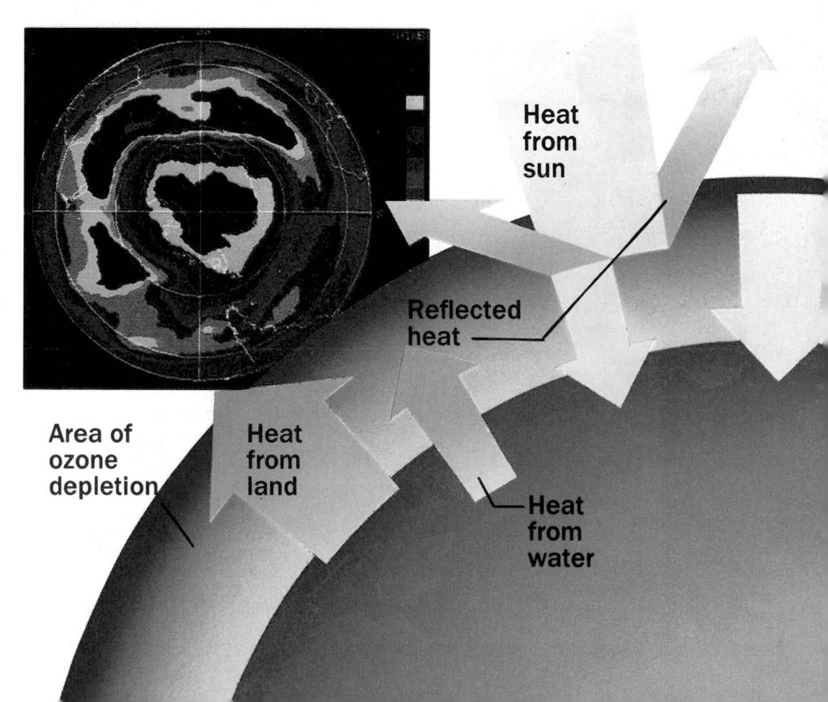

THE GREENHOUSE EFFECT

One of the trace gases in the atmosphere is carbon dioxide (it forms only 0.03 percent of air). This gas is an essential part of the carbon cycle. It is released when animals breathe out and organic matter burns or decays, and is the raw material used by green plants in photosynthesis to form carbohydrates.

Burning of trees releases carbon dioxide.

GREENHOUSE GASES

The wholesale burning of the tropical forests releases too much carbon dioxide into the atmosphere. The burning of fossil fuels such as coal and oil has a similar result. Excess carbon dioxide in the atmosphere increases the greenhouse effect. Normally, rays from the sun that reach the surface of the earth warm the ground and are then re-emitted as heat back into space. But carbon dioxide in the atmosphere and the other greenhouse gases (shown below) trap some of the heat. The layer acts like the glass in a greenhouse: it lets warming rays through, but blocks heat trying to get out. One result could be global warming – a gradual increase in temperatures throughout the world. The climate would change dramatically.

Carbon dioxide from burning of fossil fuels etc

CFCs from aerosols, refrigerators etc

Carbon dioxide from volcanoes

Trapped heat unable to escape

Methane from cattle

Nitrous oxide from fertilizers

Carbon dioxide from sea and land

RISING SEA LEVELS

One possible result of an increasing greenhouse effect is a rise in average temperatures – by as much as two degrees Fahrenheit by the end of the century. As we have just seen, this in turn could start melting the ice of the ice caps at the poles, something that has happened before in the earth's history between the various ice ages. Sea levels would then rise. Many of the world's major cities are built on the coasts. A general rise in sea level of only a few feet would drown many cities near coasts, and some islands in the Pacific would disappear.

△ Erosion of coastlines would increase rapidly if sea levels were to rise. In many places, the sea would encroach on the land, flooding cities and ruining farmland.

▽ Increasing the carbon dioxide content of the atmosphere through pollution and cutting down trees may increase the greenhouse effect to a disastrous degree.

Carbon dioxide in atmosphere

Carbon dioxide from burning wood and deforestation

Carbon dioxide from marine animals

The earth 18,000 years ago

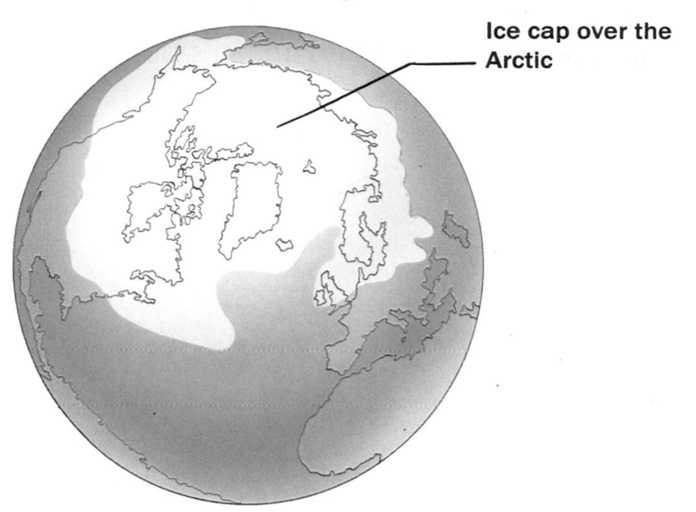

The earth today

Ice cap over the Arctic

▷ The average temperature today is only 7° F warmer than the last ice age 18,000 years ago. Due to increasing carbon dioxide levels, the temperature could rise further.

OTHER ATMOSPHERES

The earth is not alone in having an atmosphere. All the other planets, and even some moons, also have them. But none of them is anything like the atmosphere on earth. None contain oxygen levels required for life like that on earth. And most atmospheres are totally poisonous.

GIANTS AND EARTH'S DOUBLE

The largest planets in the solar system are Jupiter and Saturn. Jupiter's atmosphere consists mainly of the light gases hydrogen and helium, with traces of poisonous ammonia and methane. Violent storms rage in the atmosphere, with winds of up to 200 miles per hour. Saturn's atmosphere is similar, and like Jupiter has bands of counterflowing easterly and westerly winds. Venus is a similar size to earth, and is covered by a dense atmosphere consisting mostly of clouds of carbon dioxide and sulfuric acid.

△ The most distinctive feature in Jupiter's atmosphere is a whirlpool of gases known as the great red spot. It has been there for at least 300 years.

▽ The mainly carbon dioxide atmosphere of Venus is so dense that, at the surface of the planet, atmospheric pressure is 90 times as high as it is at sea level on earth.

▽ The famous ring system of Saturn consists of millions of particles of dust and ice, probably coming originally from the planet's atmosphere.

ATMOSPHERIC MOONS

Earth's moon has no atmosphere at all. But some of the moons of the giant planets have retained an atmosphere. Saturn's largest natural satellite, Titan, is much larger than our moon and has a substantial atmosphere consisting of thick clouds of methane. Io, also slightly larger than our moon, is the closest of Jupiter's large satellites and is dotted with active volcanoes. These throw various gases into its atmosphere, and even coat neighboring Amalthea with sulfur. Scientists wonder if the composition of its atmosphere is similar to that of primitive earth's.

△ Voyager space probes took close-up pictures of Jupiter's moon Io, revealing its active volcanoes with streaks of ash and sulfur.

▷ Titan, the largest moon of Saturn, is the only body in the solar system other than a planet to have a proper atmosphere. It is so thick that it hides Titan's surface.

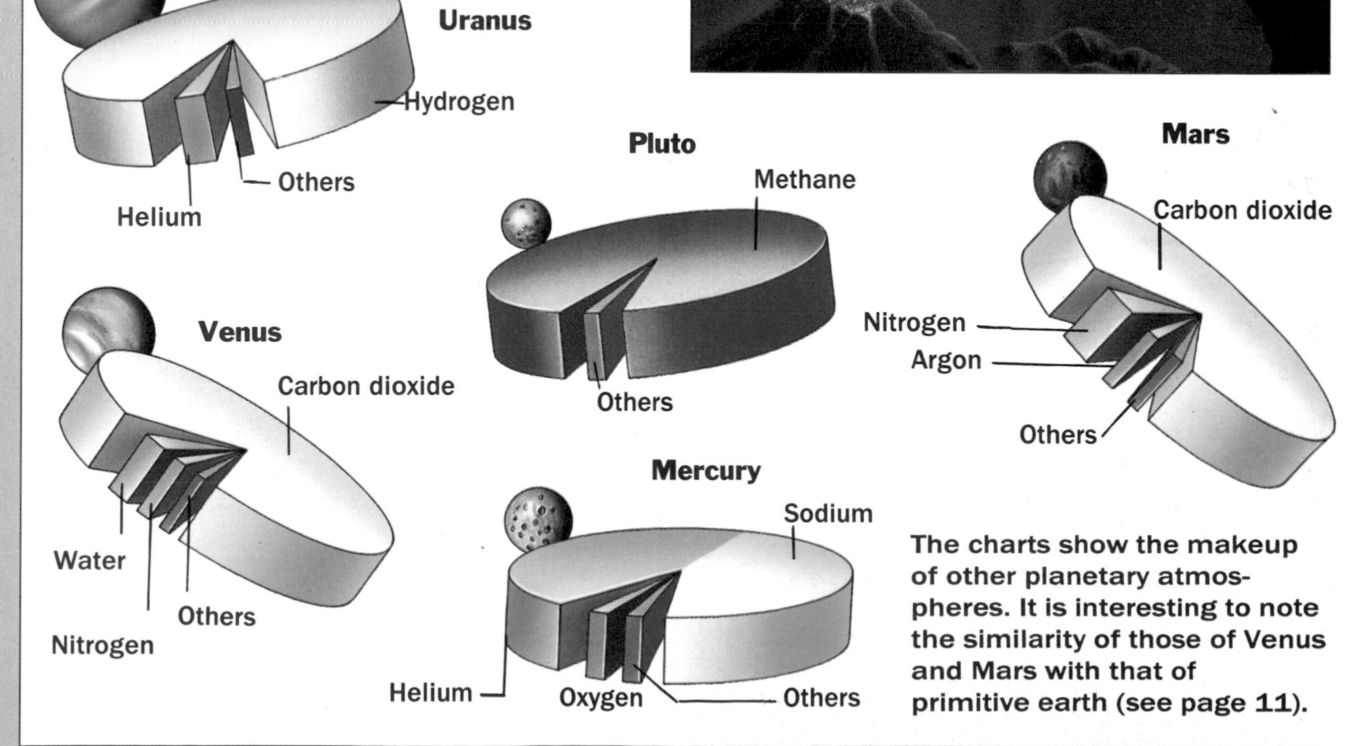

The charts show the makeup of other planetary atmospheres. It is interesting to note the similarity of those of Venus and Mars with that of primitive earth (see page 11).

In the total absence of air or any other gas, we are left with a vacuum. Vacuums have their drawbacks – sound will not travel through them. But they also have their uses, some of which are described on this page. But the best vacuums produced on earth are still not as "perfect" as the vacuum of outer space.

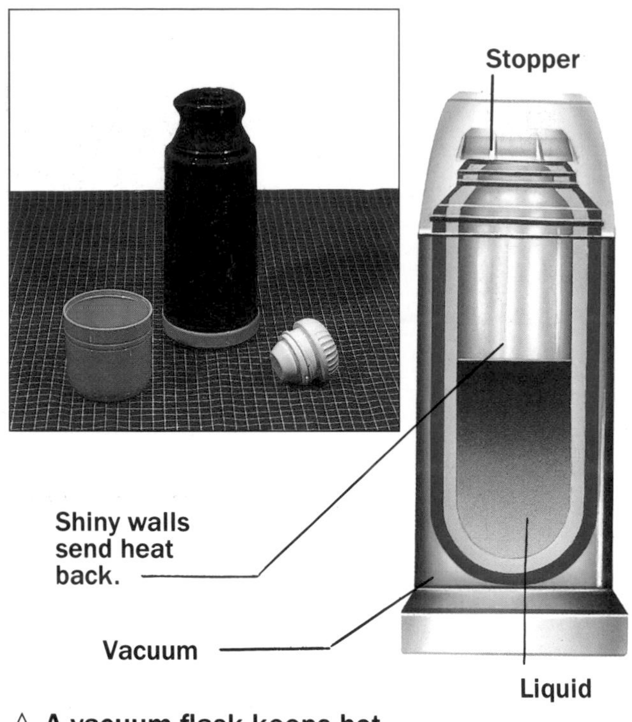

△ A vacuum flask keeps hot liquids hot, or cold liquids cold, by eliminating all three ways that heat can travel.

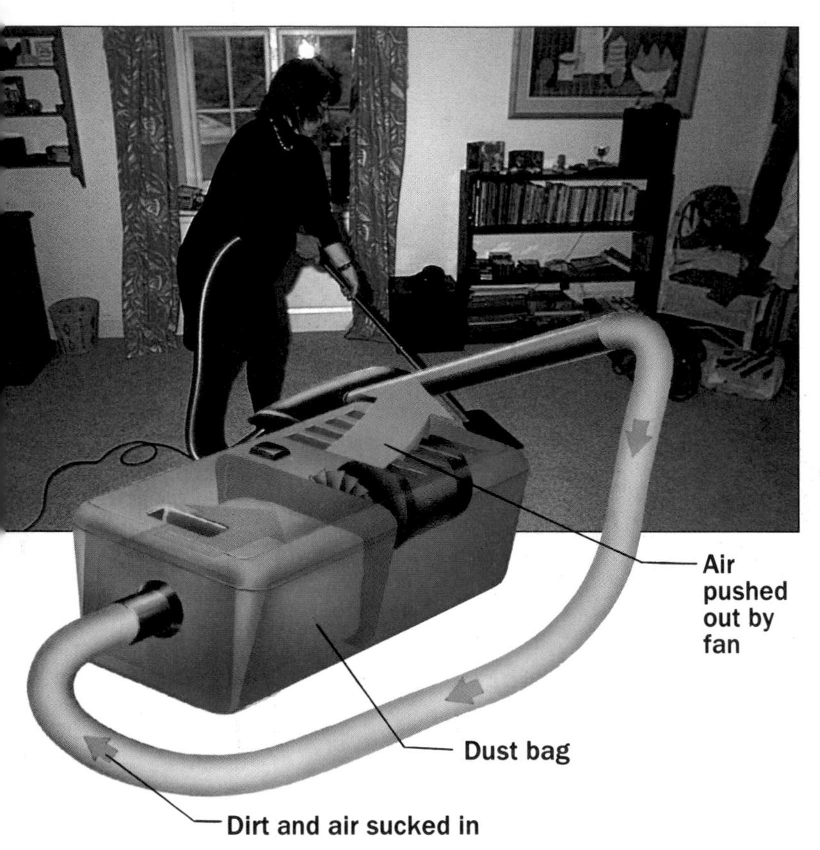

△ A vacuum cleaner uses a motor-driven fan to force air out of the back. Air rushing in brings with it dust and dirt.

The vacuum flask was invented at the end of the last century by the British scientist James Dewar. The vacuum between two thin glass walls prevents heat transmission by conduction (through contact between a hot object and something else) or convection (movement of heat by a liquid or gas). Silvering prevents transmission by radiation.

A vacuum cleaner is better described as a suction cleaner. It does not create a true vacuum, just a low-pressure region which external air rushes into carrying dust and dirt. A removeable collecting bag catches the dust from the air.

In the absence of radio communications, astronauts cannot communicate with each other no matter how loud they shout. The vacuum of space will not carry sound. But if they touch helmets, sound vibrations (and speech) travel from one to the other.

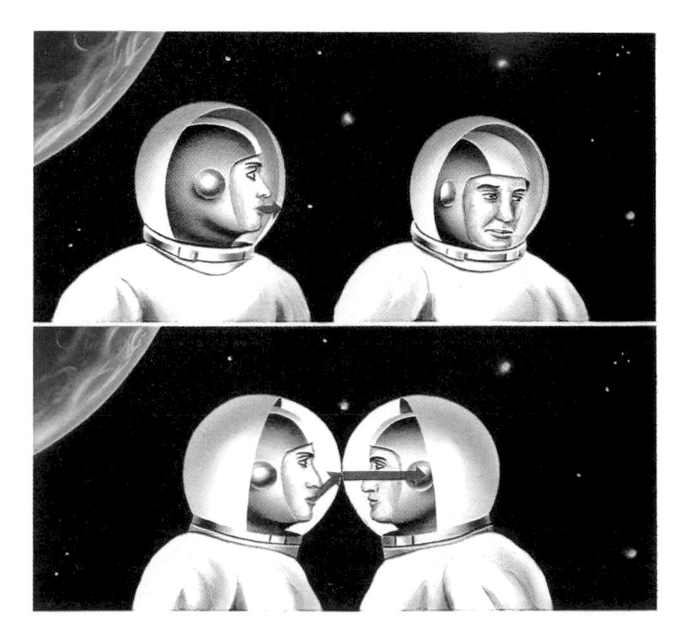

THE
OZONE
LAYER

THE OZONE LAYER

Ozone is a form of oxygen. It is created when ultraviolet radiation from the sun meets oxygen in the atmosphere. The ozone layer occurs throughout the stratosphere, but is most dense between about 12 and 19 miles above the ground. It absorbs most of the dangerous ultraviolet radiation reaching the earth from the sun. The ultraviolet that does get through to the surface of the earth has important effects. It is the radiation which gives people their natural skin coloring. However, too much ultraviolet radiation can have harmful effects on plants and animals, including humans.

▼ Many people take their vacations in hot and sunny climates. They spend long periods lying in the sun, absorbing the sun's radiation and often getting burned. They receive some ultraviolet radiation, but most has been absorbed by the ozone layer.

The ozone layer in balance

The way ultraviolet radiation, ozone, oxygen and other chemicals act together in the atmosphere is extremely complicated, but under normal circumstances everything is in balance. Ozone is being made and broken down all the time in the atmosphere. The amount of ozone in the atmosphere stays more or less the same.

The threat to the ozone layer comes from pollutants which can destroy the ozone, and this upsets the balance in the atmosphere. The amount of dangerous ultraviolet radiation reaching the earth may increase if this balance in the ozone layer is disturbed.

Ultraviolet radiation is one of the "rays" that we receive from the sun. It travels through space into the atmosphere, until it reaches the ozone layer.

When the ultraviolet meets ozone in the atmosphere it is absorbed by the ozone, and at the same time breaks down the ozone into a different form of oxygen. But these forms then reunite with others that have similarly been broken down, to reform as ozone. In this process a large amount of dangerous ultraviolet radiation is absorbed.

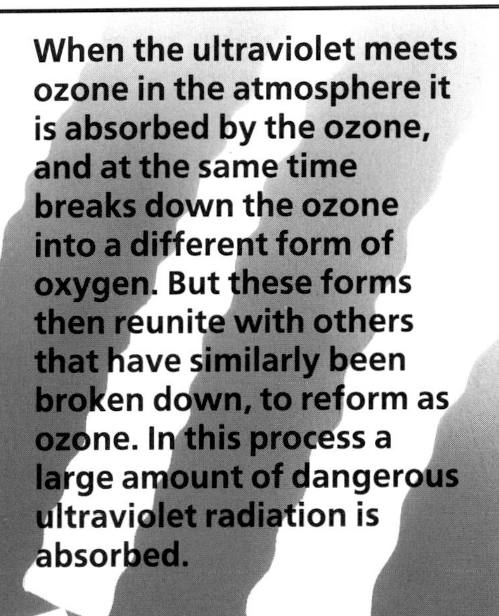

Once the ultraviolet radiation has been filtered by the ozone, a reduced amount penetrates the remaining atmosphere to reach the surface of the earth.

THE OZONE-EATERS

Scientists expect the sun to keep shining for at least another 200 million years. The earth has its umbrella of gas – the atmosphere – to protect it from the dangerous radiation that the sun produces. But, unfortunately, the composition of the atmosphere is changing as a result of human activity.

Part of the atmosphere – the ozone layer – is under threat from chemicals that we use on earth. The guilty chemicals are chlorofluorocarbons (often called CFCs for short). They can last for more than 100 years in the atmosphere, slowly moving up through the atmosphere before breaking down to produce the chemicals that destroy the ozone layer. Although the best–known culprits are CFCs, which are the most important of the ozone–destroying chemicals, other chemicals can also help to break ozone down. On earth these chemicals are inert – they never change, and nothing happens when they meet other chemicals. But very slowly they drift upward into the atmosphere. When they get high enough into the atmosphere something does happen to them – ultraviolet light from the sun breaks them down and changes them.

What are CFCs
CFCs are chemicals called chlorofluorocarbons. They have a number of applications. They are used in a variety of aerosols, refrigerators, some air-conditioning systems and some packaging materials.

The way CFCs react with ultraviolet and ozone in the ozone layer is complicated. When the CFC reaches the ozone layer, the ultraviolet strikes the CFC and releases chlorine from it. This reacts with the ozone, breaking up ozone into different forms of oxygen. The chlorine itself remains unchanged, so it continues to destroy ozone, turning it into different forms of oxygen, over and over again.

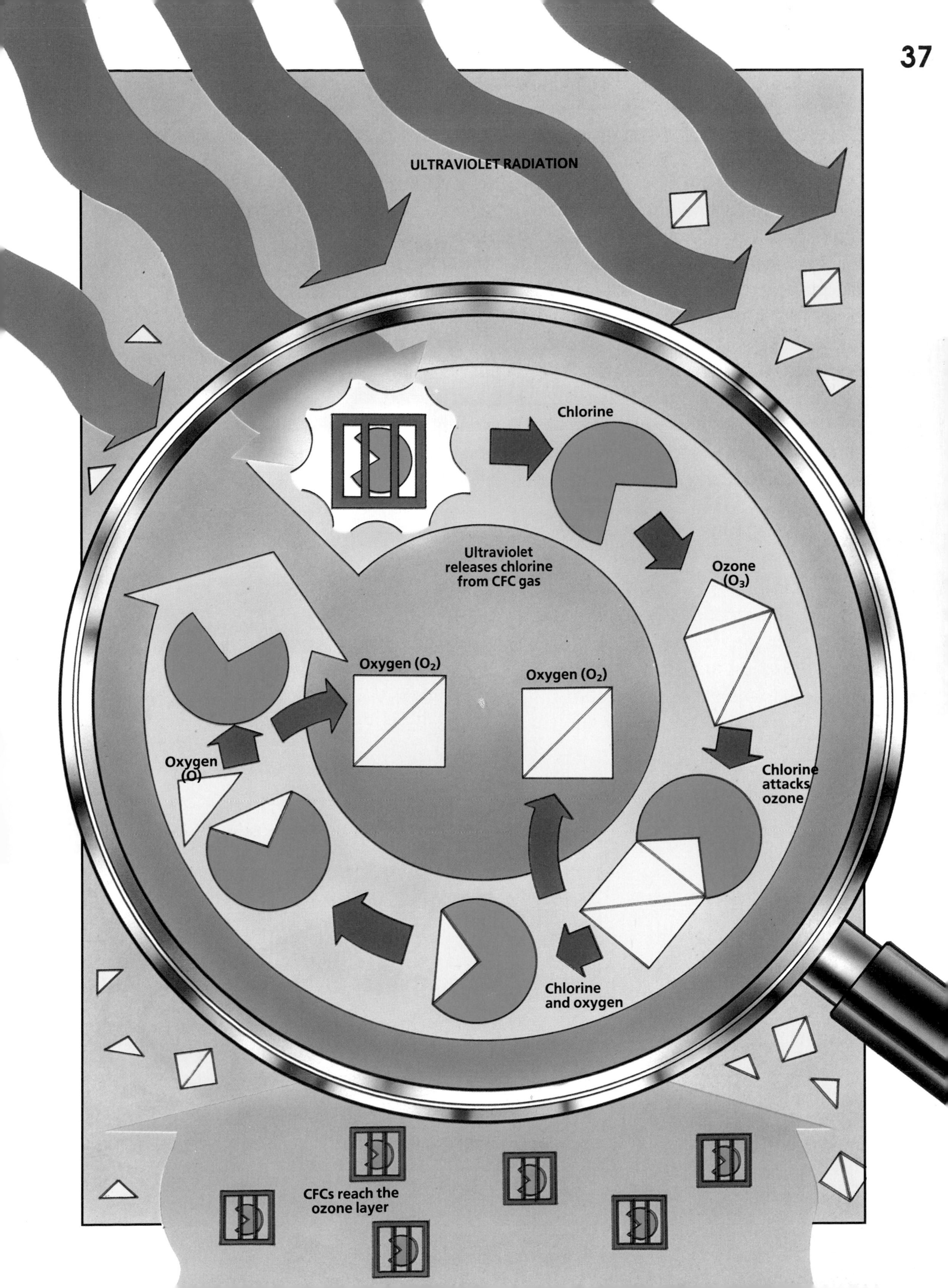
ULTRAVIOLET RADIATION
Chlorine
Ultraviolet releases chlorine from CFC gas
Ozone (O_3)
Oxygen (O_2)
Oxygen (O_2)
Oxygen (O)
Chlorine attacks ozone
Chlorine and oxygen
CFCs reach the ozone layer

WHERE THEY COME FROM

Ozone-eaters come from a variety of sources. Aerosols are made for all kinds of personal and household uses. Hairsprays, anti-perspirants, insect spray and spray paint are all aerosols and all use CFCs. In the United Kingdom alone, 800 million aerosols were used last year. CFCs are used in the manufacture of some types of foam packaging, where they are used to inflate the foam. Sometimes CFCs remain trapped in the bubbles of foam packaging and escape when it is crushed and burned.

In refrigerators and some air-conditioning units, especially those used in cars in hot climates, CFCs are used as the cooling fluid that circulates to keep the temperature down.

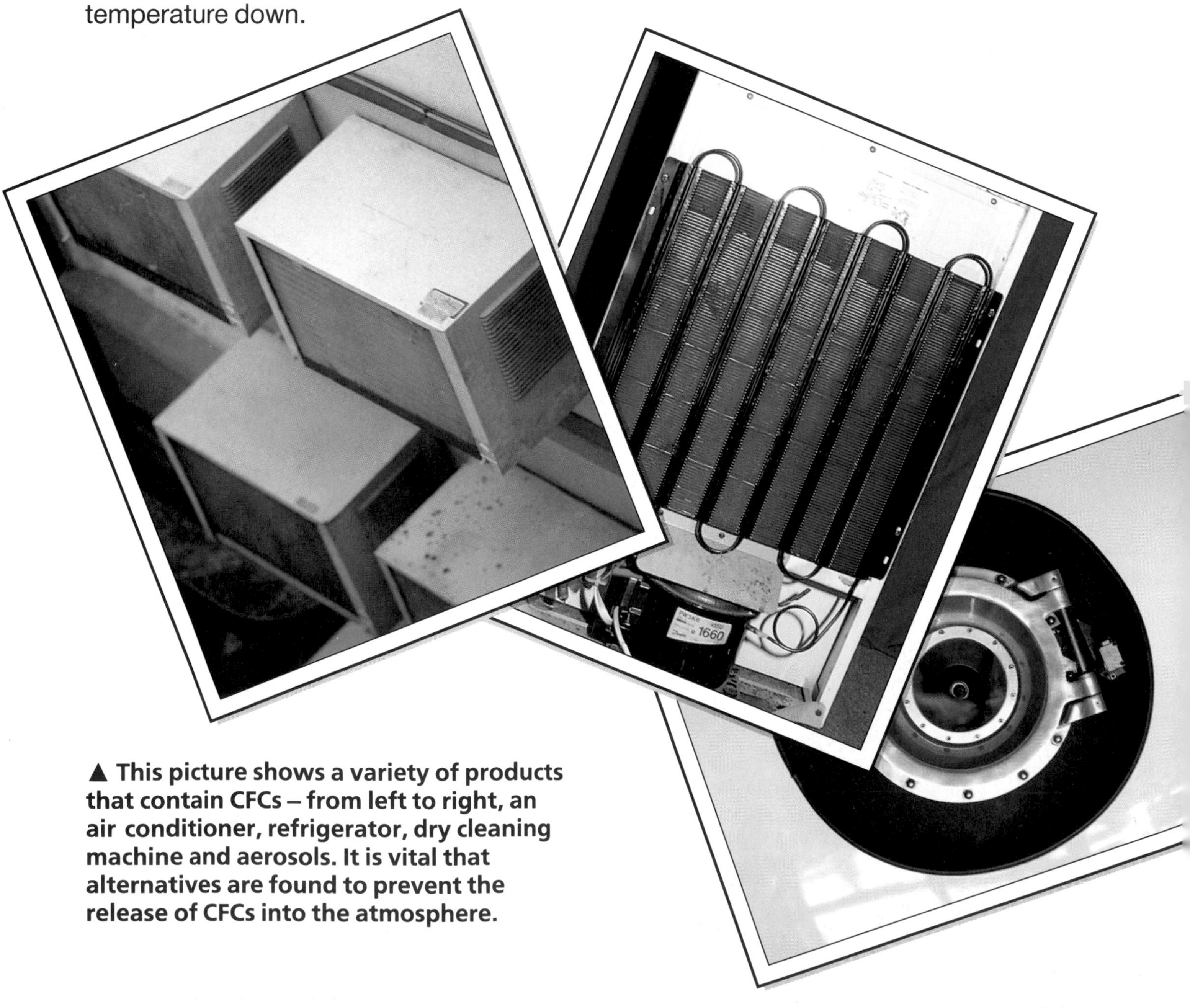

▲ This picture shows a variety of products that contain CFCs – from left to right, an air conditioner, refrigerator, dry cleaning machine and aerosols. It is vital that alternatives are found to prevent the release of CFCs into the atmosphere.

All the other ozone-eaters

Ozone-threatening gases do not only come from these sources. The factories that make aerosols also release CFCs into the atmosphere. Other chemicals threaten the ozone layer too, such as carbon tetrachloride – a chemical used in the manufacture of CFCs, and sold in some countries as a solvent – even though it has been banned in many places because it has been connected with liver cancer. Halons, which are used in fire extinguishers, are ozone-eaters, as is methylchloroform, which is used as a solvent. Solvents are found in many products which we use every day, such as glues and spirit-based pens, and in paints. And trichloroethane is used in typist's correction fluid.

▲ **This industrial complex produces chemicals.**

CFCs

CFCs, and the other chemicals that are endangering the ozone layer, take time to drift up into the ozone layer. They may also last a very long time – on average for 70-110 years, although for up to 23,000 years in some cases. They also drift higher than other substances like methane and hydrocarbons. Because of this, scientists find it difficult to predict what damage is ultimately likely to result.

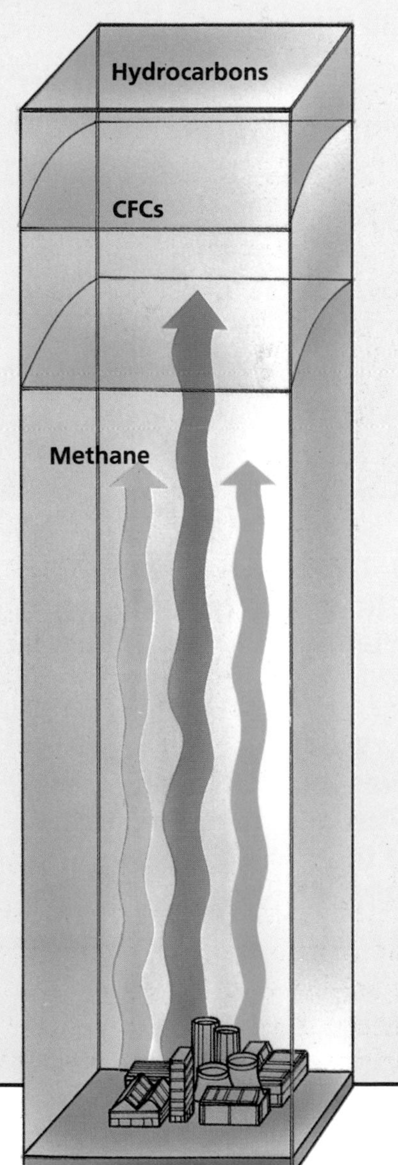

THE HOLE

At certain times every year, over Antarctica, the levels of ozone in the ozone layer fall drastically. There is an area where the layer is so sparse that there is virtually a hole.

During the Antarctic spring, which is at the same time as our autumn, there are some areas over Antarctica where as much as 40 percent of the ozone has disappeared in some years. The hole is as big as North America and as deep as Mount Everest.

Records show that the levels of ozone in the Antarctic atmosphere do vary naturally from year to year. But the hole has been observed in recent years to be greater than that which occurs naturally. Scientists have collected samples from the atmosphere where the hole occurs, and have found high levels of ozone-eating chemicals. These are almost certainly responsible for the hole.

The hole in the Antarctic
Scientists use high-level reconnaissance aircraft, balloons and satellites to gather their information. This satellite picture (right) shows quite clearly the hole that is appearing in the ozone over the Antarctic pole. The blackish area in the middle confirms the existence of a hole.
No hole has yet been found over the Arctic, although the chemicals that could cause it are present. But the ozone layer has certainly been found to thin out over the northern hemisphere in general. In a band that stretches around the globe in the latitudes of Canada where Hudson Bay lies, up to 7 percent ozone depletion has been found in winter.

▲ This NASA ER-2 high-altitude aircraft is being prepared for flight.

▶ Satellites orbit regularly over the Arctic and Antarctic, taking pictures of the earth with sophisticated cameras.

Nimbus

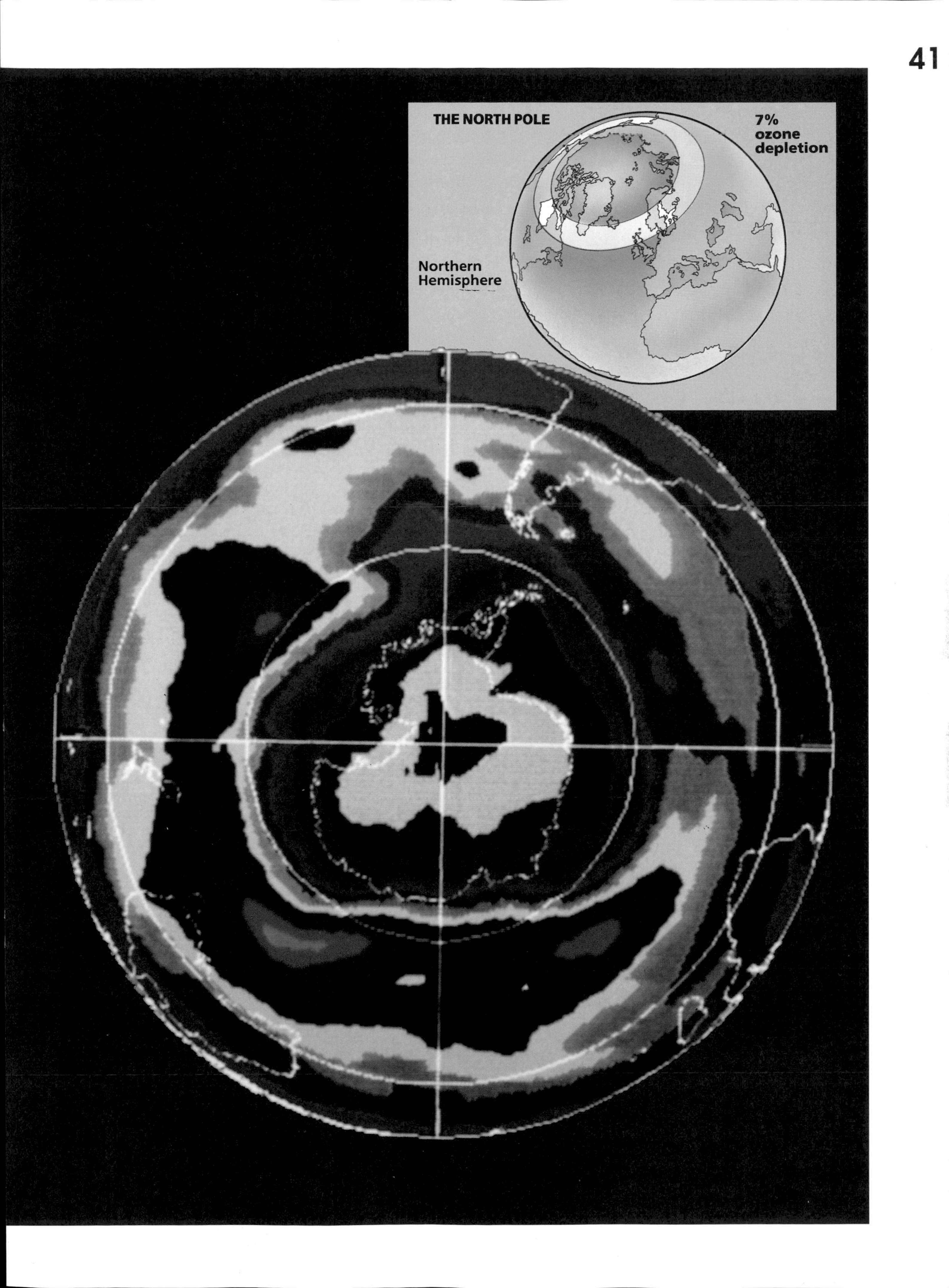
THE NORTH POLE
7%
ozone
depletion
Northern
Hemisphere

WHAT COULD HAPPEN

The ozone layer absorbs most of the dangerous ultraviolet radiation. If more of this radiation got through it would cause an increase in skin cancer and cataracts – a major cause of blindness in the countries where modern medical treatment is unavailable. It has been estimated that a one percent depletion of the ozone layer would result in an extra 70,000 cases of skin cancer every year worldwide. But the increased ultraviolet radiation would not just affect us – it would affect all life on earth. There would be damage to crops and to the plants and trees which form the basis of the food chains that support life on earth. So there would be a threat to the world's food supply. In the sea, if the plankton – tiny plants and animals in the surface waters – were killed, the fish would starve, the seas would die, and a major source of human food resources would be lost.

▼ Plankton (see photo inset) is the basis of the food chain in the sea. Plankton consists of tiny plants and animals, and is eaten by marine creatures such as fish and squid. The bigger fish and sea mammals eat other fish. The Baleen whales such as the Blue whale, the Humpback whale, and Gray whale (below), bypass the chain and feed directly on large amounts of plankton.

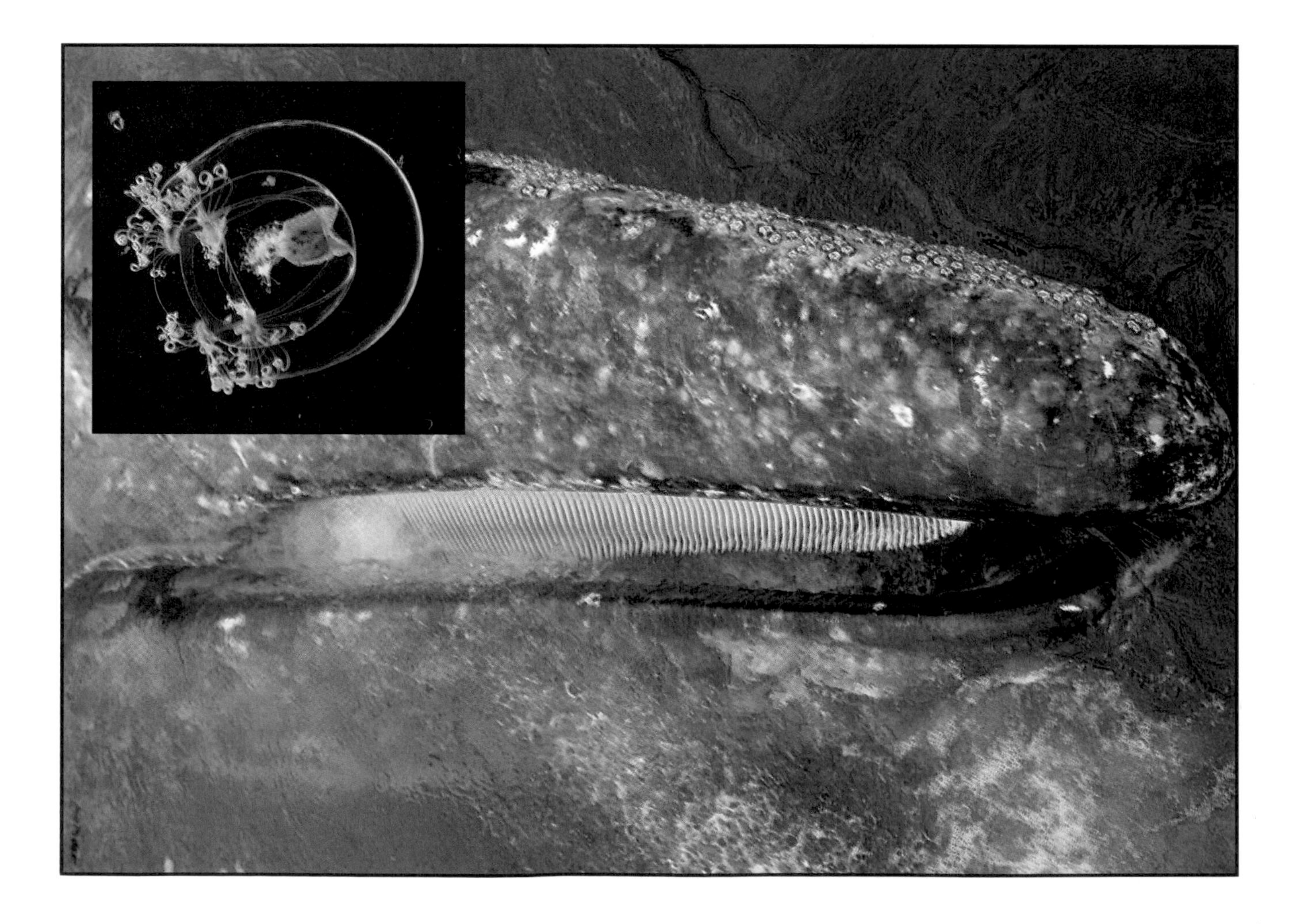

PHOTOCHEMICAL SMOG

Increased ultraviolet radiation reaching the earth could raise the likelihood of photochemical smog over heavily built-up areas. Smog is formed when ultraviolet radiation comes into contact with air pollution produced by cars.

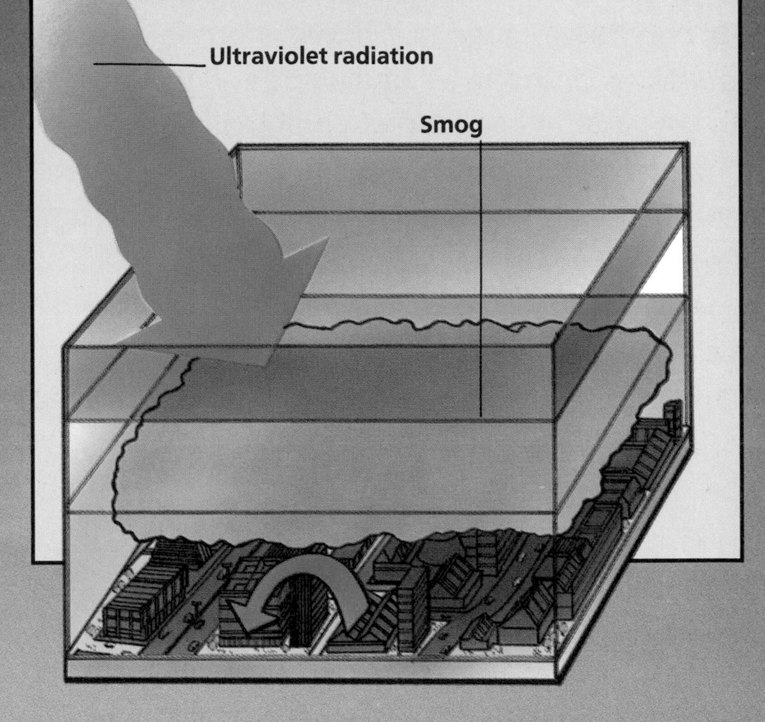

ALTERNATIVES

Risking the destruction of the ozone layer is unnecessary. There are alternatives for virtually all the uses of CFCs. For example, aerosol sprays which use CFCs can be replaced by harmless pump-action sprays which do no damage to the environment. Moreover, foam-packaging insulation material can be made without the use of CFCs. People are beginning to wonder whether we really need all the packaging that goods come in – a lot of it is only decoration and serves no useful purpose. The CFCs in refrigerators can be recycled – they can be sucked out of an old refrigerator and put into a new one.

"Release of CFCs could be prevented if consumers and businesses were offered cash incentives to return broken-down air conditioners and refrigerators to auto and appliance dealers. Then the units could be sent back to the manufacturers so that the CFCs could be reused."

Time January 1989

"Much of what reaches the atmosphere is not coming from industrial sources. It's things like sloppy handling of hamburger containers."

Senator Albert Gore of Tennessee, USA

"It has also been suggested that environmentally-damaging substances like CFCs should be made more expensive to encourage recycling and a switch to less harmful alternatives."

Which? October 1989

▶ While the developed and heavily industrialized countries of the world can afford to look at the long-term dangers of a thinning of the ozone layer, the problems of developing countries are very different. Their priorities lean toward the provision of basic food supplies, and a general increase in their standard of living. Whereas refrigerators and aerosol sprays are commonplace items in a developed country, they are often luxury items in developing ones. It is therefore difficult for developing countries to accept that they are not entitled to such luxury items, and it is harder for them to agree to ban CFCs.

Banning CFCs
To protect the ozone layer it will ultimately be vital to ban harmful CFCs on a worldwide basis. Even now, manufacturers are beginning to look for alternatives. There is growing opposition to the general use of CFCs worldwide.

Recycling refrigerators
The disposal of refrigerators is a major problem. By leaving them on a dump or by crushing them, the CFCs are released into the atmosphere. It is now possible to extract the CFCs from refrigerators and to recycle them.

Alternative gases
Not only can the CFCs in some cases be recycled, but they can also be replaced by other chemicals and gases. CO_2 is now widely used for foam fire-extinguishers. Others can be replaced by harmless pump-action sprays.

WHAT'S BEING DONE

In September 1987 many countries signed an agreement called the Montreal Protocol. They promised to reduce the production of CFCs by half, by the end of the century.

It is now realized that the situation was worse than people imagined and that the Protocol did not go far enough. It is currently under review. If the ozone layer is to survive, many scientists believe that the countries must agree to reduce their CFC production to zero by the end of the century. Scientists are discovering more and more ozone-destroyers all the time. If the ozone layer is to be maintained we must plan for the future and completely stop using all the ozone-destroyers. It is vital that all countries work together to provide the goods people want, without destroying our environment.

► Some products such as aerosols have symbols printed on the can to inform you the propellant is not harmful to the ozone layer. However, alternative propellants are often greenhouse gases, and add to the greenhouse effect. The safest are pump-action sprays.

▼ Margaret Thatcher, former Prime Minister of Great Britain, speaks out at a conference on the ozone layer, organized to protect the environment.

► In this Greenpeace demonstration outside a well-known West German chemical factory, protesters are demanding an end to the production of CFCs.

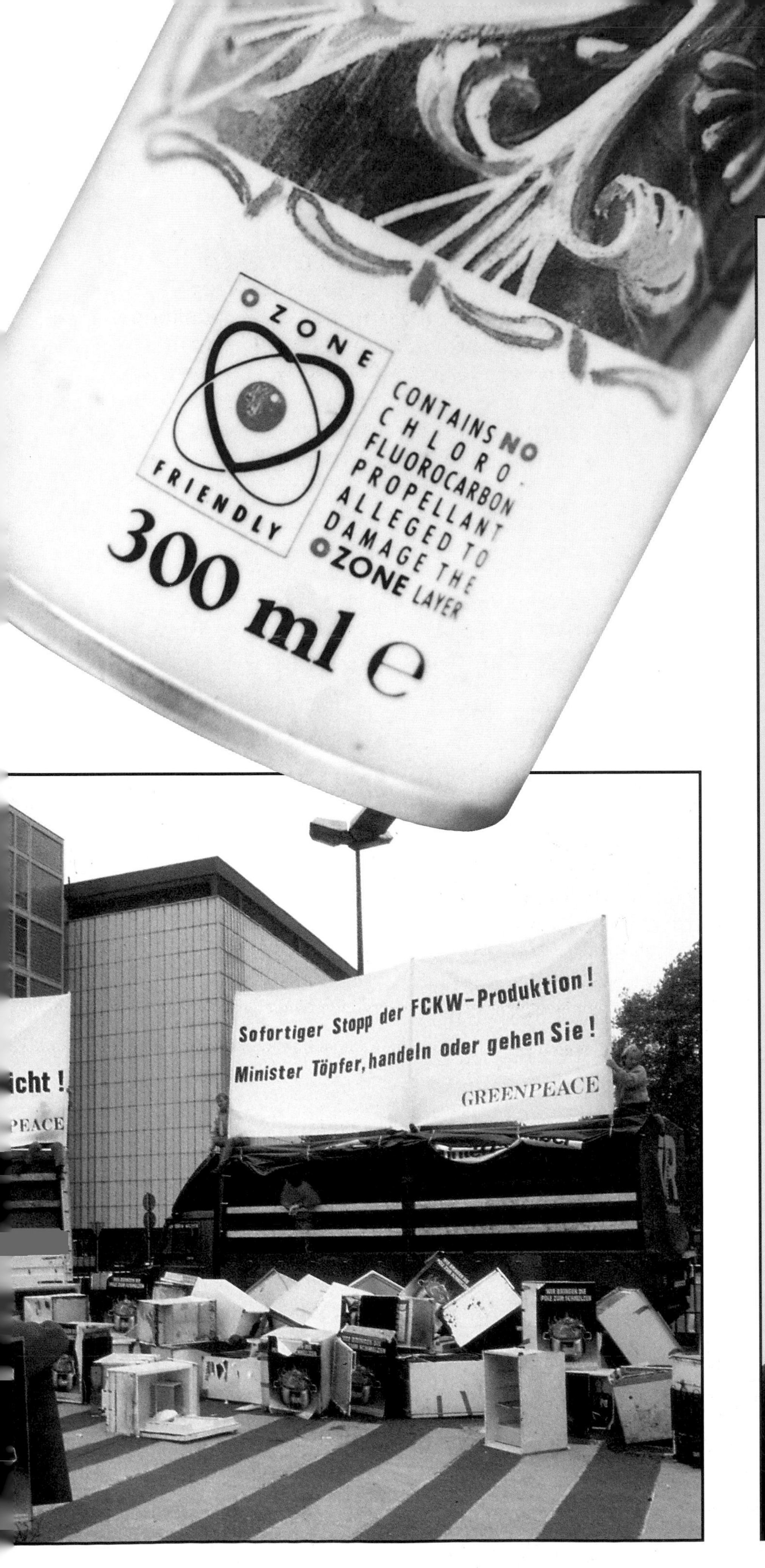

TAKING ACTION

Organizations like Greenpeace and Friends of the Earth (FOE) are aiming campaigns at consumers, industry and governments, to try to alert them to the great dangers of pollution and to encourage them to help protect the ozone layer. These organizations demonstrate outside government buildings and factories to voice their concern. This is already having considerable effect. Manufacturers are influenced by public opinion, and are beginning to cut down the use of CFCs in their products.

It also helps when prominent people, like Prince Charles, support the ozone layer by refusing to use CFC aerosols.

FACT FILE 1

How big is the ozone layer?
The ozone layer spreads right out over a thick layer of atmosphere. But if you brought it down to earth, to ground level, where there is a lot more air above to flatten it down, it would only be about 0.2 inches thick.

CFCs and the greenhouse effect
CFCs do not just threaten the ozone layer. They are also greenhouse gases. This means that they help trap heat close to the earth's surface. Greenhouse gases cause the greenhouse effect, which is responsible for keeping the earth warm. It is also responsible for a gradual increase in temperatures throughout the world. Global warming could have devastating effects on climate, sea level, crop production and wildlife. Although they are present in smaller quantities than the best known greenhouse gas – carbon dioxide – some CFCs are more than 10,000 times as powerful.All the more reason to stop using them as soon as possible.

The origin of the ozone layer
The sun's ultraviolet radiation plays a vital role in maintaining the ozone layer. When the sun's ultraviolet hits the atmosphere it meets oxygen and causes a chemical reaction to take place which forms ozone. Oxygen exists as molecules, which are made up of atoms – an oxygen molecule is made up of two oxygen atoms. When the ultraviolet strikes an oxygen molecule it splits it in two. The end result is that some ultraviolet radiation has been stopped from getting any further, and two oxygen atoms are free in the atmosphere. A single oxygen atom may meet another oxygen atom, and the two may join to form an oxygen molecule; or it may bump into an oxygen molecule, and join up with it to make a molecule with three atoms – ozone. Then, when ultraviolet strikes the ozone molecule, it breaks it up again, setting the oxygen atom free again in the atmosphere. More ultraviolet has been stopped on its way, and prevented from reaching the earth.

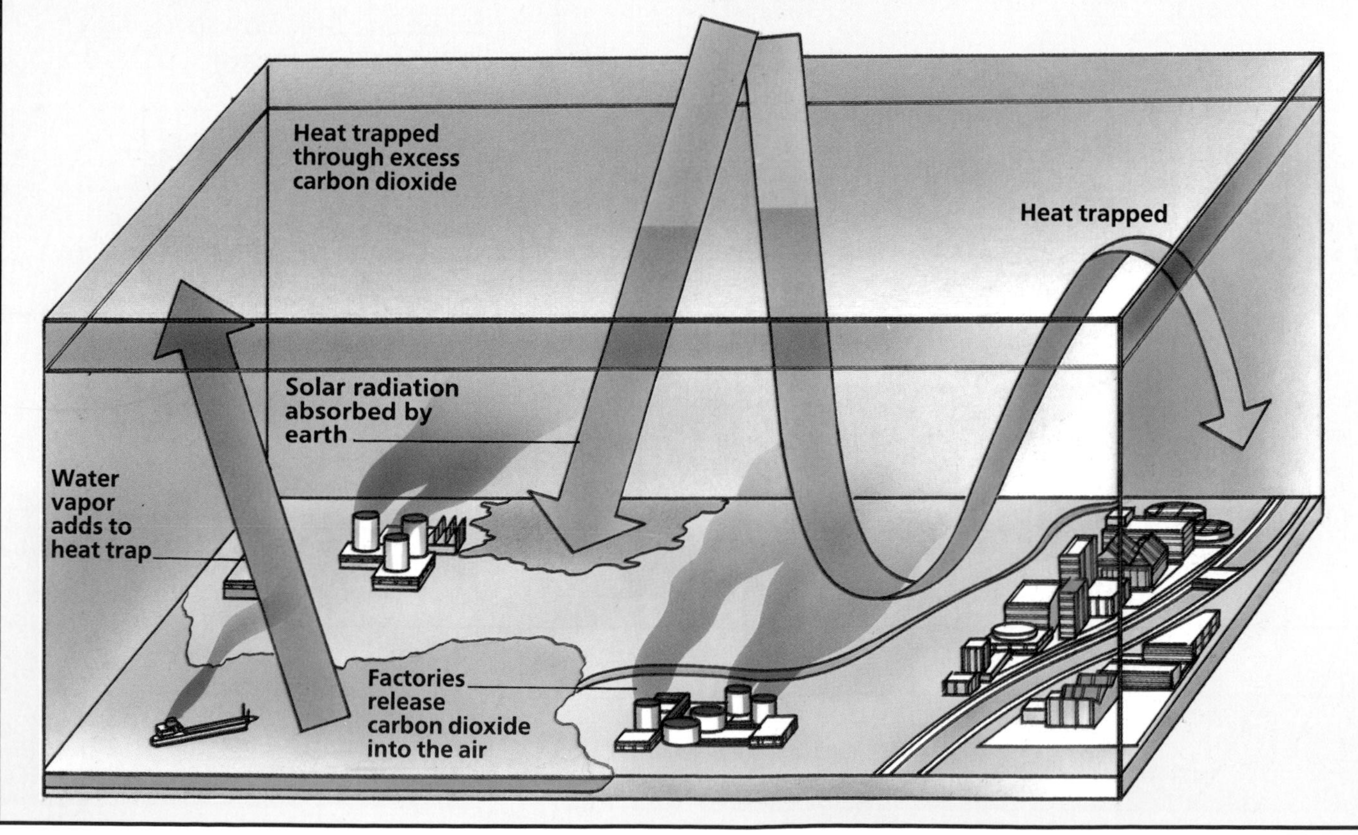

For an oxygen molecule and an oxygen atom to combine to make ozone, a catalyst (normally nitrogen) needs to be present. Ozone is being made and destroyed all the time, and most of the ultraviolet radiation is being stopped from reaching the surface of the earth. But when the ozone-destroyers are involved, there is more ozone being broken down than made.

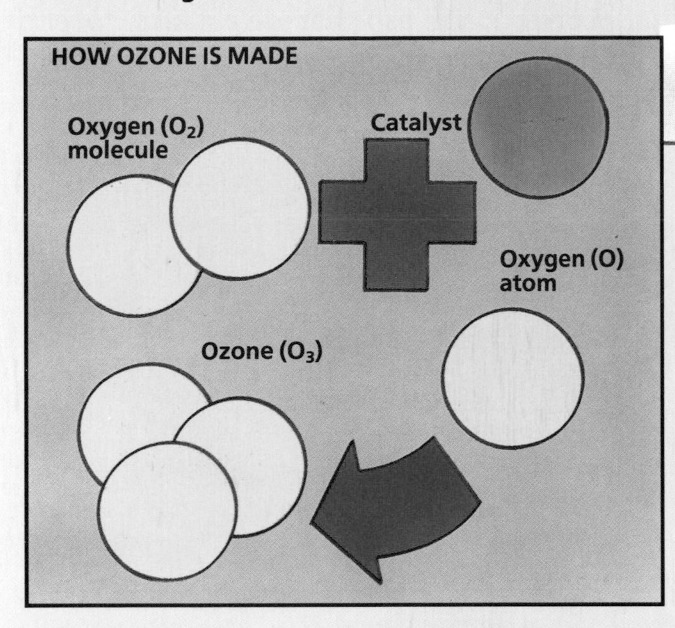

How can scientists tell that the ozone layer is under attack?

An instrument called a spectrophotometer shows them how much radiation is getting through. When they see that there is more ultraviolet getting through than there should be, they know that there has been a reduction in the amount of ozone in the ozone layer

What do CFCs do?

When CFCs are used in aerosols, they act as the propellant mixed with the product – they are put into the can under pressure, and when you press the button they force the product out.

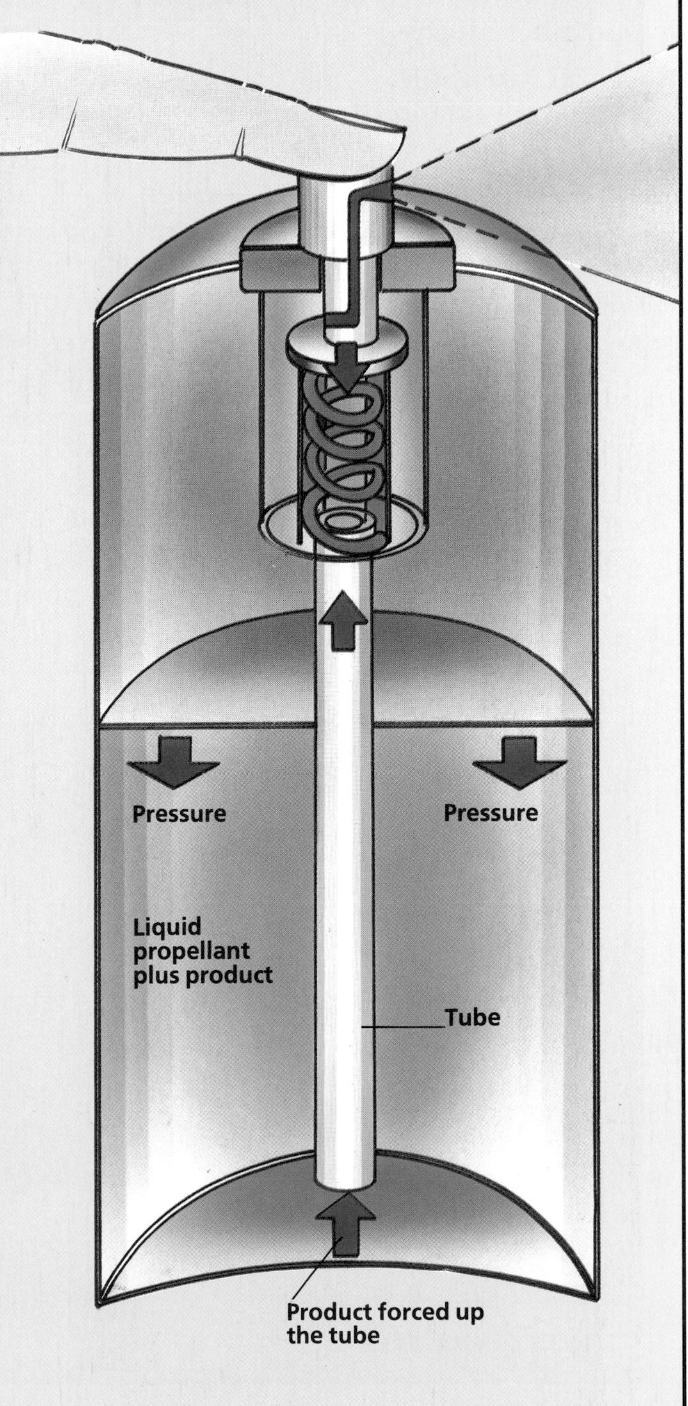

FACT FILE 2

Unfriendly replacements

Some manufacturers are replacing the CFCs in aerosols with other gases. The cans are often labeled "ozone friendly". The gases used – hydrocarbons – may be safe for the ozone layer, but they are greenhouse gases. So they – like CFCs – are bad for the environment. The only really environment-friendly spray is a pump-action one.

Useful radiation

The sun's radiation has many uses besides photosynthesis. Along with the little infrared radiation that gets through, it helps to keep the planet warm. Light in the visible spectrum allows us to see. Radio waves that come through from the sun and other more distant stars are used in the science of radio astronomy. This helps scientists to find out about distant galaxies. We can put radiation similar to that produced by the sun to many different uses. Infrared radiation can be used in burglar alarms. Even radiation that is dangerous to life on earth can be put to valuable use. Ultraviolet is used in health lamps, and X rays in hospitals.

Marine food chains

About 70 percent of our earth is covered by the seas, and there are food chains in the seas as well as on land. In the upper parts, the sun's light penetrates far enough for tiny plants and animals to live in the surface waters. They are called plankton. Some of the sea's great giants, such as manta rays and many whales, eat plankton. The fish that we eat also depend on plankton, either directly or indirectly.

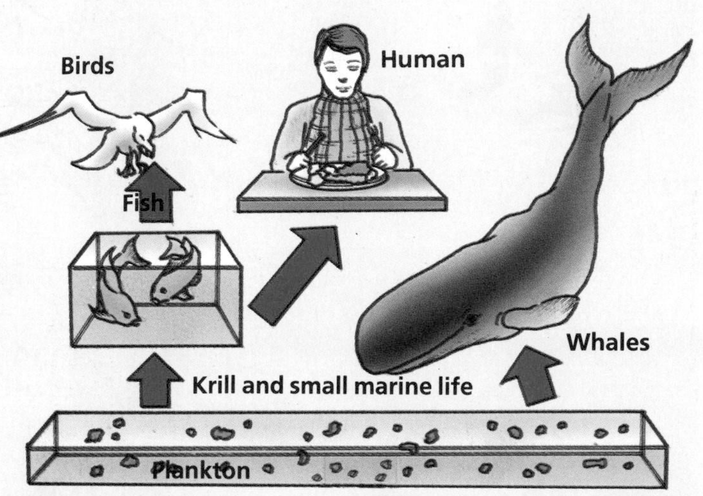

WEATHER AND CLIMATE

CHAPTER 2

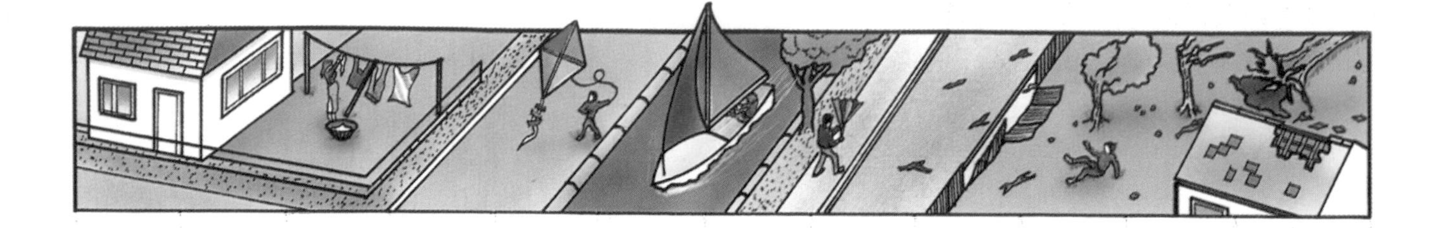

CHAPTER TWO:
WEATHER AND CLIMATE

INTRODUCTION

Weather is news. Every day, millions of people tune into the weather forecast on television and radio or check the newspaper and telephone-line forecasts. Droughts, hurricanes, floods and storms are all news. Many people such as farmers, sailors, airline pilots, coast guards, construction workers and sportspeople all take an interest in how the weather is likely to affect their lives. For example, it is important for farmers to know if the weather will be good for planting seeds, or for a sailor to know whether there will be dangerous storms at sea.

The weather also gets into the news because many scientists say the world's weather is changing and getting hotter. They think this is a result of increasing pollution.

This chapter is an introduction to the basic ideas about weather — why the wind blows, why it rains, why fog forms, why hurricanes develop, and how the world's climate is changing.

Clouds take many shapes and forms.

HOT AND COLD

Temperature is the word we use to describe how hot or cold something is. Where we live and how we feel will change our idea of what is warm and what is cold. So to measure temperature we use a thermometer, which shows degrees Fahrenheit or Celsius (sometimes known as degrees centigrade).

▷ The North and South Poles are cold and always covered by snow and ice. The frozen surface makes life difficult for people and animals in these places. But snowmobiles make getting around easier.

▷ Camels are ideally suited for getting around in hot, dry deserts. They can go for long periods without food or water, and their thick, wiry hair protects them from the heat. People who live in deserts wear long, loose clothes.

FEWER RAYS

Different places on the earth's surface receive different amounts of heat and light from the sun. This is because the sun's rays spread out more on the surface at the poles than at the equator. As a result, places near the equator are hotter than those near the poles.

1 In both polar regions (1 and 5), light is at its weakest.

2 The sun's rays travel parallel to each other in straight lines.

3 Light is least spread out on the earth's surface at the equator.

4 Light is more spread out farther from the equator.

5 Light rays at the poles (1 and 5) also have to travel farther through the atmosphere.

TEMPERATURE EXPERIMENTS

To measure the air temperature you need an ordinary, household thermometer. But you must keep it in a shaded place, like the box shown here. Cut out the shapes using strong cardboard. Put the thermometer inside the box, balanced on the supports. The flaps in the side of the box let air flow through. It is best to put flaps on both sides. Paint the box white. This will reflect away any direct sunlight.

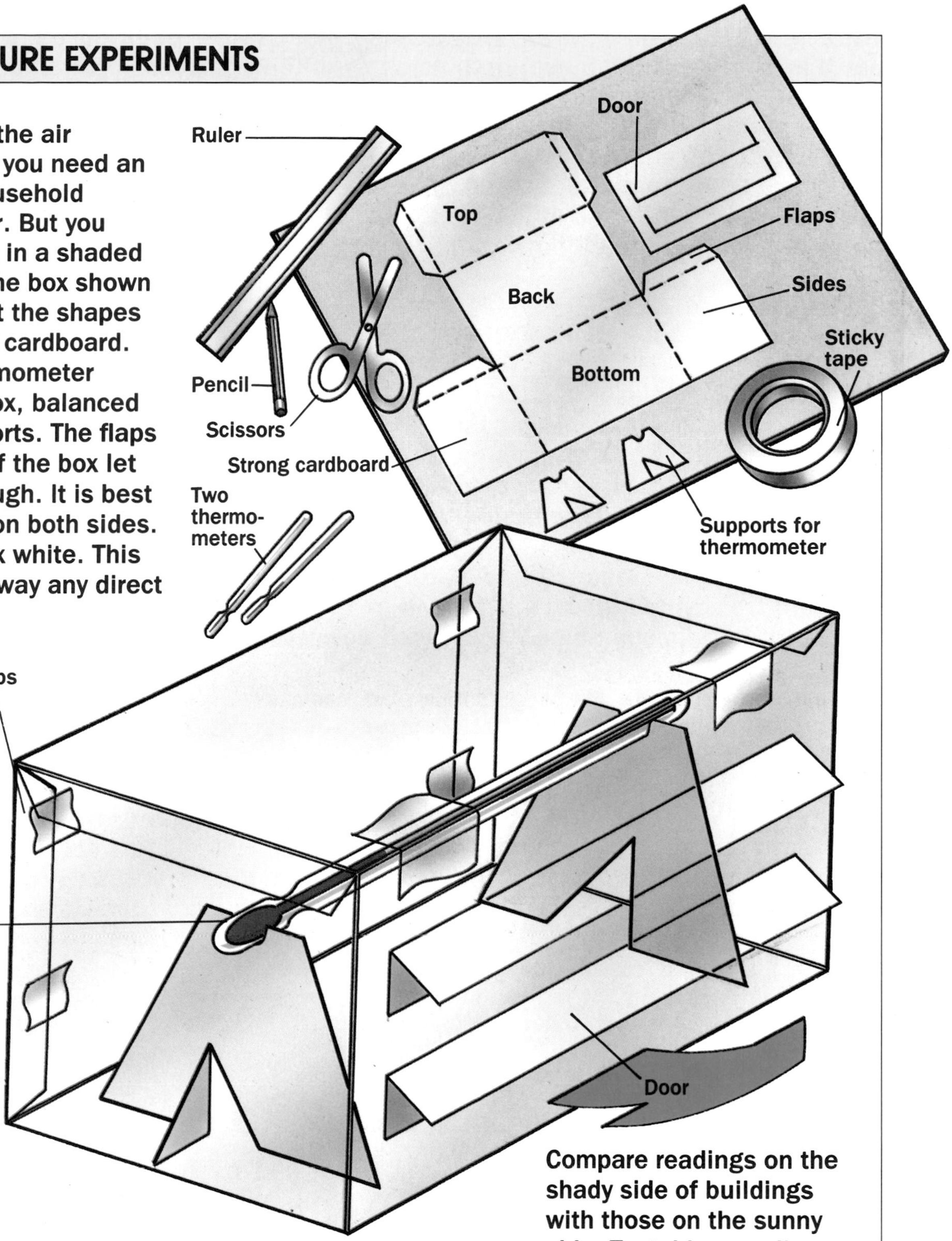

Compare readings on the shady side of buildings with those on the sunny side. Try taking readings close to the ground and then at a height of three to six feet. Compare readings taken in the box with readings when the other thermometer is left out in the open, in either shade or sunlight.

WIND

Wind is moving air. The air around the earth is always on the move, both across the surface, and up and down in the atmosphere. Sometimes we can tell where the winds have come from. For example, dust from the Sahara Desert has settled in northern Europe. There are patterns of wind around the world.

WORLD'S WINDS

At the equator, air is heated, causing it to rise. This creates low air pressure. On each side of the equator – about 2,000 miles north and south – cool air sinks to the earth's surface. This creates high air pressure. Winds blow from the high pressure to the low. Because the earth is spinning, the winds also swirl around in the patterns shown below. The winds around the equator cause other wind patterns farther north and south. All this means that in many parts of the world there is one direction in which the wind usually blows.

▽ The steady, reliable winds once used by sailing ships making regular journeys are known as trade winds.

△ Strong winds can easily make trees bend. Stronger winds can cause a great deal of damage.

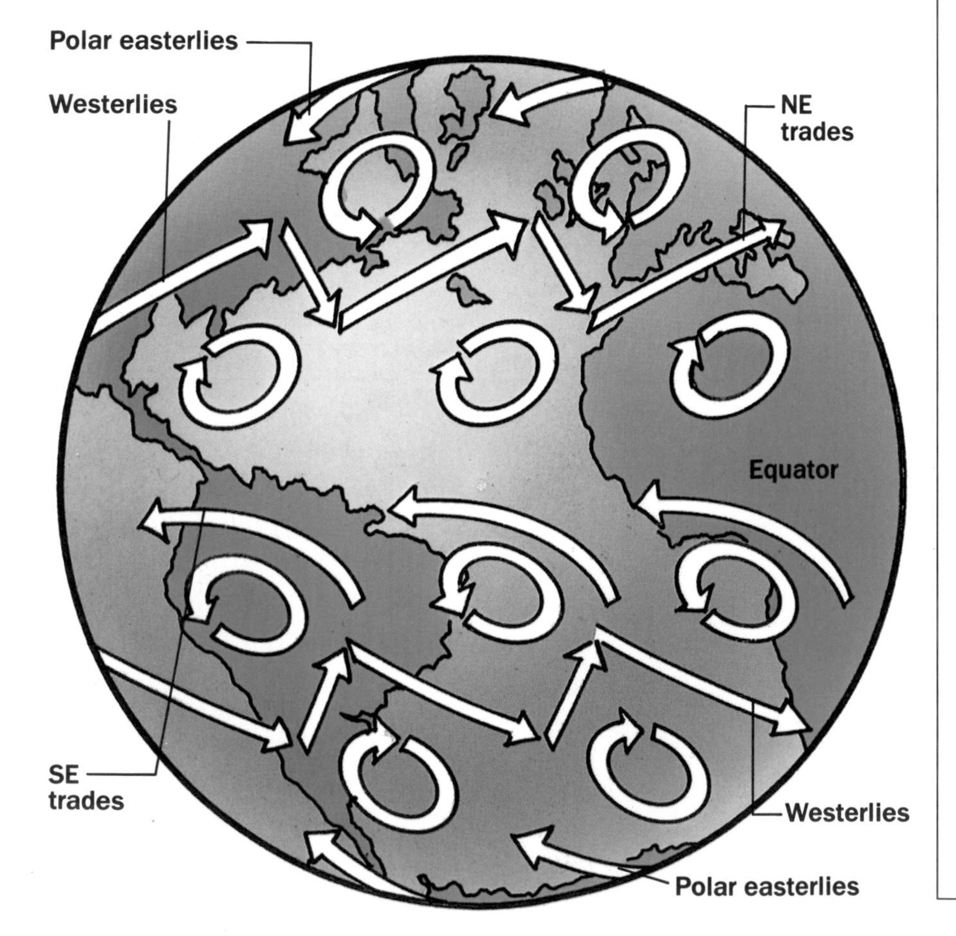

WIND PROJECT

To make a weather vane, fix two triangular pieces of cardboard to a drinking straw (the tail piece should be larger than the head). Pin the straw to the end of an eraser-ended pencil. Fix the pencil into a hole in the bottom of a plastic bottle. The arrow will point to the direction from which the wind is blowing.

Wind speed is measured by an anemometer. This can be made in much the same way as a wind vane, but with four arms and with a counter added. Check how many times the anemometer turns in a period of time – say 20 seconds.

BEAUFORT SCALE

In the early nineteenth century, Sir Francis Beaufort developed a system for judging wind speed. He was a Rear Admiral in the British Navy and wanted a guide to wind speed for use at sea. He made up a scale, and at each point he gave the wind a number, a name, a speed and a description of its effects. His original descriptions were mostly related to the effects of wind on sailing ships. For example, at 2 on the scale a ship would travel at 1 to 2 miles per hour.

The Beaufort scale has 18 points (0 to 17). Zero on the scale represents no wind at all, and 1 is a very slight breeze. At 5 on the scale, small branches on trees sway and paper blows about. Force 8 on the scale is a gale, and it is very difficult to walk against the wind.

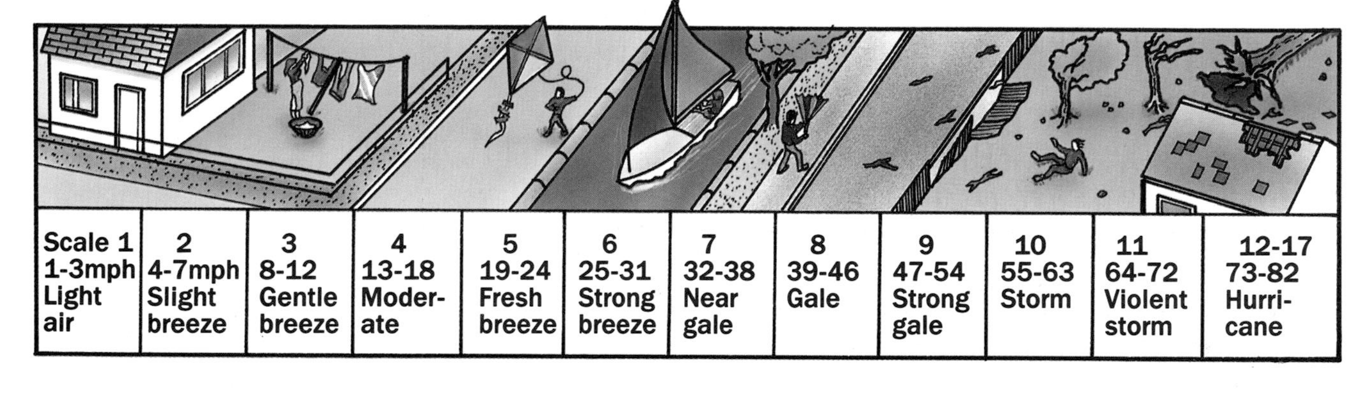

Scale 1	2	3	4	5	6	7	8	9	10	11	12-17
1-3mph	4-7mph	8-12	13-18	19-24	25-31	32-38	39-46	47-54	55-63	64-72	73-82
Light air	Slight breeze	Gentle breeze	Moderate	Fresh breeze	Strong breeze	Near gale	Gale	Strong gale	Storm	Violent storm	Hurricane

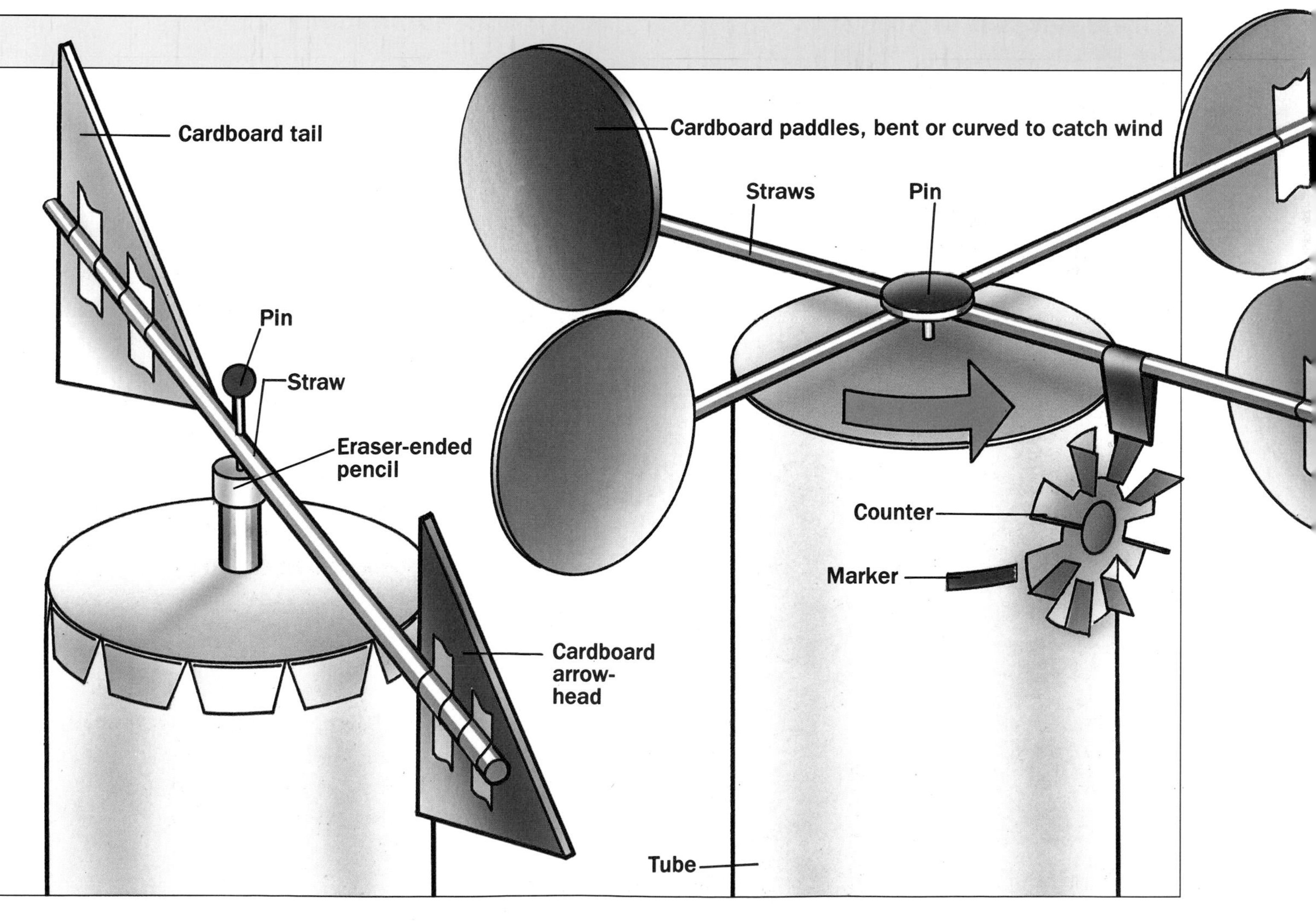

Clouds are made up of millions of tiny droplets of water or ice. Pilots of airplanes inside clouds can see nothing but cloud. Being inside a cloud is like being in a very thick fog. Each cloud droplet is smaller than a grain of flour. The water droplets are so small and light that they can float in the air.

△ Different types of cloud bring different types of weather. These cumulus clouds often indicate fine weather.

FORMATION OF CLOUDS

All air contains at least some water vapor. Water vapor is a gas. When air rises, it cools and the water vapor condenses (turns into tiny drops of water) to form clouds. Air may start to rise for various reasons. For example, in some places air is heated by the warm ground and so rises. In other places air rises to pass over hills and mountains. In other cases cold, heavy air pushes under warm air and forces it to rise.

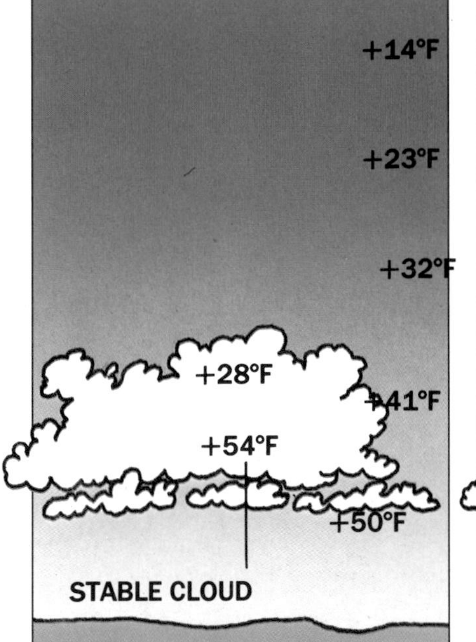

△ As air rises it cools and the water vapor in it condenses to form clouds. When the atmosphere around the cloud is warmer than the cloud itself, only stable clouds are formed. A stratus cloud is a typical sort of stable cloud.

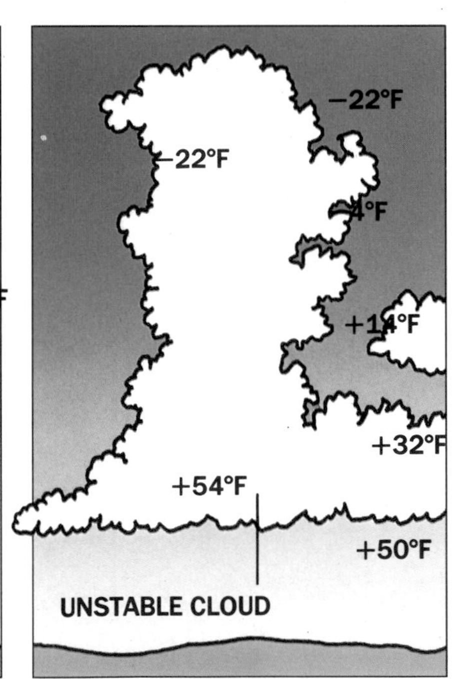

△ If the rising air that is forming a cloud is much warmer than the air around it, it rises to a considerable height. The cloud cools down, but it remains warmer than the surrounding air. A cumulonimbus cloud is of this type.

▷ There are many types of cloud, and cloud names are often joined together. For example, a cumulonimbus is a cumulus that gives rain, or an altostratus is a high stratus.

Cumulus

DID YOU KNOW?

There is an old saying that a red sky in the evening means good weather the next day. Meteorologists say there is some evidence that this is true (see page 13).

DIFFERENT TYPES OF CLOUD

Clouds vary in shape and in their height above the earth. Clouds that look like cotton balls are called cumulus. They have flat bases and tops shaped like cauliflowers. Stratus are layers of cloud that look like even sheets, covering all or part of the sky. They are usually quite low in the air. Cirrus are thin wisps of cloud, high up in the atmosphere. They are made up of ice crystals. Clouds that give prolonged rain are called nimbostratus. The base of a cumulonimbus cloud is often low, but it may tower to great heights.

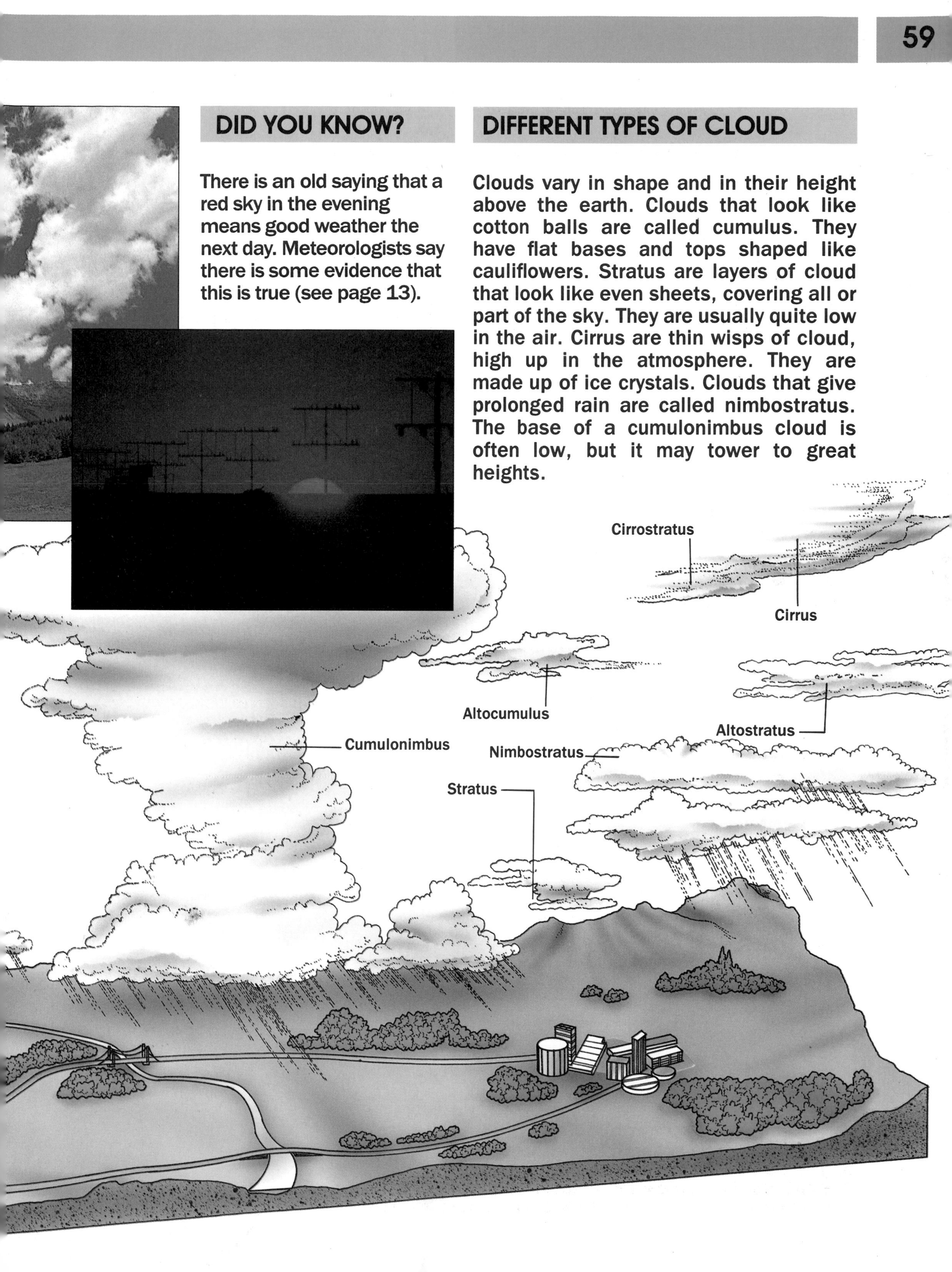

RAIN, SNOW AND HAIL

Water is constantly on the move in a process called the water cycle. Winds pick up water vapor that has evaporated from the sea, and which forms clouds. When the clouds reach land, often the water falls as rain or snow. This drains into rivers and streams that flow back to the sea, and the process starts again.

Vapor blown inland

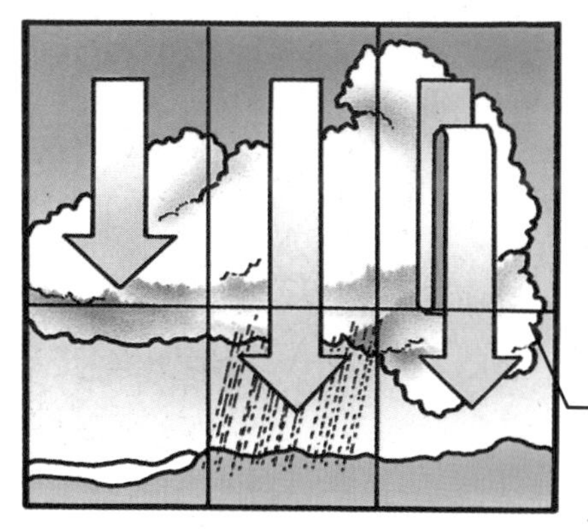

Water droplets move in clouds.

Evaporation from oceans and lakes

Vapor condenses as it rises and cools, making rain.

RAIN AND SNOW

Rain or snow starts in clouds. The tiny droplets of water floating in a cloud stick to particles of dust, salt from ocean spray, or ice. The water droplets inside the cloud grow bigger and bump into each other, growing even larger. Eventually, the droplets become too big and heavy to be held up in the air any longer, and they fall from the cloud as rain. If the temperature of the cloud is below freezing, the water vapor turns into ice crystals, which form snowflakes.

▽ Rain gives water for drinking, for farms and for factories. Too much leads to floods, too little brings drought.

▽ Snow can get very deep and cover a whole landscape. But in most parts of the world it soon melts to provide water.

HAIL

Hail falls only from tall cumulonimbus clouds. Inside the clouds there are very strong vertical air currents. Raindrops that form inside a cloud are carried up and down by these air currents. At the top of the cloud it is very cold and the raindrops freeze. Then, as they fall, more water sticks to them and freezes a layer at a time so that the frozen drops get bigger and bigger. They may travel up and down again many times inside the cloud. When the raindrop eventually falls, it is a lump of ice called a hailstone.

▷ If a hailstone is cut in half, layers of ice can be seen. Large hailstones can cause a great amount of damage.

MAKE A RAIN GAUGE

Carefully cut the top from a flat-bottomed plastic bottle. Place the top upside down inside the cut-down bottle. Then seal it in place using tape. Use a ruler to make a scale showing inches and stick it upright on one side of the bottle. You can use the gauge to find out how much rain falls in a day, week or month.

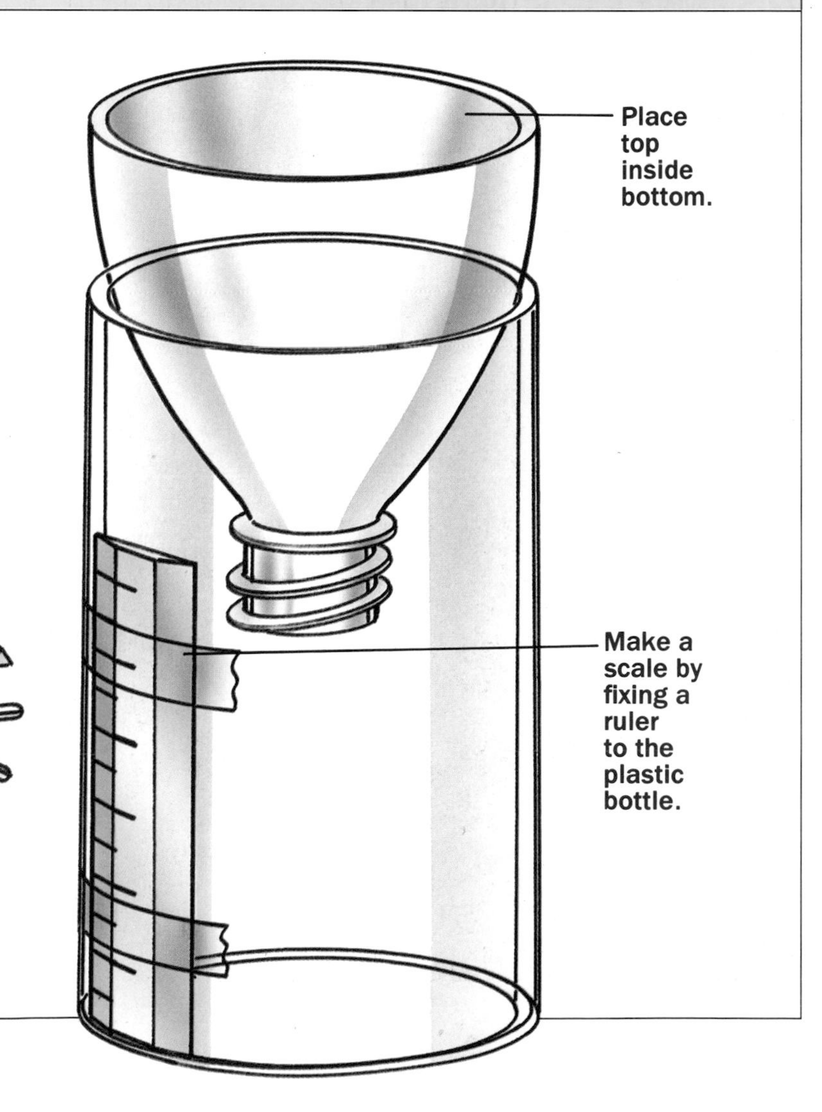

FOG AND FROST

Fog, drizzle, dew and frost all form when water vapor in the air cools until it condenses (turns to water). This process is more or less the same as that by which clouds form. But with fog, mist, dew and frost the condensation takes place close to or on the ground. And it is often the ground itself that cools the air.

FOG

Fog often forms after sunset on fine days with clear skies and no wind, although it can form in many other conditions. The surface of the ground loses heat rapidly. As the ground cools, it cools the air that is in contact with it. The cool air is heavier than the surrounding air, so it tends to collect near the ground in hollows and in the bottoms of valleys. Eventually the water vapor in the air condenses into droplets, which form the fog. To weather forecasters, the difference between fog and drizzle is that with fog, visibility (how far it is possible to see) is one half mile or less.

△ The tiny water droplets that make up fog are suspended in air close to the ground. This makes visibility a problem.

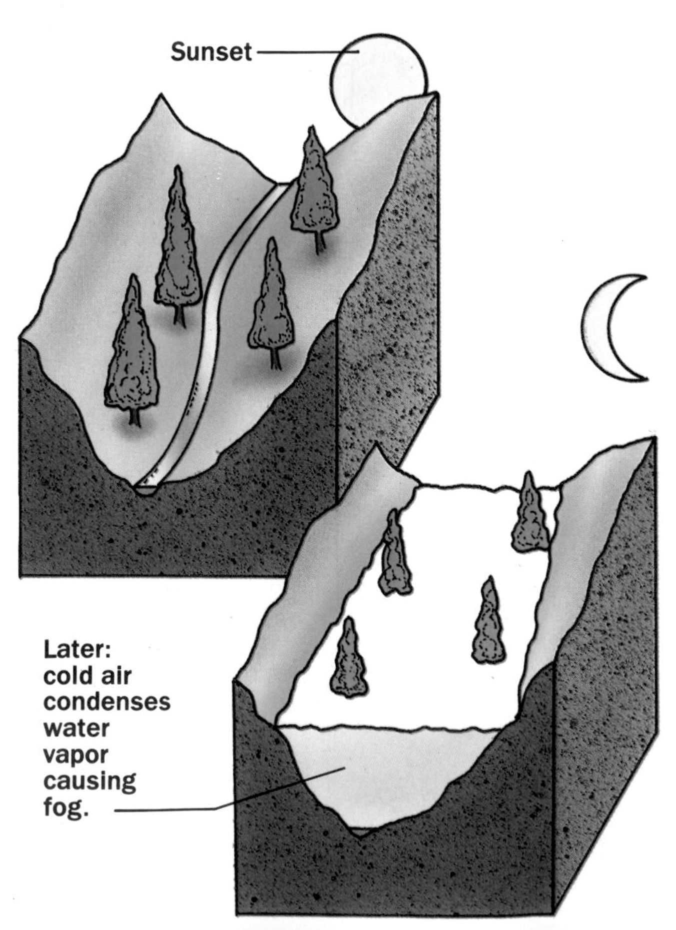

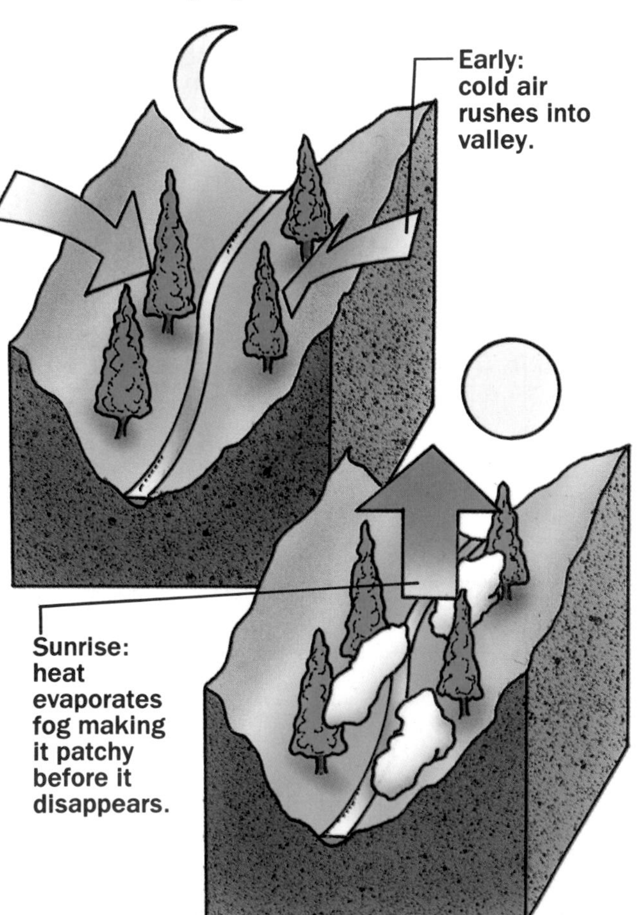

FROST AND DEW

On calm, clear nights, cold ground cools the air close to it. Water vapor in the air condenses onto cold surfaces, such as plants, forming large droplets of water called dew.

If the temperature of the ground is below freezing, then frost will form instead of dew. Cars, roads and plants may be covered by a white layer of frost. On windows, frost forms feathery crystals. Sometimes water vapor or rain freezes into a layer of clear, slippery ice, particularly on roads. This is called black ice and is a very dangerous type of frost because drivers cannot see it.

▽ Frost can form very beautiful patterns in the landscape. It can also kill plants and make roads and paths slippery and dangerous.

FREEZING PROJECT

Water expands when it freezes. This is why water pipes can burst in cold weather. Fill a plastic bottle to the rim and put on the cap. Freeze it, and it will bulge or split. **Do not use a glass bottle.**

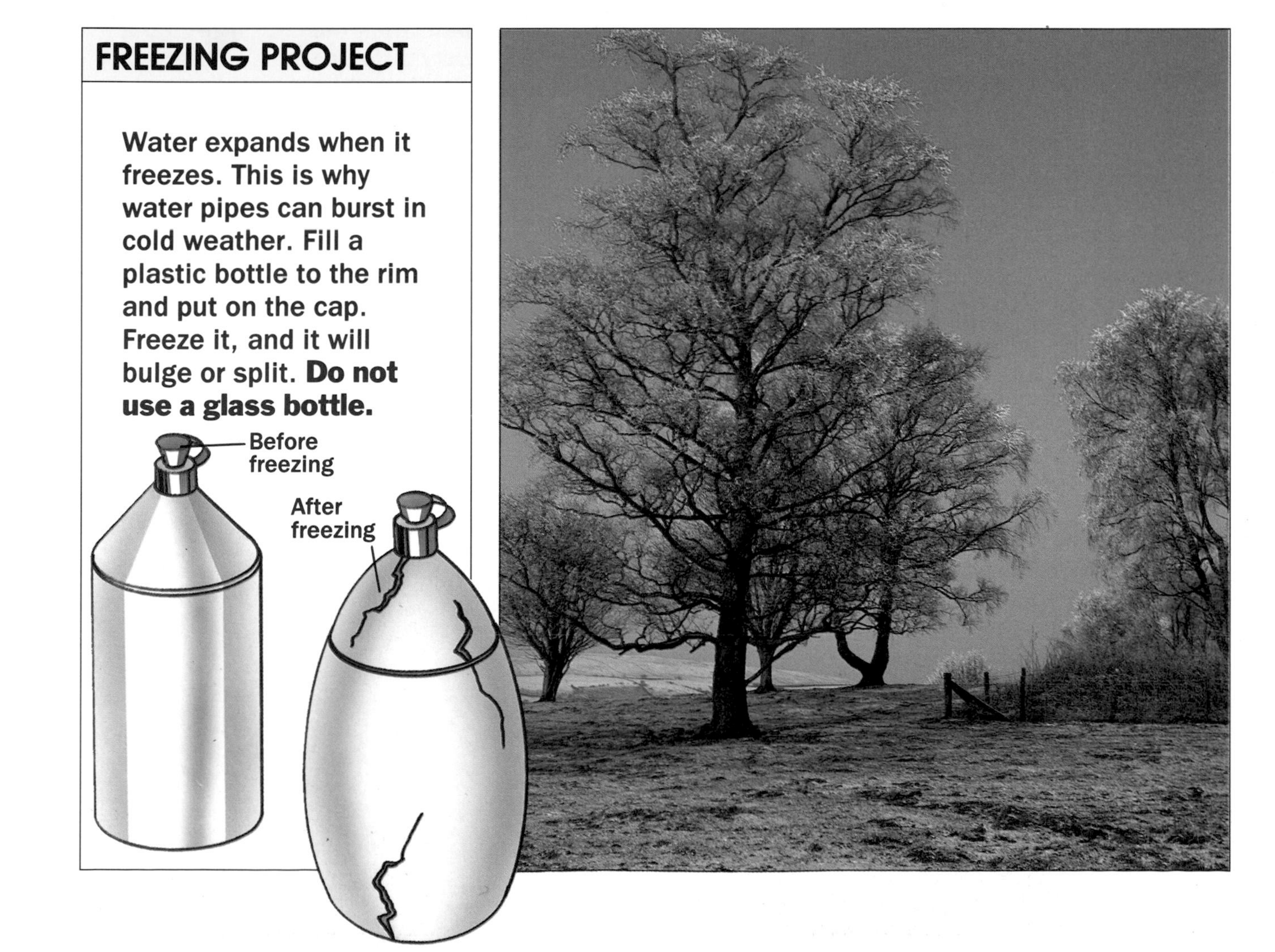

DEPRESSIONS AND ANTICYCLONES

The weight of the air in the atmosphere pressing down on the earth is called air pressure. This pressure varies from place to place, and areas of pressure often move. Areas of high pressure (called anticyclones) bring fine weather. Areas of low pressure (called depressions) bring cloud and rain.

HIGHS AND LOWS

In anticyclones, in which air pressure is high, the air is slowly sinking toward the surface of the earth. As the air descends it gets warmer and so can hold more water vapor. This means that the weather is usually fine. When the air reaches the surface, it spreads out and rotates clockwise (in the Northern Hemisphere) because of the earth's rotation.

In depressions, in which air pressure is low, air rises. As it rises, it cools and so can hold less water vapor. As a result, clouds and rain are formed. The rotation of the earth causes the air to rise in a counterclockwise spiral. The directions in which air spirals are reversed in the Southern Hemisphere.

△ When two masses of air meet, clouds form. Often the air masses are very different. If one is warm and wet and the other is cold and dry, dark clouds quickly form, often with rain, hail or thunder.

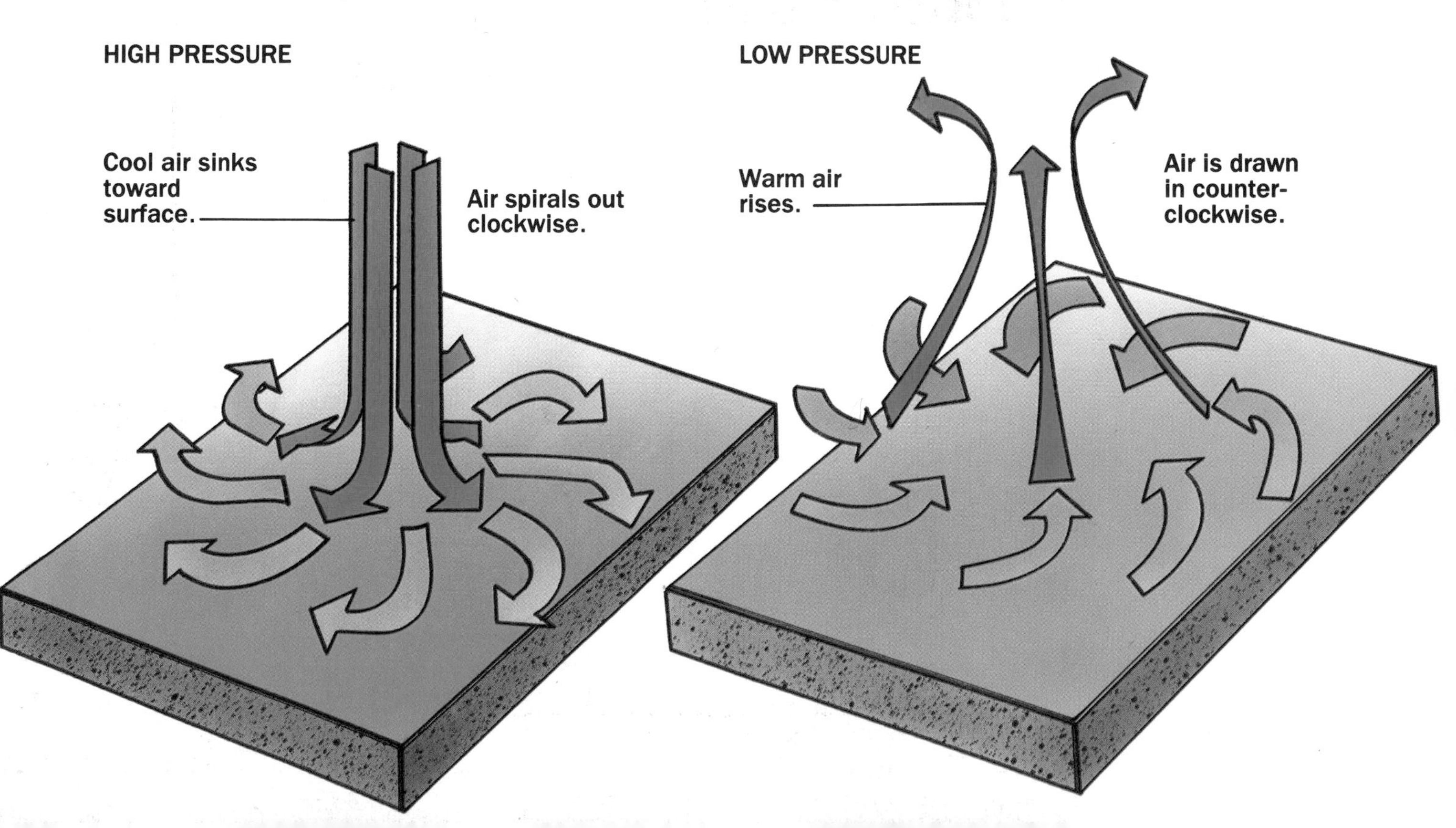

INSIDE A DEPRESSION

As the air in a depression swirls around, fronts move with it. Fronts are belts of cloud and rain where masses of warm air are rising over cold air. With a warm front, a mass of warm air catches up with a mass of cold air. The warm air rises quite slowly over the cold air, so the rain is often a light drizzle. With a cold front, cold air pushes underneath the warm air. The warm air rises rapidly, and there is often heavy rain or even thunderstorms. An occluded front is when one front catches up with another.

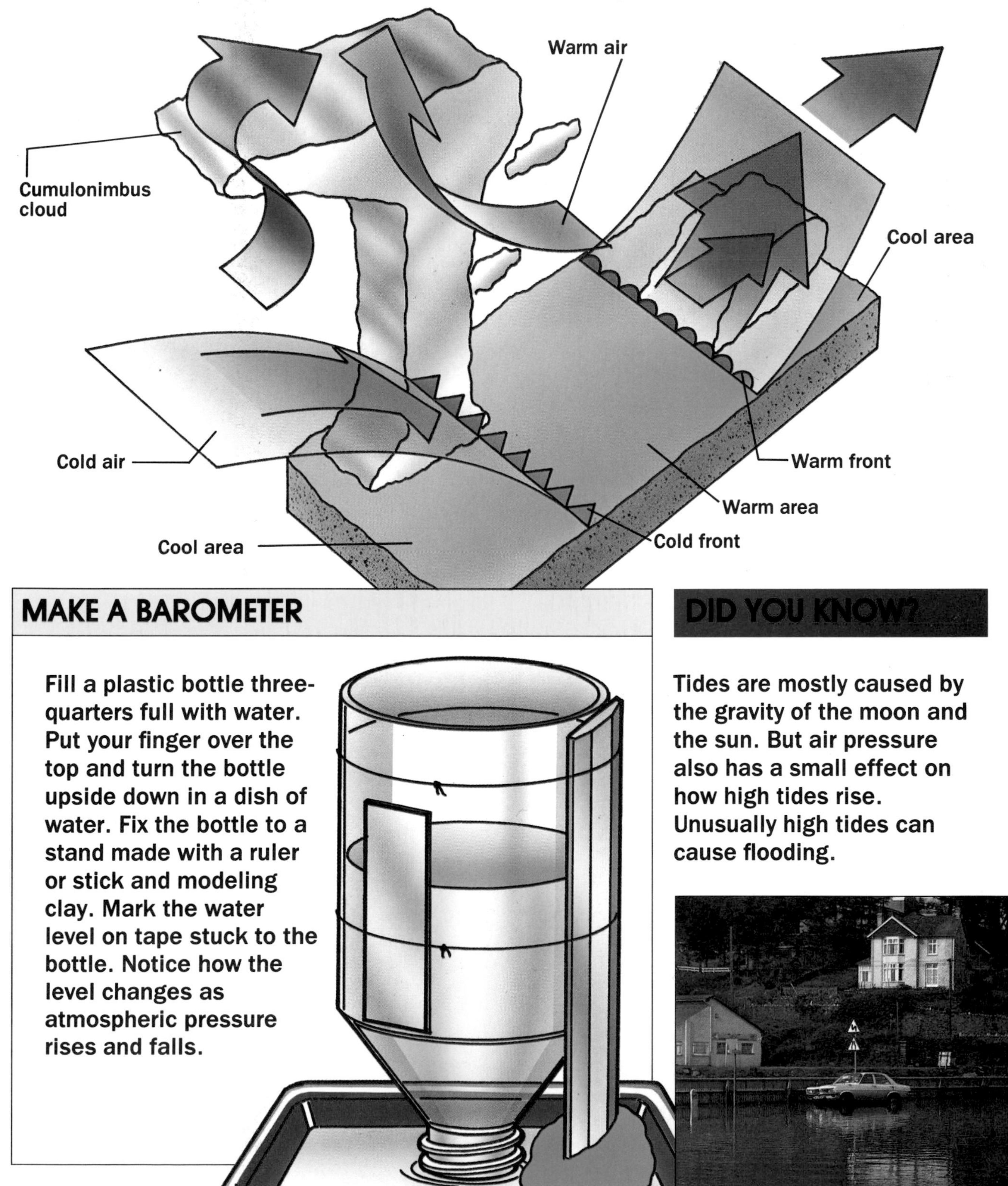

MAKE A BAROMETER

Fill a plastic bottle three-quarters full with water. Put your finger over the top and turn the bottle upside down in a dish of water. Fix the bottle to a stand made with a ruler or stick and modeling clay. Mark the water level on tape stuck to the bottle. Notice how the level changes as atmospheric pressure rises and falls.

DID YOU KNOW?

Tides are mostly caused by the gravity of the moon and the sun. But air pressure also has a small effect on how high tides rise. Unusually high tides can cause flooding.

THE WEATHER FORECAST

Forecasts are made by collecting information from around the world. This information includes temperature, humidity, sunshine, wind speed and direction, air pressure and rainfall. Computers process the information into special maps called synoptic charts. These are used to predict the weather.

△ Weather forecasters are like detectives. They use clues about the weather in order to give television forecasts.

GATHERING INFORMATION

Information for weather forecasting comes from many sources. Weather stations record information at ground level, and automatic weather stations send back data from remote places. Satellites collect data such as temperature and cloud cover in parts of the atmosphere we cannot see. Weather balloons are sent about 70,000 feet up into the air every day. They carry radio transmitters and send details about the temperature and humidity of the atmosphere at different heights. Ships often make reports on conditions at sea. Radar is used to track the progress of rain across the country, and produces maps that show the amount. Special aircraft fitted with instruments measure atmospheric changes.

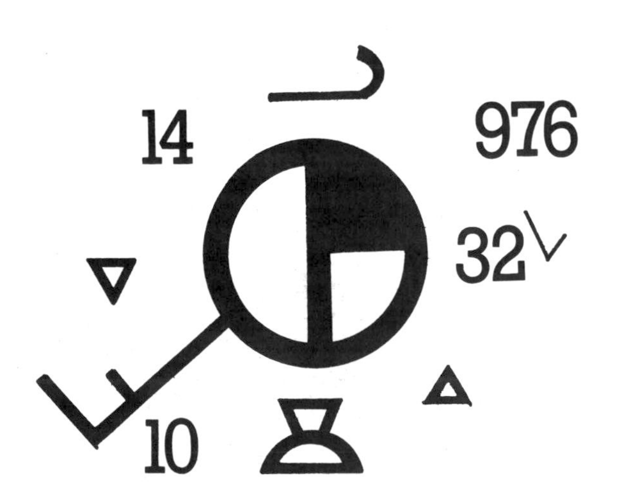

△ Symbols like this show the weather in a particular place; for example, the "F" shows where the wind is coming from.

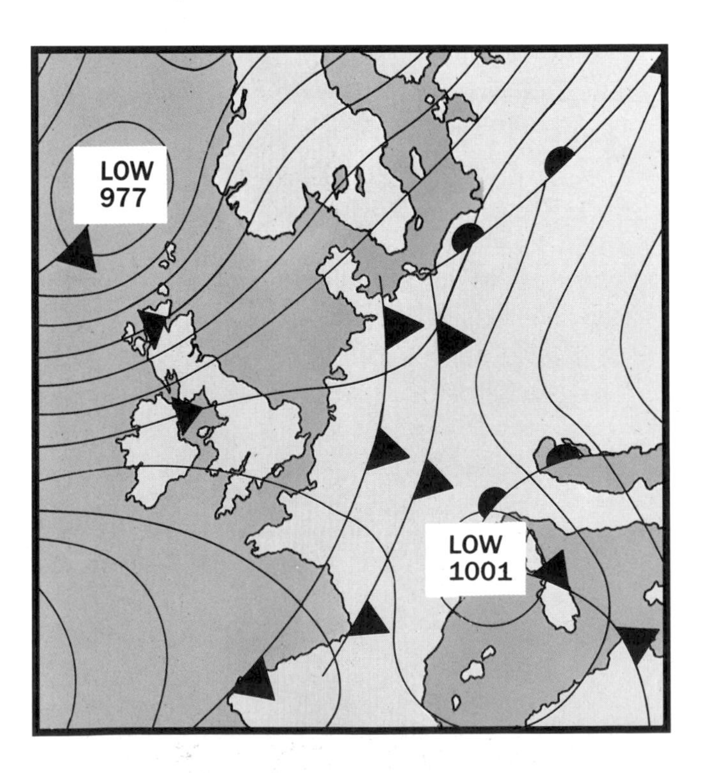

▽ Meteorologists use the information from a synoptic chart to scientifically predict the next day's weather.

USING THE FORECAST

Millions of people look at or listen to television, radio and newspaper forecasts every day. For some people this is simply to know what to wear the next day. However, many other people or organizations study the weather forecast carefully. For example, farmers need to know the best time to harvest their crops. Supermarket managers need to know if the demand for ice cream and soft drinks is likely to increase. Airlines can save money and fuel by routing airplanes so that they are not flying against wind.

▷ Knowing the positions of the main cloud formations over the earth helps forecasters to understand the weather.

▷ Satellites have helped to make modern weather observation and forecasting much more accurate.

▽ Computers track and record the movement of weather systems around the world. This is important in stormy areas.

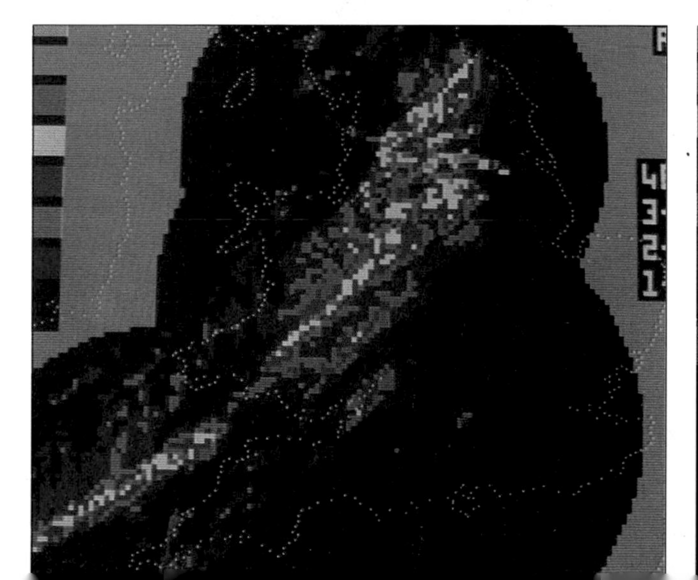

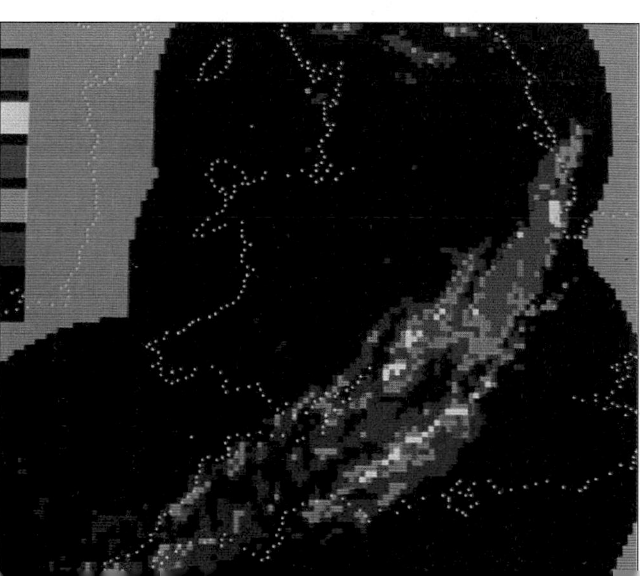

EXTREME WEATHER

Extreme weather can be very dangerous. Every year it brings disaster to many places around the world. The weather can cause millions of dollars worth of damage, and it may injure people or even kill them. As forecasting and planning improve, the worst effects of severe weather can sometimes be avoided.

HURRICANES

Hurricanes are extremely destructive storms. They usually form over warm oceans in areas where winds from opposite directions meet. Swirls of air form. These begin to create a spiral. Gradually the air in the spiral moves faster and faster, until it reaches speeds of up to 180 miles per hour. The wind is strong enough to demolish houses and whip up huge waves. The center, or "eye", of a hurricane is a calm area surrounded by violent winds.

△ Hurricanes form over the Atlantic Ocean. The same sort of wind over the Pacific Ocean is called a typhoon.

▽ Tornadoes are most common in the central parts of the United States. They suck up many things in their paths.

TORNADOES

Tornadoes form over land and are often more violent than hurricanes. They start when hot, damp air meets cool, dry air and rises extremely fast. A funnel of cloud forms, which can be up to 1,000 feet high. Winds in tornadoes blow at up to 300 miles per hour. Tornadoes are usually a few hundred feet in diameter, and swirl around a center which is about 300 feet wide. They last for between 15 minutes and five hours, and travel between 20 and 200 miles. They can destroy almost everything that is in their path. When tornadoes pass over water, they suck it up into the air to form a waterspout. In large tornadoes, small frogs, fish and other animals can be swept up into the air.

THUNDER AND LIGHTNING

There are violent air currents inside cumulonimbus clouds. These currents cause ice crystals to crash into each other. This creates friction and splitting, which cause static electricity. Positive charges build up at the top of a cloud, and negative ones at the bottom. The ground has a positive charge. The difference between charges gets bigger until lightning sparks across the gap.

Lightning almost instantly heats the air in its path to about 50,000°F. This causes the air to expand very quickly. Thunder is the sound of the hot air expanding.

▽ Lightning can damage buildings and injure or kill people. Lightning takes the shortest path to the ground.

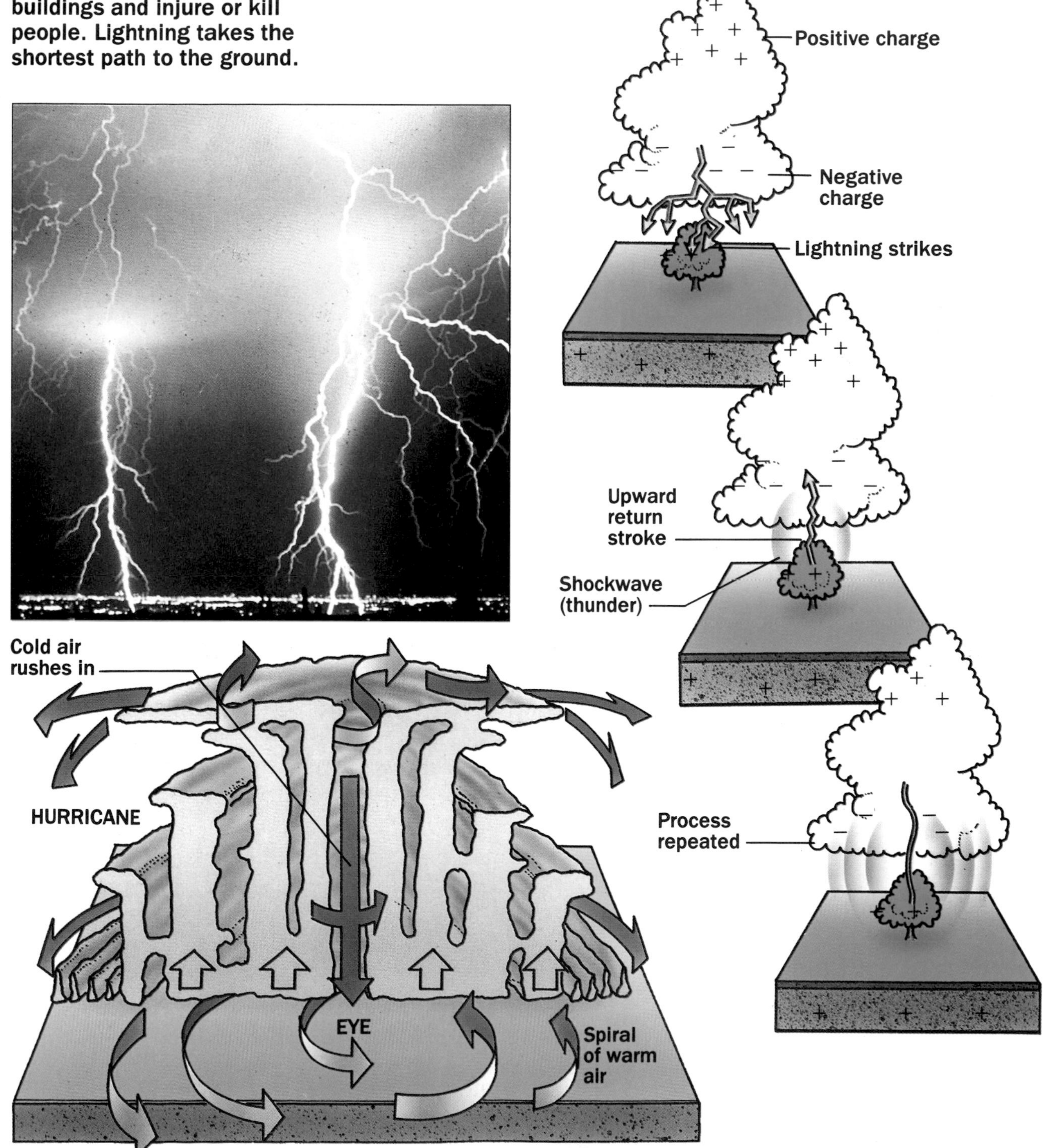

THE SEASONS

In many parts of the world, the main type of weather that occurs changes during the course of the year (as shown in the four pictures below). Each period with a particular type of weather is known as a season. Seasons have a direct effect on plant and animal life; for example, plants start to grow in spring seasons.

ALL THE YEAR ROUND

Seasons are the result of the tilt of the earth as it orbits around the sun. At one end of the earth's orbit, the North Pole is pointing toward the sun and the Northern Hemisphere has its hot summer and the Southern Hemisphere has its cold winter. Six months later, the opposite is true. In between, the weather changes during spring and autumn.

These seasons happen because the sun's rays are spread more thinly in parts of the world tilted away from the sun (in winter). Also, the length of each day is shorter. The opposite is true when that part of the earth is tilted toward the sun in summer. (Compare this to the reason why the poles are cold on page 54).

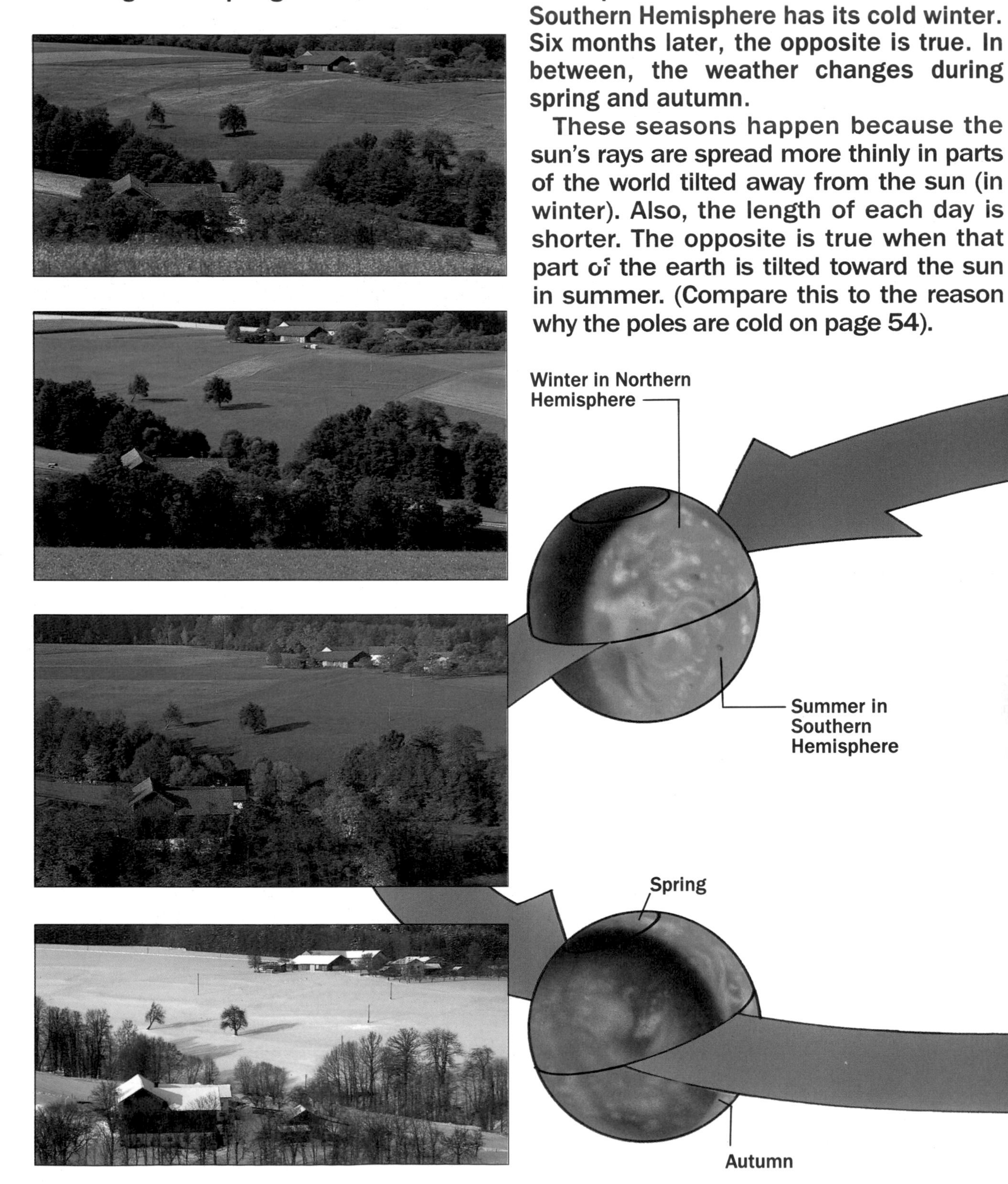

DIFFERENT PLACES

The North and South Poles have only two seasons, which are six months of winter followed by six months of summer. Places in between the equator and the poles usually have spring and autumn as well as summer and winter. Places near the equator really have only one season, which is like summer. This is because the sun is always high in the sky. In some places, particularly southern Asia, the seasons change very quickly. The wind blows from the northeast for six months then, within a day, it can turn around and blow from the southwest. These seasonal winds are called monsoons. The monsoon from the southwest brings a season of heavy rain.

△ The rain brought by the southwesterly monsoon winds in Asia is vital for rice growing. But the rain can also cause rivers to overflow and flood the surrounding land.

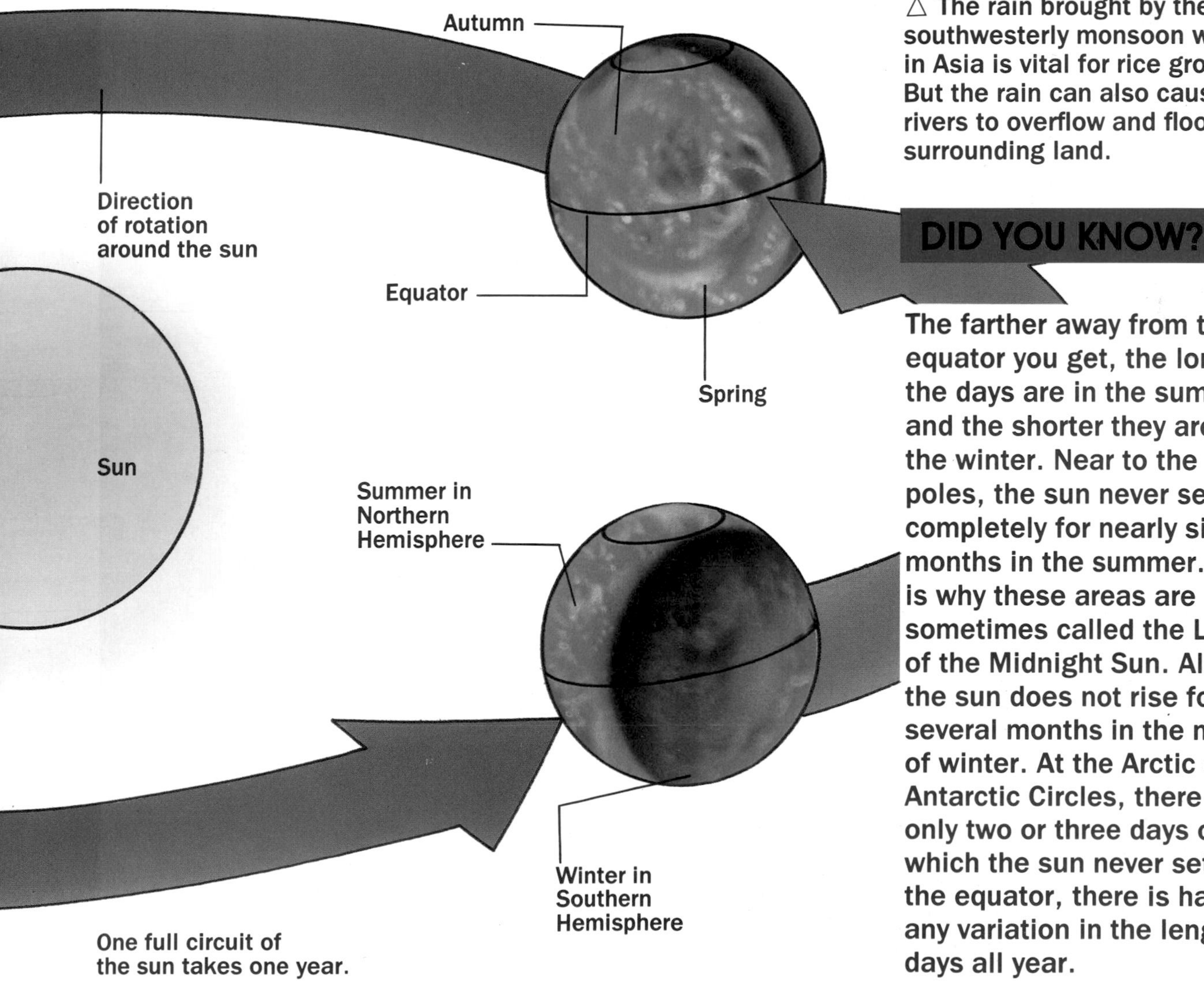

DID YOU KNOW?

The farther away from the equator you get, the longer the days are in the summer and the shorter they are in the winter. Near to the poles, the sun never sets completely for nearly six months in the summer. This is why these areas are sometimes called the Land of the Midnight Sun. Also, the sun does not rise for several months in the middle of winter. At the Arctic and Antarctic Circles, there are only two or three days on which the sun never sets. At the equator, there is hardly any variation in the length of days all year.

WORLD CLIMATES

Each part of the earth tends to have certain types of weather. These range from generally hot, dry weather in deserts to mostly cold and snowy weather at the poles. The pattern of weather in each place is called its climate. For example, the west of Europe has a generally mild climate, with few extremes of weather.

▽ Climate has a big effect on plants. These maps show the main types of vegetation in different areas.

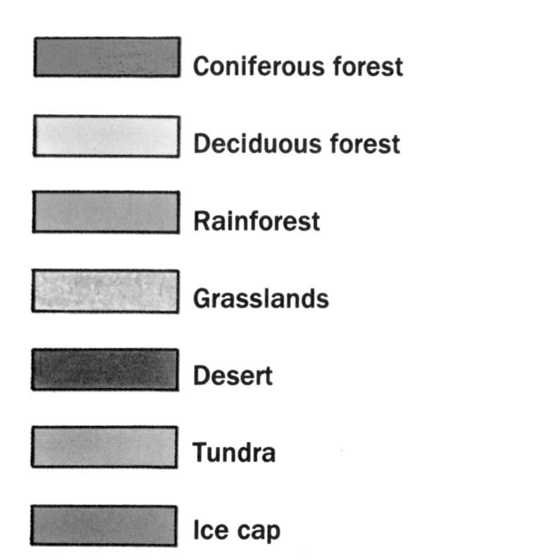

DIFFERENT CLIMATES

Geographers divide the world into areas with different types of climate. The climate in each place depends on very many factors. These include how far the place is from the equator, how far it is from the sea, and how high it is.

An example of two places with different climates is Glasgow in Scotland and Moscow in Russia. These cities are roughly the same distance north of the equator. But their climates are very different. Moscow is much colder in winter and much hotter in summer. There is a difference in climate because Glasgow is very close to the sea, whereas Moscow is hundreds of miles inland. Places like Glasgow, which are near the sea, are said to have a maritime climate. In a maritime climate, temperatures do not vary much throughout the year. Places like Moscow have a continental climate, with yearly extremes of temperature.

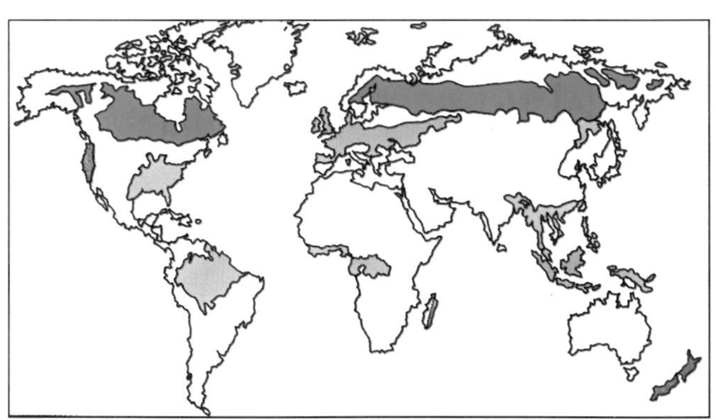

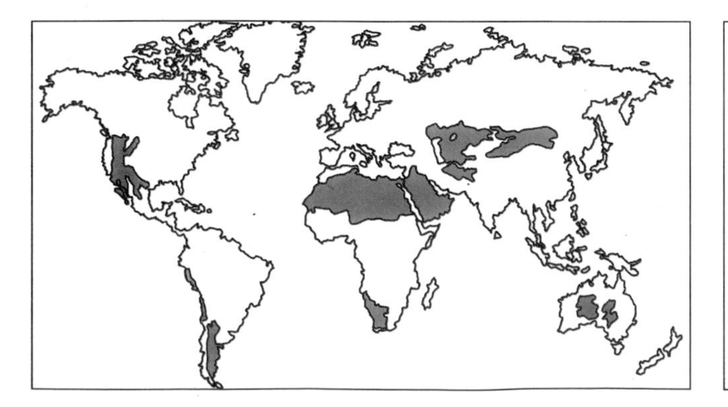

ALTITUDE AND CLIMATE

Climate changes with altitude (height) in much the same way as it changes when you travel away from the equator toward the poles. Temperatures decrease as altitude gets higher. And as the temperature changes, so does the rest of the climate and the vegetation. So on high mountains close to the equator it is possible to move through several climates before reaching snow. Above the snow line, climate is much like that at the poles!

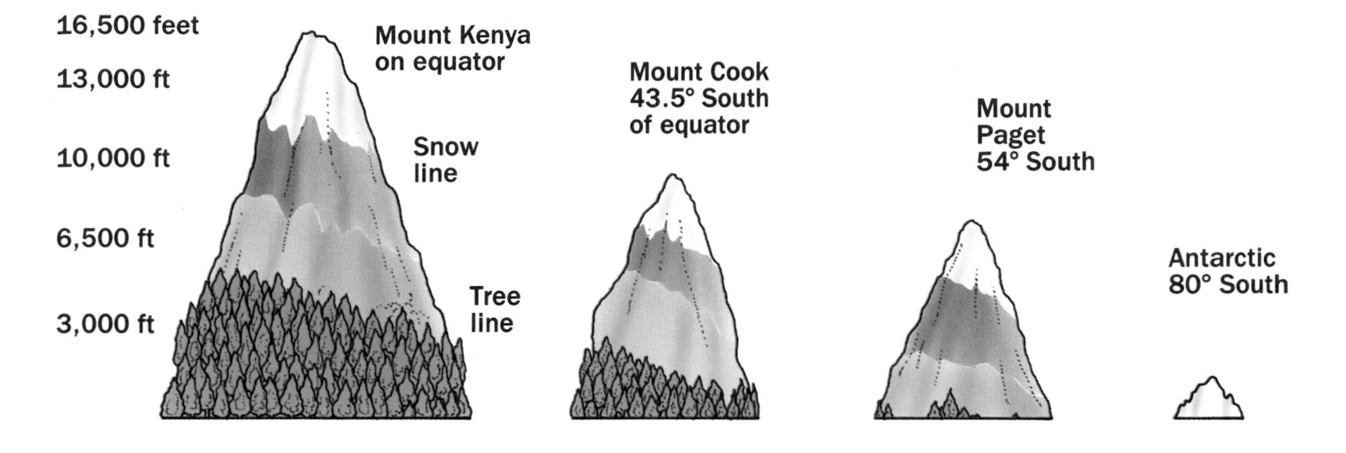

CURRENTS AND CLIMATE

Warm and cool ocean currents affect the climate of coastal areas. This happens particularly if the winds are blowing from the sea to the shore and carrying the sea's influence inland. Currents that flow toward the poles are warmer than the surrounding water, and so are called warm currents. Currents that flow toward the equator are usually colder than the surrounding water, and so are called cold currents. Warm currents have most effect in winter, when they make coasts warmer than areas farther inland. Cold currents have most effect in summer, when they cool the coasts.

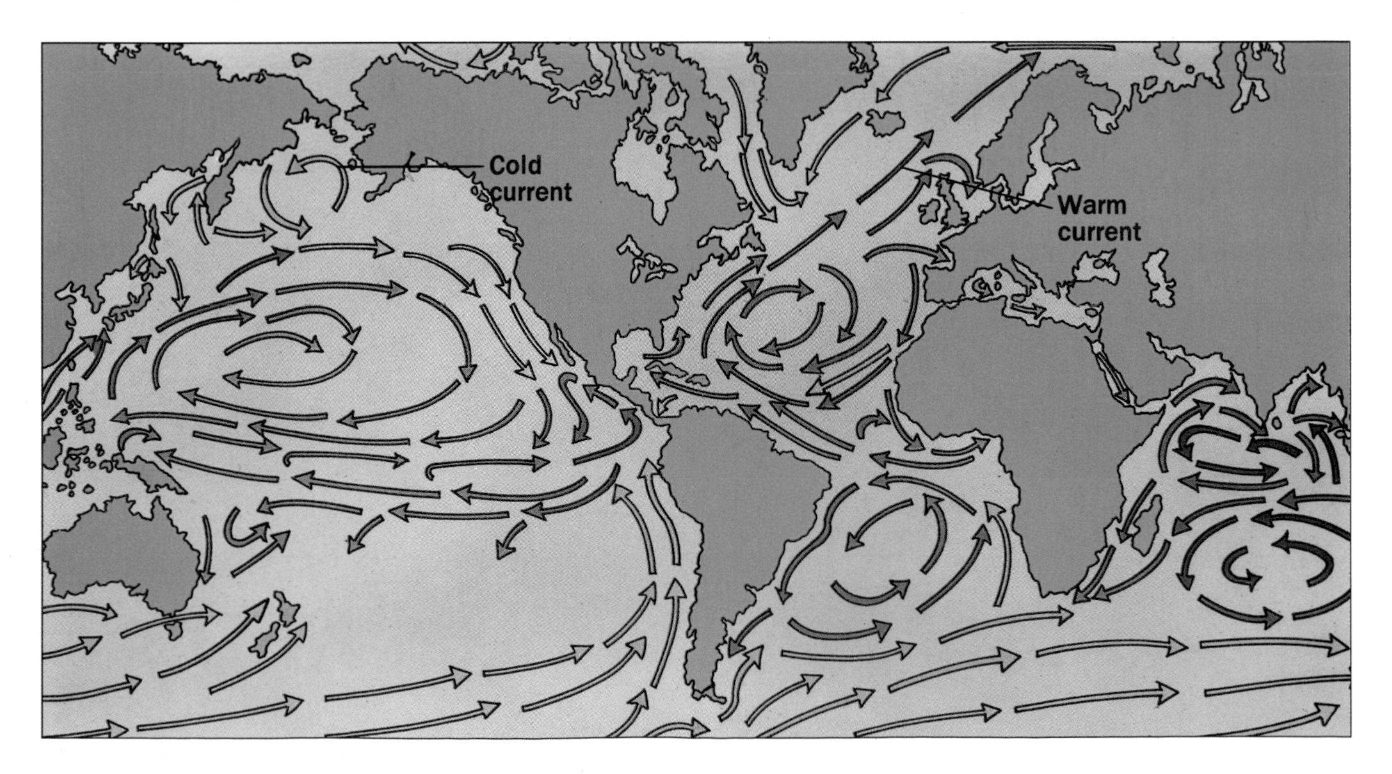

WEATHER IN THE PAST

Most of northern Europe was covered by thick sheets of ice about 20,000 years ago. This was the last Ice Age. Since then, the climate has become warmer and much of the ice has melted. There have been several Ice Ages. We are now in a warm period between two Ice Ages, which could last 40,000 years.

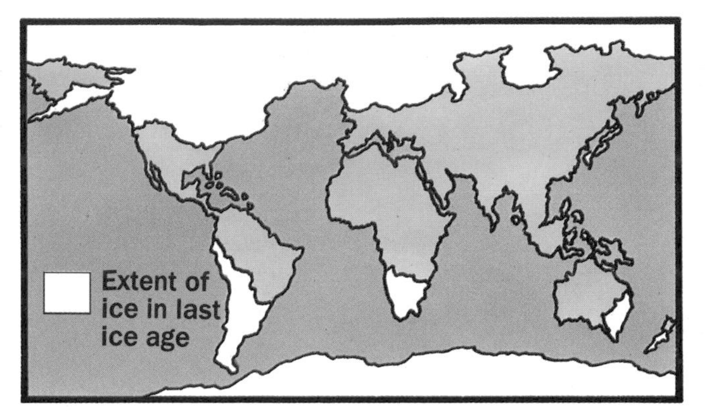

The weather 2,000 years ago was much warmer than now. This meant, for example, that grapes could be grown in Britain, which was ruled by the Romans at the time. Between 1600 and 1800 the world had a "Little Ice Age" when glaciers and sheets of ice grew thicker. It became quite common in winter to see people skating on large rivers that never freeze over now. They even held "frost fairs" in the middle of such rivers.

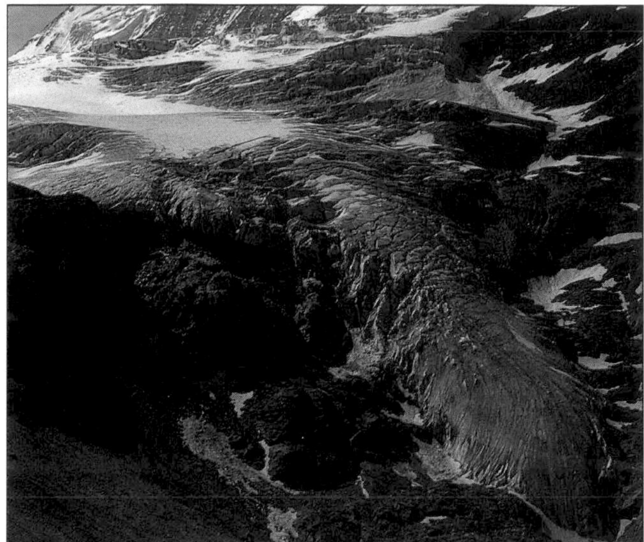

Glacier

Between 1800 and 1900, the world's weather began to warm up again. This meant ice sheets became thinner and glaciers in Europe began to retreat. As the ice melted, the bodies of explorers who had fallen into crevasses in the ice were gradually revealed. Since 1900, average temperatures seem to have continued rising. Sometimes events can have an effect on the weather. In 1883, when the volcano Krakatoa exploded, dust stayed in the air for 3 years. This had a temporary cooling effect, because the dust blocked some heat from the sun.

Krakatoa exploding

JUNGLES AND FORESTS

CHAPTER THREE: JUNGLES AND FORESTS

RAINFOREST DESTRUCTION

INTRODUCTION

Forests are an important part of the earth's landscape. They protect the land from erosion, provide homes for millions of plants and animals, and help regulate the oxygen in the atmosphere.

The dominant life-form in forests are trees, and the types of tree that thrive in a particular forest depend on the climate of the area. For example, coniferous trees, which stay green all year round, thrive in the cold climate of the north. Deciduous trees that shed their leaves in winter cover large areas of the temperate forests. Tropical rainforests have a year-round growing season, and contain an amazing diversity of plant and animal life.

Forests compete with human beings for use of the land. Ten thousand years ago, the world's forests were twice as large as they are today. But logging and agricultural activity have reduced much of the forests over the years, and many people are worried about the rate at which forests are being cut down.

Beautiful ancient oak trees in a forest in Dartmoor, England

Today, about one-quarter of the earth's land surface is covered by dense, green forest. Stretching over millions of square miles, trees are the most dominant life-form. The world's forests can be divided into three main types — the tropical; rainforests, the temperate forests, and the boreal forests.

Polar regions are too cold for forests to grow.

WHERE THEY GROW

Forests develop over many years, and different types of plants and animals live in the forest until it reaches its climax stage. For example, after a few years, pines may start to grow in a grassy meadow. These are finally replaced with wholly deciduous trees, the final stage in the forest succession.

The types of tree that grow in a particular area depend on the temperature and rainfall. In common with other plants, trees need average temperatures of at least 59°F (15°C) during the summer growing season. Trees also require substantial amounts of rainfall.

Deserts are too dry to support dense forests.

BOREAL FORESTS

Boreal forests are the coldest and driest in the world, and are found in areas that have very cold winters and a short growing season. The word boreal means northern, and the forests stretch across Asia, North America, and Europe. High mountain slopes on these continents are also covered with boreal forests.

To the south, boreal forests merge into temperate forests and grasslands. Despite abundant snowfall, boreal forests suffer from drought. Conifers and a few hardy trees such as birch and some willows, are the only trees that can withstand these cold, dry conditions.

◁ Coniferous trees such as spruce and pine retain their needles (leaves) throughout the year. Instead of bearing fruits, the trees bear cones.

△ Temperate, deciduous trees have a full, bushy shape. In autumn, the trees shed their leaves before they can be damaged by frost.

TEMPERATE FORESTS

Temperate forests grow in areas with moderate climates. Most temperate regions have warm summers and cool winters, and trees vary from broadleaf, deciduous trees to evergreen trees.

In the Northern Hemisphere, temperate deciduous forests extend across eastern North America, western Europe, and eastern Asia. Temperate evergreen forests are found in western North America.

In the Southern Hemisphere, evergreen forests occur in southeastern Australia and New Zealand. These forests lie on steep slopes that have very high rainfall.

TROPICAL FORESTS

Tropical forests include both dryland forests, in much of East Africa, and rainforests. Tropical rainforests are found in South and Central America, West and Central Africa, and all over Southeast Asia and tropical Australasia.

The tropical rainforest zone is characterized by an abundance of rainfall and very high temperatures. These conditions have made them the most spectacular forests on earth today. Tropical rainforests consist mainly of broadleaved trees that do not shed their leaves annually, but have a year-round growing season.

▽ Tropical trees tend to have very tall trunks with the foliage (leaves) right at the top of the tree. The trees normally support lianas (creepers).

NATURAL COVER

Forests form the natural vegetation for a large part of the earth's land surface. Ten thousand years ago, forests were more extensive than today. For example, western Europe was covered by an unbroken chain of trees. Since then, increasing human activity has drastically reduced the size of the earth's forests.

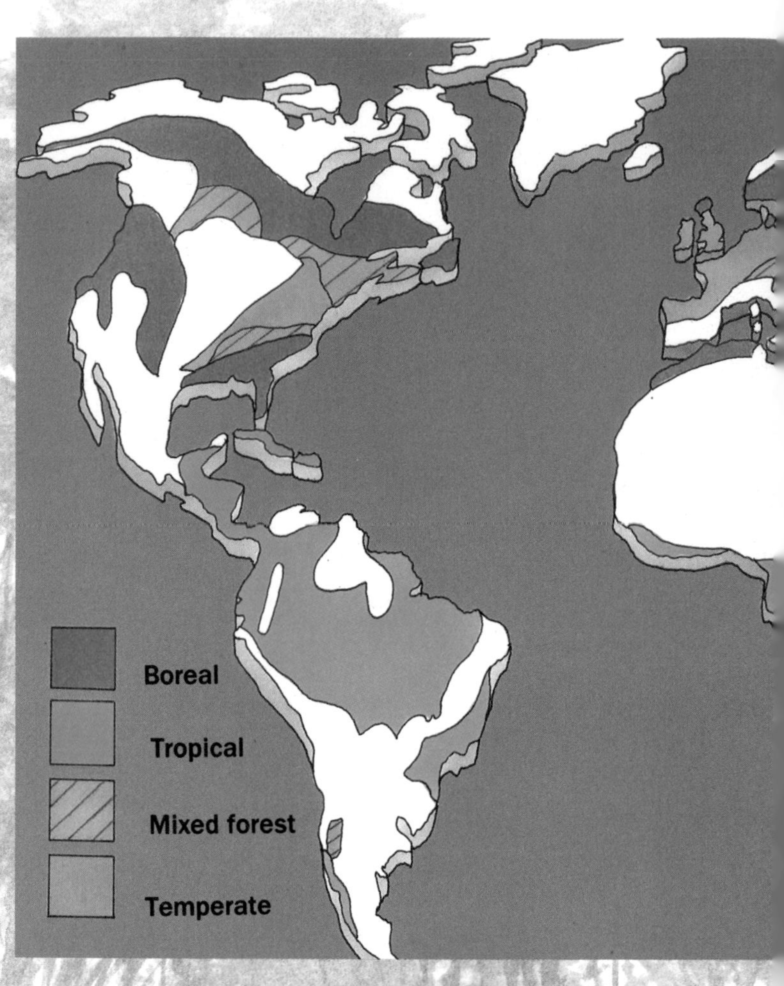

△ The natural forest zones – temperate, boreal, and tropical – covered a large part of the earth's land surface some 10,000 years ago.

PEOPLE VERSUS TREES

Farmers have a difficult relationship with trees. While other people may think that trees are a valuable natural resource, farmers sometimes feel land that the trees occupy could be used to plant crops and raise cows and sheep.

Trees are incredibly useful. Wood is a superb construction material. The same tree that provides strong lumber for building bridges also provides delicate struts for tables and chairs. Humans also discovered other uses for wood, most importantly that of making paper. The newspapers, magazines, notebooks, and envelopes we use today are all made from trees.

Trees are also a very important source of fuel. Billions of people all over the world still rely on firewood for everyday cooking and heating.

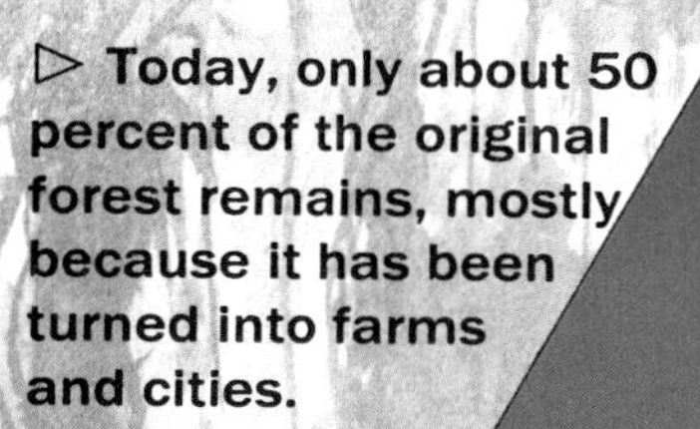

▷ Today, only about 50 percent of the original forest remains, mostly because it has been turned into farms and cities.

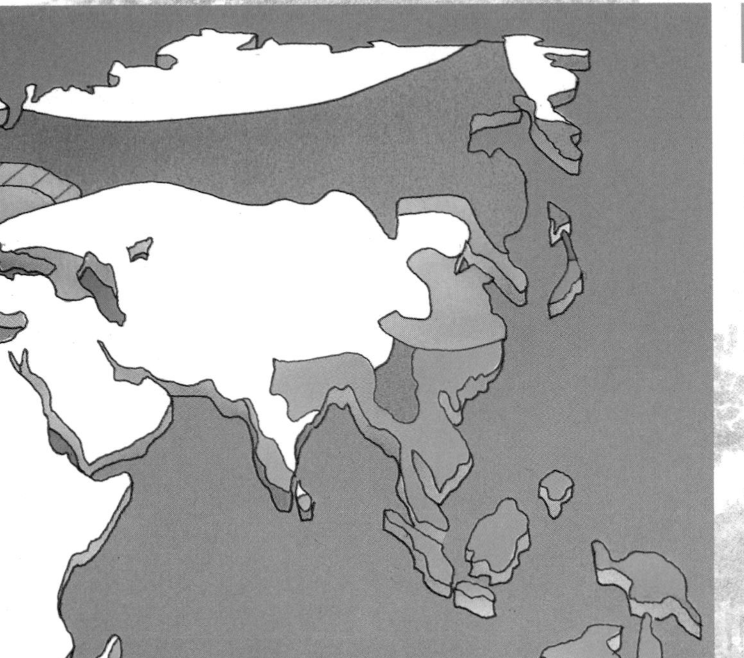

PACE OF DESTRUCTION

As people spread out all over the world, forests began to shrink. The first phase of destruction began with the spread of agriculture about 6,000 years ago. The best land was cleared and trees were replaced with cattle and crops.

The second phase of destruction began about 2,000 years ago. Metalworking, which used up huge amounts of charcoal (half-burned wood), became widespread. Other new industries also required wood. For example, the oak forests of England were used to build the wooden ships of the Royal Navy.

By about the 1800s, temperate forests had been substantially reduced in Europe. Soon after, similar losses occured in North America and Australasia. Within the last 80 years, about half of the tropical rain forests have been cut down.

◁ Forests were cleared using stone tools and fire. Crops were then sown on the clearings made by this slash-and-burn agriculture.

Forest
Land

◁ As metal tools, the plow, and grazing animals were introduced, farmers were able to clear even larger areas of land for their own use.

Forest
Land

▷ Forest destruction increased at the beginning of the industrial age. Today, the greatest enemy of forests is the portable chain saw.

Land
Forest

Because of the favorable climate around the equator, tropical rainforests have become the most complex and diverse places on earth. These forests contain the greatest variety of plant and animal species. But due to unrestricted logging, these forests have also become the most threatened places on earth.

EXTENT

At the beginning of the 20th century, there were about 6 million square miles of tropical forest. Today, less than 3 million square miles remain.

The destruction of tropical forests began with large-scale logging operations. Many tropical species, such as teak and mahogany, were felled because they provided valuable lumber for humans. However, such logging is very inefficient. Because the forests are so dense and diverse, about 50 other trees are cut down for every lumber tree.

When forests are cleared for agricultural purposes, the trees are often burned down. Huge areas have been cleared in this way for agriculture and cattle ranching, and during the 1980s, tropical forests were being cut down at a rate of 2 percent a year.

Petrified logs found in Arizona

Palm trees in Brazilian rainforest

HISTORY

Tropical forests are a product of their climate, and this has not always been as it is today. Between 400,000 and 14,000 years ago, our planet experienced a series of Ice Ages, when the climate was much colder and drier. As the climate got colder, the tropical forests shrank.

At the height of the Ice Ages, there were probably no tropical forests in South America or Asia. However, in Africa, conditions were better. Scientists have identified areas of forest in West Africa which they believe existed through the Ice Ages. This survival means that they are the oldest on earth.

When the climate became warmer the tropical forests began to grow again. They probably reached their maximum extent just before humans commenced their large-scale destruction.

LOCATION

Tropical forests grow well around the equator where temperatures rarely rise above 95°F or drop below 68°F. The forests also receive about 80 inches of rain a year. The air beneath the trees is always humid, and in areas where sunlight reaches the ground, dense growths called jungles occur. Most of these are found near rivers.

The largest area of tropical forest in the world occurs in the vast Amazon River Basin of South America. Smaller stretches extend north to the West Indies. In Africa, the forest follows a similar pattern, and is mainly confined to the basin of the Zaire River.

In Asia, the tropical forest zone is more widespread. In eastern Asia, the natural forest extends from southern China to northern Australia, and covers most of the islands in between. In western Asia, there is a narrow rain forest zone down the west coast of India.

Equator

Rainforest

△ The tropical rainforest zone occurs around the equator in South America, Africa, and Southeast Asia. Rainforests also cover parts of Australia.

Part of the Zaire rainforest in Africa

CREATE TROPICAL CONDITIONS

Plant two seedlings in pots. Place one in a cool place. Cover the other with a transparent plastic bag, and keep it warm. Give both seedlings equal light and water. After a week, see which one has grown the most.

Seedling in warm atmosphere with plastic bag over it

Heater

Tropical rainforests form a multilayered environment. Contrary to popular opinion, not all rainforests contain the dense tangled undergrowth that is known as jungle, although most of them have a dense growth of trees. The most crowded part of a tropical rainforest is high above the ground, in the treetops.

LIFE AT THE TOP

A tropical rainforest can be divided into three distinct layers, one above the other. About 130 feet above the ground, the leaves and branches of the trees form the first forest canopy. The trees grow so close together that their branches often intertwine. Occasionally a taller tree, known as an emergent, will tower an additional 33 to 65 feet above the rest of the canopy.

A second canopy normally reaches a height of 65 feet, and the third reaches 33 feet. The shrub and herb layers of tropical rain forests are quite thin. This is because very little sunlight penetrates to the forest floor. The canopies also have many climbing plants and epiphytes growing in the branches.

Aerial view of rainforest in Venezuela

Rainforest vegetation in Surinam

▽ Tropical rainforests have three distinct canopies. Tall trees, called emergents, sometimes grow higher than the first canopy. The undergrowth is normally thin.

GROWTH FACTOR

Tropical rainforests need plenty of sunlight for them to survive. The tall trees in the canopies use their green leaves and the sunlight to make food. This process is known as photosynthesis. There is a lot of competition for sunlight, and this makes the canopy quite crowded. Beneath the canopy, trees cast a very dense shade. Less than 2 percent of the sunlight reaching the canopy filters down to the forest floor. Few plants can grow in such darkness, and the warm, moist conditions mean that the rate of decomposition is extremely rapid.

A natural forest canopy has some spaces within it. When a large tree dies it collapses, often bringing down other trees and producing a small clearing. At any given time, about ten percent of the forest consists of such clearings. Here, sunlight penetrates to the ground, and the undergrowth becomes dense. Eventually, a few trees grow to reach the canopy, and the clearing disappears.

RESTRICTED LIGHT

You can demonstrate the effects of the canopy with two seedlings. Plant one seedling high in its pot, and place it on a windowsill. Plant the other seedling low in its pot, and construct a cardboard shield as shown in the picture. Place the shielded pot alongside the other one, and give both the same amount of water. Measure the seedlings every few days, and keep a record of how much each one has grown.

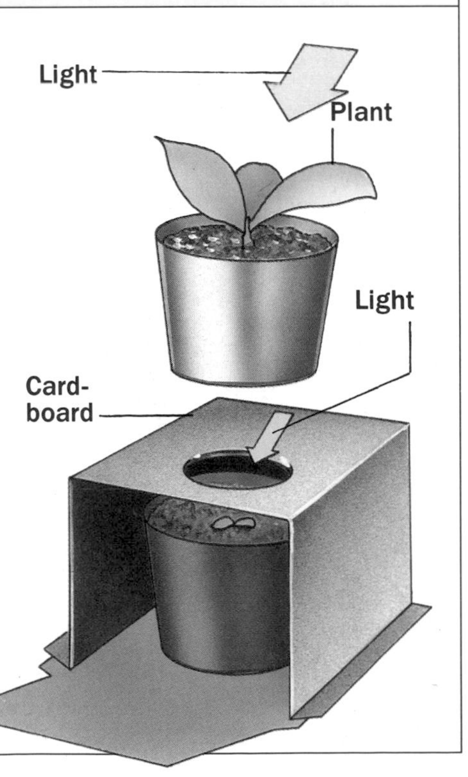

Tropical rainforests contain plant and animal life at its most abundant. We will never know how many species the forests originally contained, because species are becoming extinct faster than we can count them. A safe estimate is that they now contain at least one million different species, most of which are insects.

VARIETY OF LIFE

In terms of plant species, the richest forests are those of Southeast Asia. The Malay Peninsula contains more than 2,500 tree species, including teak and palm. A single square mile of tropical rain forest may contain more than 100 different types of trees and hundreds more smaller plants. By comparison, other forests have far fewer species.

This great diversity of plant life and the layered structure of the forests have given rise to an even greater diversity of animal life. A single tree might easily support hundreds of different insect species and a variety of animals. Most animals spend their lives in the trees, feeding on the nuts and fruits in the upper two canopies.

Rainforest epiphyte

Bromeliads growing on fallen tree trunk

▽ Tropical rainforests are the most diverse forests on earth. In South America, the forests contain more than 70 different species of tree in just one acre.

WAYS OF LIFE

Tall trees dominate the forests, taking up most of the available space, light, and nutrients. Competition between smaller plants is intense, and forest trees support numerous epiphytes and parasites.

Epiphytes are plants that grow on tree branches without harming them. As leaf litter decays to form a thin soil, many plants take root there. Typical epiphytes are bromeliads, which have large, cup-shaped flowers that are able to collect rainwater.

Parasitic plants send out roots to absorb water and nutrients from the tissues of a host plant. Some plants, such as the strangler fig, start out harmless, but later turn parasitic, enveloping the host completely and killing it.

Many saprophytes live on the forest floor. Saprophytes are plants that absorb nutrients from decaying organic matter. Some tropical orchids and many types of fungi are saprophytes. Bacteria and other decomposers on the ground speed up the process of decay.

Orchid in Peru's tropical rainforest

As their name suggests, tropical rainforests depend upon a high amount of rainfall. This abundant water is the key to the lushness of the forests. At the same time, the forests also protect the earth from the damaging effects of the rain and wind. Without the forests, the land would rapidly turn into a wasteland.

RAINFALL

Rainforests are generally found where the rainfall is higher than 60 inches a year and the dry season is no longer than two months. An exception to this rule is found in parts of Southeast Asia, where most of the rainfall is concentrated in the annual monsoon.

Heavy rainfall is a result of global climate patterns. However, rain forests also contribute to the amount of moisture in the atmosphere. Some of the rain that falls evaporates from the tree canopy. The rest is absorbed by the roots and transported to the leaves. The leaves give off water through their pores, and this process is known as transpiration.

Above the forest, the evaporated water condenses to form thick clouds that produce brief thunderstorms on an almost daily basis.

Monsoon rain falling on the Ujung river in Indonesia

▽ Although rainforests recycle much of the rainfall back into the atmosphere, a considerable amount of water seeps away into the soil.

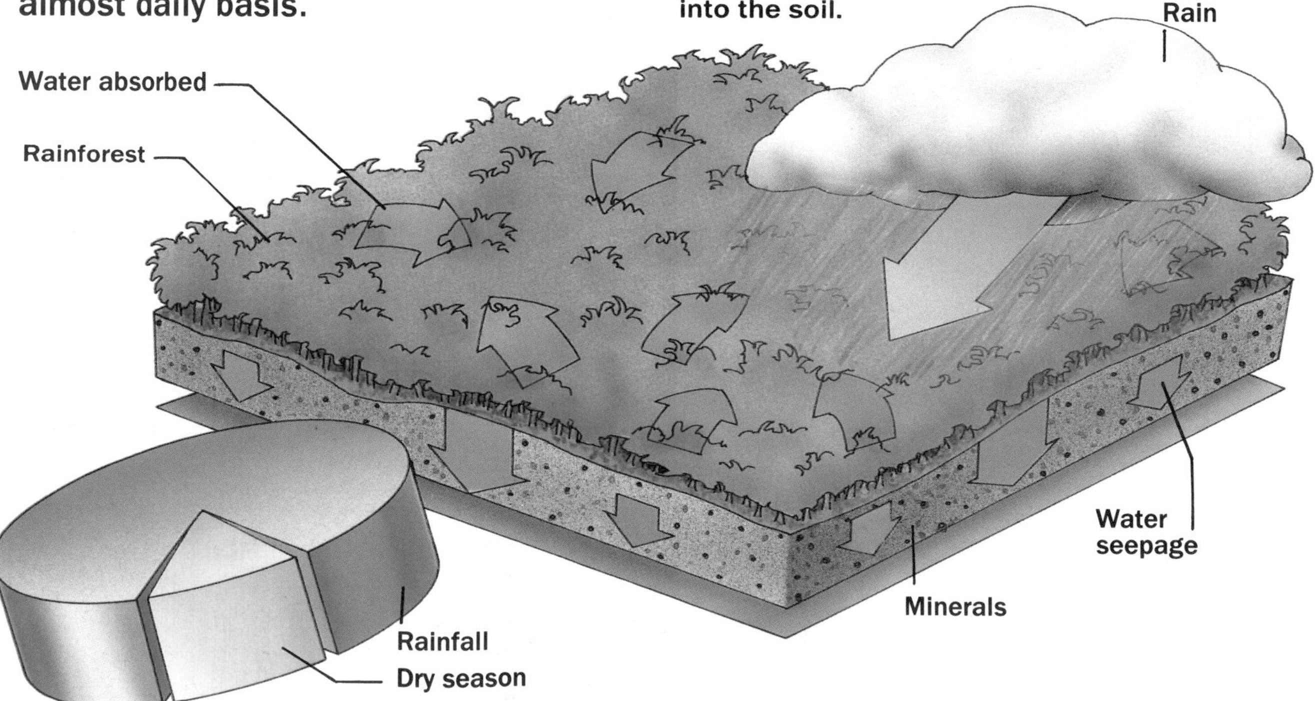

▽ Without the protection of trees, tropical soils deteriorate very rapidly. Within a few years the soil becomes filled with mineral nodules that turn into laterite.

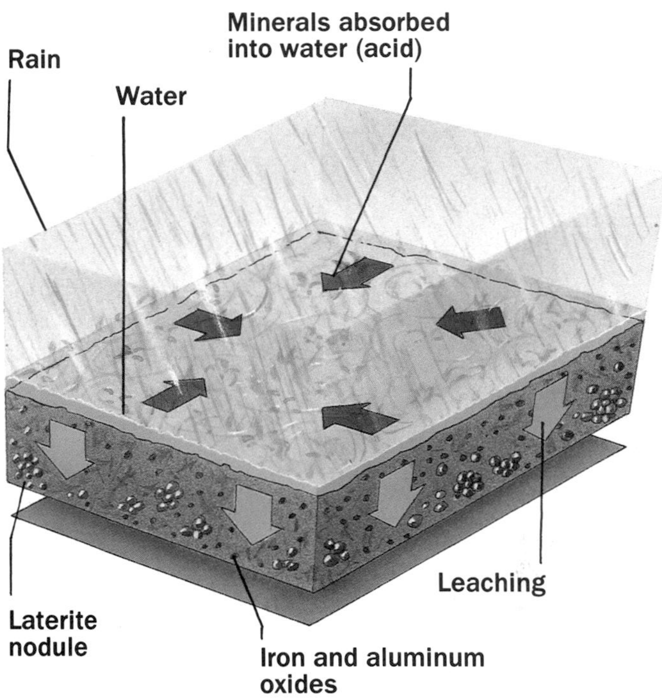

LEACHING PROJECT

Half fill a flowerpot with gravel and sprinkle on some sand. Now add a layer of salt crystals, and cover with 1 inch of sand. Water the pot every day. See how much salt is left after one day; one week.

SOILS

Surprisingly, tropical forest soils are relatively poor and infertile. About 95 percent of the available nutrients are locked into the tissues of the giant trees.

Because of the rapid rate of decomposition, there is only a very thin layer of decomposing organic matter on the forest floor. Any nutrients released are either absorbed by the trees or washed down through the soil by rainwater. This process is known as leaching.

In tropical regions, leaching also makes certain minerals (notably iron and aluminum) rise to the surface. These minerals turn the soil acidic, inhibiting plant growth.

When trees are cut down, the process of leaching speeds up because there is less evaporation. The action of sunlight on the exposed soil often turns it into a useless red dust called laterite. Laterite is easily blown away by the wind.

TEMPERATE FORESTS

Most temperate forests lie between hot, wet tropical forests and cold, dry boreal forests. Their most important feature is their ability to adapt to seasonal changes in climate. During autumn, they lose their green color when the trees shed their leaves, and by winter they seem bare and lifeless.

LOCATION

Temperate forests are mainly confined to the Northern Hemisphere and occur in Europe, northern Asia, and North America. Trees need at least 28 inches of rainfall per year, so areas with less rainfall are unable to support this type of forest. Temperate forests tend to occur within about 600 miles of the coast. Further inland, the weather is generally too dry to support them.

Temperate trees grow much farther apart than those in tropical forests. The leaves and branches of adjacent trees are not as tightly packed, and a reasonable amount of sunlight is able to reach the forest floor.

The sunlight that reaches the ground encourages growth of a large number of other forest plants, mainly herbs and small shrubs. The undergrowth in some places can become quite thick and tangled. Near the forest floor conditions are often humid, and this encourages ferns and fungi.

Woodland scene

▽ An example of the type of plant life that grows on a temperate forest floor: (1) wild mushrooms, (2) ferns, (3) shrubs, and (4) undergrowth.

DECIDUOUS HABIT

In temperate regions, the winters are short but often severe. Short days bring a sharp reduction in the amount of heat and light. When temperatures fall below freezing, very little rain falls on the trees and delicate plant tissues may be fatally damaged by frost.

Many small forest plants die away completely at the onset of winter and grow again from seed the following year. Trees, however, are much longer-lived and have to survive the harsh conditions. Most temperate trees have adapted themselves by becoming deciduous – shedding their leaves in autumn and virtually shutting down for the winter. Without leaves, there is no photosynthesis and the tree becomes dormant. In spring, leaf buds appear on the branches and the forest grows again.

Year 1: land covered with cornfield

Year 5: undergrowth and shrubs

Year 25: trees

FOREST REGROWTH

Throughout history, huge areas of temperate forest have been cleared for agricultural purposes. Occasionally, fields have been abandoned and the natural vegetation allowed to regrow. Scientists have been able to observe the stages of succession – the various types of vegetation that grow before the climax community is established.

The first plants to invade the abandoned fields were wild grasses and herbs, including most common weeds. These provided sufficient shelter for woody plants and shrubs to take hold. Trailing plants such as wild roses, blackberries, and ivy covered the ground. After about 25 years, young broad-leaved trees became well established.

◁ The annual deciduous cycle. 1) Spring: leaves grow. 2) Summer: tree is in full leaf. 3) Autumn: leaves dry out and fall. 4) Winter: most trees are bare.

Temperate forests are much less diverse than tropical forests, and the number of species per square mile is measured in tens, rather than hundreds. Temperate forests usually contain a mixture of tree species, but local weather conditions can lead to one particular species becoming dominant.

SPECIES

Typical trees of the European temperate forests include oak, ash, elm, beech, horse chestnut, lime, willow, and hazel. North American and north Asian forests contain a wider range of species, including magnolias, maples, and hickories.

In cooler, drier areas, temperate forests often have abundant numbers of silver birch trees. In places with poor climate and soil, coniferous trees which are able to resist the harsh climate thrive.

The temperate forest zone once covered almost all of the Northern Hemisphere. Over the centuries, most of the trees were cut down to provide lumber and fuel, and make room for farms and cities. Humans also have some part to play in the present species distribution. For example, the sycamore is not native to the British Isles, but was probably introduced by the Romans. In areas with mild winters, evergreen species are able to develop. Their leaves have a waxy coating that helps them withstand winter drought. The evergreen rhododendron, native to the Himalayas but now widespread, can survive winter beneath an insulating blanket of snow.

Bamboo forest in China

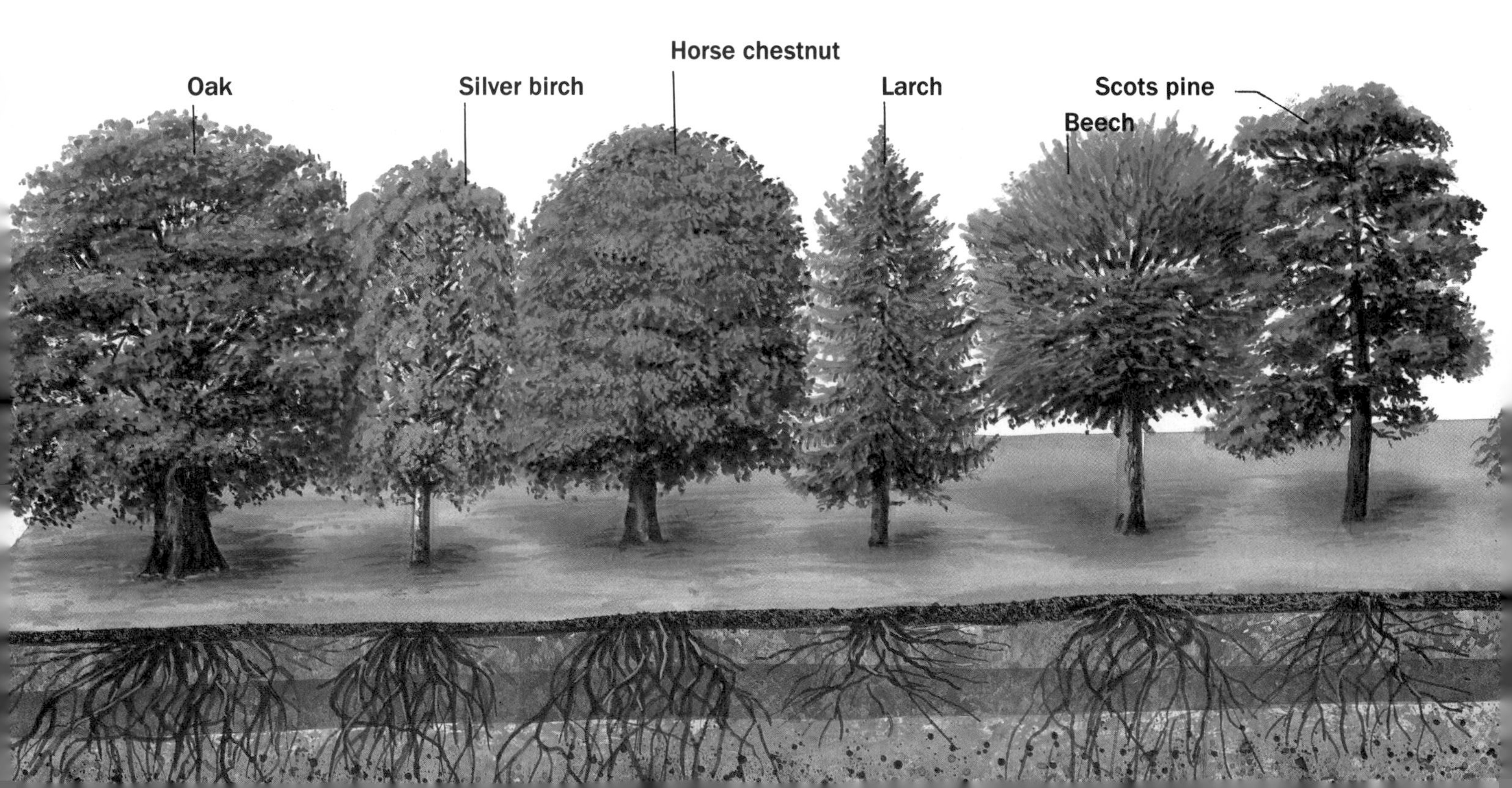

SHADE AND SOIL

Trees vary in the amount of light they require, and in the amount of shade they cast. Beech trees absorb the most amount of sunlight. For every square yard of land beneath a beech tree, there may be almost eight square yards of beech leaves above. As a result, beech trees cast the densest shade, and few other species can survive under them. Beech forests are usually clear of undergrowth.

Shade from forest trees is also responsible for the timing of the first flowers of spring. Plants such as the bluebell have to complete their annual cycle of flowering and fruiting before the shade becomes too dense.

In autumn, the forest floor becomes covered with a carpet of fallen leaves. These leaves build up to form a thick layer of decomposing leaf litter, which eventually rots to form humus and soil.

Leaves sink to surface
Leaf litter
Dead leaves absorbed into earth
Roots
Nutrition from dead leaves absorbed back into roots

△ Dead leaves that fall to the forest floor add nutrients to the soil. These are absorbed by the trees.

Shedding leaves is also a way of storing nutrients until the following year. During winter, the low temperatures slow down decomposition and nutrients are preserved until the next growing season.

Small animals such as earthworms and insects mix the decomposed leaves with the soil. Nutrients released into the soil are absorbed by the tree roots, and over a long period of time, temperate forests develop very fertile soils.

▽ Temperate forests create fertile, well-mixed soils as tree roots gradually break up the bedrock. Many types of trees, from old oaks to horse chestnuts and sycamores, grow in the forests.

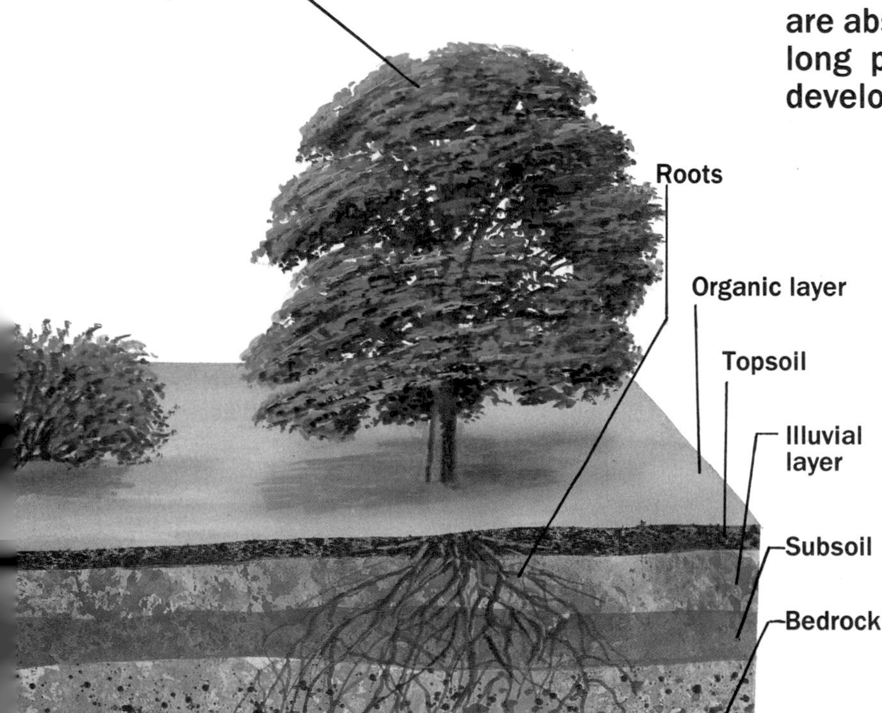

Bluebells growing on the clear floor of a beechwood forest

Boreal forest are the cold, coniferous evergreen forests of the Northern Hemisphere. Most of them contain conifers, an ancient group of trees that evolved long before broad-leaved trees and other flowering plants. However, the present-day boreal forests are the youngest forests on earth.

Coniferous trees are extremely hardy and can tolerate the cold northern winters. They are also well-suited to the poor clay and sandy soils left behind by glaciers. Once established, conifers tend to dominate the landscape because they withstand conditions that most other plants cannot tolerate.

EXTENT

Boreal forests form a wide belt around the top of the globe. In Eurasia, the forest is often known by its Russian name, taiga. To the north, boreal forests are limited by the tree line. Beyond this, the polar regions are too cold for any trees except dwarfs a few inches high. To the south, boreal forests merge into temperate forests and grasslands.

Most boreal forests grow on areas of land that were once covered by ice sheets. As the glaciers retreated, coniferous trees occupied the newly exposed landscape. In some places, such as Alaska, boreal forests cover areas that were glaciated only 200 years ago.

Boreal forest is the most northerly of the forest zones.

▽ The boreal forest zone covers much of the northern Arctic regions. Most of the trees in the forest stay green throughout the year.

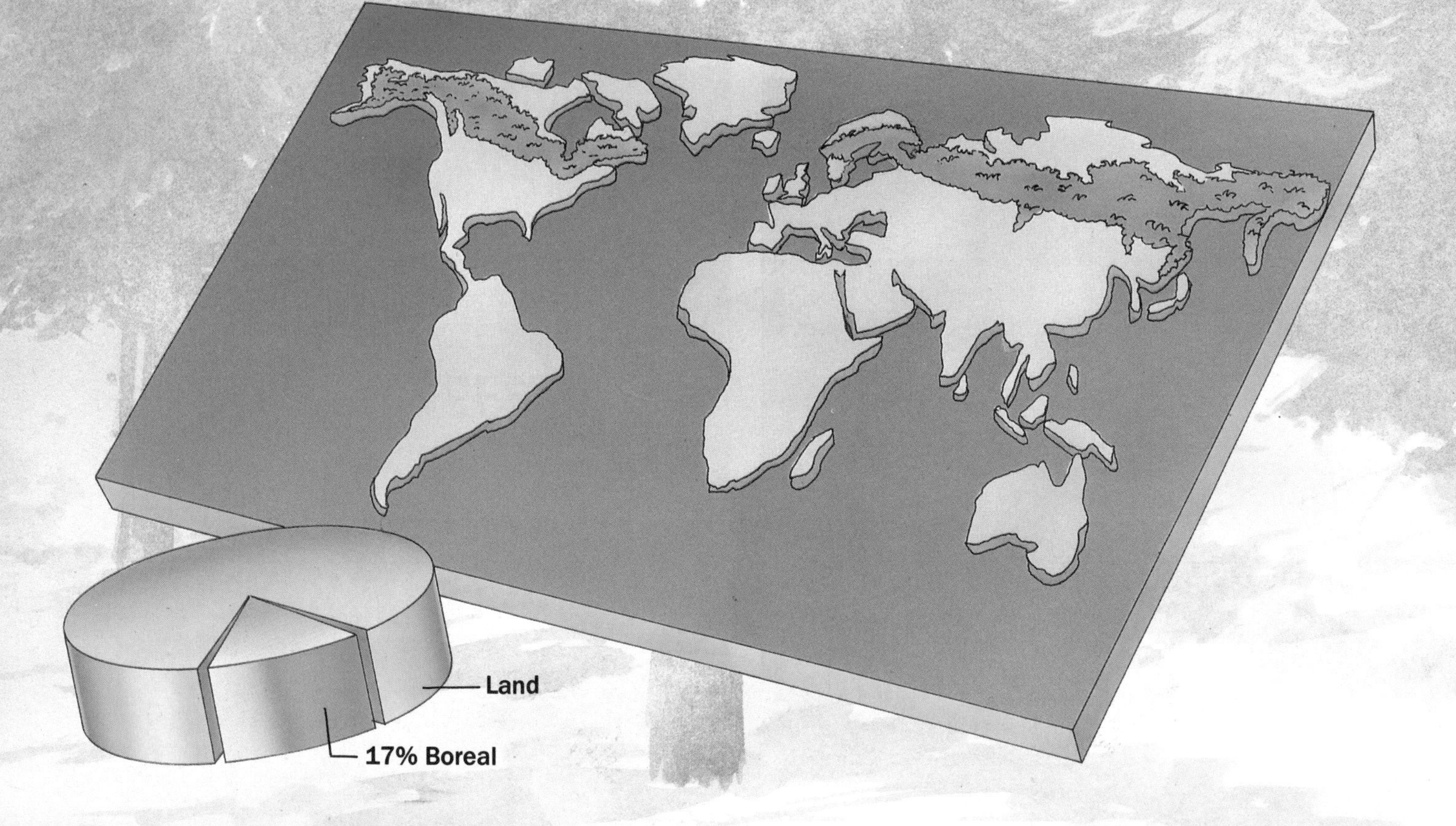

SPECIES

Boreal forests consist mainly of the various species of fir, spruce, and pine. In drier areas, and especially in Siberia, larches are the dominant species. Boreal forests are less diverse than other forests, and although areas of mixed species do occur, it is more usual to find the same tree species covering hundreds of square miles. This uniformity is characteristic of boreal forests.

Coniferous trees grow much closer together than broad-leaved trees. Spruce, for example, often grows as densely as 12 trees per 100 square yards. This close-packing creates extremely thick shade, with no light for other plants. Spruce forests are usually entirely clear of undergrowth. Pine forests, however, are much less shady and many grasses grow on the forest floor.

Conifers are not the only trees in boreal forests. Around lakes and clearings, hardy trees can be found. But they are soon smothered by the conifers.

A boreal forest in Norway

▽ Trees in a boreal forest belong to several coniferous families. Conifers make up 15% of the world's tree species.

Scots pine
Balsam fir
White spruce
Larch
Other species
Conifers

DID YOU KNOW?

Coniferous trees are the tallest and largest living organisms. One redwood tree in northern California, measures over 367 feet high. A specimen of the giant sequoia species is shorter but thicker, and is the heaviest living thing, weighing more than 2,100 tons.

The trees of boreal forests have to endure very harsh winters. Most of the time the temperatures remain below freezing point, and may fall as low as −40°F. Winter also brings severe drought to the area, and groundwater becomes totally frozen. The land ends up being covered in snow, with water in very short supply.

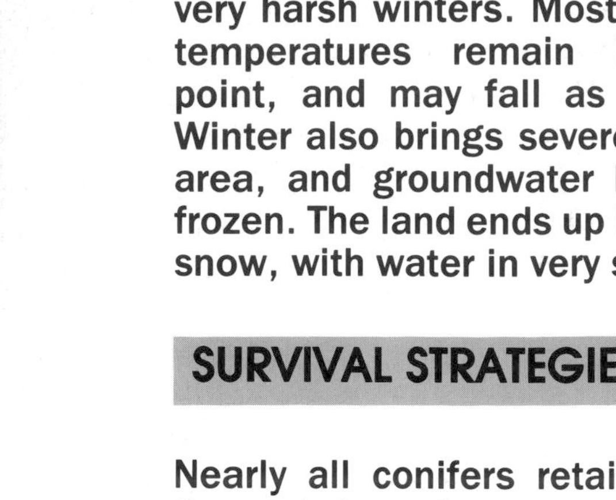

SURVIVAL STRATEGIES

Nearly all conifers retain their needles (leaves) throughout the year, so that they can make their own food. Individual needles have a small surface area and are coated with wax. These adaptations help prevent water loss through evaporation. Natural antifreeze produced in the needles prevents them from being killed by frost.

In the coldest, driest regions, larches lose their needles in winter to keep water loss to a minimum.

Coniferous trees have shallow, spreading root systems that collect water from a wide area. These roots enable conifers to take advantage of the available nutrients during early spring, when only the top few inches of soil thaw out.

The close packing that creates such dense shade also helps keep the trees warm. Air trapped between needles and branches forms a layer of insulation around each tree. The trees' conical shape allows snow to slide down before its weight breaks the branches.

▽ Conifers make maximum use of winter sunlight. Their shape allows some sunlight to reach each tree. Heat reflected up from fallen snow is trapped beneath the trees.

Conifers covered in winter snow

NEEDLES AND SOIL

Dead needles fall to the ground at a steady rate. Over many years, these needles build up to form a thick carpet. Because of the cold climate, needles decompose very slowly. Acidic chemicals in the needles also deter decomposing organisms in the soil.

Dead needles contain few nutrients. Their acidic chemicals discourage earthworms and other burrowing animals from mixing them into the soil. The result is an acidic, infertile soil, unsuitable for plants other than conifers. By affecting the soil in this way, conifers increase their own domination of the landscape.

Not even conifers can flourish in these conditions without assistance. Most owe their success to mycorrhizalic fungi that live in the soil. These fungi supply the tree roots with vital minerals and receive food in exchange. Mycorrhizal fungi are found associated with many trees in all types of climates.

A pinecone from a conifer

▽ Coniferous trees produce infertile soils. The shallow root systems of the trees are able to collect water during the spring thaw.

Permafrost

Mineral rich layer

Pine needles

There are several other forest regions that do not fit the main forest zones. These forests owe their existence to a variety of local climatic conditions. There are warm, dry forests; cool, damp forests; and even saltwater forests. Together they demonstrate how adaptable and widespread trees have become.

ALTITUDE

The temperature of the atmosphere drops by about 1°F for every 1,000 feet above sea level. In the tropics, mountains provide areas of cool weather in an otherwise hot climate. The sides of a mountain can be graded into a series of vegetation zones. At the top of the mountain, it is too cold and icy for plant life. Further down, as conditions get warmer and wetter, herbaceous plants and trees start to appear. Conifers are often found on the higher slopes, with temperate species growing farther down. Cloud forests occur where bands of permanent low cloud create cold, damp conditions.

Mountain forests are not confined to the tropics. In North America, the Rocky Mountains enable boreal species to grow much farther south than they could on low-lying land.

Alpine meadow in France during summer

▽ Bands of vegetation on a mountain. (1) Snow and ice, (2) Alpine meadow, (3) Coniferous forest, (4) Deciduous forest, (5) Tropical forest, (6) Deciduous forest, (7) Coniferous forest, and (8) Tundra meadows.

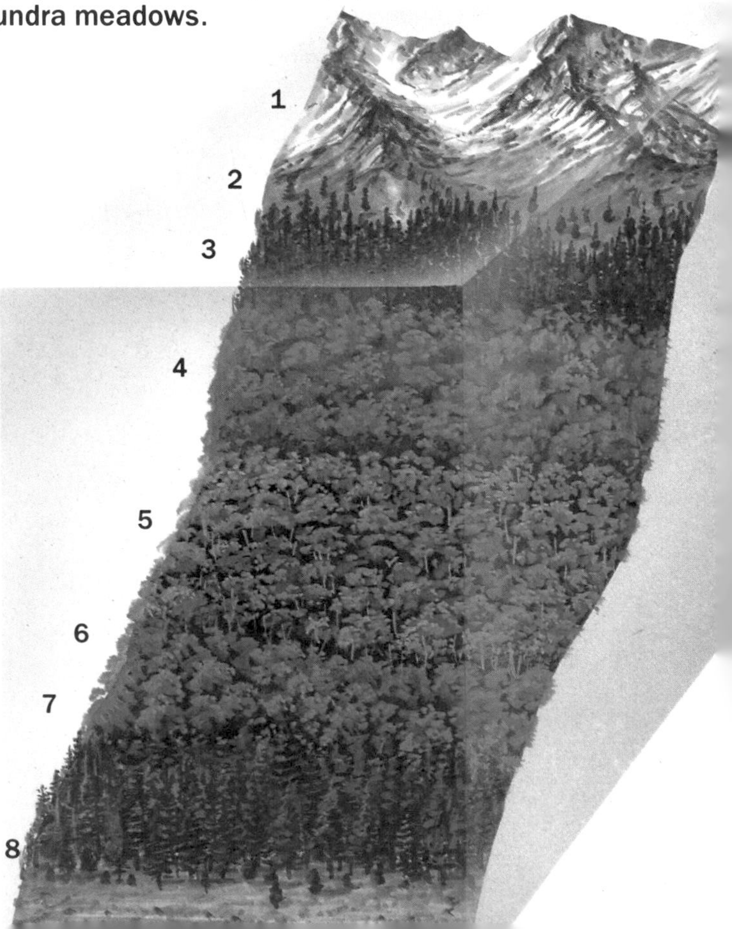

Mountain forest in Nepal

ARID FORESTS

Around the shores of the Mediterranean Sea, there once was a belt of widely-spaced trees that could withstand the hot summers. Much of this forest was cut down to provide farmland for vineyards and olive groves. In areas that have been abandoned, the landscape is now covered with a dense layer of low evergreen shrubs. Some extensive forest areas remain. One of the most unusual trees of the Mediterranean forest is the evergreen cork oak. It is rarely found growing wild, and is extensively cultivated for its bark which is the world's major source of natural cork.

Around tropical grasslands, similar areas of open woodland can be found. In Africa, the dominant species are the acacias. Well adapted to arid conditions, acacias are often covered with thorns to discourage grazing animals.

A Mediterranean forest in May

Waipoura Kauri forest in New Zealand

COASTAL FORESTS

In New Zealand, Canada, and the northwestern United States, climatic conditions have produced temperate rain forests on the slopes of coastal mountains. Warm, damp air from the sea ensures a high rainfall that supports very lush forests. In New Zealand, the temperate rain forests are notable for their many species of tree ferns. American forests contain more conventional temperate species, and many trees are covered with a thick blanket of moss.

Along many tropical and subtropical coastlines are narrow belts of mangrove swamp. Mangrove trees can tolerate salty water, and some species grow out into tidal waters. Arched aerial roots enable the trees to survive the waterlogged conditions. Farther inland, where the coastal swamps are less salty, other water-tolerant species, such as swamp cypress, may be found.

Deforestation, the loss of natural forest, is now the focus of worldwide attention. Tropical rainforests are being cut down at the rate of about one square mile every eight minutes. Many countries have now placed strict controls on the use of their forests, but in many cases the damage has already been done.

A deforested hillside in Nepal, now used for agriculture

LOST TREES AND LOST SOIL

Logging, oil drilling, agriculture, human settlement, gold mining, road construction and many other activities all contribute to the continuing pressure on rainforests. In Brazil and India, for, example, the coastal rainforests have almost disappeared completely.

Other forest zones suffer from different pressures. In arid regions, extended drought and the human need for firewood combine to threaten the scant remaining forests. In Southeast Asia, vast areas of mangroves have been cut down to make disposable chopsticks.

The effects of deforestation are worse in hilly, tropical areas. Without trees to anchor the soil, the heavy rain soon washes the soil from the hillsides, leaving steep-sided gullies. The soil is washed into rivers, carried downstream and deposited, choking irrigation channels and smothering fields.

A deforested area in Brazil

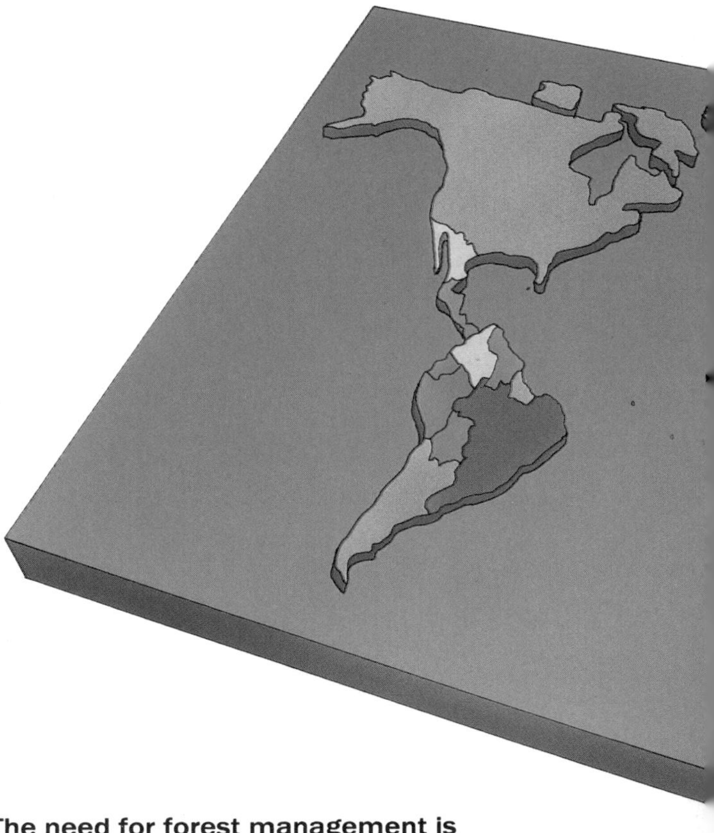

△ The need for forest management is highlighted by the rate of deforestation throughout the world. The rate is most severe in the tropics. The rainforests of Brazil are being cleared at an alarming rate. Environmentalists now fear for the survival of many forests.

TREE COVER PROJECT

Make two mounds of sand and sprinkle one with lettuce seeds. After the seeds germinate, water both mounds each day. Over two weeks, see which mound holds its shape better. Notice what happens to the other mound.

△ Careful planting projects can generate trees in deforested areas. This picture shows the results of reforestation in Nepal. In the background is a deforested area.

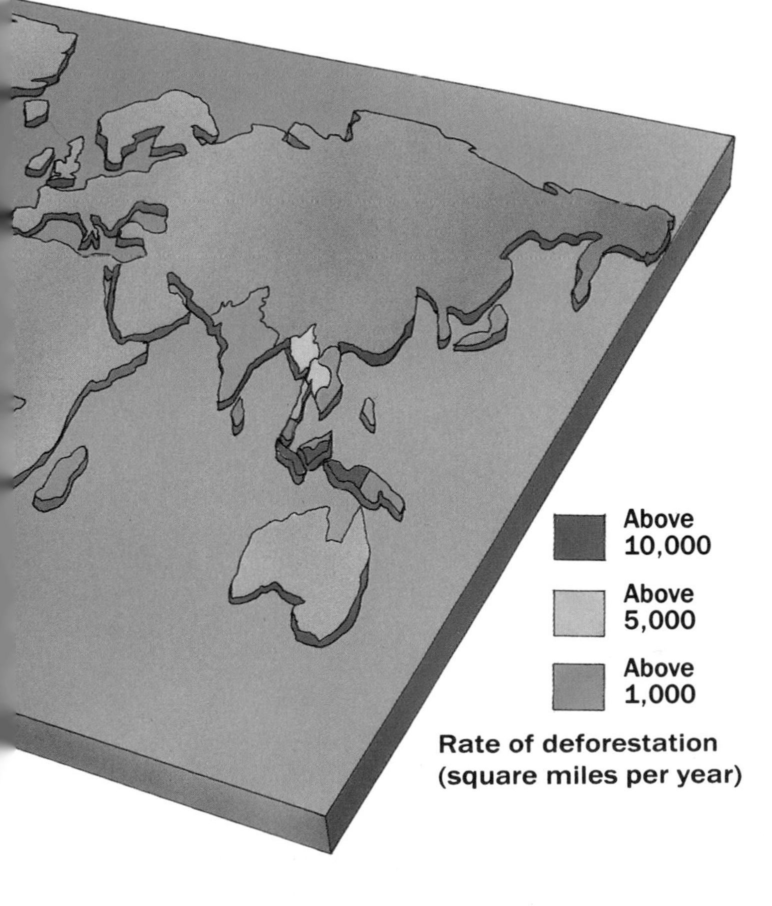

PRESERVATION AND REPLANTING

Several countries have now banned logging, and their remaining areas of rainforest are protected by law. Environmental groups have played an important role in making people aware of the need to preserve the rainforests.

Halting the destruction is much easier, however, than replanting the rain forest. In many areas, soil erosion is already so severe that the land can no longer support tall trees. Even where conditions are favorable, regrowth is a very long process. It can take up to 600 years for a rain forest to reach a climax community.

In temperate regions, large areas of former deciduous forest have been replanted with quick-growing coniferous trees. Although these conifers provide a renewable source of lumber, they are not a good option. Coniferous trees turn the soil acidic and can have a harmful effect on drainage patterns. If the conifers are not native to the region, they do not support much wildlife.

Trees are an ancient life-form, and they have existed on our planet much longer than human beings. Individual trees now grow much larger and live for much longer than human beings. The oldest trees are over 2,000 years old. In ancient times, people treated trees with greater respect than they do today.

The Green Man is a pagan spring god associated with the May Day festival.

Throughout history, most people considered forests to be very scary places. The dark, gloomy interiors of forests were thought to contain fierce animals, wicked trolls, and evil spirits. In many myths, folktales, and legends, forests feature as strange, uncivilized places where the unexpected can happen. By contrast, forest peoples often regard the forest trees and animals as individuals just like themselves.

A carving from a church in Norway

In ancient India, villagers often selected one particular tree for special attention. As long as the village experienced good fortune, the inhabitants continued to respect the tree. If their fortunes declined, then they would abandon the tree to the wild forest.

Ancient Europe had many tribal religions that paid special attention to trees. Often, trees were planted in sacred rings or groves, which could only be entered by druids and priests. In North America, Ojibway Indians did not like to fell living trees, because they did not want to cause them pain.

In Tolkien's imagination, forest trees became semihuman, with individual personalities.

Forests are a powerful symbol in human art and literature. Few people have not heard a version of "Little Red Riding Hood", who is menaced by a forest wolf. Tolkein's "Lord of the Rings" turns giant trees into creatures called Ents, that can walk around. Much more important are the real forests of the world. They are vital and irreplaceable, providing homes for some of the world's rarest plants and animals.

RAINFOREST DESTRUCTION

RAINFOREST DESTRUCTION

The reason why the rainforests now cover only a portion of the area which they did in the past is because they have been destroyed by people. Every day huge areas of rainforest disappear, particularly in the Amazon and Southeast Asia, as the trees are felled, bulldozed, or burned down.

Many temperate forests (forests which grow in moderate climates, with no huge extremes in temperature or rainfall) in North America, Europe, and Asia have been felled over the ages for farming and settling, leaving the tropical rainforests as the last great treelands on earth. The clearing of the temperate forests was done gradually, but the rainforests can now be cleared at a frightening rate: with a chainsaw, felling a tree can be done in minutes.

The rainforests are rich in plants and animals, many of which occur in just one tiny patch of forest. Some scientists estimate that as many as one species every half hour is made extinct by rainforest clearing.

▼ The fires raging through the tropical rainforests are so huge that they can be easily picked out from space by satellites, as can the clearings made in the Brazilian Amazon. On either side of a highway cut through a rainforest lies some 12 miles of destruction.

▶ Every minute an average of 100 acres of rainforest, which is equivalent to about 60 football fields, is lost. Over a year this amounts to an area the size of the whole of Great Britain being destroyed.

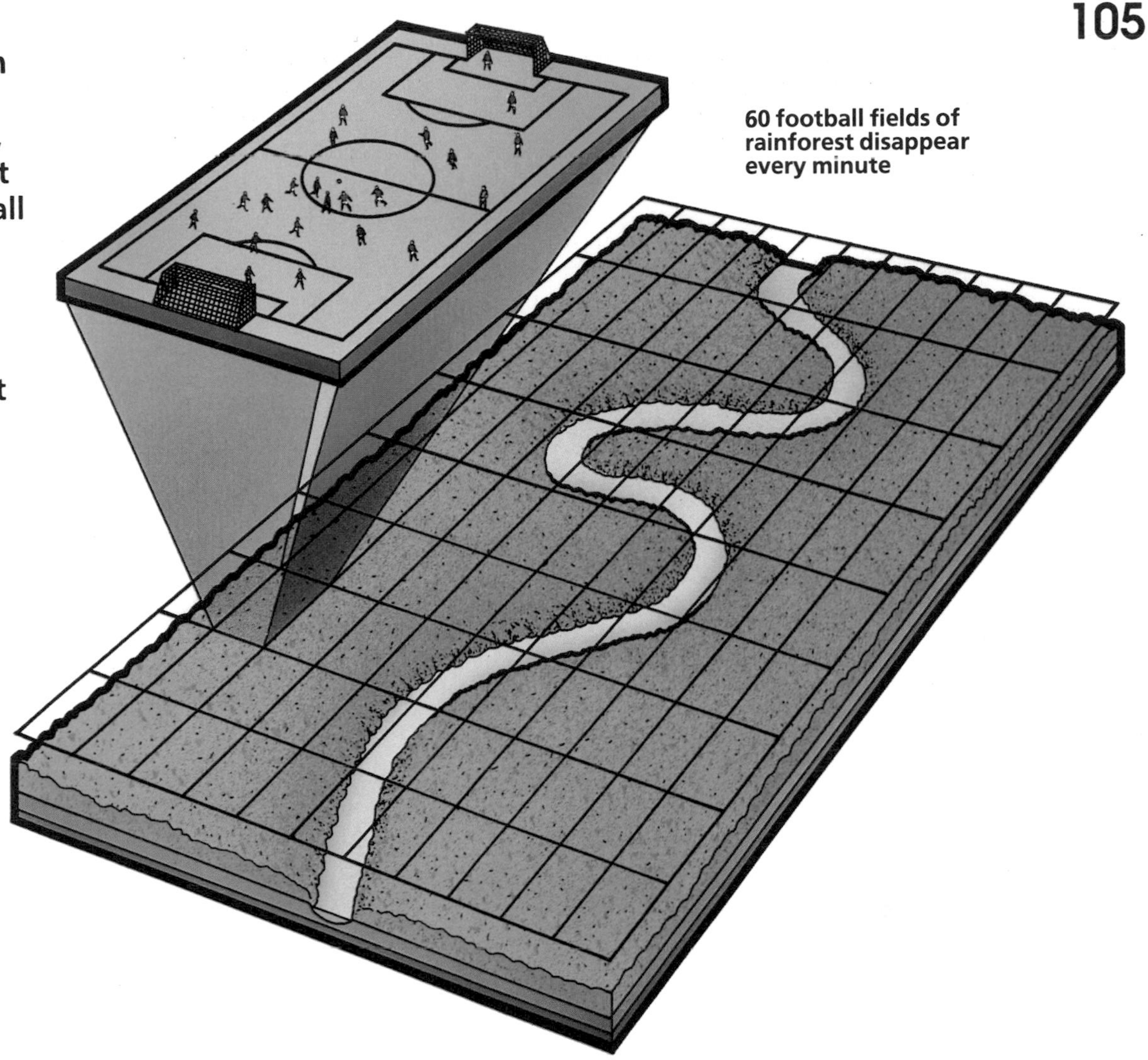

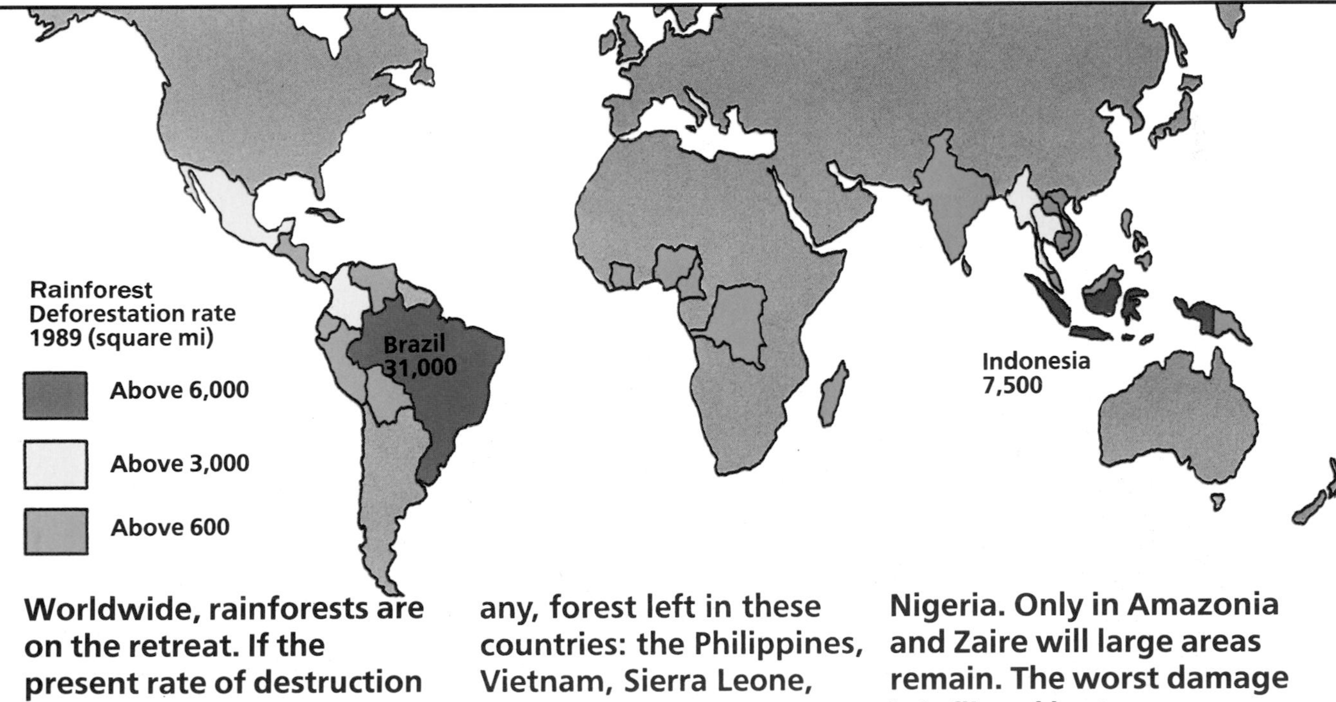

Worldwide, rainforests are on the retreat. If the present rate of destruction continues, it has been estimated that by the year 2000 there will be little, if any, forest left in these countries: the Philippines, Vietnam, Sierra Leone, Thailand, Sumatra, Madagascar, Myanmar, Ecuador, Ivory Coast, and Nigeria. Only in Amazonia and Zaire will large areas remain. The worst damage is inflicted by Japanese logging companies in Southeast Asia.

WHY IS IT HAPPENING?

Money and survival are the two main reasons why people are destroying the rainforests. Some people fell the forests to make large profits, while others clear them because it is the only way for them to survive.

Some forest land is cleared for mining minerals that lie beneath the ground. Other land is cleared for cattle ranching, or to be replaced by eucalyptus plantations for the paper pulp industry. Also, many tropical trees are felled for their timber.

In many parts of the tropics poverty is the reason for rainforest destruction. People are forced to move into the forests to make a living because there is nowhere else for them to go. They chop down and burn the forest, and plant their crops in the cleared ground. Rainforest soils are not very fertile, and after a few years of intense cultivation all the nutrients in the soil are used up. The people have to move on to a new patch of forest. This is called "shifted cultivation" or "slash and burn".

▼ Eucalyptus plantations can bring greenery back to devastated rainforest areas. Yet in many countries rainforest has been cleared in order to plant eucalyptus. It is grown for paper pulp, but it also drains nutrients and water from the soil.

▲ Many of Brazil's cattle live on ranches which were once rainforest. Forests are burned and replaced with grass for the cattle; some end up as hamburgers.

▼ Tropical woods like mahogany and teak are often used for furniture and other objects. Usually the timber is obtained with no thought for the forest. When loggers fell a tree for its timber, the surrounding forest is damaged by the loggers and their bulldozers.

◀▶ Parts of Brazil's rainforests are remote and difficult for settlers to reach until roads are driven through. Roads are made by governments improving transportation, and by loggers exploiting new areas for timber. People who have nowhere else to go follow the new roads to cultivate the land before moving on. Their method of farming, called shifted cultivation, saps the nutrients from the soil and destroys the surrounding forest so it cannot grow back. The impact on the forest grows as more people move into it.

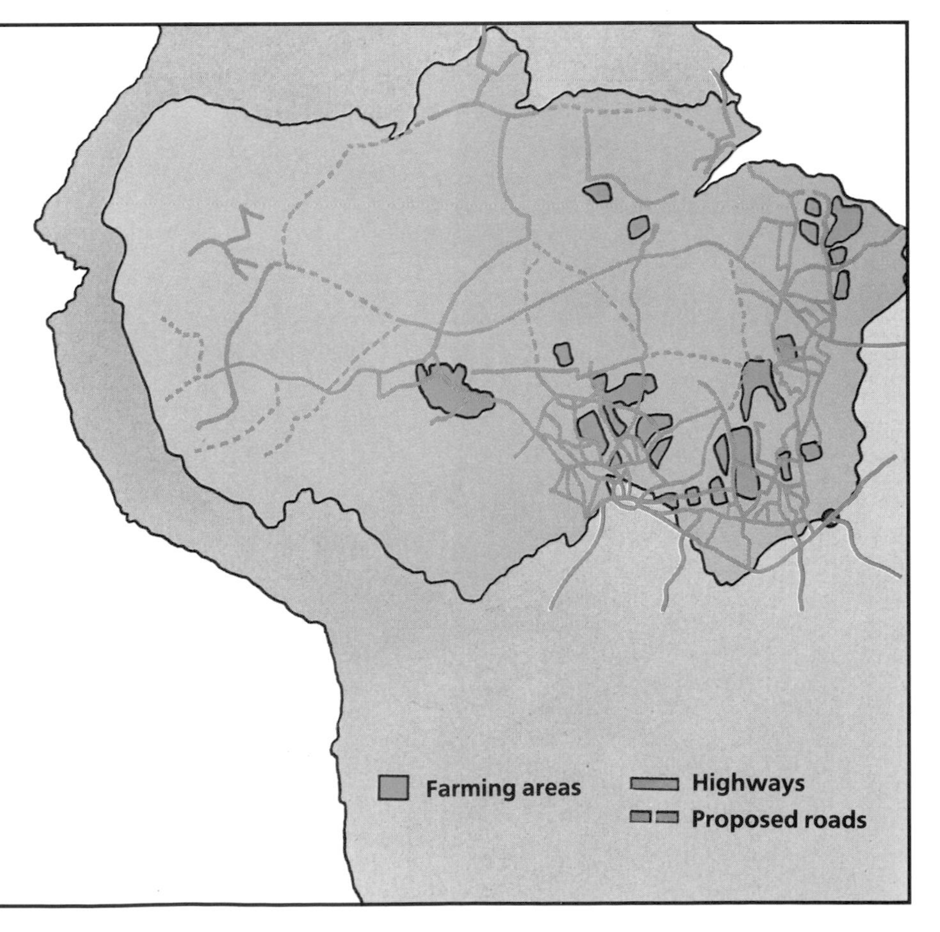

PARADISE LOST

Because the temperature of the rainforest stays fairly constant, life reproduces all year round. Tropical rainforests are home to at least half of the species of plants and animals in the world, although they occupy only seven percent of the earth's land surface. They teem with life, from the ground all the way up to the canopy. Animals and plants of all kinds live in the forests, from ants to jaguars, and from the mighty emergent trees to the tiniest fungi.

A rainforest is a web of life. Trees are covered with other plants; some of them are climbers, that twist and turn around the tree's trunk. Other plants find rootholds among the branches. Among the plants live the animals. Some are leaf-eaters like sloths and monkeys, while others are hunters, like the anteater searching out ants, and big cats like tigers hunting larger prey.

Many of the forest animals live in the canopy, and are more often heard than seen. The forest is a very noisy place, especially at night. Along with the drumming of the rain, the air is full of the buzz of insects, the howls of monkeys, the croaks of frogs and the calls of birds.

▼ (From left to right), *toucans* are typical rainforest birds of South American forest canopies. *Insects* (this one is a frangipani caterpillar from Panama) abound in all rainforests, but *lemurs* live only in Madagascar's rainforests. This *three-toed sloth* mother with young lives in South and Central American rainforest, and *gorillas* inhabit Africa's rainforests.

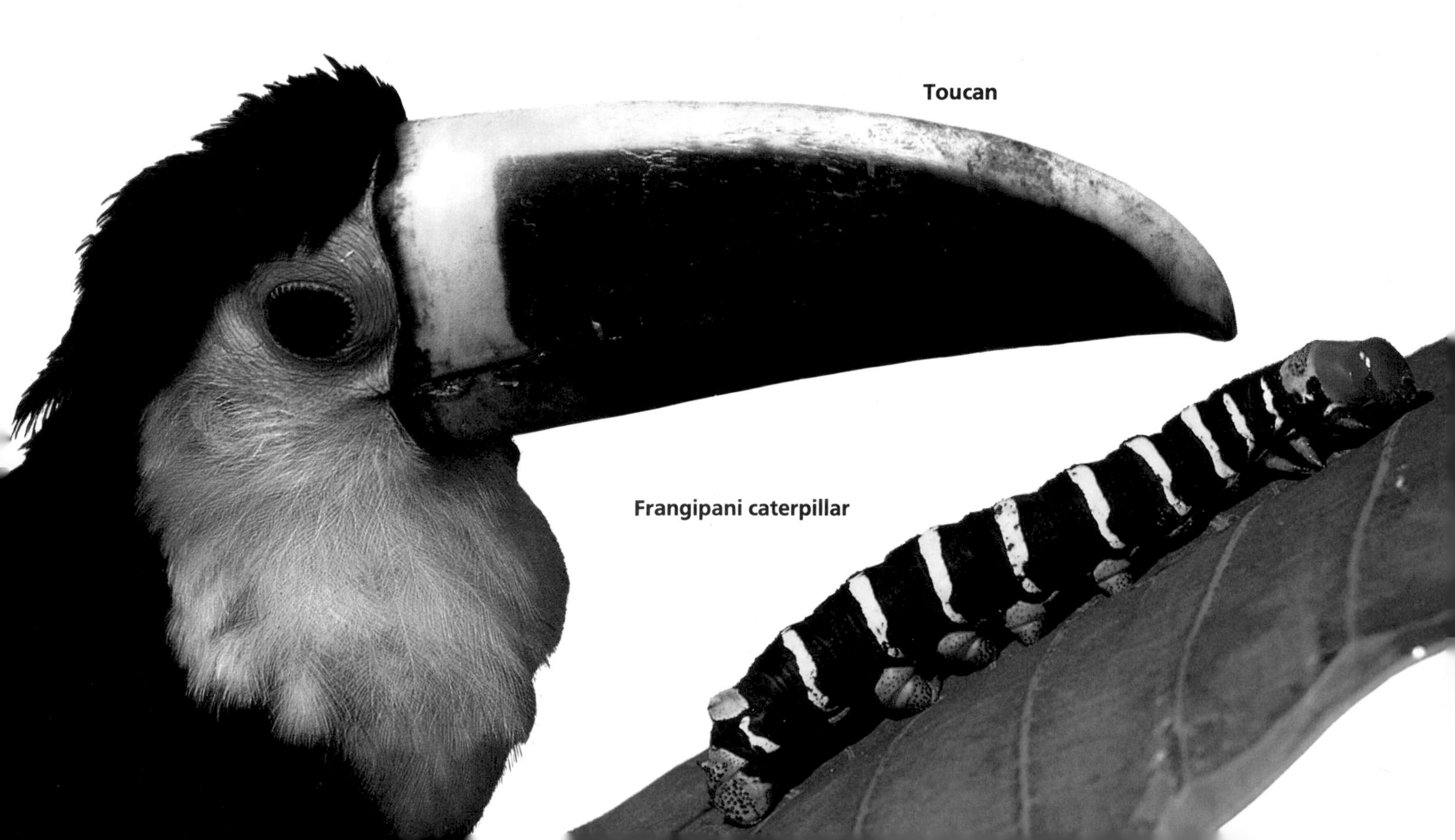

Toucan

Frangipani caterpillar

The gorilla, along with the chimpanzee, is the wild animal most closely related to us. Even so, it is badly treated in its restricted range in Africa. It is killed for food, its skull is sold, it is shot as an agricultural pest and its forest habitat is being destroyed. Luckily, some gorillas live in protected National Parks, but more protection is necessary to ensure their survival.

RAINFOREST MEDICINES

Some of the plants of the rainforests have proved to be of great importance to people because they provide vital medicines. At least one quarter of the world's most important medicines are based on rainforest plants. The variety of treatments from these tropical products includes painkillers, cough mixtures, drugs that relieve anxiety, birth control pills, anesthetics, antibiotics and cancer-fighting drugs.

Only one percent of tropical plants have yet been carefully tested for their potential as medicines. Some scientists believe that as high as ten percent of untested plants may have the potential to fight cancer. Also, a species of tree found in the Amazon and in Australia contains a substance which is being researched in London as a possible treatment for AIDS.

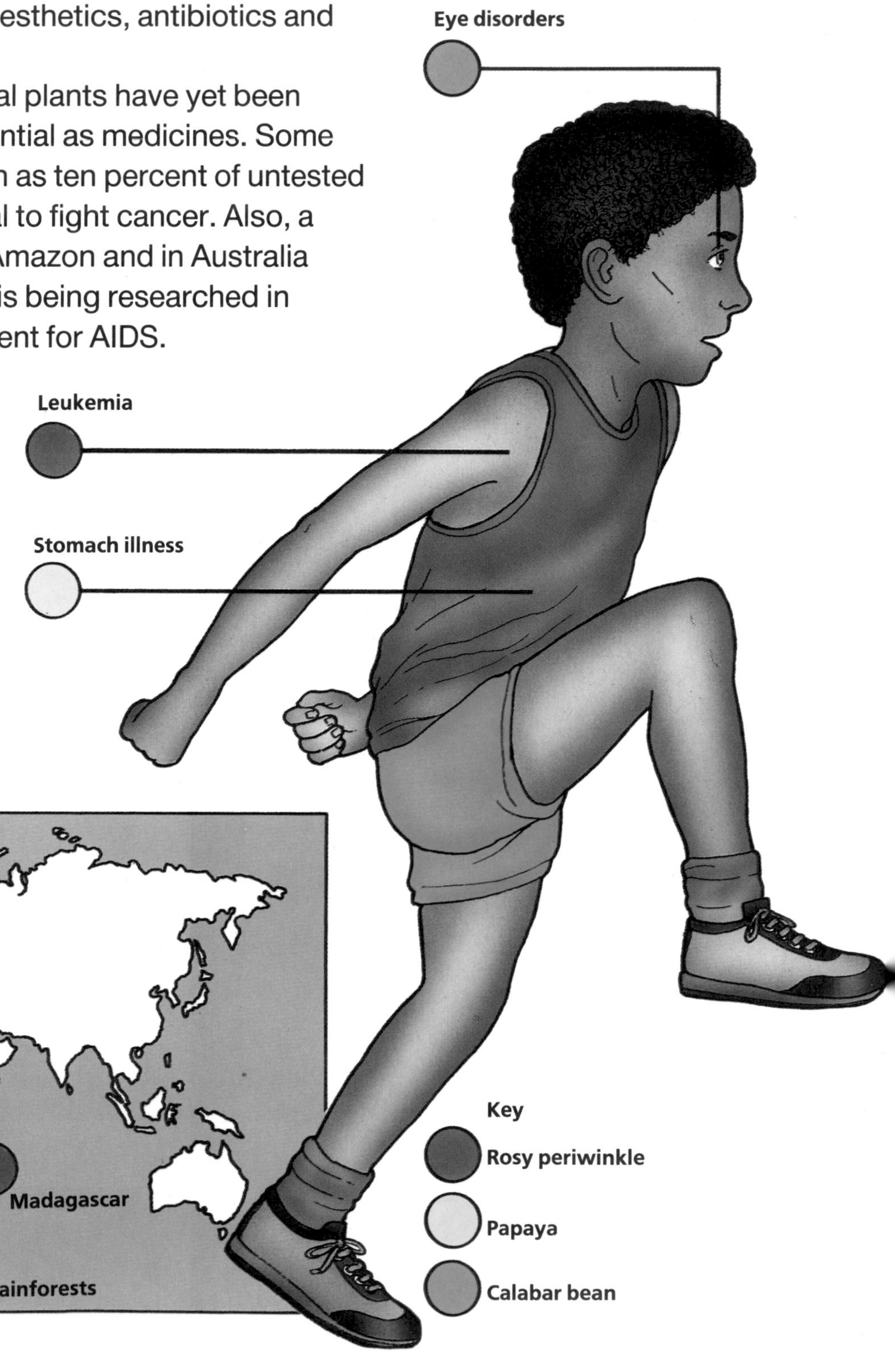

▼▶ The following rainforest plants provide medicines for illnesses: the rosy periwinkle of Madagascar for leukemia; the calabar bean of West Africa for eye disorders; and the papaya of Latin America for stomach illnesses.

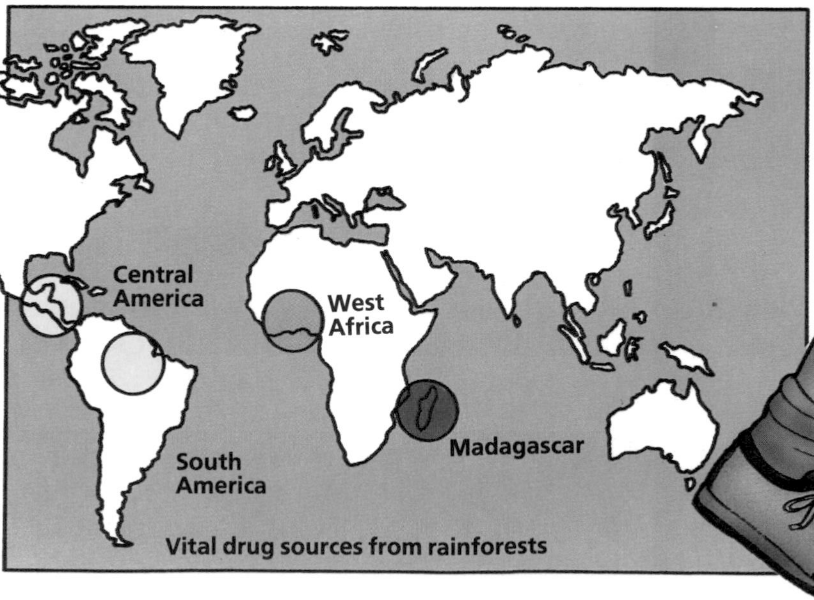

Vital drug sources from rainforests

When Amazonian Amerindians hunt, they often use poison-tipped darts shot from blowpipes to kill their food. The poison, known as *curare*, works by stopping the muscles from working. The animal cannot breathe and soon dies. When scientists saw the poison's effect they used it to develop a powerful muscle relaxant. It is given to people to make their bodies relaxed for surgical operations. *Curare* is still harvested in the Amazon and helps patients worldwide.

◀▲ Traditional healers around the world, like this South African witchdoctor, employ hundreds of different kinds of plants to treat people. Madagascan herbalists have long used the rosy periwinkle (shown above) as medicine, which led western scientists to discover how useful it could be against leukemia.

THE FOREST LARDER

An amazing number of foods and drinks that we find in our grocery store originally came from rainforest plants. Coffee, bananas, cacao (which makes chocolate), avocados, rice, tea, oranges, and pineapples all grow naturally in the world's rainforests, as do the plants which provide spices like cinnamon, clove, cardamom, nutmeg and ginger. Other commodities also come from the forests: high-quality chewing gum, from the chicle tree of Central America, and some perfumes depend upon rainforest plants for their manufacture.

Nobody knows how many more useful materials might be waiting to be discovered in the rainforests. Already some native rainforest crops with great commercial potential are being tried out, such as the pummelo, a large relative of oranges and lemons, and the mangosteen, said to be the tastiest fruit in the world.

▼ Forest lands provide profit for loggers and ranchers, but they can also prove very valuable without being destroyed. If forest areas are allowed to remain wild, fruit, nuts, and other products can be harvested while leaving the forest itself intact. This is called sustainable harvesting, and is employed by native rainforest peoples like this Amazonian boy.

◀ Many food crops that originally came from the rainforests are now grown in plantations rather than harvested wild in the jungle. But domestic crops still need their wild relatives. Wild plants often have qualities which cultivated varieties lack, like especially good flavor or disease resistance. People, like this botanist, search for the plants' relatives in the forests so they can introduce their qualities to the cultivated crops by crossbreeding them.

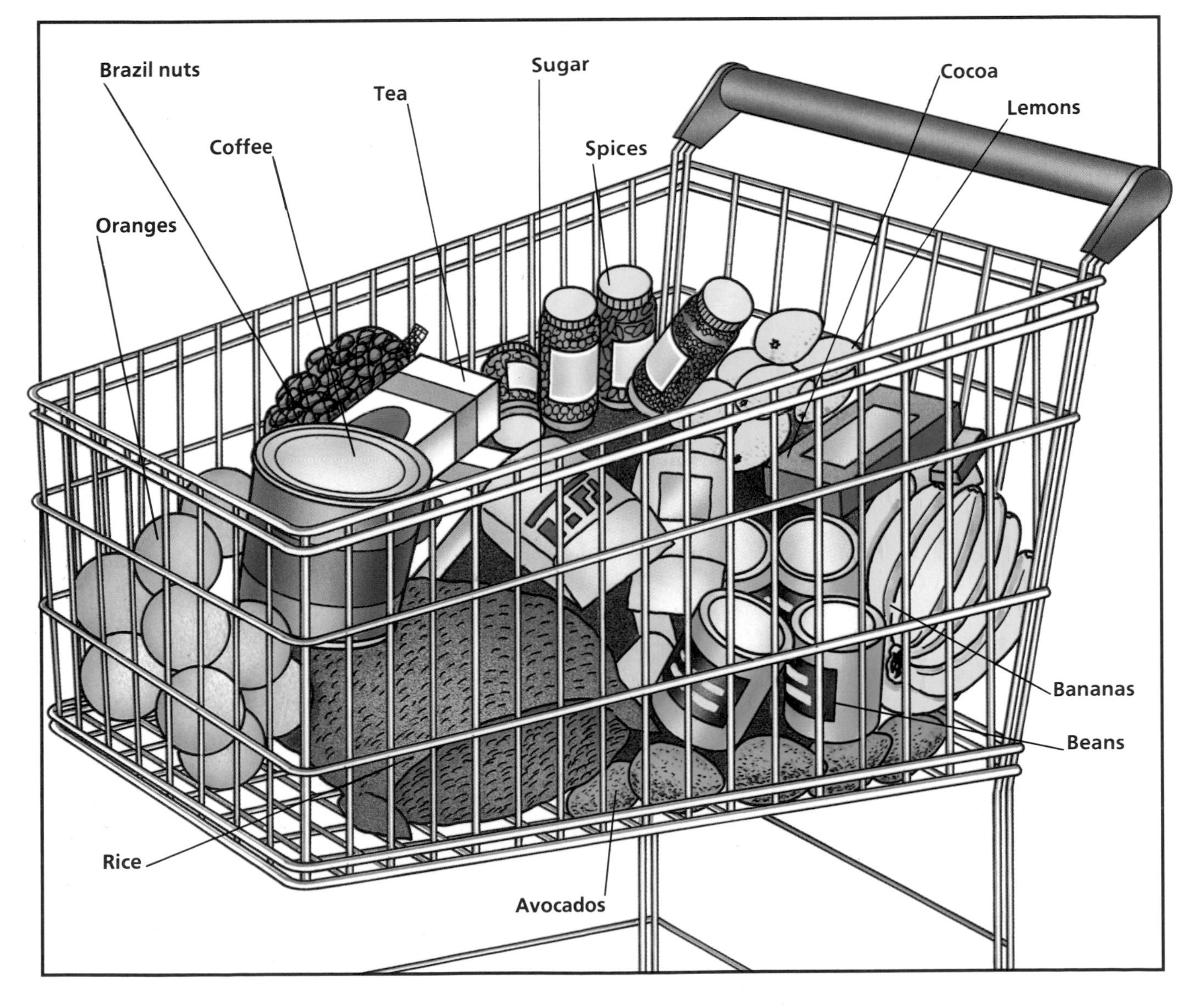

DEFORESTATION EFFECTS

Scientists warn that large-scale rainforest destruction could have devastating effects upon life on our planet. Burning the rainforests releases gases into the atmosphere which add to the greenhouse effect. This process, in which heat is trapped in the atmosphere by certain gases like CO_2, threatens to raise the earth's temperature, with potentially disastrous results.

Another serious impact of the destruction is that the removal of rainforests leaves behind bare earth. In hilly areas this means that large amounts of water run off the land instead of being trapped by the forests, so soil is washed away and floods occur. Flooding of this type has occurred in many places, like Madagascar and the Philippines. Disastrous floods, caused by forest destruction, led Thailand to ban all logging in 1989.

Rainforest plants, like other plants, take up carbon dioxide (CO_2) from the atmosphere and turn it into substances that are vital for growth and life. But when they are burned the CO_2 is released again. Carbon dioxide is a "greenhouse gas" and it adds to the greenhouse effect, helping to cause global warming which threatens to disrupt the climate worldwide. Over a billion tons of CO_2 are estimated to be released from rainforest burning every year; this is second only to the amount released from burning coal, oil, and gas in contributing to global warming.

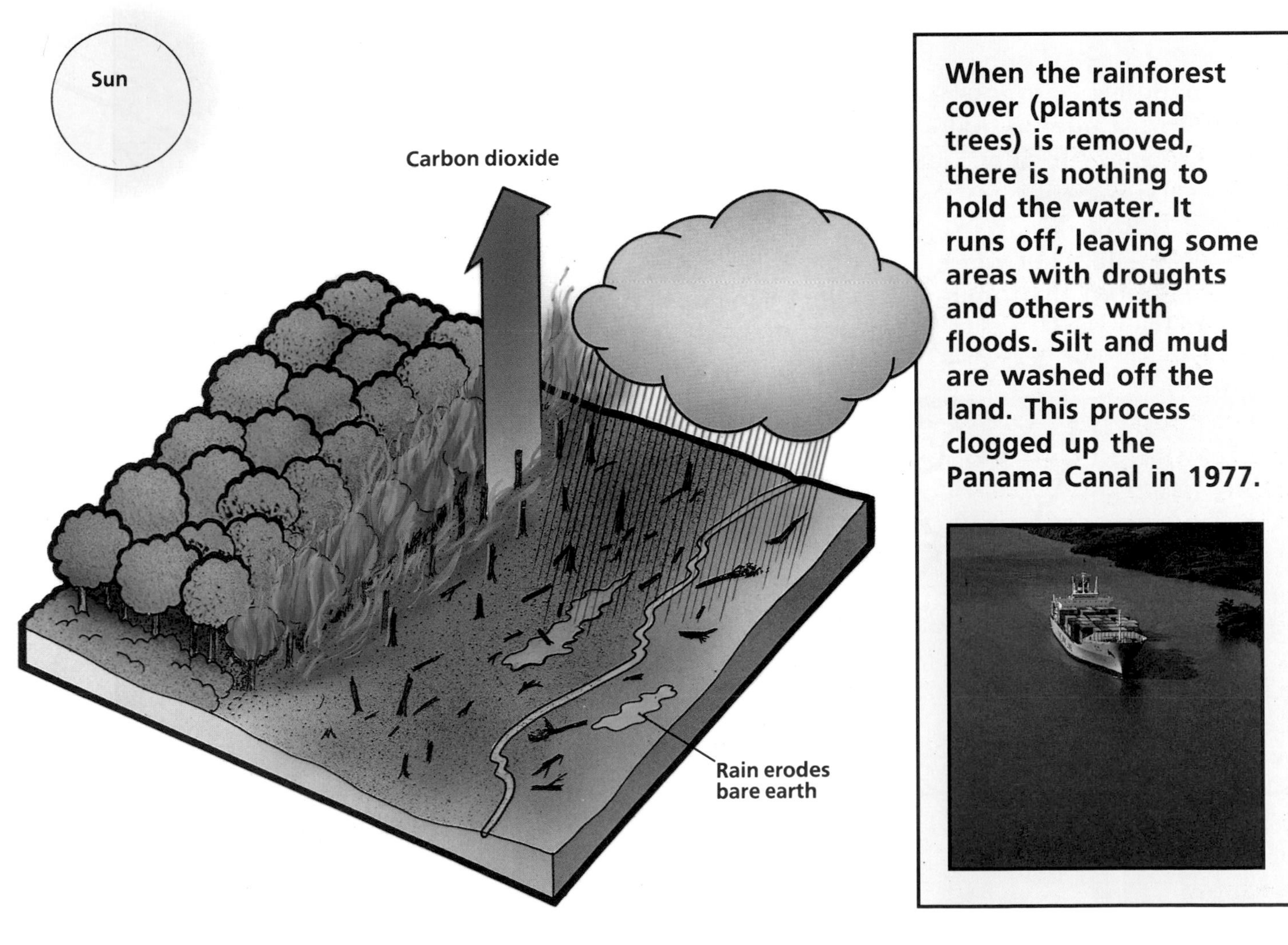

When the rainforest cover (plants and trees) is removed, there is nothing to hold the water. It runs off, leaving some areas with droughts and others with floods. Silt and mud are washed off the land. This process clogged up the Panama Canal in 1977.

FOREST PEOPLES

For thousands of years people have lived in the world's rainforests. They have lived in harmony with the forest, using its products for food and shelter, and not overexploiting or destroying it. They are the people who know most about the forest and its plants and animals.

Since other people have started to demolish and invade the rainforest the forest peoples have suffered badly. Their forest homes have been destroyed. They have died from epidemics of diseases like malaria brought in by settlers from outside. They have even been murdered by people coming into their lands. Worldwide the forest peoples have protested to stop others from destroying them and their homes. Sometimes they succeed, but too often they are overwhelmed by bulldozers, roads, and people with guns.

▼ Across the world there are probably about a thousand tribes of rainforest peoples. Pygmies are rainforest people that live in parts of Africa's rainforests. The tribe below is from Zaire. Pygmies are very knowledgeable about the forest they live in.

▶ Despite continual invasions, the Kaiapó tribe of Brazil has maintained its culture, such as the traditional dancing shown here. In 1989 they organized the first meeting of Brazilian Indian tribes to protest against a planned government dam project.

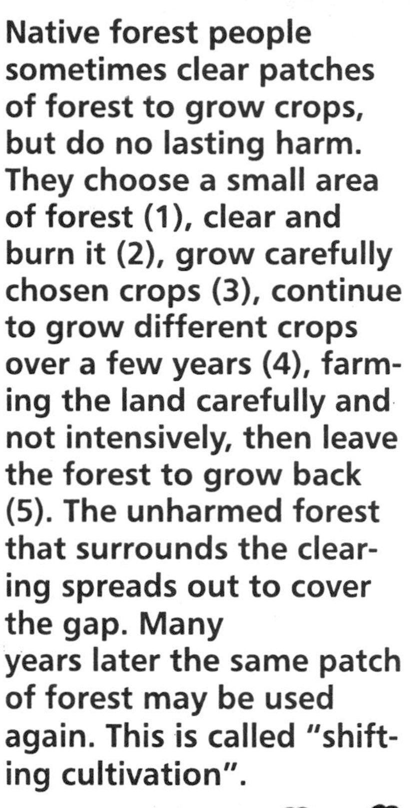

Native forest people sometimes clear patches of forest to grow crops, but do no lasting harm. They choose a small area of forest (1), clear and burn it (2), grow carefully chosen crops (3), continue to grow different crops over a few years (4), farming the land carefully and not intensively, then leave the forest to grow back (5). The unharmed forest that surrounds the clearing spreads out to cover the gap. Many years later the same patch of forest may be used again. This is called "shifting cultivation".

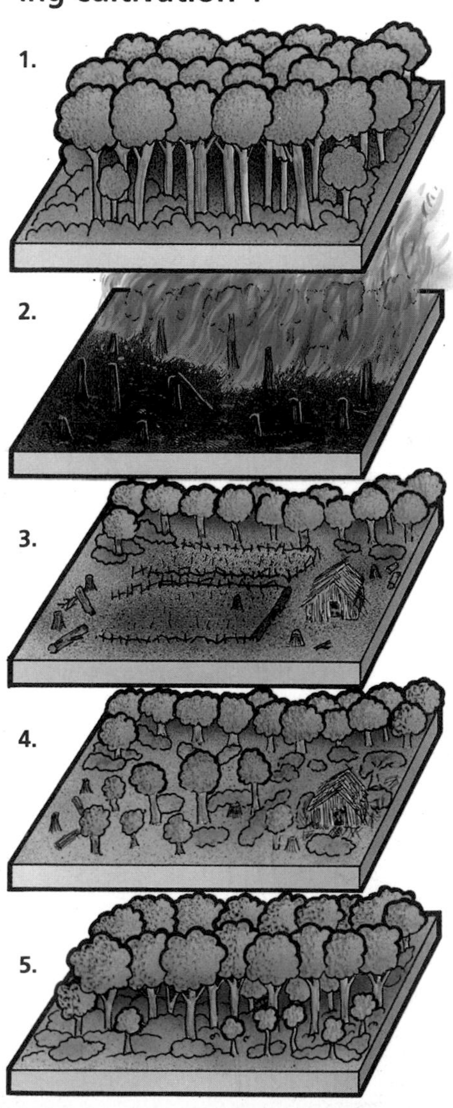

WHAT CAN BE DONE?

Saving the rainforests is a difficult problem, but it can be done. It demands a major effort by the countries of the world working together to make sure that the forests remain a habitat for millions of animals and plants, a source of food and medicines for the future, and a home to tribal peoples.

One of the most important priorities lies in educating people all over the world about the value of the rainforests and the precious resources they hold. We must ensure that the governments in countries with rainforests become committed to saving them. Other countries have to help and, if necessary, give economic support to the rainforest countries.

For the rainforests to survive they must have complete protection in National Parks where possible, and sustainable use, instead of overexploitation, of unprotected forests. This is possible if the rainforest peoples are allowed to protect and manage their own forests. The global consequences will be disastrous if the current rate of destruction is not slowed.

Huge organizations, like the World Bank, and rich Western countries help to fund development programs such as roads and dams in the tropics. Sometimes these programs benefit the people in the area, but not always. Some projects, like roads through the Amazon, can do more harm than good. Now the World Bank is beginning to look at the environmental effects of such programs before it supports them.

▶ Rubber is collected by cutting grooves in the bark of the rubber tree so that the latex (raw rubber) runs down into a cup. Although there are human-made rubber substitutes, none of them are as elastic or as heat-resistant as the natural product. Rubber is particularly useful in tires because it enables them to withstand potholes and emergency stops. This rubber is being collected at a Malaysian plantation, but rubber tapping in the wild is preferable because some rainforests are cleared for rubber tree plantations.

◀ It is possible for people who live in rainforests to use the land in non-destructive ways. These Kenyan women are planting trees to ensure soil protection in the future. Trees shelter soil from the rain thus preventing it from being washed away. They also provide building materials and firewood, fruit and nuts for food, and rubber and other substances for industry. Trees live for many years and, if species compatible with the habitat are used, they do not exhaust the soil as other crops do. This means that people do not have to keep moving on and clearing new areas of forest. Useful trees can be planted within the rainforest, or grown in areas where rainforest has been cleared.

FACT FILE 1

Temperate rainforests

There are some rainforests outside the tropics. In temperate lands where there is a great deal of rain, and where the weather is mild, with few or no frosts, temperate rainforests grow. In southeast Australia and Tasmania there are temperate rainforests, like those below in New South Wales, where eucalyptus trees and tree ferns flourish. Australia also contains tropical rainforests.

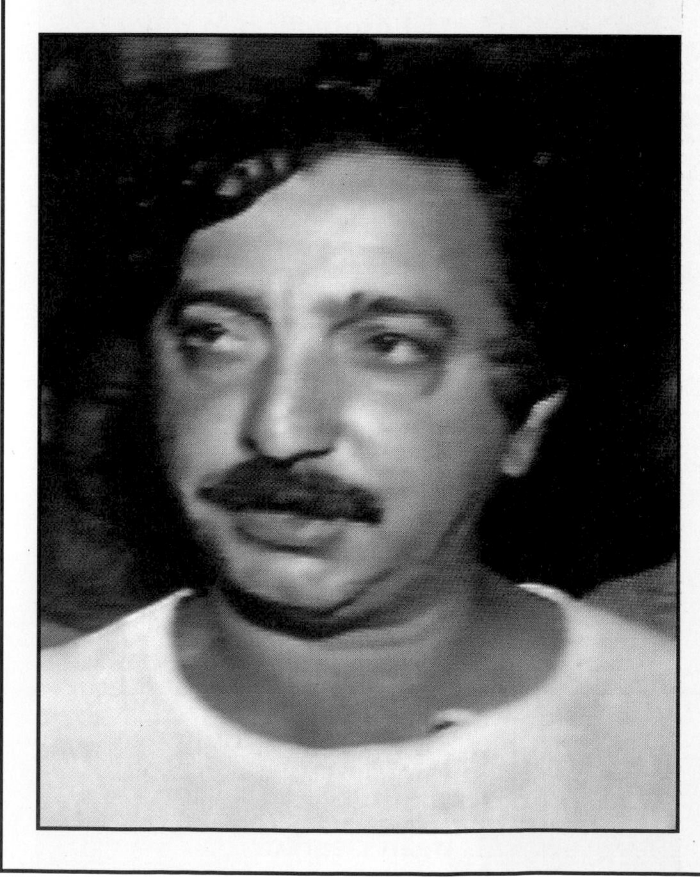

Chico Mendes

Chico Mendes was a rubber tapper in the Amazon jungle. The rubber tappers collect or "tap" rubber from the rubber trees that grow wild in the forest; they exploit the forest's resources in a sustainable way. Mendes and the other rubber tappers resisted the attempts by wealthy landowners in Brazil to clear away the forests for ranching land. The Amazonian Indians supported and joined Mendes and others in the rubber tappers' union to try to save the forest. But Mendes non-violent struggle earned him many enemies among those who destroy the forest and exploit its riches. On December 22, 1988 Mendes was shot dead by his enemies. Even though he was gone, the Amerindians and the rubber tappers will not give up. At Chico Mendes' funeral a banner was carried that read "They killed our leader, but not our struggle".

Rainforest climate

Tropical rainforests thrive where the temperature is fairly constant all year at about 18-30°C (64-86°F) and where rain falls fairly regularly throughout the year. Rainforests get at least 200-300 cm (80-120 in) of rain a year, and some get as much as 1,000 cm (395 in). The climate never fluctuates to extremes like cold or drought. Nottingham, England, by comparison, has an average annual temperature of about 9.1°C (48°F) and an annual rainfall of about 71 cm (28 in), which does not fall regularly throughout the year.

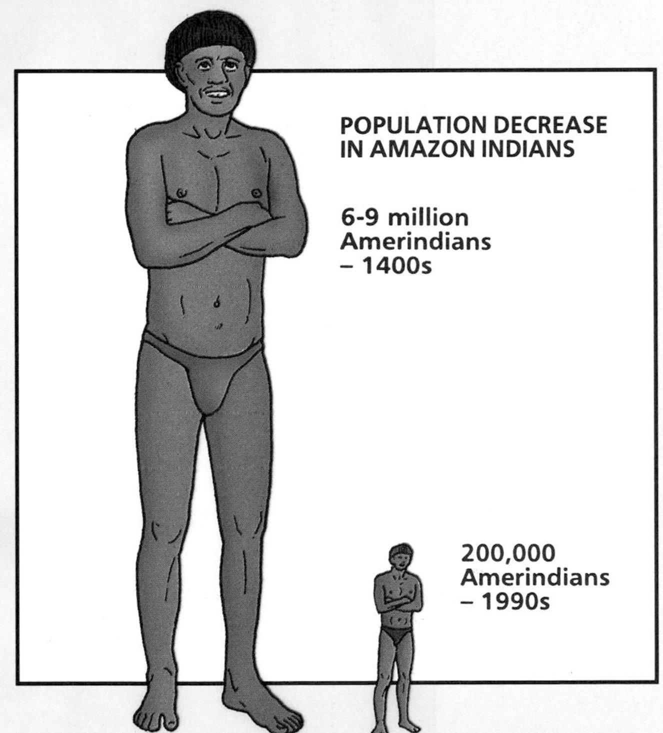

Amazon Indians

The destruction of the rainforests and the diseases brought in by people from other places have drastically reduced the number of native people in the rainforests. In the Amazon, there were probably between 6 and 9 million Amerindians in the 1400s. Now there are about 200,000, and they are threatened on all sides.

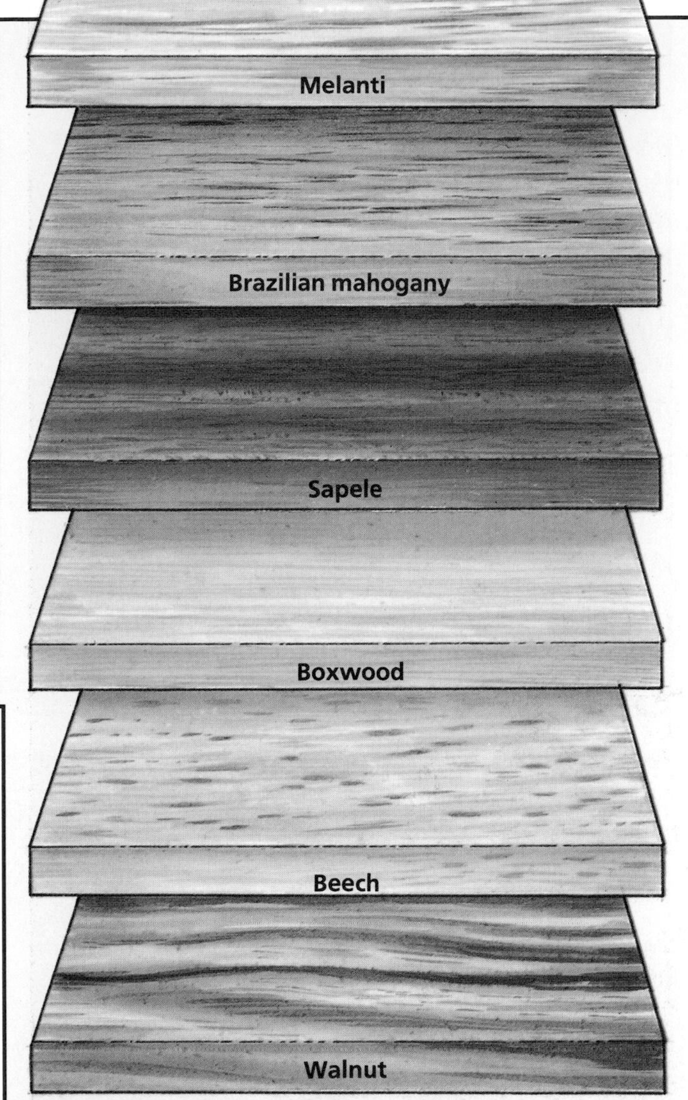

Types of wood

Woods like mahogany, sapele and melanti are from rainforest trees. Their felling damages the forest and the surrounding environment. In the future, there may be sustainable harvesting of these woods, perhaps from plantations. Until then, the use of tropical timber nearly always means the destruction of rainforests. For virtually all uses of tropical timber there are good alternatives, like walnut and beech from Europe and North America, and boxwood from the Mediterranean countries. These woods come from trees that are harvested in a more sustainable way than tropical rainforest timber.

FACT FILE 2

The water cycle

Nothing goes to waste in the rainforest. Most of the rain is taken up by the plants, used, and then released back into the atmosphere through their leaves. For the rest of the water, the roots of the trees in the rainforest act like a huge sponge, releasing water slowly into the streams and rivers. the water that returns to the atmosphere falls again later as rain. Rain may be recycled up to 5 times as it passes from east to west across the Amazon, but deforestation stops this process and threatens to cause droughts

Dead animals and plants decay quickly in the hot and humid conditions, their nutrients being taken up by the web of roots that grow a close to the surface. Because everything is recycled quickly, a thick soil like that of cooler temperate forests does not form. This is why the soil can be easily washed away or lose its fertility under shifting cultivation when the forest is cleared

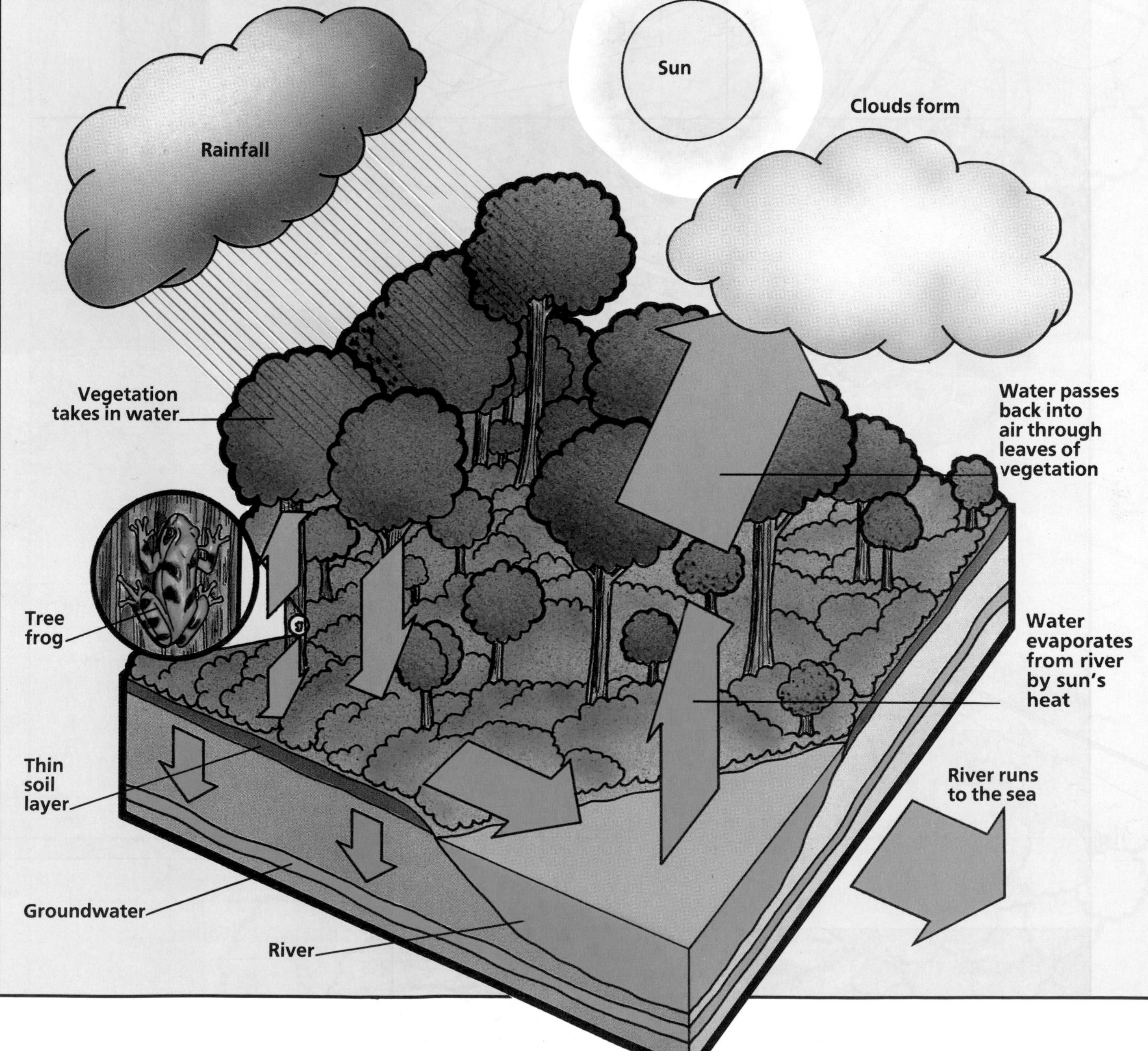

ICE CAPS & GLACIERS

CHAPTER 4

CHAPTER FOUR:
ICE CAPS AND GLACIERS

INTRODUCTION

Although the earth's climate is fairly warm, some parts, such as the poles and high mountain ranges, remain covered with glacier ice all year round. Glaciers vary greatly in size and depth. Some of them are quite tiny and measure only a few hundred feet long. Others cover vast areas of land and may be thousands of feet deep. Glaciers rarely remain still. Their massive weight causes the ice to flow slowly downhill, scraping the rock beneath and creating new landforms.

Less than 10,000 years ago, the earth's climate was much colder than it is today. Glaciers extended over much of North America, Europe, and Asia, and huge sheets of ice covered Greenland and Antarctica. Even in warmer parts of the world, such as Africa, South America, and New Zealand, glaciers formed in the high mountain areas. These glaciers gradually formed many different geographical features, such as the Great Lakes and valleys of North America.

Glaciers are an important source of water and electricity.

Some parts of the world are so cold that they are covered with permanent layers of ice. The largest layers occur around the North and South Poles, where they spread out to form ice caps thousands of feet thick. Smaller glaciers are found in mountain valleys all over the world. These are known as valley glaciers.

EXTENT TODAY

Glacier ice covers about 6.5 million square miles of the earth's surface, just over ten percent of the total land area. Nearly all of this ice (98 percent) occurs at the poles. Valley glaciers account for the remaining two percent.

Huge ice sheets have advanced across Europe and North America during successive glacial periods, and at one time the whole of Britain was covered with a large mass of ice.

Today, glaciers can be found in areas that have very cold winters and short, cool summers, such as Greenland and Iceland. Glaciers can also be found in mountains that have very high altitudes, such as Mount Kilimanjaro in Tanzania, and in high mountain chains like the Alps, Andes, Rockies, and Himalayas.

Extent of ice

90% land

10% ice

▽ The nearer you get to the equator, the less ice there tends to be. This is because it is much hotter near the equator.

A view of a glacier and icebergs.

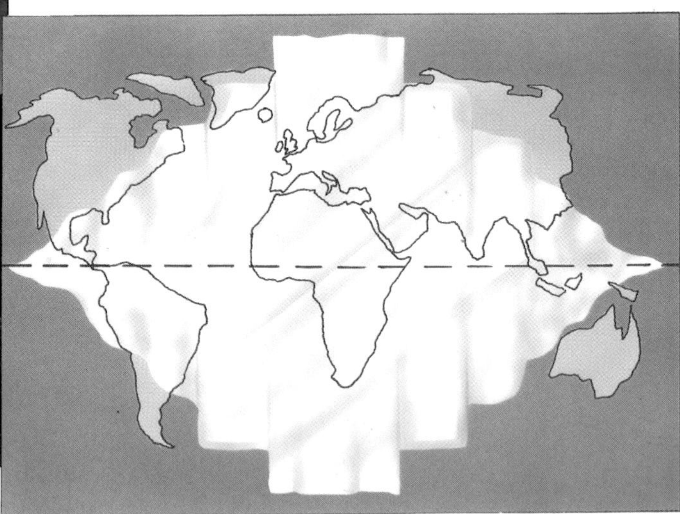

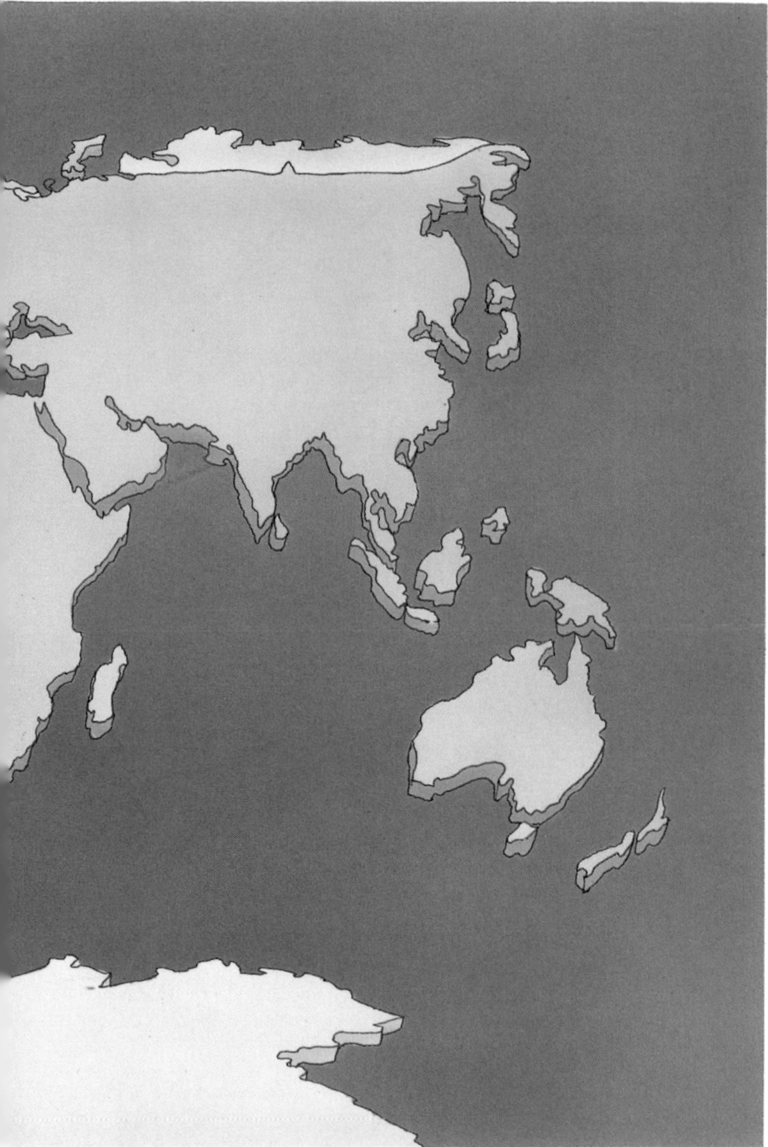

THE POLES

The poles are very cold because of their geographical position. Situated at the very top and bottom of the globe, the poles receive sunlight for only half of the year. The remaining six months are spent in complete darkness. Even at the height of the polar summer, the sun never reaches its full height in the sky. As a result, it shines at an angle on the poles, and the amount of heat reaching the land is very much reduced.

Glaciers are made up of snow, and at the poles, snow falls throughout the year. This snow does not melt but becomes compressed into glacial ice. The ice and snow that collect have an extra cooling effect, for the white surface reflects a high proportion of the sunlight and absorbs little heat.

The region around the North Pole is known as the Arctic, and the ice covering in this area extends southward over most of Greenland. Around the South Pole, ice completely covers the continent of Antarctica, making it the coldest and iciest region in the world.

△ Today, ice covers ten percent of the earth's land surface. Nearly all of this ice can be found at the poles.

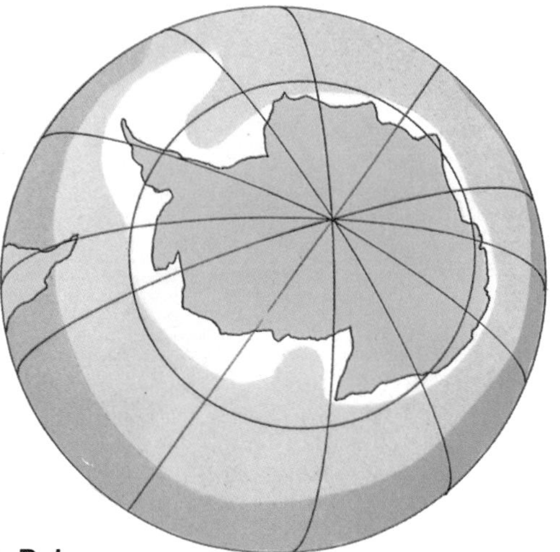

South Pole

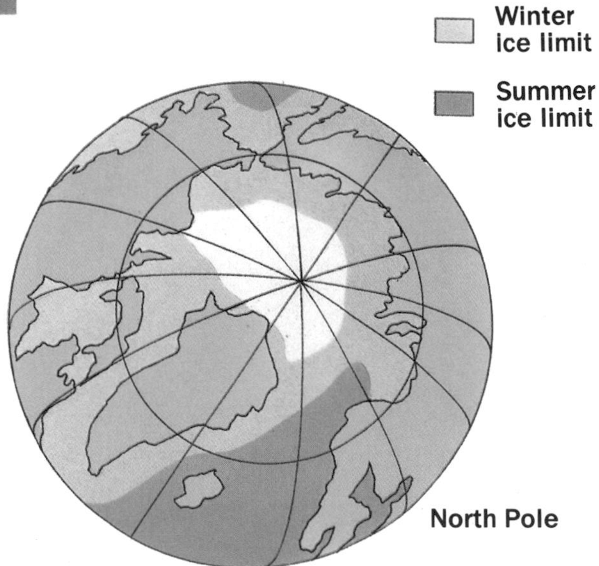

North Pole

△ About 99 percent of the world's fresh water is locked into the ice sheets of Antarctica and Greenland.

In the past, the earth's climate was much colder than it is today. The polar glaciers extended much further south and north, and vast areas of land were buried under a half-mile-thick sheet of ice. These periods are known as the Ice Ages, and the most recent one ended only about 10,000 years ago.

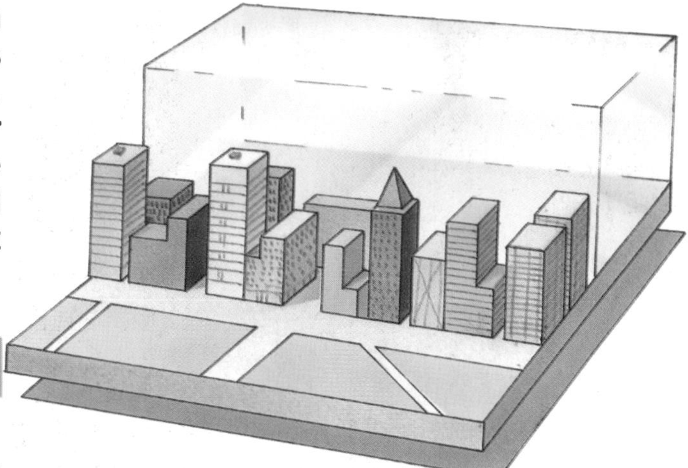

△ The illustration above shows the size of a glacier against the high-rise buildings of New York City.

EXTENT OF THE ICE

Between 400,000 and 10,000 years ago, our planet experienced a series of Ice Ages separated by warm periods. We are probably living in one of these warm periods, called interglacials, today. During the last Ice Age, the glaciers reached their furthest extent and covered about 30 percent of the earth's land surface.

The effects of the Ice Age were greatest in the Northern Hemisphere, where huge sheets of ice covered much of North America, Europe, and parts of Asia. South of the equator, the glaciers covered about one-third of South America, and parts of Australia. One major effect of the last Ice Age was a fall in sea levels. Millions of tons of water were used in forming glaciers, and in many parts of the world, land that had been submerged under water became exposed. The Black Sea was turned into a lake, and around the Pacific, New Guinea was connected to Australia. As the glaciers melted, sea levels rose and the landscape took the form it has today.

At their greatest extent, glaciers covered about 30 percent of the earth's land surface.

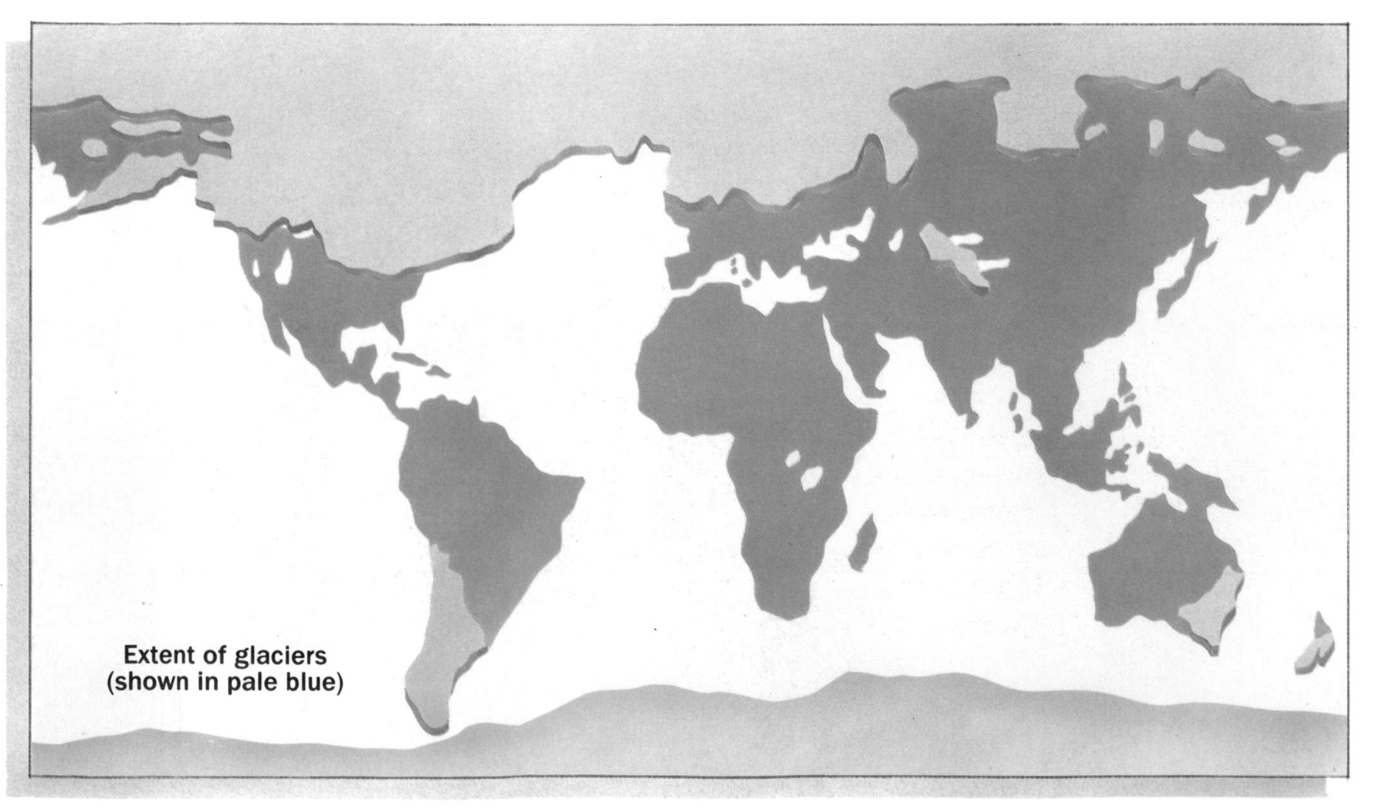

EFFECTS ON LAND

During the last Ice Age, the amount of habitable land on earth was greatly reduced. Animals, including our ancestors, were forced to move away from the advancing glaciers toward the equator. With so much water turned into ice, the climate was much drier than it is today. The rainforests shrank so much that they almost disappeared completely.

Further north and south of the equator, the effects of the glaciers were even more dramatic. The large masses of thick ice hid the features of the land beneath. Glaciers also helped to form new landscapes, as they are among the most powerful land-shaping forces on earth. North America and northern Europe are full of features carved out by glaciers. When the glaciers melted, the flood of water released added new features, such as lakes and valleys, to the landscape.

Death Valley in California.

ICE TO WATER

The effect of melting glaciers does not alter sea levels. You can demonstrate this for yourself. Fill a margarine tub with water and place it in a freezer until the water has completely turned to ice. Remove the ice block from the tub and place it in a shallow bowl. Add water until the ice block floats. Measure the level of water in the bowl with a ruler. Wait until the ice has melted and measure the depth again. The "sea level" in the bowl should not have risen.

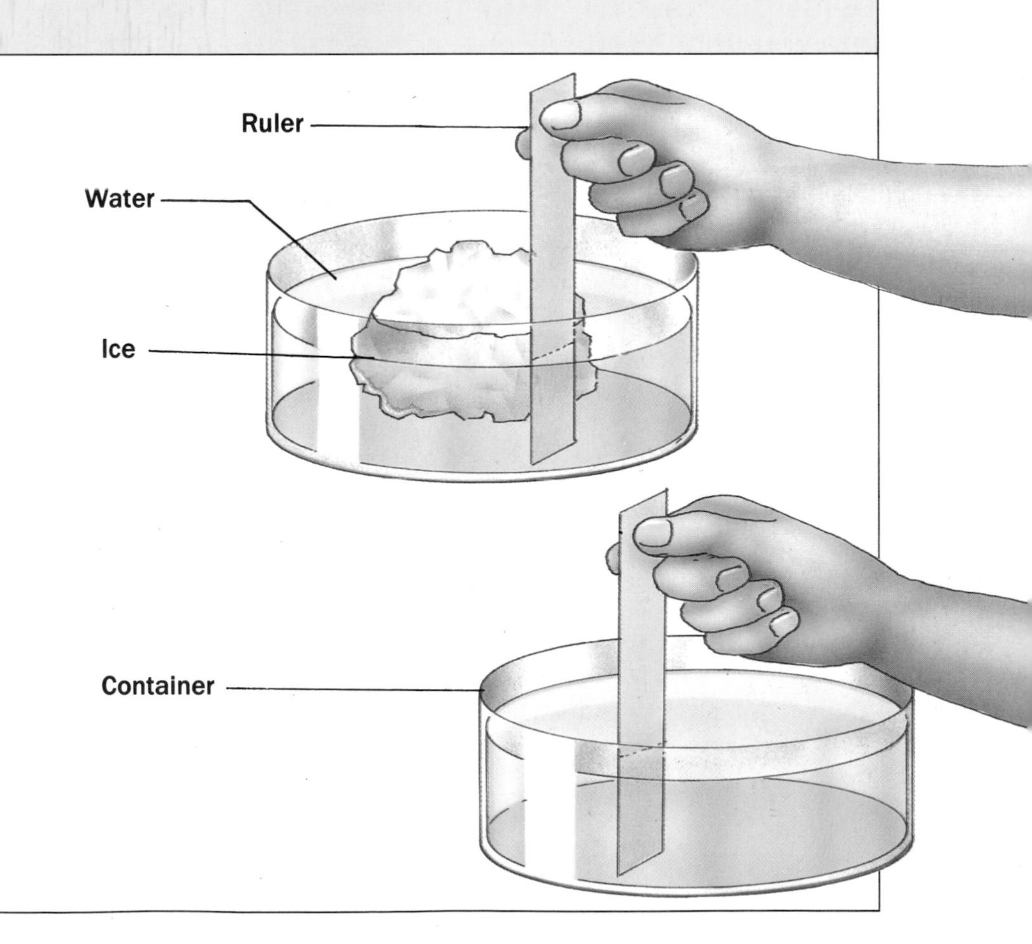

Altogether, the polar regions around the world contain several million cubic miles of ice. This represents almost all of the fresh water found on our planet. Most of the ice at the poles lies on solid rock, Floating ice in the sea makes up less than one percent of the total volume of ice at the poles.

ANTARCTIC

In the continent of Antarctica, ice covers over 4.6 million square miles, and in some places it is more than 13,000 feet thick. Beneath the ice lies a varied landscape of mountain ranges, lowlands, and valleys. The massive weight of the ice has depressed the earth's crust, and many parts of Antarctica have been pushed down below sea level. In places where these depressions open out into the sea, ice shelves have formed. An ice shelf is a thick layer of ice that starts on land and extends out into the sea. Apart from a few plants and insects, Antarctica is completely uninhabited. There are also 30 science and weather stations on the continent.

△ The Arctic is comparatively warm. At the North Pole, the average midsummer temperature is 32°F. On Greenland, temperatures may drop to 5°F.

ARCTIC

In contrast, much of the Arctic ice consists of an island of pack ice floating in the middle of the Arctic Ocean. The ice has an average depth of seven feet, but in some places it is considerably thicker. Even so, there is clear water under the North Pole, and submarines are able to travel beneath the ice.

On Greenland, however, a thick layer of ice extends for nearly one million square miles, covering almost all of the land. Only the narrow strips along parts of the coast are free from ice, because these areas are washed by warm ocean currents. Most of the people of Greenland live in the southwest where summer temperatures average 40°F.

◁ Antarctica is the coldest place in the world. The midsummer temperatures rarely rise above −22°F. In winter, temperatures fall below −90°F.

ICE CAPS

The term ice cap is usually used to describe ice that can be found at the poles, because they "cap" the top and bottom of our planet. But the ice on Antarctica and Greenland is most often called ice sheets.

An ice cap is an extensive glacier that covers less than 20,000 square miles. The term ice sheet is used for larger masses of ice. A large area of permanent pack ice is known as an ice field, because of its flat surface and uniform thickness.

Glaciers are frequently thought of as frozen rivers. Despite being frozen and compressed into dense ice, they still tend to flow downhill. Within the vast polar ice sheets, great rivers of ice slowly flow over the underlying landscape toward the sea. These rivers of ice are called continental glaciers.

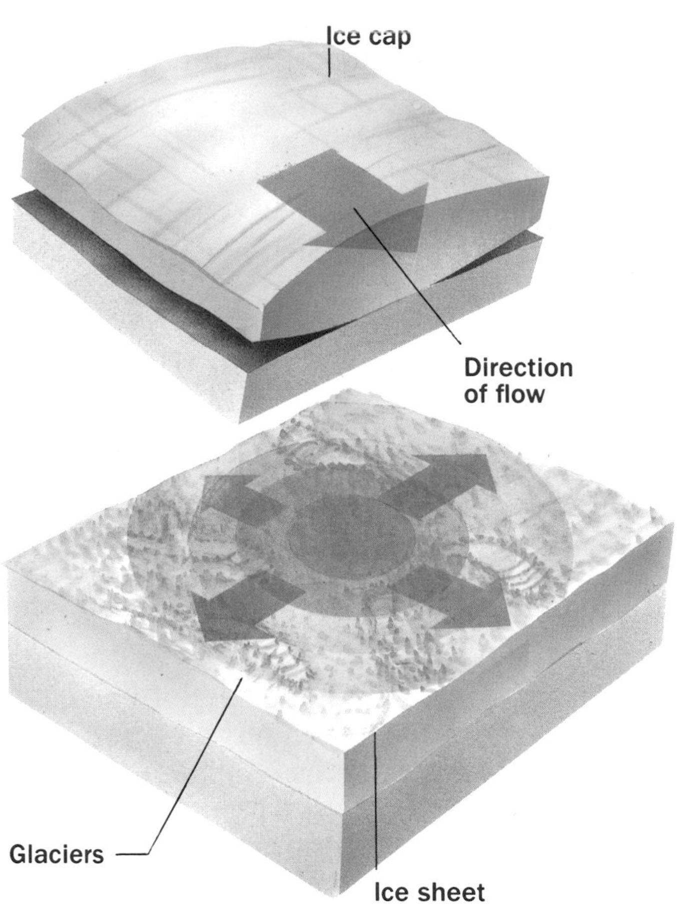

△ Glaciers are given different names, depending on how large they are. Ice caps and ice sheets can cover thousands of square miles of land.

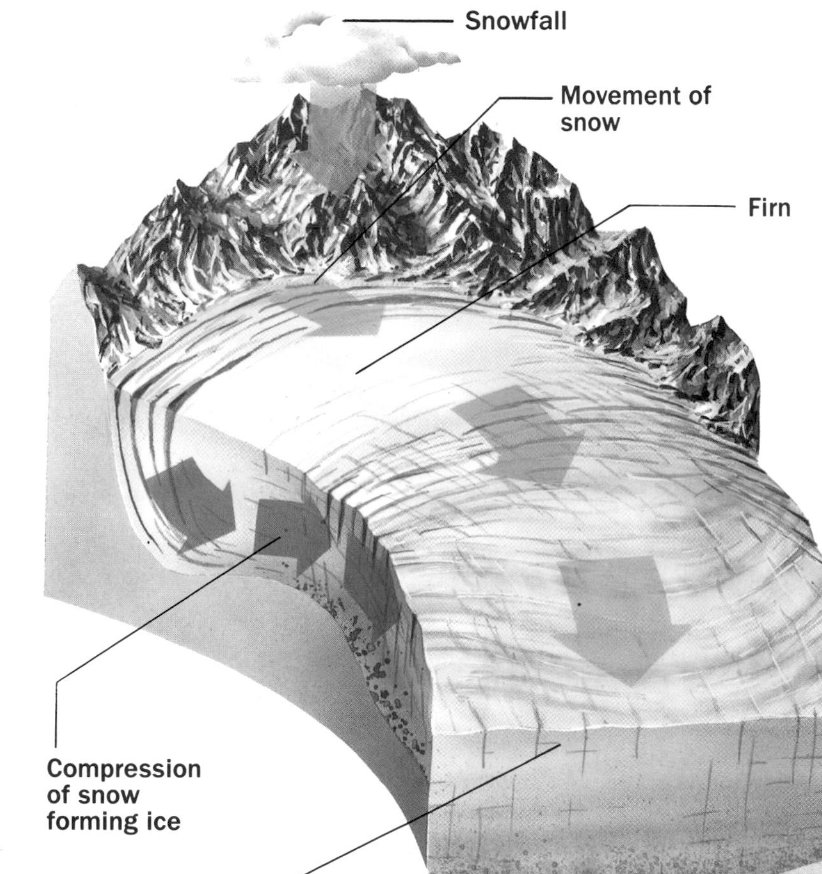

◁ All glacier ice comes from snow. Snowflakes melt very slowly in the intense cold around the poles. It takes about one year for the snow to turn into the hard dense crystals known as firn. As more snow falls, the firn begins to turn into larger crystals of ice.

▽ A cross section through an ice core shows layers of snowfall.

The ice sheets at the poles receive about 12 inches of fresh snow every year. Combined with the force of gravity, the weight of the accumulated snow drives continental glaciers toward the sea. Most of the water lost from the polar ice sheets occurs when the masses of ice (icebergs) break off the sheet and float out to sea.

JOURNEY TO THE SEA

Buried beneath the ice sheets are mountain ranges that are as high as the European Alps. The largest glaciers are found in Antarctica. The Lambert Glacier is more than 40 miles wide, and over 250 miles long.

Where the amount of snow falling on the glacier is the same as that lost through icebergs, the glacier remains almost stationary. But when the snowfall is more, the glacier moves forward a few feet a day. One example was the Hubbard glacier in North America, which advanced at around 32 feet a day in 1986. The fastest-moving glacier is the Quarayaq in Greenland, which moves about 72 feet a day.

In Greenland, glaciers flow straight into the sea and begin to melt. Cracks appear in the glacier, and large ice blocks form. These break away to form icebergs which can be found in the North Atlantic. This process is known as calving.

Ice cliffs at the edge of Svitjobreen glacier in Spitsbergen.

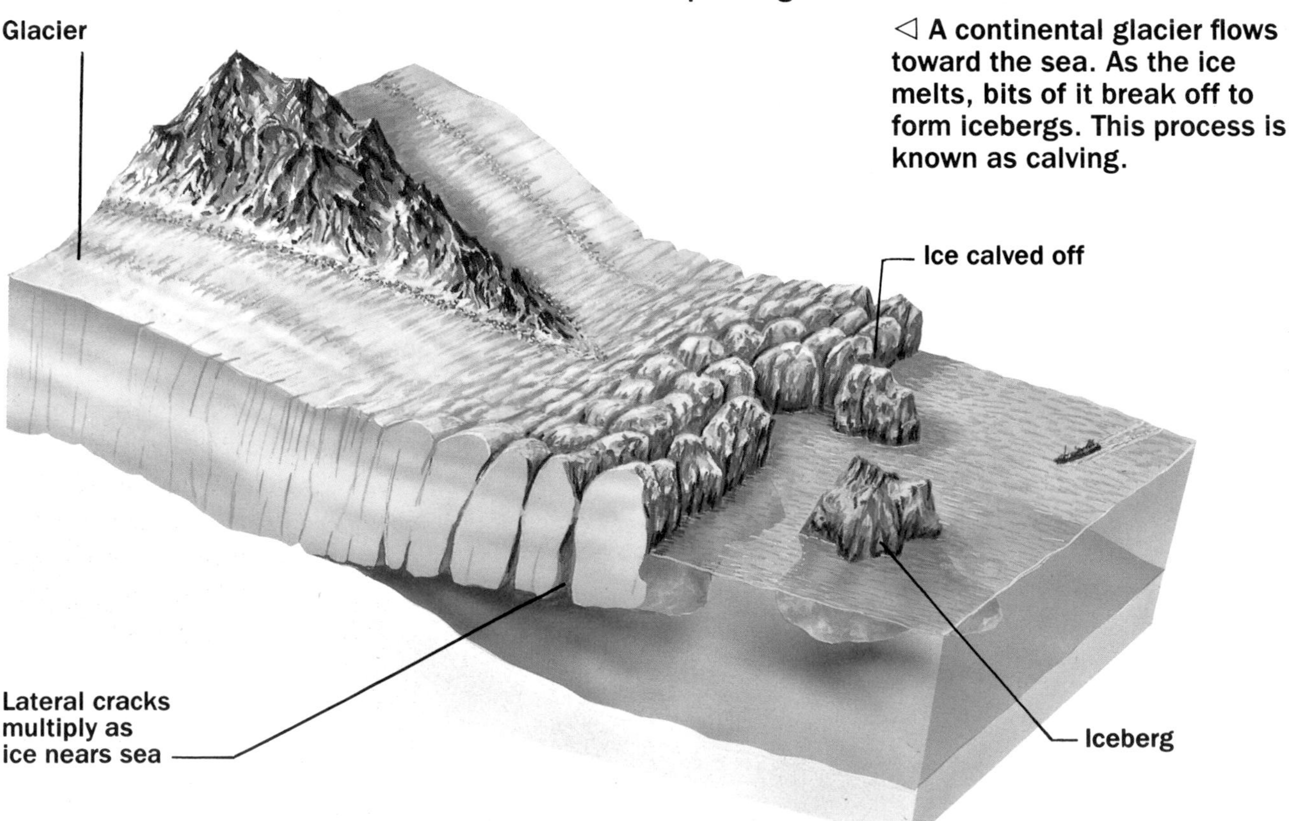

◁ A continental glacier flows toward the sea. As the ice melts, bits of it break off to form icebergs. This process is known as calving.

BERGS

In the Northern Hemisphere, icebergs tend to be relatively small. Although some measure a few miles, the vast majority are only a few inches long. Very small icebergs are called growlers. Smaller lumps of ice are known as "bergy bits". Northern icebergs usually have a very irregular shape, and even the largest melt within a year or two.

Around the edges of the Antarctic ice sheet, huge tabular icebergs can be found drifting in large numbers in the ocean. Icebergs more than 12 miles long are common. These massive ice-islands remain intact for many years, and only begin to melt when they eventually drift toward the equator.

△ An iceberg floats with 80 percent of its bulk underwater. There is usually a groove on them at sea level caused by wave action.

HOW MUCH BELOW

Ice floats at different depths in fresh water and salt water. You can measure the difference for yourself with an ice cube in a glass. Dissolve some salt in a glass of water. See how much of the ice cube sticks out above the surface of the glass. Now use fresh water and compare the results.

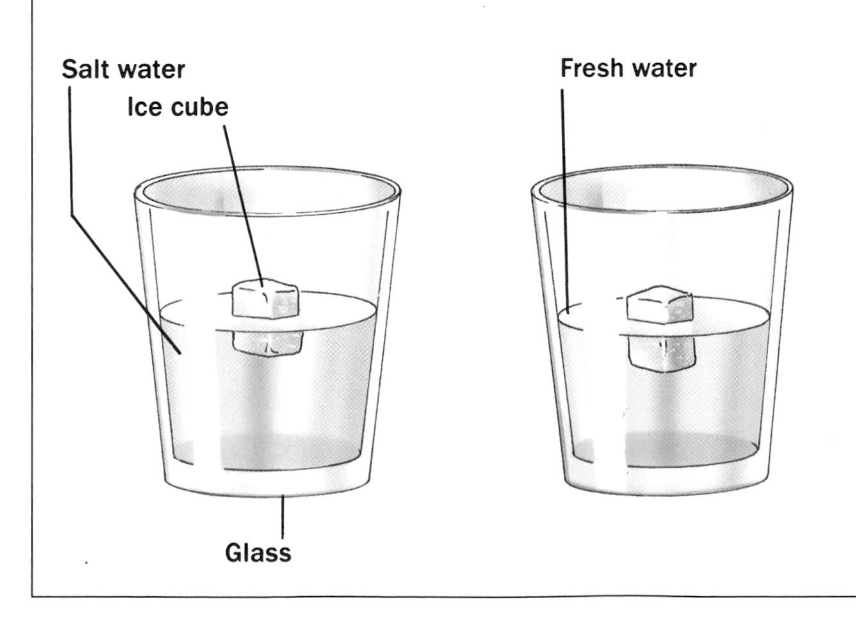

The largest icebergs produced in the continent of Antarctica measure more than 60 miles (100 km) in length. Three tabular bergs that calved from the Filchner ice shelf in 1986 had a combined area of more than 4,000 square miles. Each of them was bigger than the country of Luxembourg, and had ice more than 1,600 feet thick.

The formation of glaciers and ice sheets requires abundant snowfall. Around the fringes of the Arctic is an area where it is too dry and windswept for much snow to fall. The main feature of this tundra climate is frost, and the ground is always frozen into permafrost hundreds of feet deep.

PERMAFROST

The permafrost zone stretches across Alaska, northern Canada, Lapland, and northern Russia. Beneath the surface, the ground is frozen solid and in parts of Siberia, the permafrost extends to a depth of 1,600 feet. During the spring and summer months, only the top few inches of ice ever thaw out completely, and then only for the brief period before the autumn freeze.

One of the main effects of this freeze-thaw cycle is to flatten out the landscape. In winter, the surface layer expands as it freezes, raising the soil. During spring, the thawing process makes the surface layer muddy, and it slides down the gentlest slope. This allows the soil to settle more evenly. Tundra soils are usually well graduated, with the smallest particles at the surface.

A pingo in Alaska.

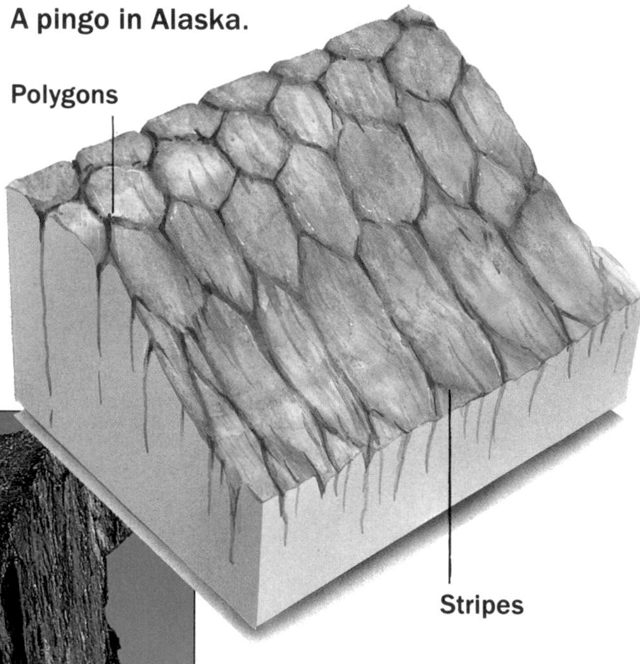

△ On level surfaces, frost action often shapes the ground into frozen polygons with almost regular sides. On slopes, the sides extend into stripes.

◁ A large rock near the summit of Bella Tolla in Switzerland. The ground here always remains frozen.

ICE ACTION

The freeze-thaw cycle of ice has a destructive effect on rocks exposed at the surface. Water that seeps into cracks in the rocks expands as it freezes, shattering the rocks. A similar process extends all the way into the permafrost.

During the winter freeze, narrow cracks appear in the soil surface. In spring, water seeps into these cracks and as the water freezes, the cracks widen and deepen. In time, these cracks develop into subsurface ice wedges up to 50 feet deep and 10 feet across. When the ice wedge finally melts, the resulting depression it leaves may slowly fill up with fine sediment.

The most dramatic feature of permafrost landscapes are pingos, small conical mounds which may be up to 330 feet high. A pingo is formed when underground water accumulates just below the surface. As the water freezes, it pushes the surface up into a dome shape. When the water melts, the enlarged cavity accumulates even more water. Eventually the ice breaks through the surface and melts. Then the soil covering collapses and produces a crater shape.

▽ This stone in northeast Greenland has been shattered by frost.

Ice

Gas pressure

△ Below ground level, expansion due to freezing can push soil up to the surface of a glacier.

VALLEY GLACIERS

A valley glacier is a long, narrow mass of ice that fills high mountain valleys. In total, there are about 10,000 valley glaciers scattered throughout the world, from the Andes in South America to the European Alps. Altogether, valley glaciers account for about two percent of the world's ice.

FORMATION

Whatever their size, all valley glaciers form in the same way – from a small hollow high up in the mountain filled with snow. Over the years, freeze-thaw action enlarges the hollow, and the snow turns into firn. As more snow accumulates, the firn turns into glacier ice. At this stage, the hollow is known as a cirque. Eventually the glacier overflows the lip of the cirque and begins to slide downhill.

Although it flows much slower than liquid water (on average only about 40 feet a day), a valley glacier behaves rather like a river. Where one glacier runs into another, they converge just like rivers do. Many valley glaciers are hundreds of miles long. For example, the Bering Glacier in southern Alaska is 125 miles long.

Not all the ice within a valley glacier moves at the same speed. Ice in the center of a valley glacier moves quite fast. But at the edge of the glacier, the ice is slowed down by friction against the sides of the mountain. Also, the underlying bedrock beneath the glacier tends to slow the moving ice down.

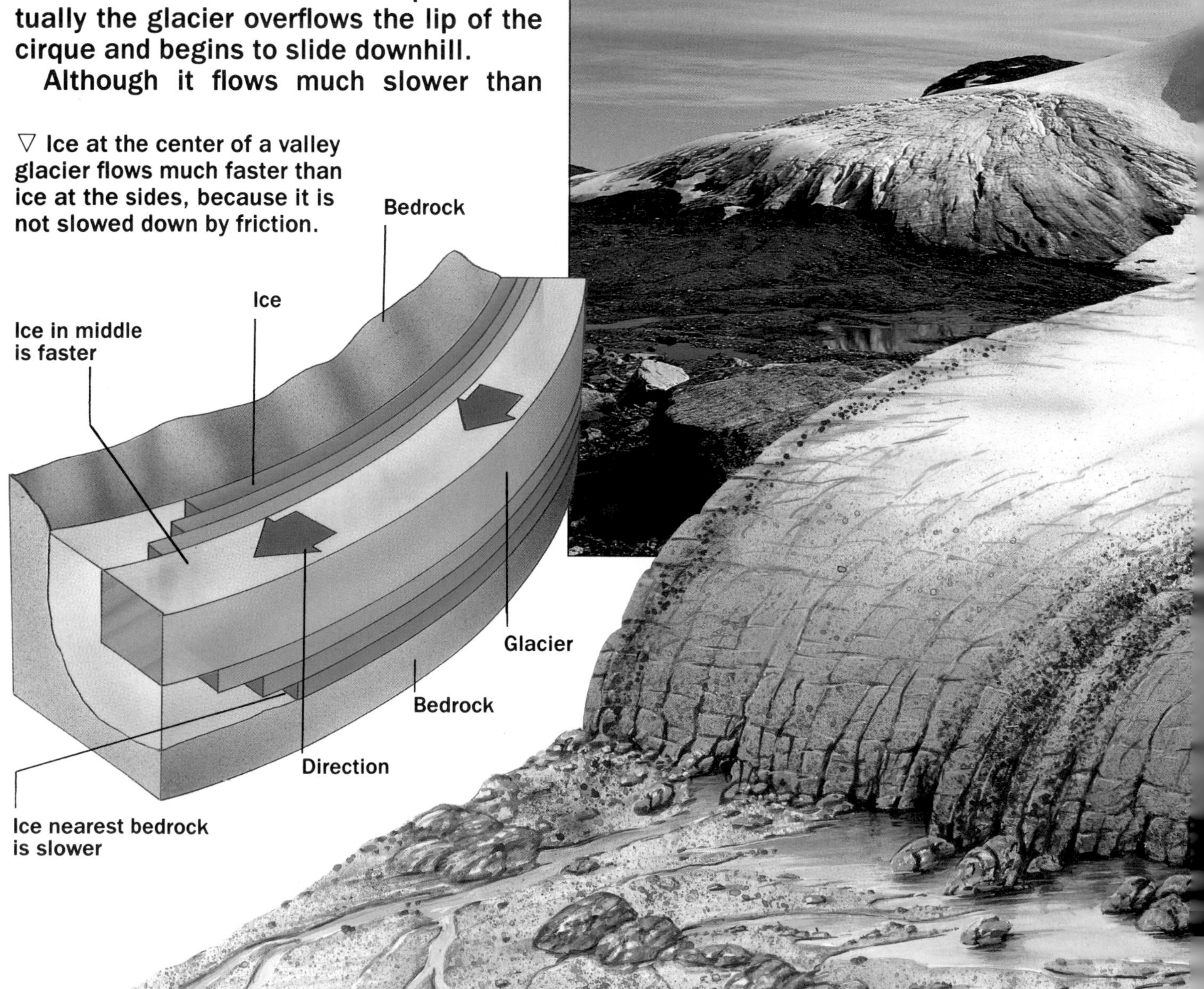

▽ Ice at the center of a valley glacier flows much faster than ice at the sides, because it is not slowed down by friction.

Hardangervidda glacier in Norway

EROSION

Glaciers are extremely powerful agents of erosion. As they creep along a valley, they change the shape of the underlying rock. Glaciers erode the landscape in two ways – by plucking and by abrasion.

At the sides and bottom of a valley glacier, friction melts some of the ice, and the water seeps into cracks in the underlying rock. As the water freezes, the glacier plucks fragments of rock away as it slides downhill.

Rock fragments become incorporated into the ice, and get dragged along with the glacier. The rocks make the glacier act like an enormous file. As it moves downhill with the rocks, the glacier cuts and shapes the rock beneath.

▽ A valley glacier accumulates snow at the top of a mountain. As it flows downhill, it erodes the landscape by plucking and abrasion.

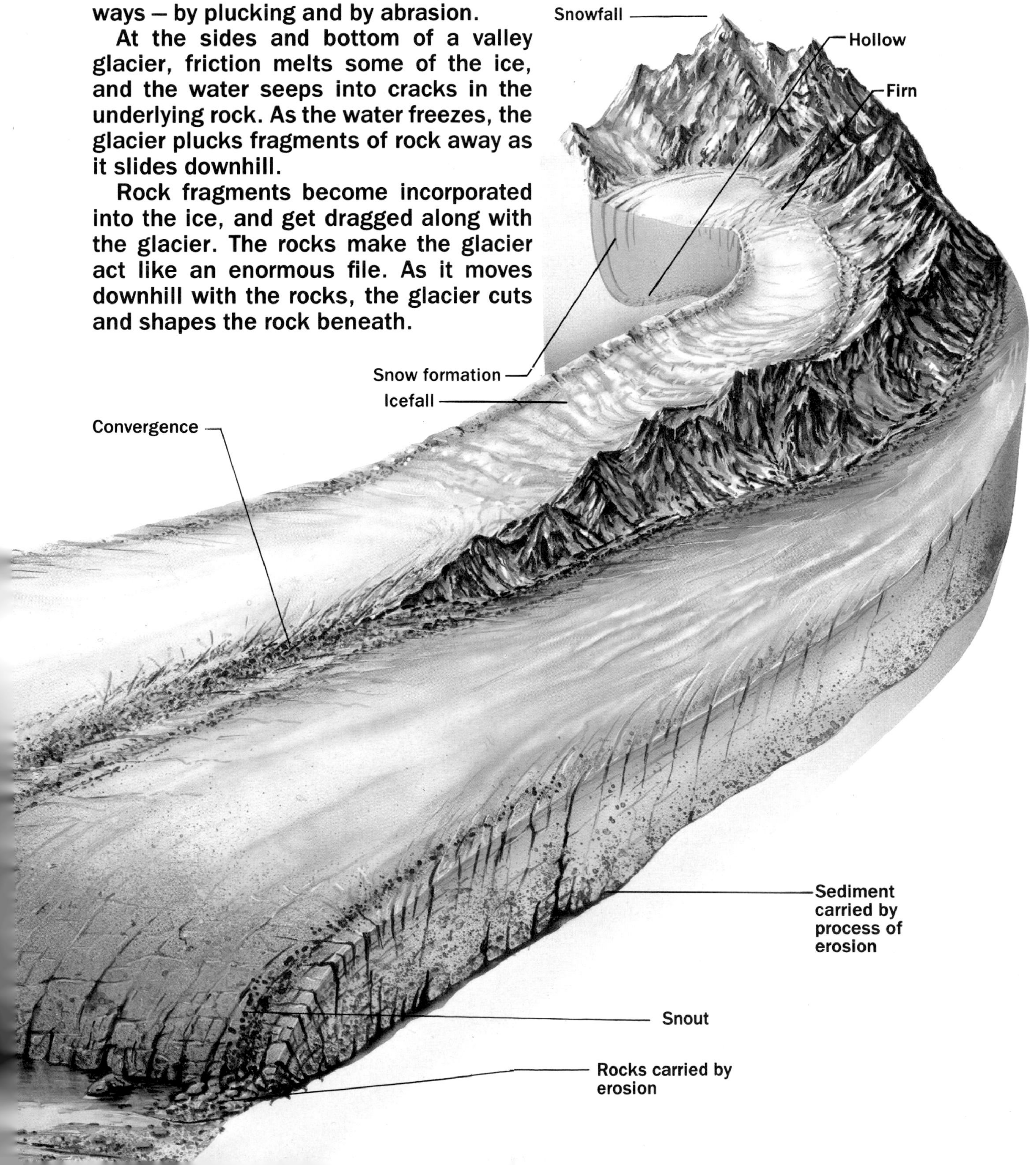

Snowfall
Hollow
Firn
Snow formation
Icefall
Convergence
Sediment carried by process of erosion
Snout
Rocks carried by erosion

During glaciation, ice conceals the action of a glacier on the land beneath. But after the glacier melts, the full effects of glaciation become apparent. The most distinctive feature of mountain glaciation is the "U-shaped" valley, which can be found in many hilly and mountainous regions of the world.

BEFORE

A river running down a valley normally cuts a V-shape with sloping sides. Viewed from above, the valley often has a zig-zag shape with the river flowing around rocks projecting from the mountain. When a glacier forms, the ice fills most of the valley and buries the rocks. The valley also appears much straighter.

At the lower end of the valley glacier, the snout (end) of the glacier tapers toward the ground as the ice begins to melt. Along each side of the glacier, a pile of rock fragments collect. These piles of rock fragments are known as a lateral moraine. When the glacier flows over bumps in the bedrock or around a bed, deep, V-shaped clefts may form. These clefts are known as crevasses. Crevasses can be up to 100 feet deep, big enough to swallow a house.

The U-shaped valley created by a glacier moving downhill in Wales.

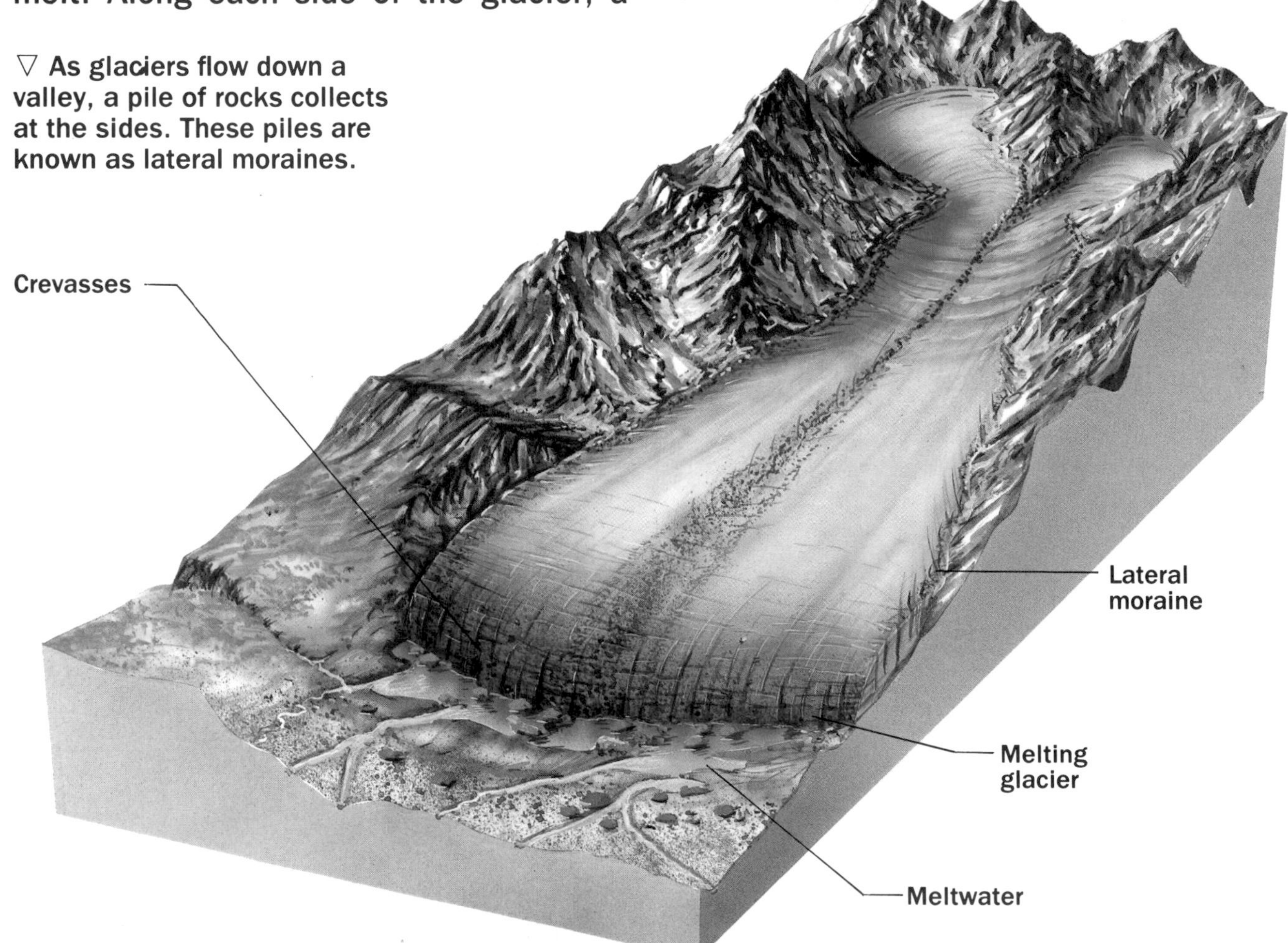

▽ As glaciers flow down a valley, a pile of rocks collects at the sides. These piles are known as lateral moraines.

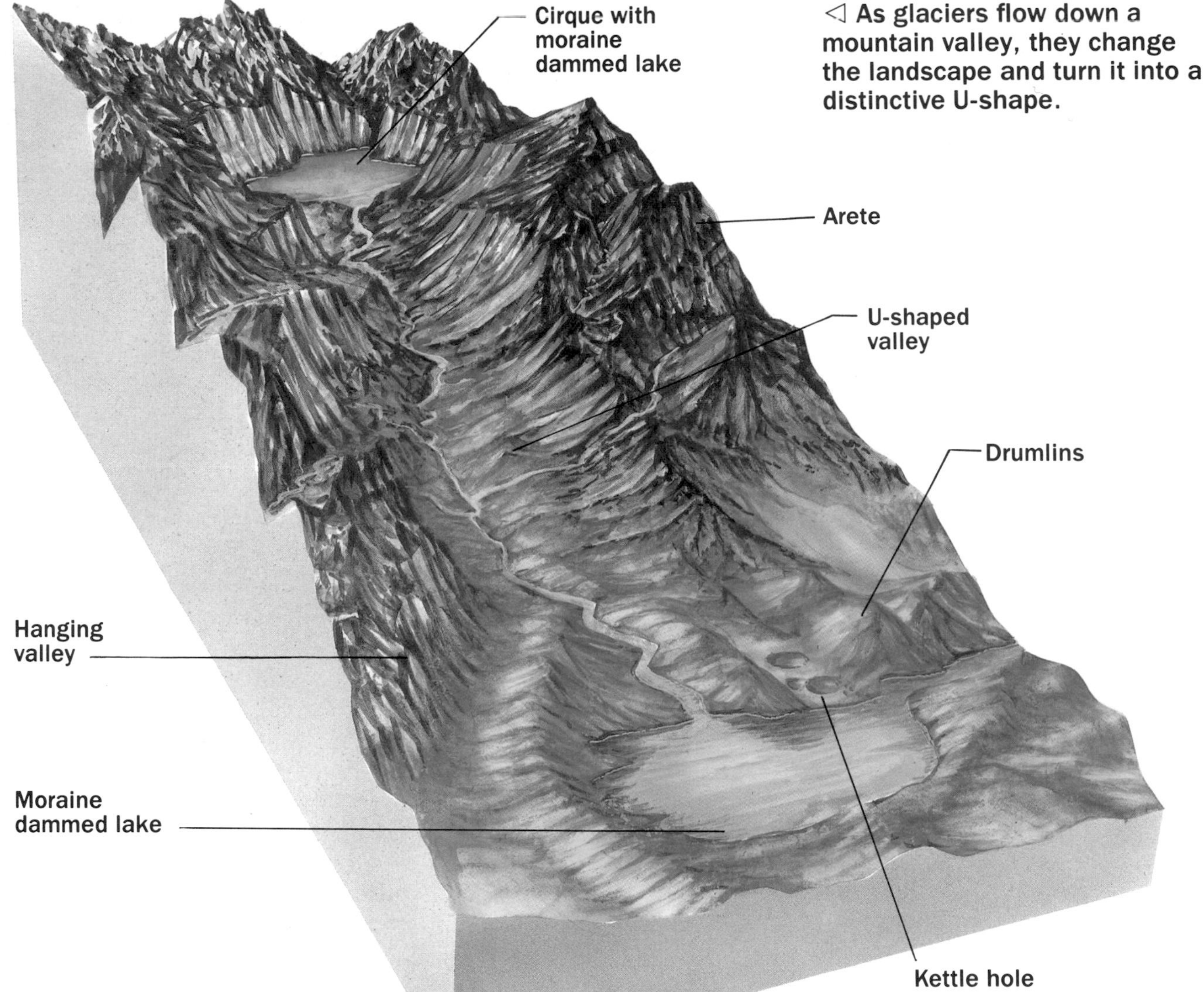

◁ As glaciers flow down a mountain valley, they change the landscape and turn it into a distinctive U-shape.

GLACIER PROJECT

Make a U-shaped valley in a sand tray. Firmly push an ice cube (glacier) down the valley. What shape is the valley now?

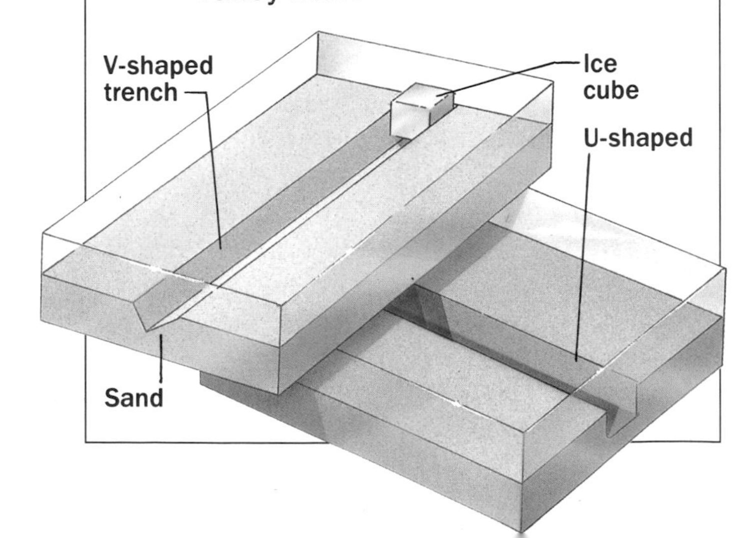

AFTER

As the glacier moves down the valley, it erodes the valley floor and cuts through the rocks. When the glacier melts, the valley looks much deeper and has much steeper sides. The glacier has created its distinctive U-shaped valley.

There are few features visible on the valley floor. The most dramatic signs are along the sides of the valley. The jutting rocks are all cut off and between them, tributary valleys enter the main one half-way up the sides. These hanging valleys are often marked by a waterfall. At the very end of the valley, a lake may have formed behind a terminal moraine, the pile of rocks and debris left behind by the glacier.

GLACIAL TRANSPORT

Apart from erosion, glaciers also alter the landscape through transport and deposition of rocks. Glaciers contain frozen water and thousands of tons of rock fragments plucked from the valley sides and floor. These fragments are transported by the ice, and are deposited when the glacier finally melts.

TRANSPORT

The rock fragments carried by a glacier vary in size from large boulders to tiny particles of sand. The smaller fragments are collectively known as glacial drift.

Although the fragments are spread throughout the glacier, they tend to be concentrated in the narrow bands of moraines. When two glaciers converge, their lateral moraines combine into a single moraine which runs down the center of the glacier. This is known as a medial moraine.

Dark rock fragments on the surface of a glacier are able to absorb more sunlight than the surrounding white ice. This makes the rocks warm up much faster, and the rate at which the ice melts increases.

Glacier and moraine in the Himalayas

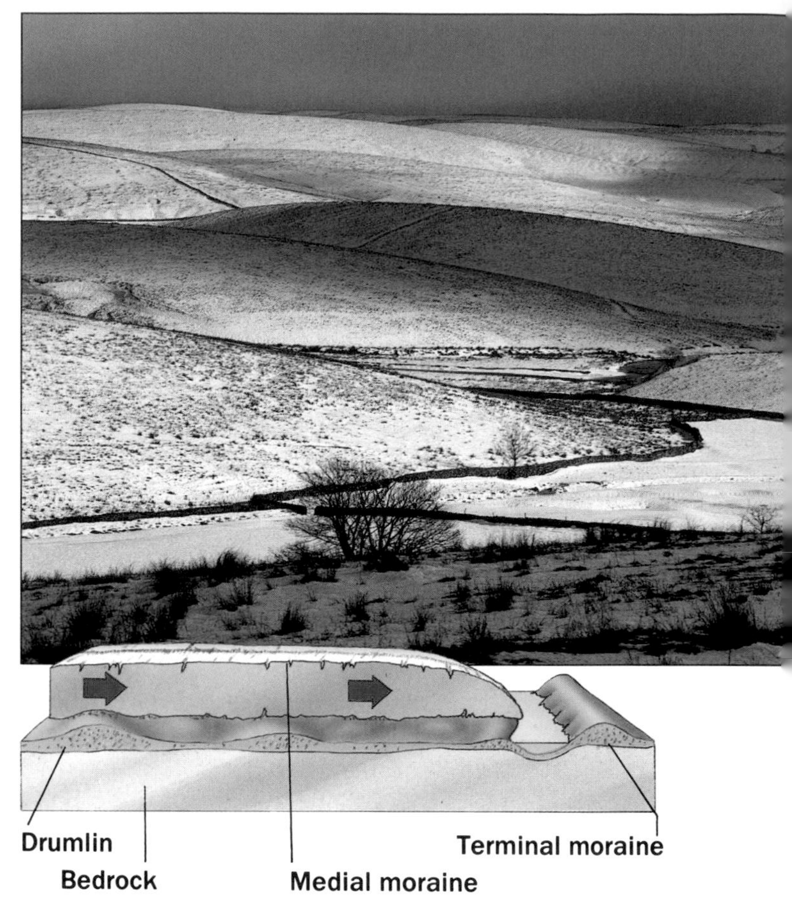

△ Glaciers create many different landforms. The drumlins in the picture are in a field in Britain.

LANDFORMS

The most distinctive feature of glacial deposition is the terminal moraine. If the glacier remains at a standstill over a long period, the moraine will build up into an impressive height. If the glacier melts in stages, a series of terminal moraines may occur across the whole valley.

Drumlins are clusters of low, egg-shaped hills that form behind the snout of a glacier. As a glacier slows down at the snout, it loses much of its power. Instead of smoothening out irregularities in the bedrock, the glacier deposits glacial till around these bumps, producing rounded hills. The shape of the hill indicates the direction of the ice flow, and the blunt end of the drumlin points toward the glacier's snout.

ERRATICS

An erratic is a pebble or boulder that is made of a completely different type of rock from those found nearby. Many erratics were carried to their present location during the last Ice Age. Instead of being turned into glacial drift, erratics were transported whole and frozen inside the ice. When the glaciers melted, the erratics were deposited many miles away from their original locations.

Erratics provide valuable clues to the movement of glaciers during the Ice Age. By finding the source rock (the original location) of the erratics, scientists can trace the path of the glacier on a map. For example, some erratics found in Poland have been traced back to Norway. Others have been traced to a different source in Finland. These results indicate that two huge glaciers must have moved into Poland before flowing down either side of the Baltic Sea.

▽ The map shows the location of some erratics. The picture above shows an erratic resting on a pavement near Black Head in Ireland.

MELTWATER

Beyond a glacier's snout, meltwater continues the process of transport and deposition. Streams and rivers fed by glaciers carry glacial drift far beyond the limits of the ice. Wind may then extend the effects of glaciation on the landscape. Glaciers are also indirectly responsible for sand dunes.

DEPOSITION

The most extensive surface feature created by meltwater is the outwash plain. As temperatures rise and fall during the summer and winter months, streams form within the glacier which sort and redistribute fluvioglacial deposits, creating an outwash plain. An outwash plain is a flat area in front of a glacier composed of rocks and fluvioglacial sediments. In lowland areas, the plains can be tens of miles wide.

The continuous flow of meltwater causes deposits in an outwash plain to become graded according to size. The smallest fragments are transported over the greatest distance. Close to the glacier snout the plain consists of gravel beds. Further away, the gravel in the outwash plain turns to coarse sand.

As the outwash plains dried up at the end of the last Ice Age, huge amounts of powdered rock were carried away by the wind. Deposits of this wind-blown material (called loess) are found in many parts of Europe and the United States.

▽ Glacial debris in Scotland

▷ Glacier meltwater creates many types of landforms, including streams, outwash plains, and steep hills which are known as kame terraces.

RIDGES AND MOUNDS

Around the snout of a glacier, the strong flow of meltwater creates a series of distinctive features. For example, meltwater running down the sides of a glacier deposits drift along the valley sides. This drift builds up into rounded terraces that are known as kame terraces.

Streams of meltwater running beneath a glacier form long, low ridges of sand and gravel known as eskers. If the rate of melting increases so does the rate of deposition, and the eskers grow in size. Several periods of melting create eskers that vary in height and width. Eskers also vary greatly in length, and may wind for hundreds of feet across the landscape. The sand and gravel from eskers, kames, and outwash plains are used in the construction industry in Europe and North America.

A glacial valley

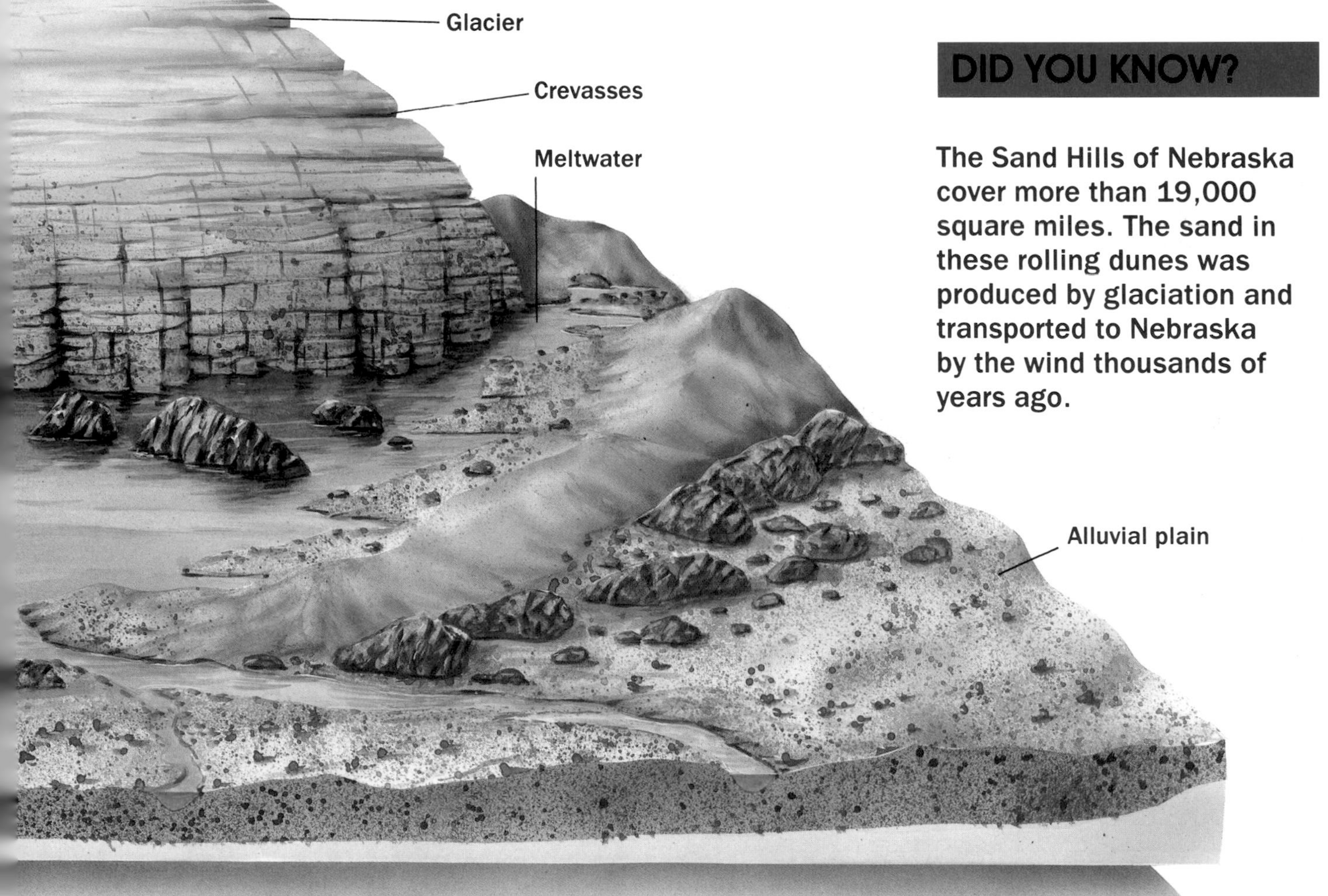

DID YOU KNOW?

The Sand Hills of Nebraska cover more than 19,000 square miles. The sand in these rolling dunes was produced by glaciation and transported to Nebraska by the wind thousands of years ago.

GLACIAL LAKES

When the glaciers melted after the last Ice Age, most of the water flowed back into the oceans. However, some of it remained behind in glacial lakes. There are thousands of such lakes scattered across areas that were once glaciated. The most famous of these are the Great Lakes.

Moraine in Wester Ross, Scotland

FORMATION

Many glacial lakes, including the Great Lakes, formed when meltwater flowed into the natural hollows and basins of the landscape. Other lakes formed on the floors of glaciated valleys, which were much deeper than before. Sometimes the lakes were held back by a moraine, which acted like a natural dam.

Along the coasts, water flowing back to the sea flooded glaciated valleys, creating deep fjords. Norway has many fjords along the coast, the longest of which is Sognefjord at 125 miles. Another kind of lake created by melting ice were the small kettle lakes. These form when bits of ice buried in glacial drift melt, filling up the resulting hollow.

▷ Fjords occur along the coasts. Fjords are often surrounded by cliffs that are over 655 feet high.

Valley

Fjord

Basin eroded by glacier

Aerial photograph of fjord in Norway

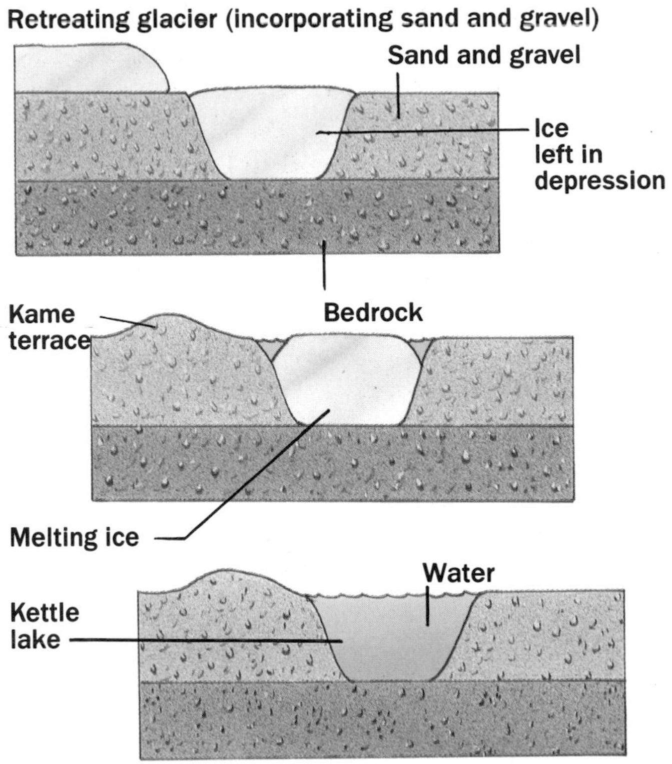

△ Kettle lakes form when buried ice melts in glacial deposits. They are often small and circular.

MORAINE LAKES

Moraine lakes reveal a great deal about the behavior of glaciers during the Ice Age. As glaciers melted, lakes often formed between the snout and terminal moraine, the pile of rock debris at the end of the glacier. As more of the ice melted, glacial drift often collected on the bottom of the lake, forming a shallow, cross-valley moraine.

If the rate of melting suddenly increased, the lake could overflow the terminal moraine or the valley sides. When this occurred, the meltwater cut an overflow channel that can still be seen on the landscape today.

Where the meltwater entered a lake from glacier-fed streams, drift was laid down in layers known as varves. Because the glaciers melt every year in spring, the varves occur in alternate layers of silt and sand. Each pair of layers represents one year's worth of melting. By studying varves in the ice, scientists are able to calculate how quickly a glacier melted.

MAKE A KETTLE LAKE

Place an ice block in a bowl and surround it with damp sand. Leave the bowl standing in a warm room for an hour. As the ice melts, water will be retained in the resulting hollow.

Ice
Sand
Bowl
Melted ice in hollow

Ice Ages are caused by long-term variations in the earth's climate. These variations probably occur as a result of changes in the earth's orbit around the sun. Dust clouds from volcanoes may also play some part, for they can block out the sun's rays. Scientists also feel that pollution affects the earth's climate.

TEMPERATURE CHANGE

The key factor affecting temperatures on the earth is the amount of sunlight reaching the planet. A small change in the tilt of the earth's axis would lead to a change in the amount of sunlight striking the earth. Variations in the average distance between the earth and sun would also have the same effect.

The earth's climate is also subject to short-term variations, and the average temperature is constantly rising or falling over time. During the Little Ice Age (see page 74), average temperatures fell by about 4°F, and the European glaciers began to advance over the countryside. Between 1880 and 1940 temperatures rose by about 2°F. The reason for these short-term variations in temperatures are still unclear, and scientists are not sure of present trends.

Ski resorts suffer from fluctuating temperatures.

▽ A flooded region in Bangladesh. Scientists feel glaciers might be be able to affect the world's temperatures.

SEA LEVEL

The earth's climate is delicately balanced. The amount of water on the planet remains constant, whether it is in the oceans, in glaciers, or in the atmosphere. When glaciers were at their greatest extent, sea levels were 330 feet lower than they are today. If the polar ice sheets were to melt away, sea levels would rise to some 230 feet above today's levels.

At present, sea levels are rising at about ¾ to 1 inch every ten years. Such a slow rate of increase presents little threat to human populations. However, if temperatures rose dramatically and the ice sheets began to melt, sea levels would increase much more rapidly. Millions of people who live along the coasts would be threatened by flooding. Many scientists think that pollution could cause temperatures, and sea levels, to rise in the future.

POLLUTION

The earth's atmosphere acts like a giant greenhouse, trapping the sun's heat near the planet's surface. High in the atmosphere, a layer of gases, mainly carbon dioxide, reflect heat back to the earth. These are known as greenhouse gases, and under natural conditions the level of these gases remains fairly constant.

However, over the last century, pollution from activities on Earth has increased the amount of greenhouse gases in the atmosphere. Burning hydrocarbon fuels, such as coal, oil, and gas, releases huge amounts of carbon dioxide. Other industrial gases, such as the CFCs used in refrigerators and aerosols, are extremely powerful greenhouse gases which also escape into the atmosphere. Another reason for the increase in carbon dioxide is the destruction of forests that usually turn this gas into oxygen. Scientists feel that this increase in greenhouse gases might lead to higher temperatures and global warming.

Millions of tons of pollution enter the atmosphere every year.

▽ Pollution from factories and power plants is increasing the amount of greenhouse gases in the atmosphere. Many scientists believe that the earth will get warmer as a result.

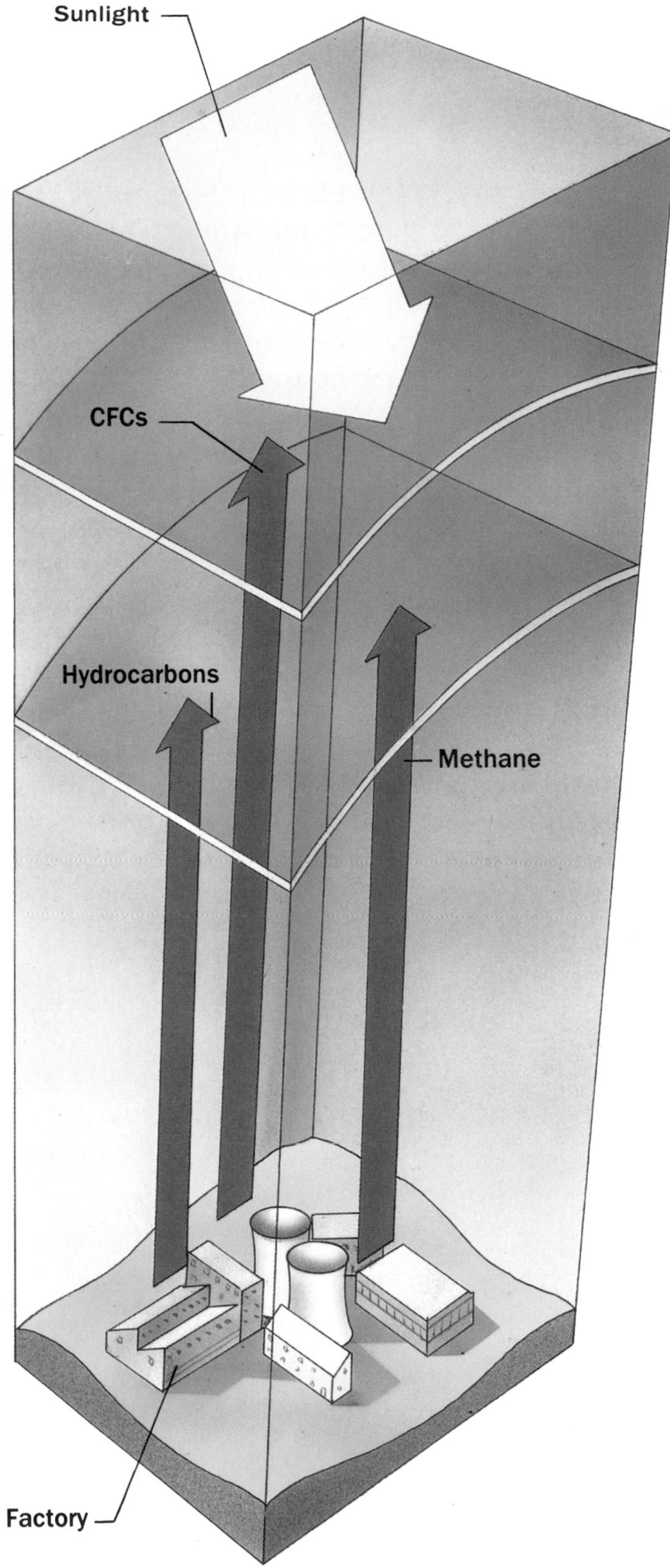

MEASURING THE ICE

Millions of years of snowfall have been compressed into the polar ice sheets. During its journey to the ground, each snowflake absorbs minute quantities of gas and dust from the atmosphere. By studying the ice sheets, scientists have made many discoveries about the earth's past climate and history.

DIFFERENT METHODS

During the first half of this century, the thickness of glacial ice was measured by echolocation. Explosions were set off, and the echoes from the underlying rocks were recorded. More recently, radar has been used to measure the thickness to within a few inches. Transmitted from airplanes or satellites, radar waves easily penetrate the ice and are reflected by the rock beneath. Using radar images, accurate maps of the Antarctic continent have been drawn.

Detailed information about the past can also be obtained by taking ice cores from the glacier depths. Scientists obtained these cores by drilling, and cores from depths of 5,000 feet have already been obtained. Such cores contain ice more than 120,000 years old.

Information about more recent years is obtained from ice nearer the surface. Ice from the base of a 100-foot crevasse would tell scientists about how the earth was 2,500 years ago. Occasionally, the ice cores or bases contain large objects. For example, in 1991, an icy region in the Alps between Austria and Italy had a 4,000-year-old human body inside it.

A scientist researching glaciers

▽ Descending a crevasse is very dangerous.

Most ice stations are located in remote polar areas, like this one in Antarctica.

▽ Ice cores provide evidence of climatic change. Minute animals alter the way their shells coil when the temperature changes.

THROUGH TIME

Snowflakes contain samples of the earth's atmosphere, and each year's snowfall is a time capsule of atmospheric conditions. When ice cores are taken to the laboratory, the first task is to separate the tightly compressed layers of ice. Each layer is then subjected to chemical analysis, releasing the various gases and solid material dissolved in it. These are then identified and quantified, before being compared with samples from different depths.

Among the first things scientists discovered was evidence of atmospheric pollution. Cores from Greenland reveal that levels of lead began to increase steadily around 1800 with the advent of industrialization. Lead levels shot up after the introduction of leaded gasoline.

Particles from volcanic eruptions can also be detected in the ice. The Greenland ice cores have been used to determine the exact date that Thera, a volcano on the Mediterranean island of Santorini, erupted. Evidence shows that Thera erupted around 1627B.C., about 100 years earlier than everyone thought.

ANTARCTICA PROTECTED FOR SCIENCE

Antarctica is a unique place – a vast and virtually untouched wilderness of ice and snow. So far, the Antarctic wilderness has been preserved through scientific cooperation between countries. However, increasing world demand for raw materials means that the future of Antarctica is by no means certain.

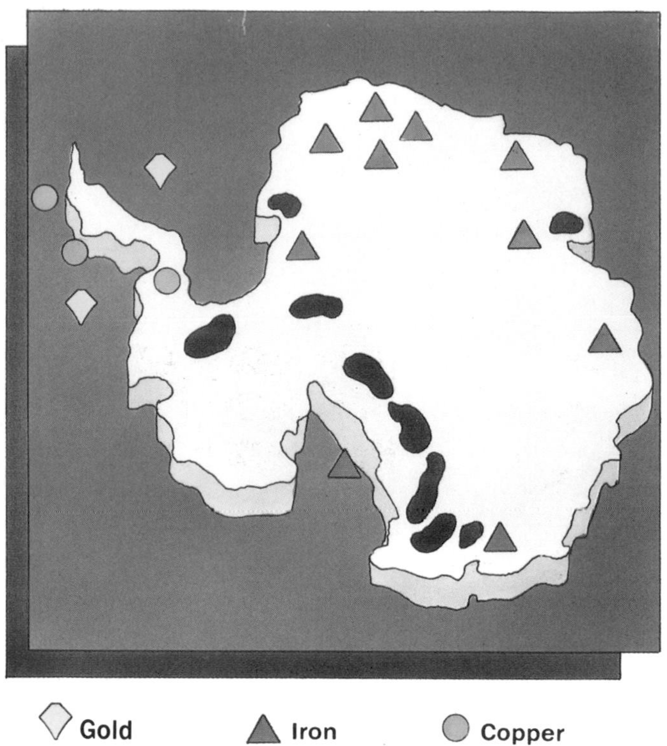

Frozen seal in Captain Scott's hut in Antarctica

No country owns Antarctica, although several of them have laid claim to parts of it over the years. Nor is Antarctica an independent state. At present, the region is administered by an international treaty which prohibits most forms of development and mining.

International cooperation in Antarctica began with scientific expeditions in the late 1950s. At that time (during the Cold War between the United States and the Soviet Union), there was considerable fear that Antarctica might be used for military purposes. The Antarctic Treaty came into force in 1961 to ensure that it was used for peaceful purposes.

Recently, fears about pollution have brought Antarctica into the headlines again. The reason for this is that once pollution reaches Antarctica, it is likely to stay there forever. The Antarctic climate will not disperse pollution, but will preserve it. The pollution also threatens the highly productive ecology around the Southern Ocean.

Beneath the ice and snow in Antarctica, valuable deposits of gold, iron ore, and other metals have been discovered. As a result, some countries are now reluctant to ban mining and other forms of mineral extraction from Antarctica.

The possibility of large-scale mining operations in Antarctica has alarmed many of the world's environmentalists. They argue that Antarctica should be declared an "earth park", free from any from of development or mining.

A British scientist measuring snow density in Antarctica.

SEAS AND OCEANS

CHAPTER 5

CHAPTER FIVE: SEAS AND OCEANS

POLLUTING THE SEA

INTRODUCTION

Seas and oceans cover nearly three-quarters of the earth's surface. Their waters are in constant motion because of powerful currents. They are also home to thousands of different creatures, from shrimps and jellyfish to sharks and whales. The bottoms of the oceans are contoured by tall mountains and deep trenches. The seabed is constantly changing as molten rock from beneath the earth's crust forces its way upward, and old rocks sink into the mantle. Volcanoes situated underwater also erupt, and help to build new chains of islands.

People have been interested in the seas and oceans for centuries. The early explorations used weighted rocks to measure the ocean depth, while modern vessels can plunge all the way to the seafloor and examine the landscape.

This chapter describes the origin, composition, and inhabitants of the oceans. It shows how the oceans can provide us with a rich source of food and energy. The chapter also explains how pollution and other activities of humans may be putting these natural resources at risk.

▽ Waves crashing into a huge rock in northern California's Pacific Ocean

Most of the earth's surface is covered by the seas and oceans. This vast area of water – about 139 million square miles – surrounds the continents. When it is viewed from space, earth appears as a blue planet with the continents appearing as occasional islands of brown land.

FORMATION

The earth has not always been covered with water, and neither have the oceans always had their present shape. When the earth first formed, it was a fiery ball of hot rock dotted with thousands of active volcanoes. As the volcanoes erupted, they emitted gases, mainly water vapor and carbon dioxide, into the atmosphere. In time, the atmosphere became saturated with vapor and as the earth cooled, it condensed and fell as rain. The volcanoes produced more and more steam, and so the cycle continued. Over millions of years, the rainwater accumulated on the surface, forming the seas and oceans of today.

During this early period, much of the land was joined together like a huge island. Then the continents separated and drifted to their present positions.

▽ Oceans on earth began as steam from volcanoes, which condensed into rain clouds in the atmosphere. This rain gradually collected to form the world's oceans.

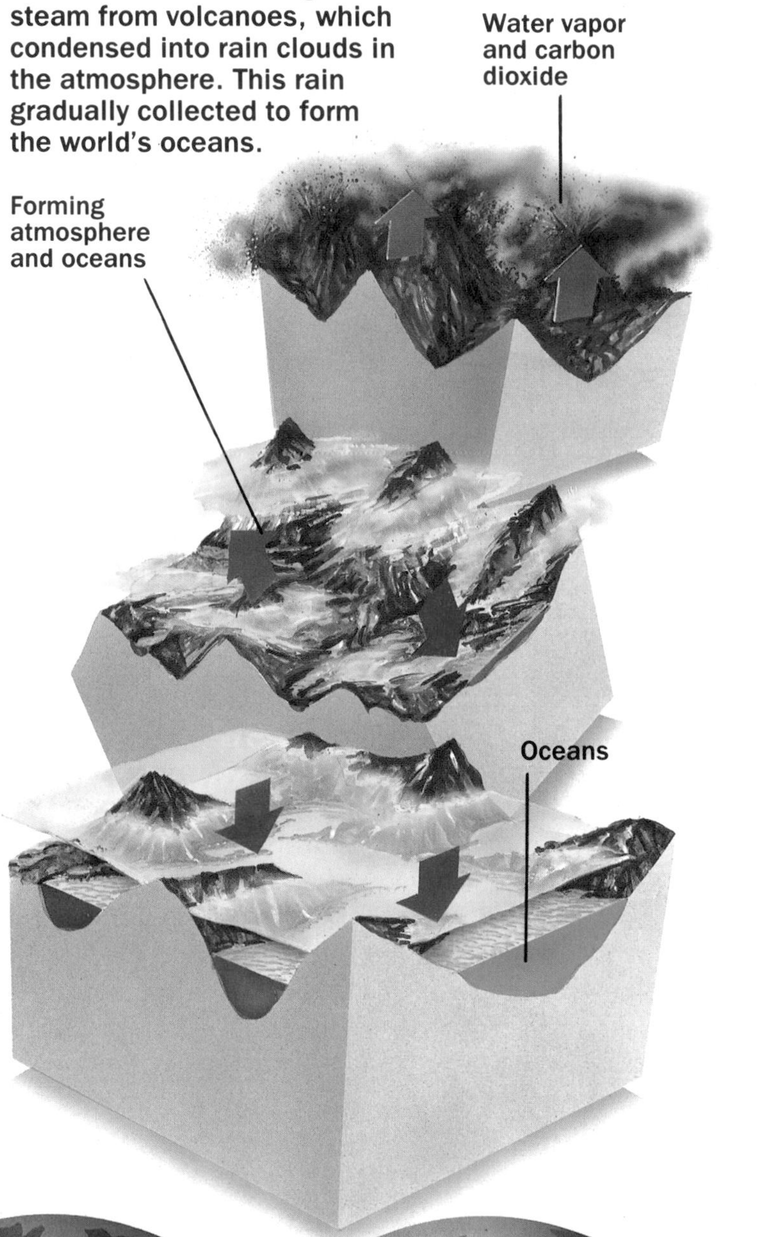

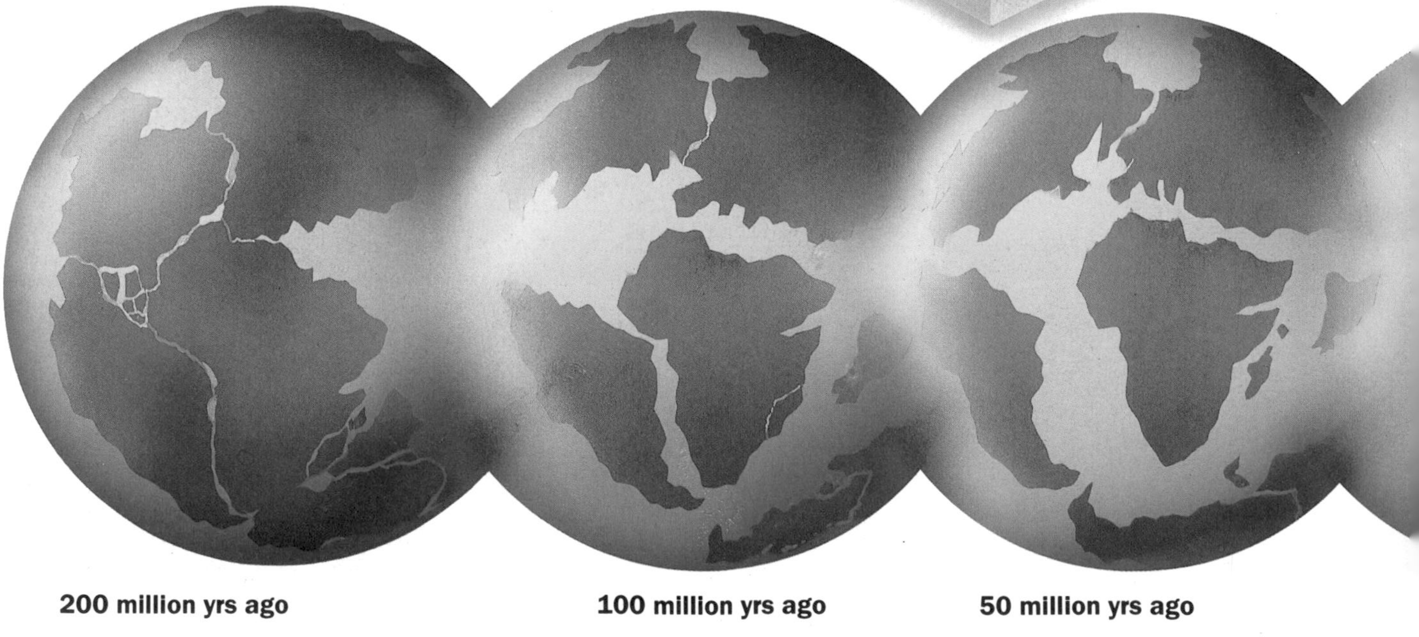

SEAWATER

The oceans still get much of their water from rain. But the water does not just stay in the oceans, it is recycled. The sun heats up the oceans and makes the water evaporate into the atmosphere as water vapor. As the vapor cools, it forms clouds which eventually release rain back to the earth. The rain flows along rivers back into the sea.

The seawater also helps to regulate temperatures on land. The sea does not lose the sun's heat as fast as the land does. So during the cold winter months, breezes from the sea carry warm air to the land.

River water also washes various minerals into the sea. The most important one is salt (sodium chloride), which makes up an average of 3.5 percent by weight of seawater. Other minerals in seawater include sulfates, magnesium, potassium and calcium; there are even small traces of gold in the sea. Seawater also contains dissolved oxygen, which is essential for the life of fish and other marine animals and plants.

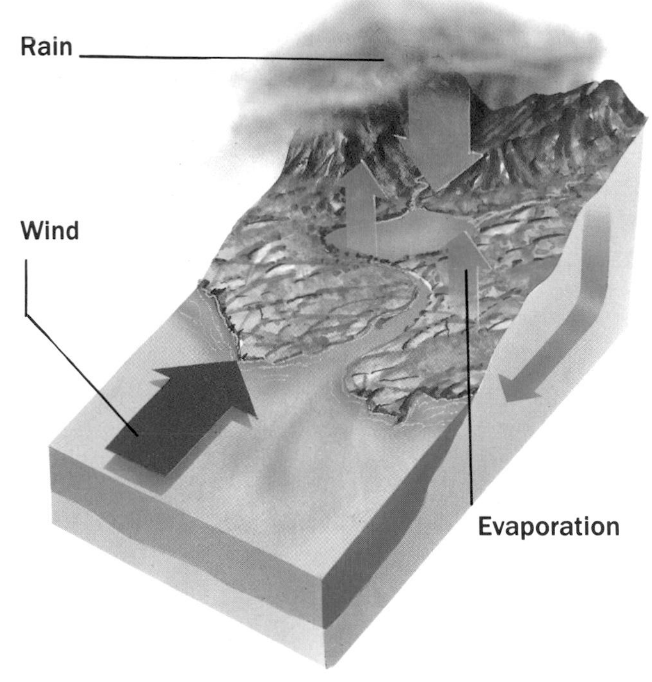

△ The water cycle circulates water on earth. Water evaporates from the oceans and forms clouds, which produce rain over the land.

▽ Water makes up 96.5 percent of the sea. The rest consists of dissolved minerals, the most important being common salt.

▽ The world's oceans changed in size and shape as the continents slowly drifted apart. The Atlantic Ocean gets 1 inch wider every year.

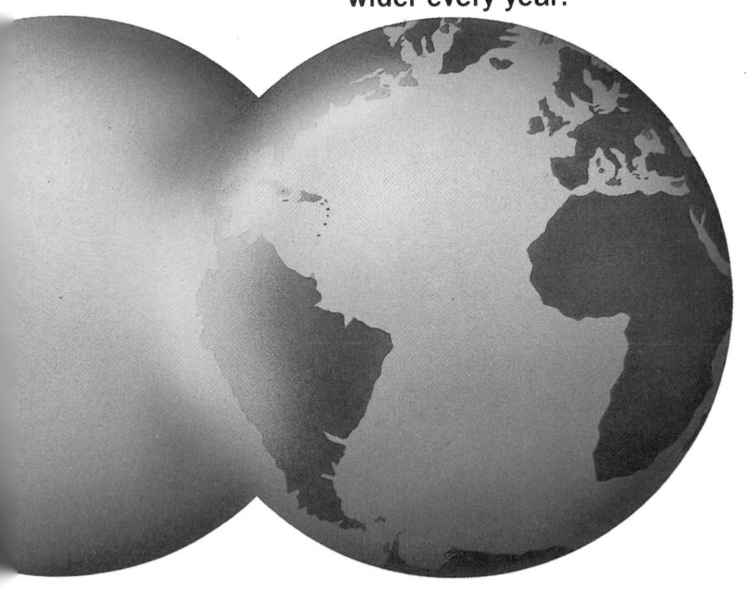

Present day

A satellite image of the Pacific Ocean

The oceans cover over 70 percent of the earth's surface, and have an average depth of 12,000 feet. Their waters therefore provide the largest available space for living things. All marine plant life, and most animals, live in fairly shallow waters near the surface. But even the ocean depths have some life.

Coelacanth: a fish that dates back 300 million years.

EVOLUTION

Life on earth began in the ocean fringes. The sea consisted of a "soup" of biochemicals which combined on rocks at the shore to form the first living cells. The first single-celled animals lived in the sea. These gradually evolved into multi-celled creatures without backbones, resembling the shellfish, worms, and corals that live in the sea today.

Meanwhile, the green plants that had evolved on land helped to add oxygen to the earth's atmosphere. The oxygen that dissolved in seawater became available to marine animals. The first animals to evolve with backbones were fishlike creatures called placoderms, whose bodies were covered in bony plates. These were also the ancestors of amphibians, the first backboned animals to move onto dry land. Fish continued to evolve in the sea, eventually giving rise to sharklike predators with skeletons made of cartilage, and modern bony fish.

(1) Jellyfish (2) Mollusk
(3) Trilobite (4) Placoderm
(5) Rachitomes (6) First shark
(7) Birkenia (8) Modern shark
(9) Holostean (10) Modern fish

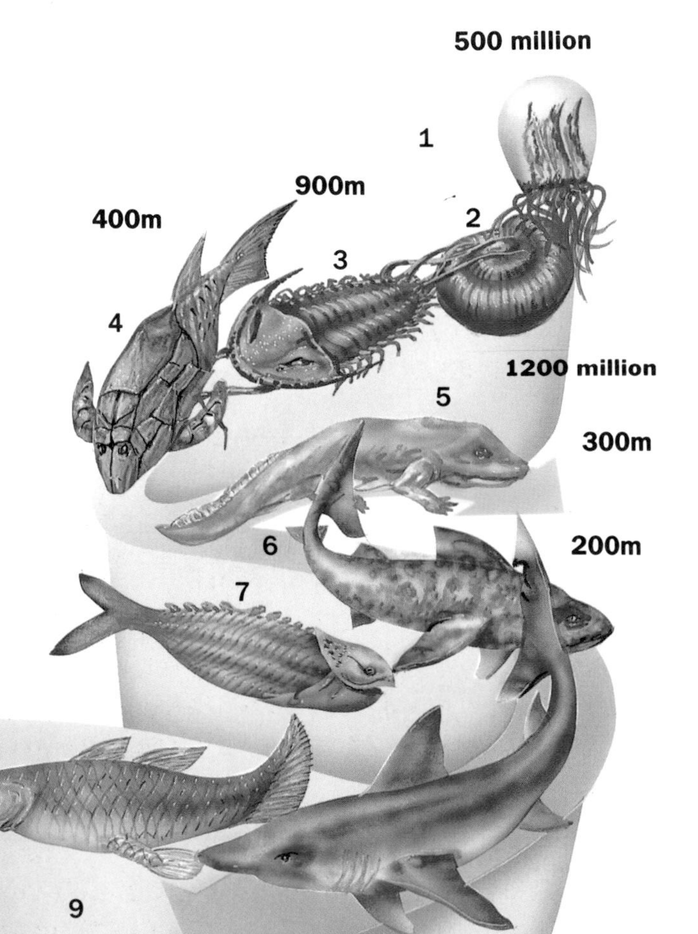

▽ The fish living in the oceans evolved over millions of years, from simple jellyfish to the more complex bony fish of today.

LIVING IN WATER

Fish come in all shapes and sizes, from the small coral fish and sardines to the long, snakelike eels and huge basking sharks. And they have evolved various unique features to suit their life in the water. Fish have fins which they use to swim, and most have internal swim bladders that enable them to float in the water without sinking or rising to the surface. Cartilaginous fish such as the shark (right), have no swim bladders and sink if they stop swimming. All fish have gills which they use to extract oxygen dissolved in the sea. This allows them to "breathe" under the water.

Fast-swimming fish have streamlined bodies that move easily through the water. For example, a 6-ft long barracuda can swim at a speed of 40 feet a second (27 mph) and turn in its own body length.

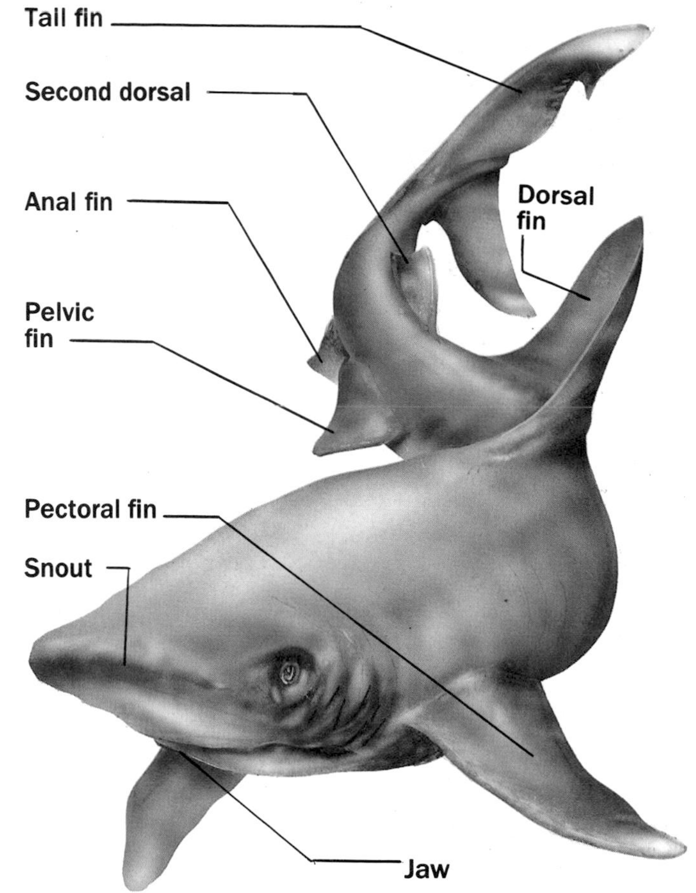

▽ Bony fish keep afloat by means of a swim bladder or air bladder. It is an elongated sac which contains air and lies above the digestive tract. The fish controls buoyancy by varying the amount and pressure of the air.

MAKE A SWIM BLADDER

You can see how a fish's swim bladder works by making a model from a small bottle with a tight-fitting top. Fill a large bowl with water, half-fill the bottle as well and screw on the top. Put the bottle in the bowl and see how it floats on the surface. Now gradually add more water to the bottle, screwing on the top and making it float each time. Eventually you will add the right amount of water for the bottle to just break the surface.

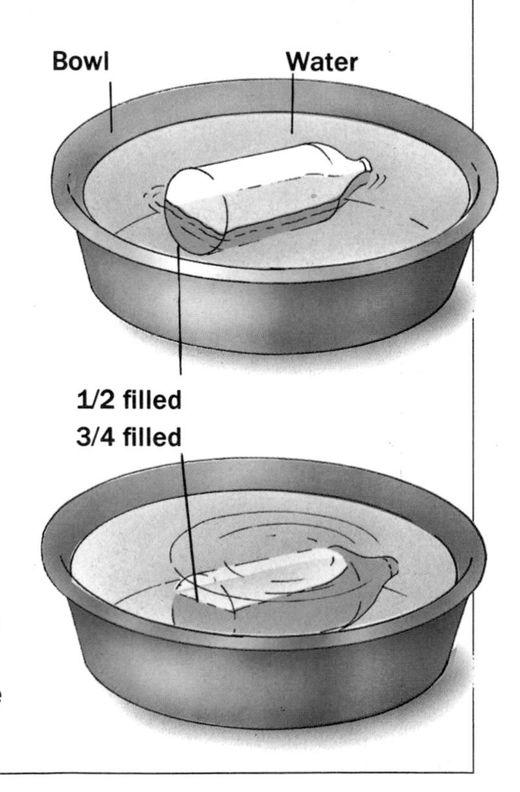

Each type of life form in the sea is found at a particular depth, from the shallow areas a few feet deep to the abyssal plain more than 13,000 feet deep. The amount of sunlight and the saltiness of the water also determine the kinds of plants and animals that are found at each ocean level.

THE CONTINENTAL SHELF

The continental shelf is the shallowest part of the sea. It starts at the edge of the continents and gently slopes downward. The shelf is seldom more than 500 feet deep, and is also known as the euphotic zone. Because sunlight reaches the bottom of the shelf, seaweed grows in this layer. The tiny animals near the surface, which are called zooplankton, consist of krill and other small shrimplike crustaceans, as well as the eggs and young of various fish.

Apart from eating microscopic plants called phytoplankton, krill are a source of food for a range of marine creatures, from surface-feeding fish to baleen whales. Jellyfish also live near the surface, drifting with the currents and using the stinging cells in their tentacles to trap and kill small fish for food.

▽ The sea depth changes as you move away from land. Nearest the shore the sea is quite shallow. It tends to be deeper further out.

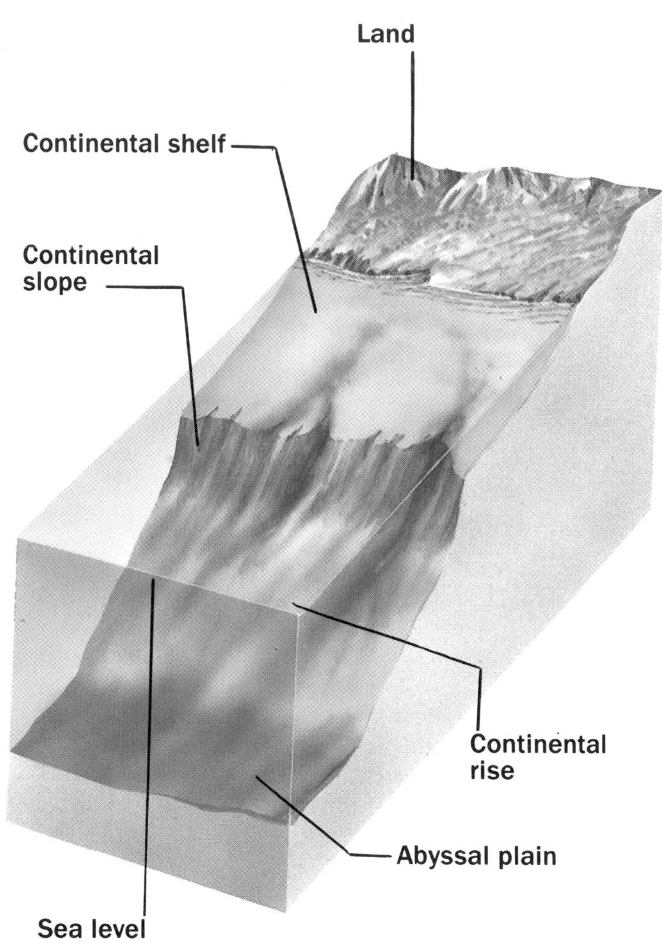

Continental shelves extend around the edges of continents.

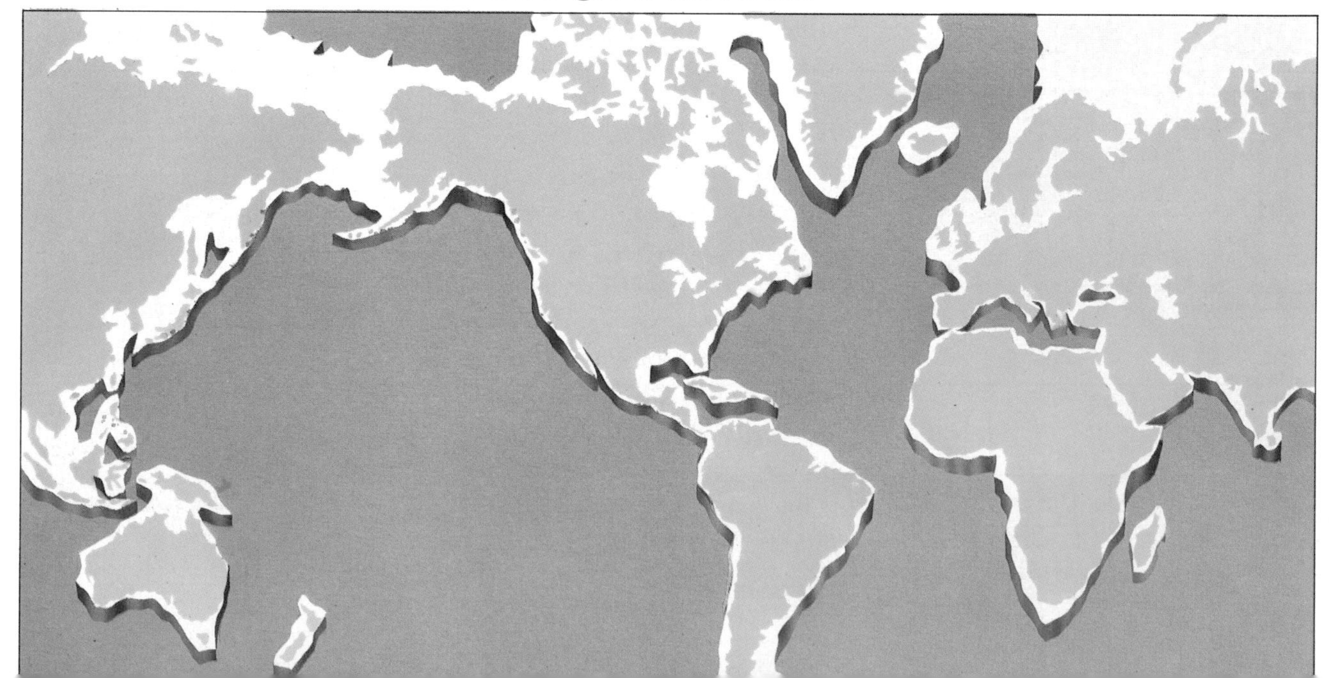

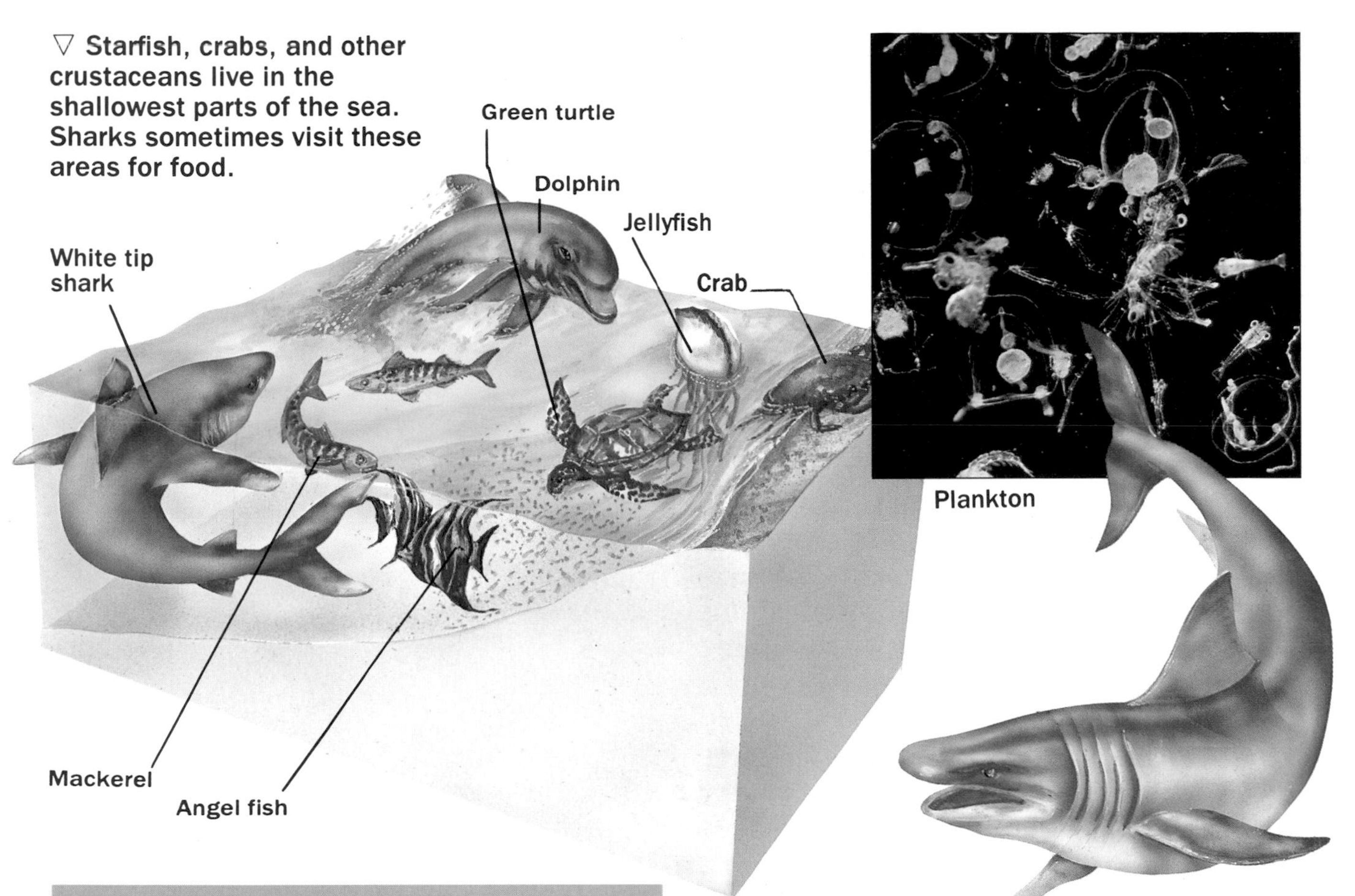

▽ Starfish, crabs, and other crustaceans live in the shallowest parts of the sea. Sharks sometimes visit these areas for food.

Plankton

△ Although usually inhabitants of deeper water, white sharks (above) swim into shallower water to feed. The large whale shark, however, feeds only on plankton.

LIFE IN THE SHALLOWS

Most fish live in the shallow parts of the oceans, and end up feeding on each other. Small fish swim in shoals for protection, while predators such as barracuda and sharks swoop in to catch their prey. Other fish, such as conger eels, wait in rock crevices for their prey to swim within range. Flatfish scavenge on the bottom, quickly burying themselves in the sand or even changing color when danger threatens.

Most of the predatory fish are active during the day. So at night, when it is less dangerous, other fish leave the deeper layers and swim upward to feed in the shallows. Some of the plankton which live near the surface give off light, and so it is never completely dark, even at night. This light helps the night feeders to find food more easily.

Some inland lakes, such as the Caspian Sea and the Dead Sea, are so salty that they resemble shallow seas.

Salt crystals in the Dead Sea area

The layer of ocean water lying beyond the shallow surface is called the mesopelagic zone. It has a depth of about 6,000 feet. The bathypelagic is the next layer and it reaches all the way to the bottom, or ocean plain, with a depth of about 13,200 feet. No light penetrates either of these layers.

THE OCEAN PLAIN

The ocean plain is not a wide, flat area, but consists of tall mountain ranges, canyons, and gorges. Mountains over 10,000 feet tall are common. Some of them were formed by mountain-building processes and erosion on land before becoming submerged under the sea. Others have been carved out by underwater currents. Sloping canyons are carved from turbid currents – resembling underwater avalanches – which sweep mud and sand further out to sea. Rivers wash silt and other sediment out to sea, and this settles at the bottom of oceans.

The continents and ocean basins "ride" on huge slabs of the earth's crust, called plates. Where the edge of one ocean plate slips under another plate, a deep trench forms. Some of the trenches drop down for more than six miles. The Challenger Deep in the Pacific Ocean's Marianas Trench, for example, is over 36,000 feet deep.

A computer-generated map of the ocean depths

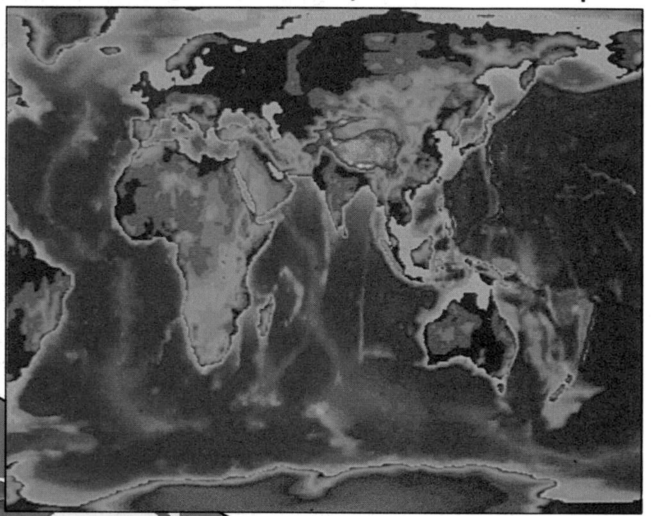

Trenches

△ Ocean trenches form at the edge of the earth's crustal plates, when one plate pushes under a neighboring one. Many trenches run roughly parallel to continental coasts.

GOING DOWN

Many factors change with increasing depth in the oceans. Sunlight is only able to penetrate to a depth of about 300 feet, and this area is known as the photic zone. By a depth of about 3,000 feet, there is a twilight zone where visibility is reduced to a few yards. No light reaches the bathypelagic zone.

The temperature of the oceans falls with increasing depth. Near the surface, temperature depends mainly on the climate, and it is hotter in the tropics than at the Poles. Evaporation and the inflow of river water also affect the surface temperatures. By a depth of about 6,500 feet however, the temperature falls to about 37°F and remains more or less constant. This is because there are few deep currents at this level to mix the water.

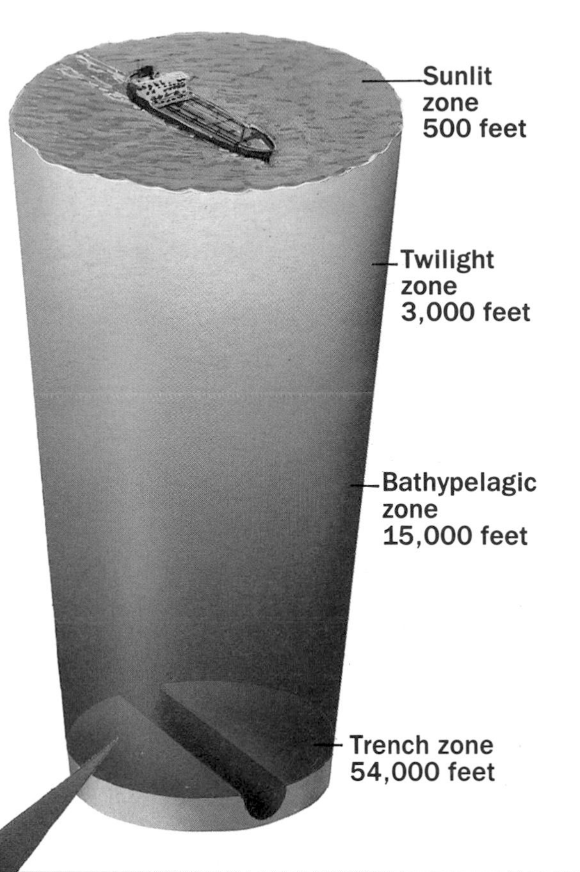

▽ The ocean is divided into four main zones. Anglers (1), Hatchets (2), Vipers (3), and Photostomias (4), all live in the deep trench zone.

DEEP-SEA LIFE

Fish that live in deep water feed mainly on the remains of dead surface animals that sink to the bottom. Some strange fish inhabit the inky blackness of the deepest oceans. Many of them have large mouths which they always keep open as they swim around, looking for prey. Others have luminous spots of light which enable them recognize each other and their neighbors. The various angler fish have a luminous blob at the end of a projection from their heads, which acts as a lure to tempt prey within reach.

A deep-sea fish underwater

The seafloor has a varied landscape, and some of the mountains that originate in the sea are tall enough to reach the surface, forming islands. Other islands are formed by the eruption of underwater volcanoes, or from the activity of corals. For example, Hawaii (right) is a chain of volcanic islands in the Pacific Ocean.

▽ Where one crustal plate rides over another, the lower one descends back into the mantle at a subduction zone. Molten rock rising up between two ocean plates creates a mid-ocean ridge.

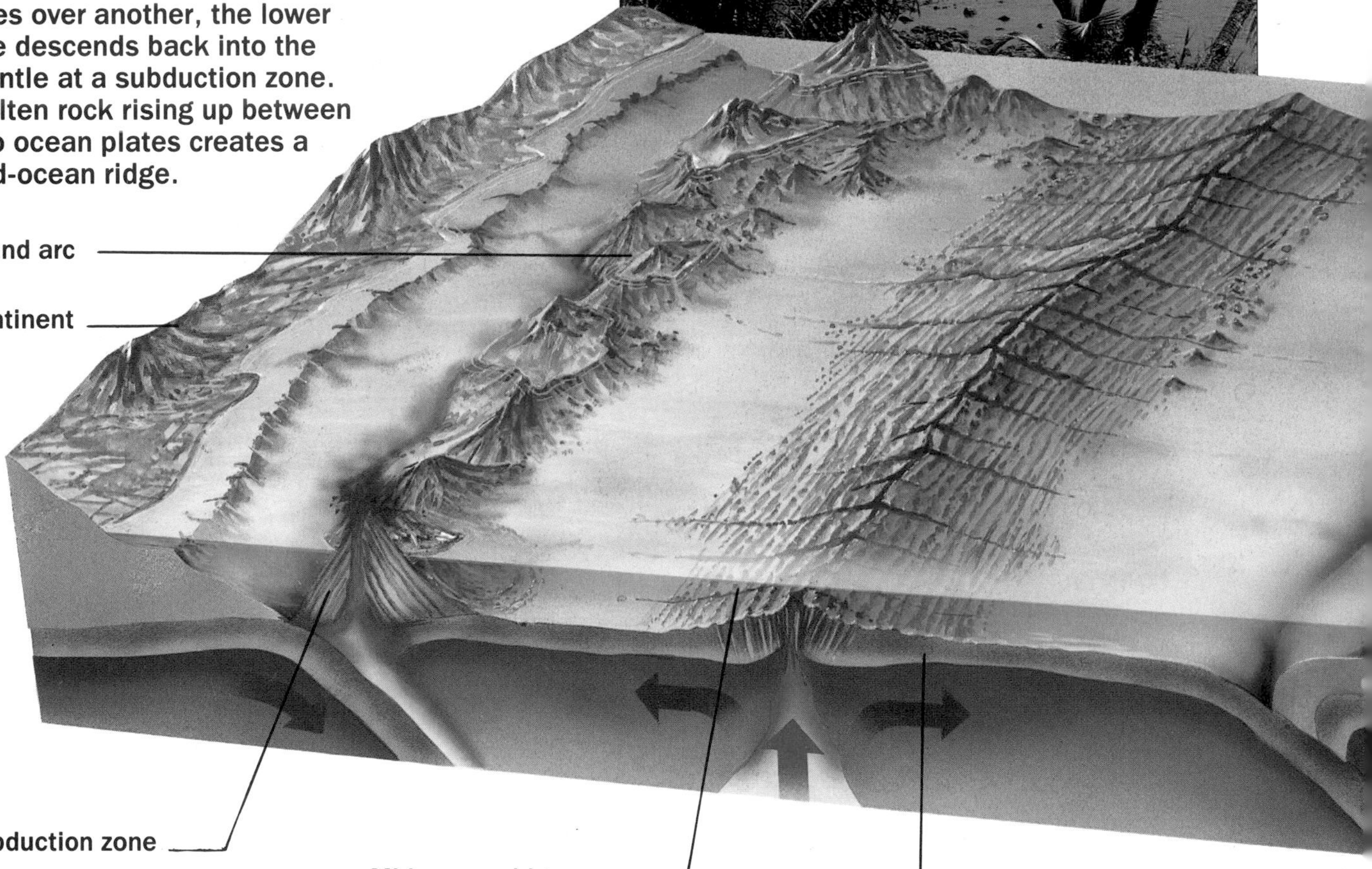

MID-OCEAN RIDGES

Down the center of the major oceans, the crustal plates are gradually moving apart. This happens because molten rock from the earth's mantle constantly wells up between them. As this hot lava cools, it forms a pair of parallel ridges. These are known as mid-ocean ridges. The whole process is called seafloor spreading, and it causes the plates of the oceans and continents to gradually move apart. The rocks in the ridges are the youngest in the earth's crust. The Mid-Atlantic Ridge, for example, runs southward from Iceland along the center of the Atlantic Ocean, until it curves eastward to join the Indian Ocean Ridge.

In some places, volcanoes rise up to 3,000 feet from the seabed to form tall, underwater mountains. In shallower parts of the ocean, the volcanoes may even be tall enough to break the surface as islands. Waves may wear away the top of a volcanic island, and such submerged islands are called flat-topped guyots, or seamounts.

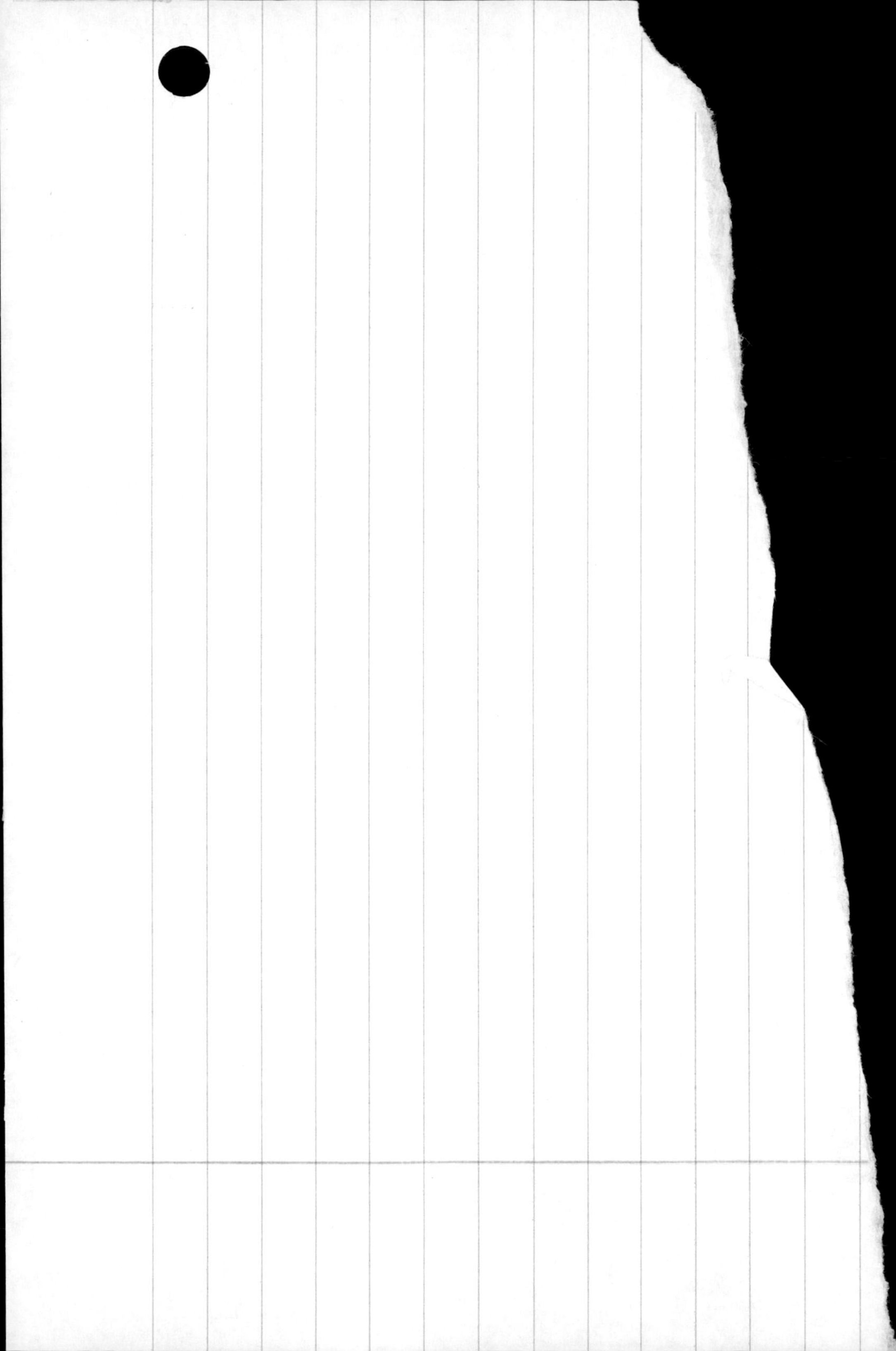

REEF FORMATION

Corals are small animals related to jellyfish and sea anemones. They extract a chalky substance, calcium carbonate, from seawater and use it to build their skeletons. When the corals die, their skeletons remain as gnarled rocky growths. Corals live only in well-lit, warm tropical waters no deeper than 180 feet. Near a shore, corals build up to form a fringing reef; further out they form a barrier reef.

Sometimes corals form a fringing reef around a volcanic island. As the volcanic peak is eroded and the sea level rises, the coral continues to grow toward the shallows. Finally the island sinks, leaving a ring of coral known as an atoll. This explains why such islands have deep, clifflike sides of coral when viewed from underwater.

The Great Barrier Reef of Australia

DID YOU KNOW?

A coral reef is a self-contained habitat for many organisms. The Great Barrier Reef in Australia, for example, is home to over 3,000 different species. In addition to fish, there are crabs, jellyfish, sea anemones, sea cucumbers (which are animals), and starfish. Even the corals themselves are animals.

MAKE AN UNDERWATER VOLCANO

You can mimic the effect of an underwater volcano. Pour cold water into a bucket until it is nearly full. Then fill a small plastic bottle with hot water, adding a few drops of colored dye. Screw the cap on the bottle and place it at the bottom of the bucket. Now unscrew the cap and watch as the less dense hot water rises to the surface.

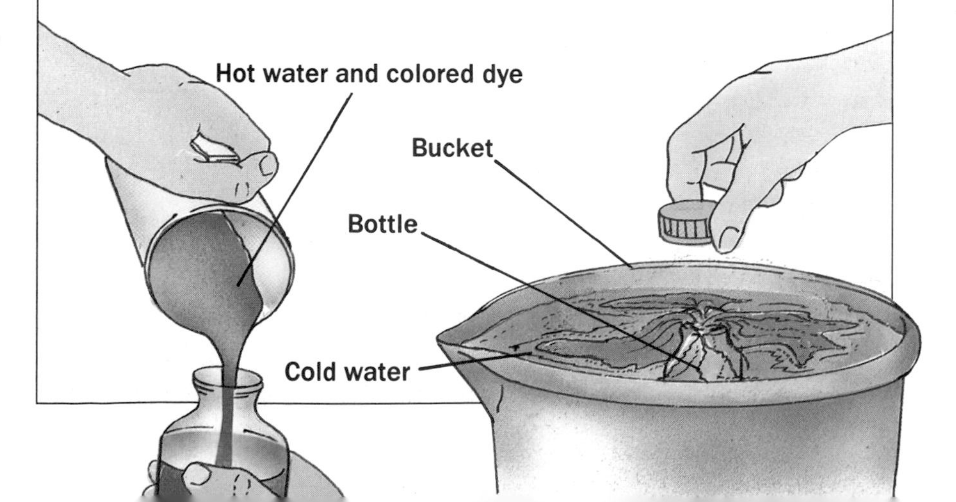

The water in the oceans is constantly on the move. At the surface, wind whips the sea up into waves that move over great distances. The gravitational pull of the moon and sun also causes tides to rise and fall each day. In addition to all these movements, underwater currents shift masses of water around the world.

WAVE MOVEMENT

Waves are caused by an up-and-down movement of water – only when waves break on the shore do they make water move along. The waves are merely large versions of the ripples you see on ponds. You can demonstrate their movement by making a cork float in a pond and dropping a stone into the water near it. As the ripples pass the cork, they make it bob up and down in the same place.

In the open sea, wind starts wave movement. Particles of water circulate immediately under the waves, and at the surface this movement may cause a wave to break, or turn over. Waves can travel over great distances and the distance between wave peaks is known as the wavelength.

Waves that reach the shore change the landscape. They form beaches, erode cliffs and gradually alter shorelines. Waves also carry beach sand away with them into the oceans.

△ Cliffs, such as these at Marsden Bay in England, are eroded by the action of waves.

Shore

Wind direction

Wave movement

Water particles

△ Wind causes waves to travel through the sea. The main movement of water is up and down, with water particles rotating in circles. Only at the shore does water move along.

TIDES

The gravitational attraction of the moon pulls the waters of the ocean into a bulge, or high tide, when the moon is directly overhead. Because the earth rotates on its axis, centrifugal forces acting on the water cause a similar bulge on the opposite side. The sun's gravity also affects the oceans and the combined effect of all these forces causes the bulge of water to move around the earth, making the sea level rise and fall as tides.

A different effect called a tidal wave is caused by underwater earthquakes. Tidal waves have very long wavelengths and travel at hundreds of miles per hour. As they approach the shore, their height increases to several feet.

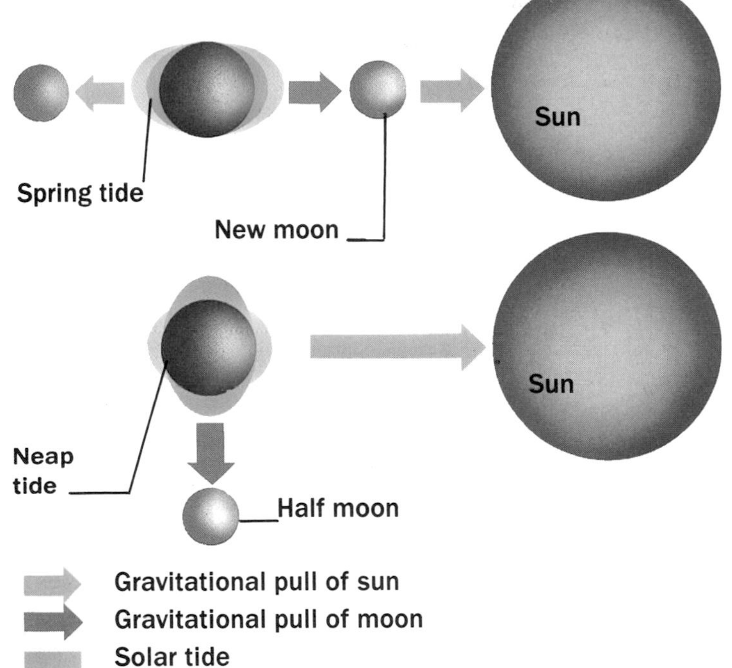

△ Spring tides occur when the moon, sun, and earth are in a straight line and neap tides when they are at right angles.

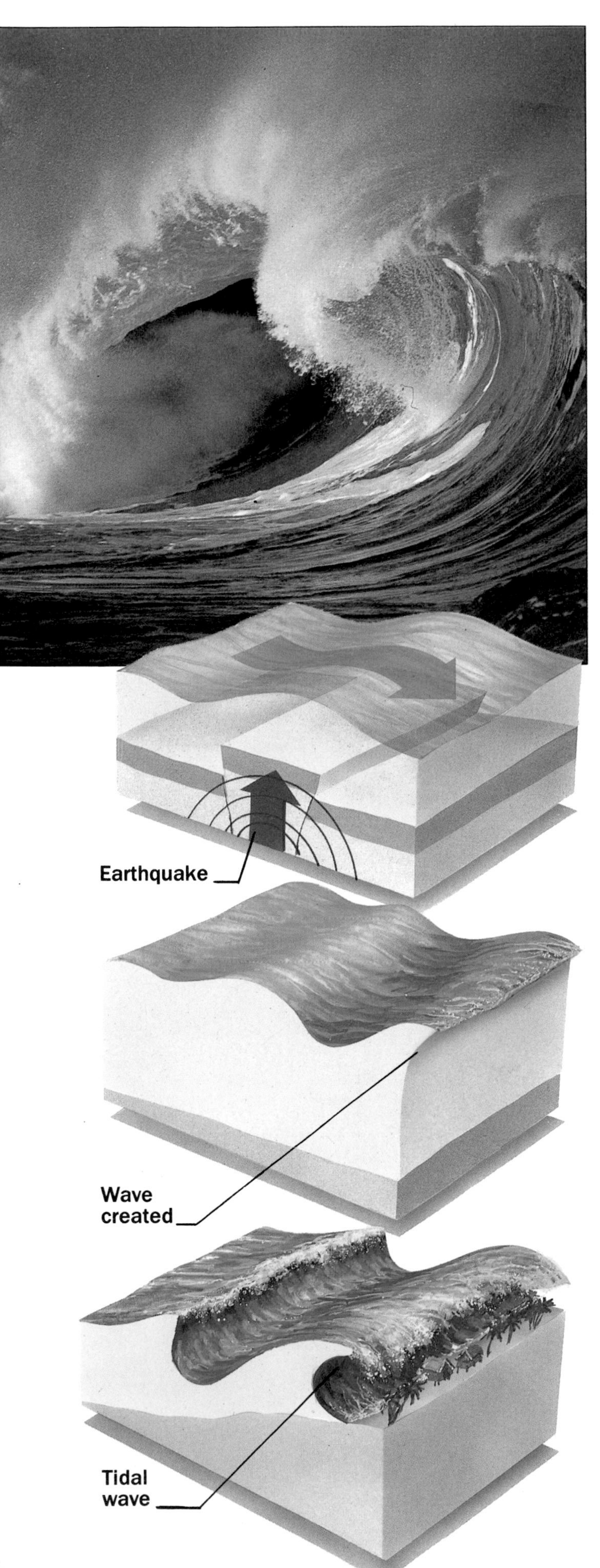

◁ Tidal waves are caused by underwater earthquakes and get higher toward the shore. They travel very fast and cause severe flooding.

Currents in the surface water of the oceans are caused mainly by the prevailing winds, and the rotation of the earth makes the currents move to the right of the wind direction (in the Northern Hemisphere) and to the left (in the Southern). The shapes of landmasses and the ocean bed also affect direction.

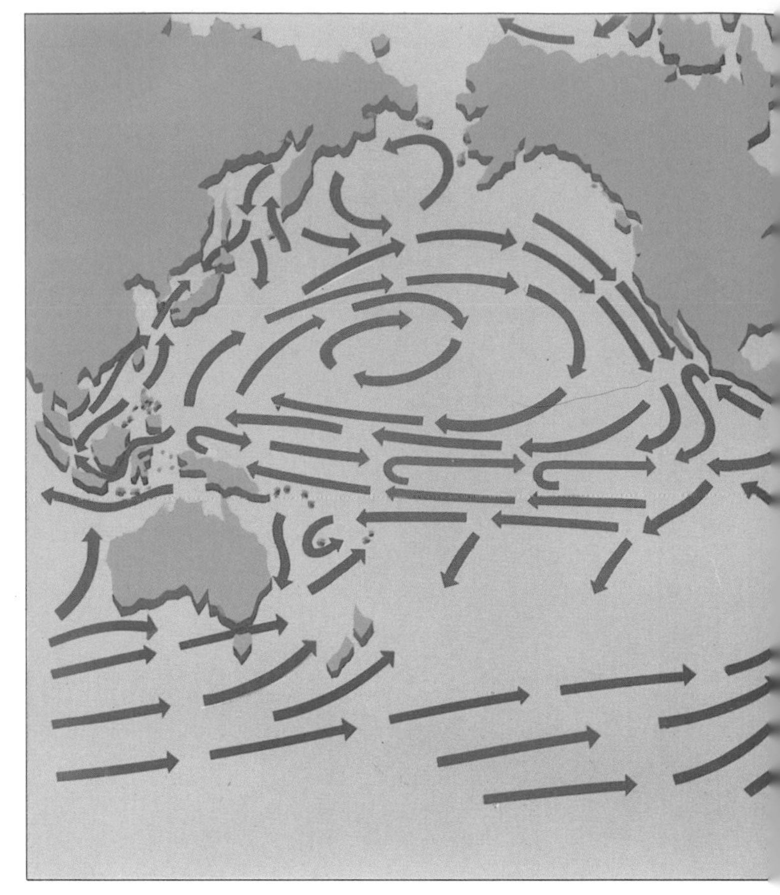

Cold currents
Warm currents
Seasonal drift during winter

△ Cold surface currents in the Northern Hemisphere flow generally southward from the North Pole. In the Southern Hemisphere, the cold water circulates around Antarctica.

CIRCULATION

Currents move in a circular pattern and are called gyres. The gyres rotate in a clockwise direction in the Northern Hemisphere, and in a counterclockwise direction in the Southern Hemisphere.

Ocean currents can be divided into two main types: cold currents and warm currents. At certain times of the year there are also drift currents, such as the Gulf Stream which flows across the Atlantic toward Europe during winter. The overall effect of all these currents is to mix the waters of the earth's oceans.

Another type of mixing occurs when wind blows warm surface water away from a shore. Cooler water from below comes up to take its place in a process called upwelling. The subsurface water often contains nutrients which plantlike organisms feed on. These organisms are then eaten by fish and other sea animals. Such upwelling regions are rich in fish.

A thermograph displays different temperatures of the Gulf Stream.

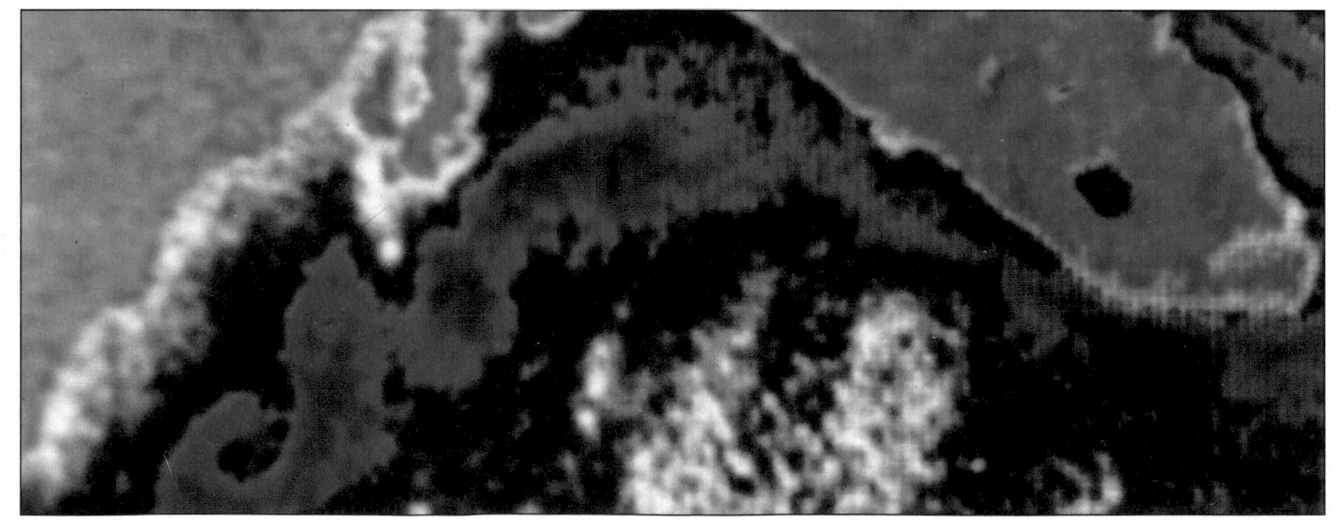

HEAT AND DENSITY

Warm water is less dense than cool water and near the equator, the sun warms the water much faster than at the poles. The salt in ocean water also affects density. As water evaporates from the Mediterranean Sea, it becomes more concentrated in salt, and therefore more dense. Currents of less salty – and less dense – water from the Atlantic Ocean and Black Sea flow in to restore the balance.

The opposite effect takes place in the Baltic Sea of northern Europe. In summer, fresh water from rivers and melting ice flows into the sea and reduces its salinity (and hence density). Then the less dense water at the surface flows southward, forming a current. At the same time an undercurrent of dense, more salty water flows in to take the place of the less dense water.

Ice flowing in the Arctic Sea

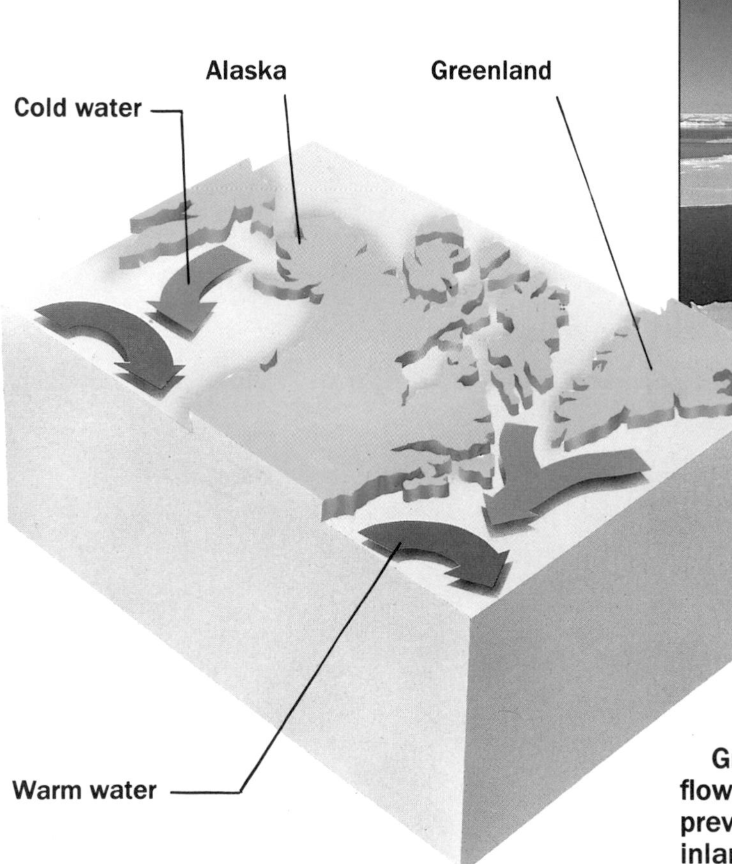

△ Cold seawater surrounds Alaska and Greenland. As warm water flows toward the land, it is prevented from reaching further inland by the cold water stream.

EXPLORING THE OCEAN FLOOR

Geographers have produced accurate maps of all the world's land surfaces. But over three-quarters of the earth lies underwater, and we know less about it than we do about the surface of the moon. The oceans could provide humankind with food and minerals, and are now being intensely studied by scientists.

MAPPING THE SEABED

Charts of the shallow areas of the ocean have been produced as an aid to navigation for many years. The charts were made using soundings (lowering a weighted rope to measure the depth of the water), and recorded the positions of sandbanks, rocks, and other hazards to shipping. Soundings could only be made far out in the ocean if the piece of rope was long enough. However, real progress was not made until the invention of echo-sounding and the development of manned and unmanned submersibles. Then the science of oceanography really took off.

Echo sounding works by transmitting ultrasonic sound waves to the seabed and measuring the time taken for the reflected waves to return to the surface. From a knowledge of the speed of sound in seawater, the distance traveled by the sound can be calculated (as well as the depth which is half the total distance). Echo-sounding is similar in principle to the sonar used by submarines for detection and navigation.

Early world map

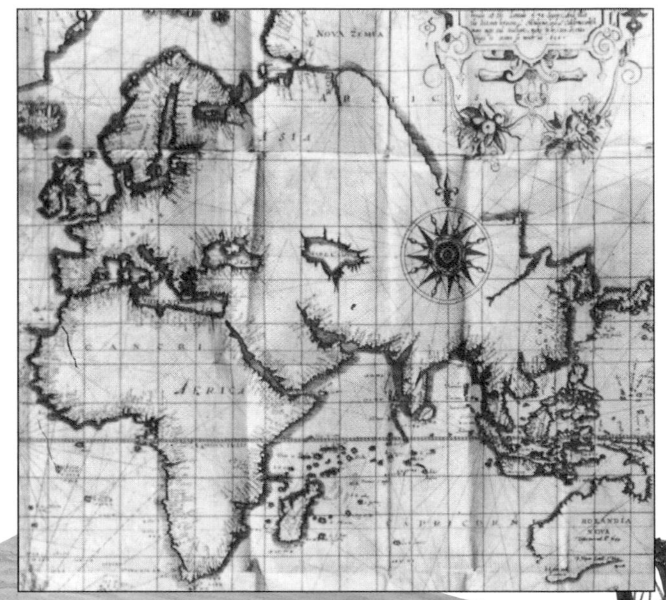

Some equipment used for deep water exploration (1) Sealink, (2) Perry chamber, (3) Deep-sea camera, (4) Trieste, (5) Box cover, (6) JIM and (7) Tech diver

SUBMERSIBLES

Oceanographers use various devices to explore the seabed, but the most versatile – and most expensive – is a manned submersible. It is effectively a small submarine built to withstand the tremendous pressures deep in the ocean. Powered by electric motors, a modern research submersible has a pilot and a crew of up to two observers. It carries lights and cameras – including a television camera to send pictures to the surface – and may have robot "arms" to collect samples from the seabed.

An alternative method of exploration uses a bathyscaphe. This is a strong, pressurized sphere made of steel. It contains various cameras and instruments. In 1960, two scientists in a bathyscaphe descended nearly 36,000 feet to the bottom of the Marianas Trench in the Pacific Ocean.

▷ The modern submersible has come a long way since the first American submarine. It used hand-operated pumps and propellers.

PLUMBING THE DEPTHS

To make a seabed map by taking soundings, put gravel and stones in the bottom of a bowl of water. Put some soil in the water and stir. Using a small weight on the end of a piece of string, measure the depth of water above the various features on the bottom and plot the results on a chart.

Water
String
Mud and gravel
Bowl

MINERAL RICHES OF THE OCEANS

The oceans are a potential source of minerals for humans — indeed, many of the mineral deposits found on land were formed originally in the sea. Today's oceans get their minerals in two ways: from minerals dissolved in seawater itself, or from deposits located on or under the seabed.

▽ Many mineral deposits are found just offshore. Rivers flowing through rocks rich in ores wash them into the sea. The ores settle in areas and form deposits.

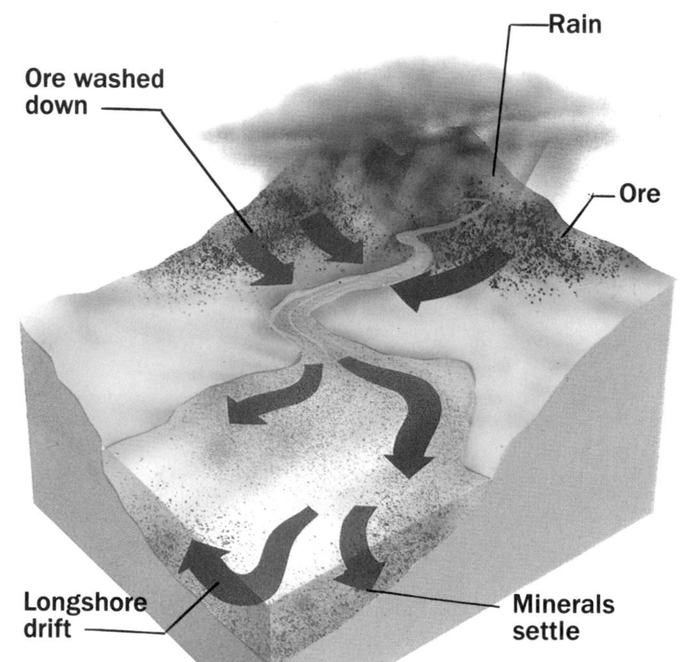

DEPOSITS

Minerals extracted from the beds of shallow waters, usually along the offshore continental shelf, include metal ores of copper, iron, tin, and titanium. Some metallic gold can also be found. Nonmetallic minerals include phosphates, sulfates, sulfur, shellsand and grit (fine gravel). Rivers that flow through diamond-bearing rocks, such as those off the coast of southwestern Africa, carry alluvial diamonds obtained from the silt and gravel near the river mouths. The minerals are scooped up by dredgers, or pumped ashore along pipes.

Minerals dissolved in seawater are extracted by evaporation – a method used for obtaining salt since ancient times – or by chemical processing. Bromine and iodine, used in medicine and by the photographic industry, are obtained chemically. The chief metal extracted from seawater is magnesium, used for making lightweight alloys.

▽ The map shows the locations of the chief minerals. Manganese is "mined" as nodules off the seabed in deep waters.

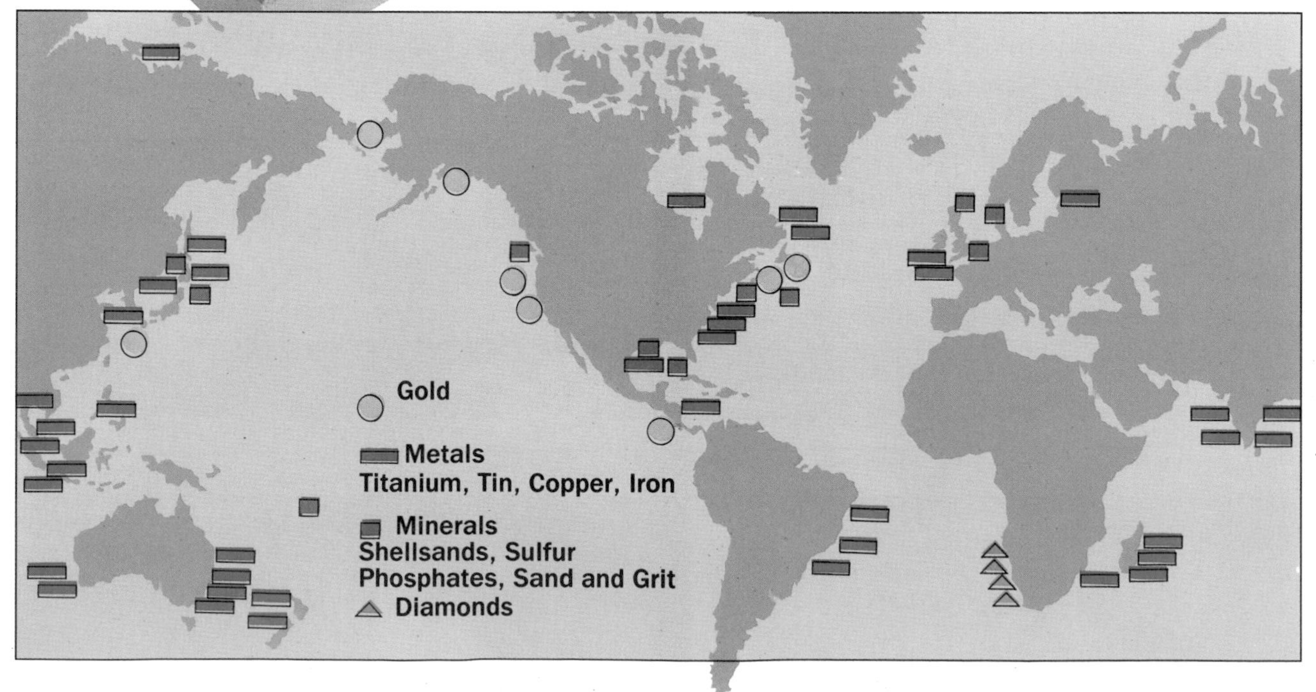

EVAPORATION

In hot parts of the world, people extract salt from seawater by running it into shallow "pans" and allowing the heat of the sun to evaporate the water away. You can copy the process by adding salt to a glass or jar of water until no more will dissolve. Pour the salt solution into another glass, and leave it in a warm place, such as near a radiator. As the heat evaporates the water, salt crystals will form.

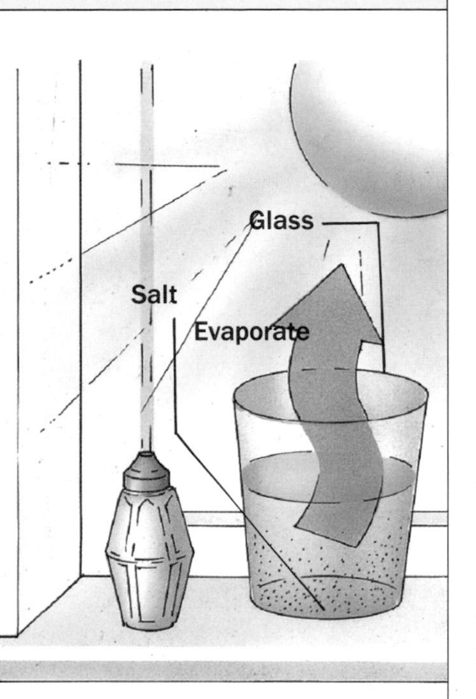

Evaporating seawater for salt

▽ Oil and gas were formed millions of years ago by heat and pressure, as the bodies of millions of small, dead animals and plants were buried at the bottom of the sea.

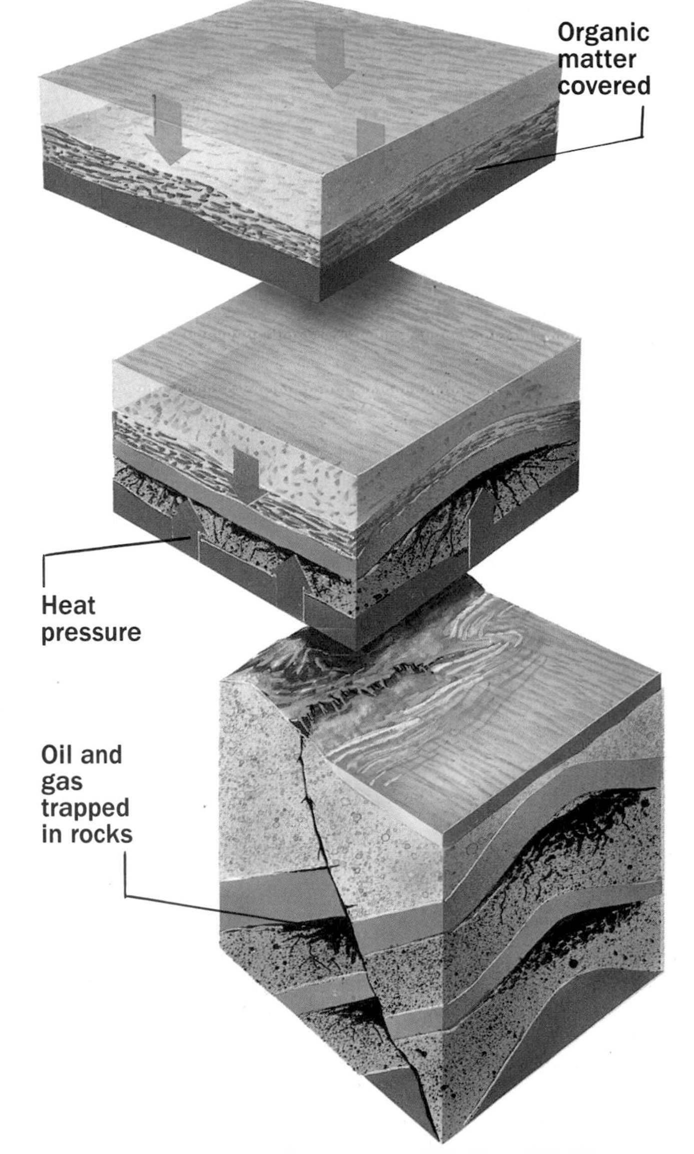

OIL AND GAS

Some of the most important minerals found under the sea – in fact under the seabed – are oil (petroleum) and natural gas. They are important sources of fuels such as kerosene and gasoline. They also serve as raw materials for various petrochemical products, ranging from drugs and dyes to plastics and explosives.

These so-called fossil fuels were formed millions of years ago from the remains of creatures that lived in the sea. Normally when a plant or animal dies, bacteria make the remains decay, or rot away. But such bacteria need oxygen in order to function, and this was unavailable in the early atmosphere. So the remains fell to the bottom of the sea, where there is little or no oxygen, and different kinds of bacteria worked on them, turning them into hydrocarbons. Layers of clay and silt settled over the hydrocarbons, and pressure and heat converted them into oil and gas. The deposits are "mined" by boring a hole and piping the product ashore.

Fish are a good source of protein, and for centuries they have been caught and used by humans and other animals. Today, fish are also processed in factories to make food for pets and farm animals. Mollusks, such as shellfish and crustaceans (crabs, prawns and lobsters), are also caught for food.

OFFSHORE FISHING

Most of the world's major fishing grounds are in shallow waters near the continents. On the continental shelves, the upwelling of nutrients from cooler, deeper water provides a good feeding habitat for the marine population. About 70 percent of all commercial fish are caught in the Northern Hemisphere. For example, herring and cod are netted in the cool northern Atlantic and sardines in warmer Mediterranean waters. The richest fishing ground in the world lies in the Indian Ocean between Japan and the Philippines.

For a long time, most of the fish caught in the Southern Hemisphere came from the offshore waters of Peru in South America, and the main catch was anchovies. But a new warm sea current disrupted the fishing grounds there.

A modern ocean-going trawler

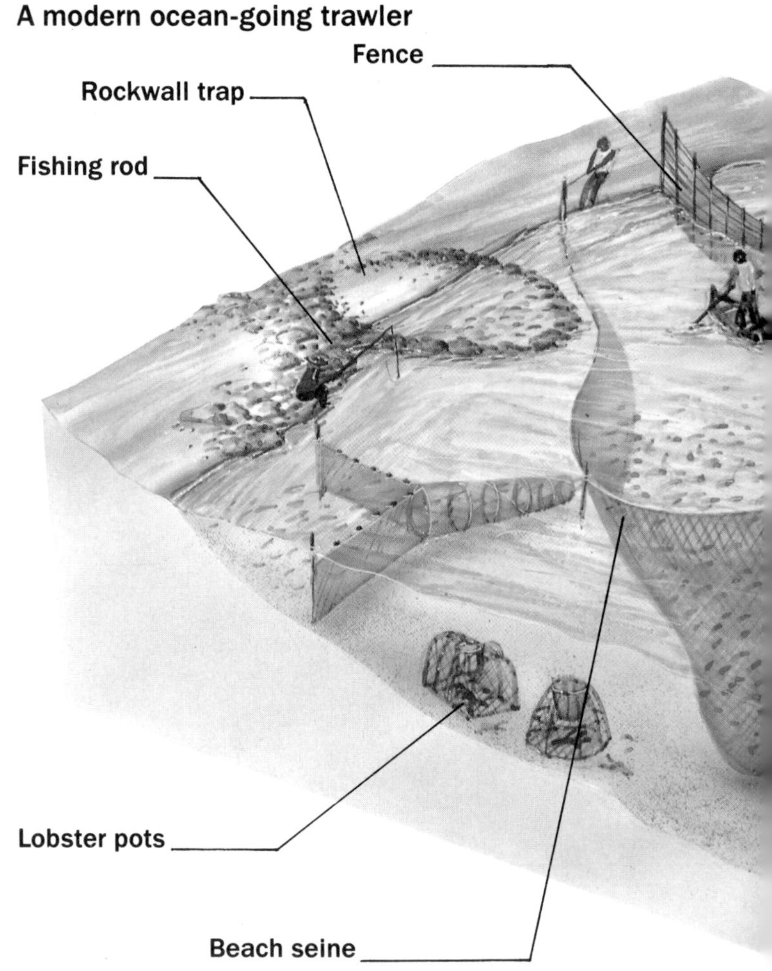

South American fishermen using simple nets

OVERFISHING

Modern fishing vessels are very efficient, and are equipped with a fish-finder (a type of echo sounder to detect shoals of fish underwater) and two-way radios to receive the latest information about the weather and the location of shoals. But the number of fish in the sea is not unlimited, and there is a danger of overfishing. This means that fish will be caught faster than the stocks are being replaced by breeding.

During the late 1980s, commercial fisheries caught almost 90 million tons of fish each year. Experts believe that with effective international control, the annual catch of all fish, crustaceans, and mollusks should never exceed 130 million tons. To enforce this, maritime nations have territorial waters around their coasts in which no foreign vessel is allowed to fish. Many countries have enlarged these waters to a zone of up to 200 miles offshore in order to protect their fish stocks.

▽ Fish may be caught by individual fishermen with rods, small nets, or traps, or by groups of men working on boats using trawls, purse seines, or gill nets.

Cast net

Gill net

Lift net

▽ The map below shows the main fishing zones. Fifty percent of commercial fish are caught along the shores outlined in red.

ENERGY FROM THE OCEANS

One of the problems facing the world today is the energy crisis. Fossil fuels (coal, oil, and gas) will not last for ever, and even nuclear power can be hazardous.The constant motion of the tides and waves, and the temperature differences in the oceans, are a vast source of untapped energy.

WATER POWER

Waves have a lot of energy. For example during a storm, waves crashing onto the shore are able to demolish sea walls. But how can this energy be harnessed? Two experiments have been set up which rely on the fact that as a wave passes, the water moves up and down. In one experiment, a long pontoon with a sausage-shaped air bag along its upper surface, is anchored out at sea. As a wave passes by, it compresses the air in the bag. The air then works a turbine that drives an electric generator.

A second type of wave-powered generator consists of a long line of pear-shaped floats. Wave action makes them nod up and down, and this movement is again made to drive an electric generator.

Tides are another source of water power. Slow-speed water turbines are placed in a dam across the mouth of a river. These turn as the tide comes in, and turn again as the tide flows out. The water turbines are used to drive electric generators.

Bay of Fundy, Canada

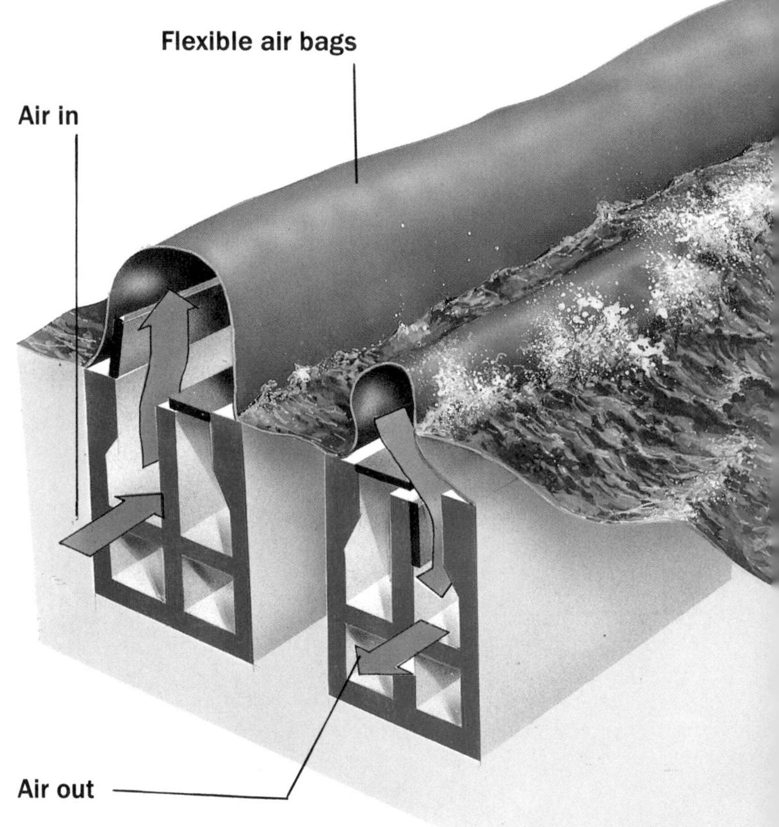

△ Experimental projects have been built which harness the energy produced by waves and tides. Wave-powered electric generators have to be located offshore, where they may be a hazard to shipping. Tidal power plants are built on the shore or at the mouths of rivers.

A Salter's duck at Edinburgh University, Scotland

THERMAL ENERGY

Below the comparatively warm surface waters, the temperature of seawater falls rapidly with increasing depth (see page 161). This temperature difference between surface water and deep water can be used to provide energy. In America, a project has been set up called ocean thermal energy conversion (or OTEC) to do just that.

The project consists of a floating power plant moored in mid-ocean, with a long pipe descending 4,000 feet into the cold water, where the temperature is about 37°F. Pumps lift the cold water up to the power plant where it is used to change ammonia gas into its liquid form. In a heat exchanger, the liquid ammonia is warmed and evaporated back to its gaseous state by warm water from the surface of the sea. The ammonia gas then goes through the same cycle as before. As the liquid ammonia flows around the system, it drives a turbine which generates electricity.

A wave energy machine in Scotland

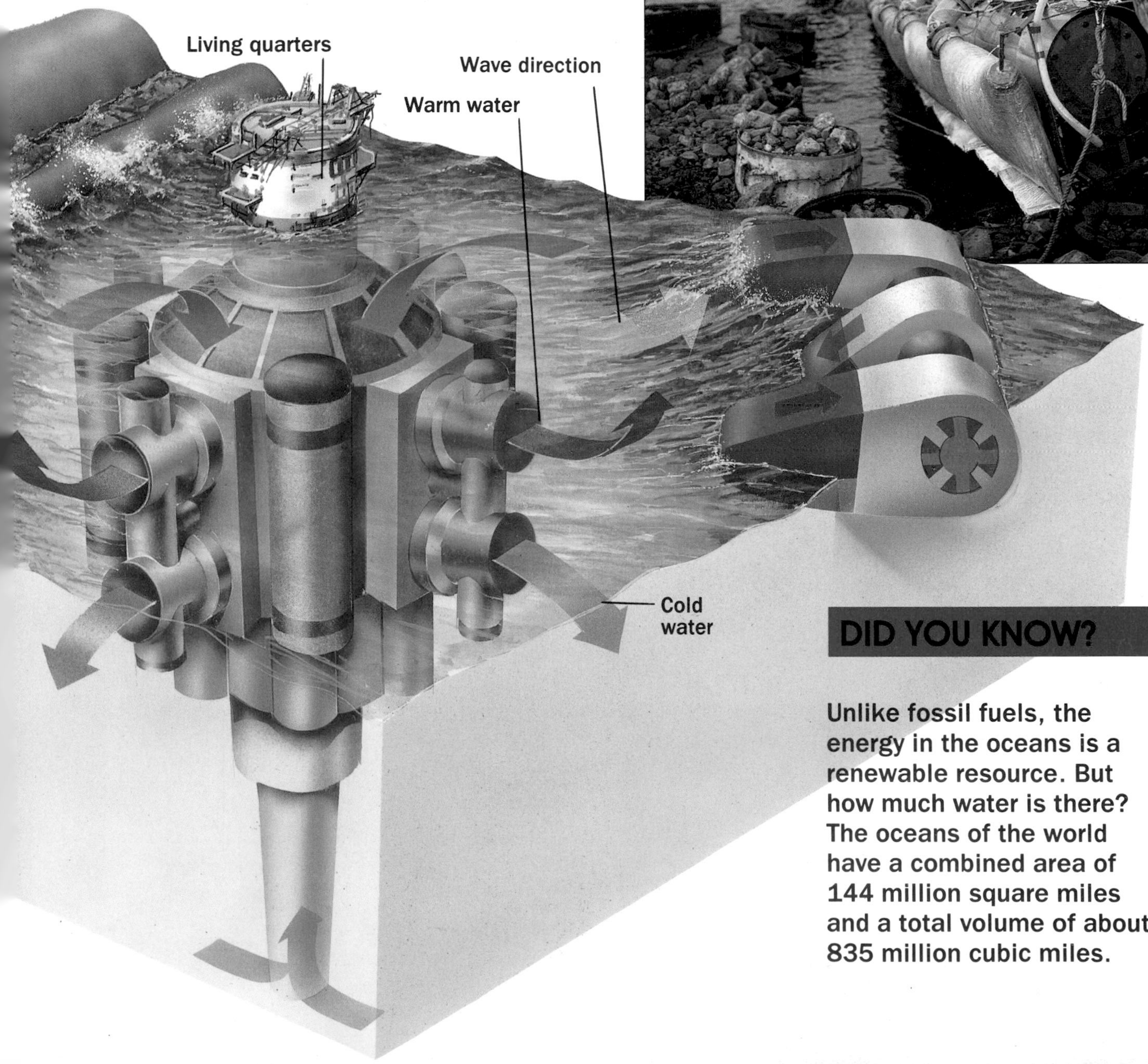

DID YOU KNOW?

Unlike fossil fuels, the energy in the oceans is a renewable resource. But how much water is there? The oceans of the world have a combined area of 144 million square miles and a total volume of about 835 million cubic miles.

Because the oceans are so vast, for years, people have been using them as a dumping ground for garbage, sewage and industrial wastes. Accidental spillages of oil have also added to the pollution. But the long-term effects on wildlife – particularly fish – could have disastrous results for humankind.

THE CHANGING OCEAN

Some human activities have an indirect effect on the oceans. Atmospheric pollution and increasing levels of carbon dioxide in the atmosphere (from burning forests and fossil fuels) give rise to the greenhouse effect. This, in turn, can lead to global warming – an overall increase in average temperatures throughout the world. One result of this warming could be melting of the ice at the poles. The salinity of the oceans would then change and sea levels would rise, flooding huge areas of land.

Dumping of sewage in the sea alters the amount of oxygen and nutrients in the water. Plankton may thrive for a while, but the phytoplankton – the tiny plants that are the ultimate source of food for sea creatures – would die off. This could lead to a mass reduction in marine life.

Plankton blooms off the New Zealand coast

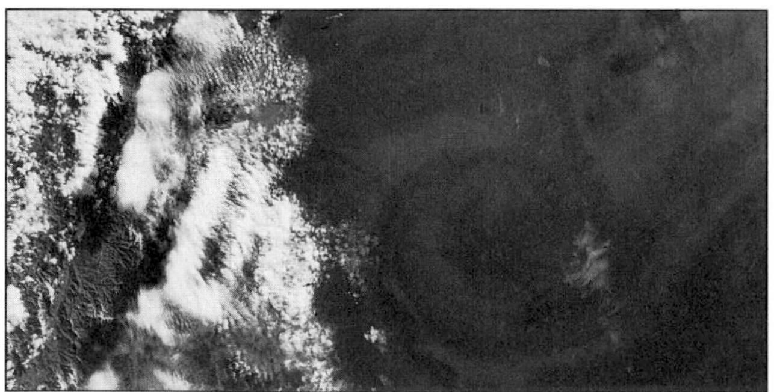

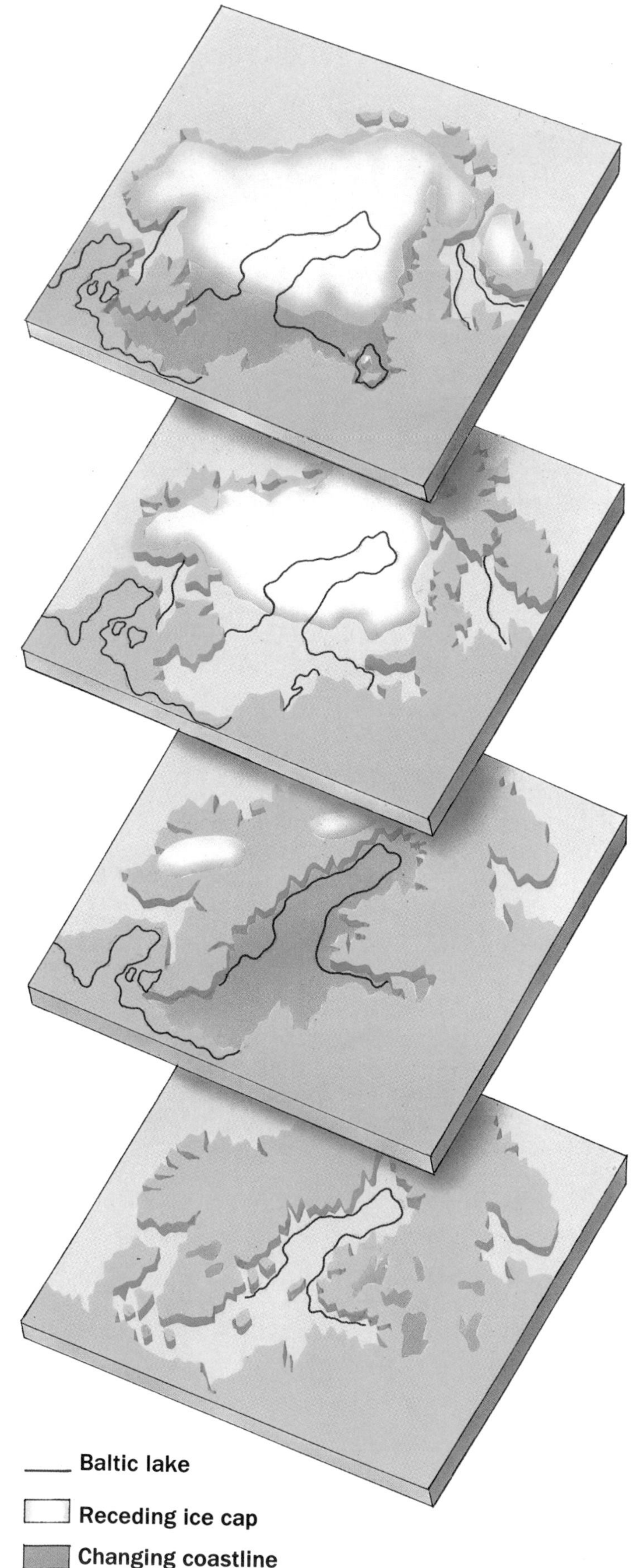

▷ At the end of the last Ice Age the huge ice cap over Scandinavia began to melt. The vast amount of melting water led to a rise in sea levels and later to the formation of the Baltic ice lake.

Cleaning up oil along the coast

PROJECT

One method of dealing with oil spillages is by using detergents. To see how it works, pour a little oil onto some water. Add some dishwashing liquid, agitate the water, and watch the oil disperse.

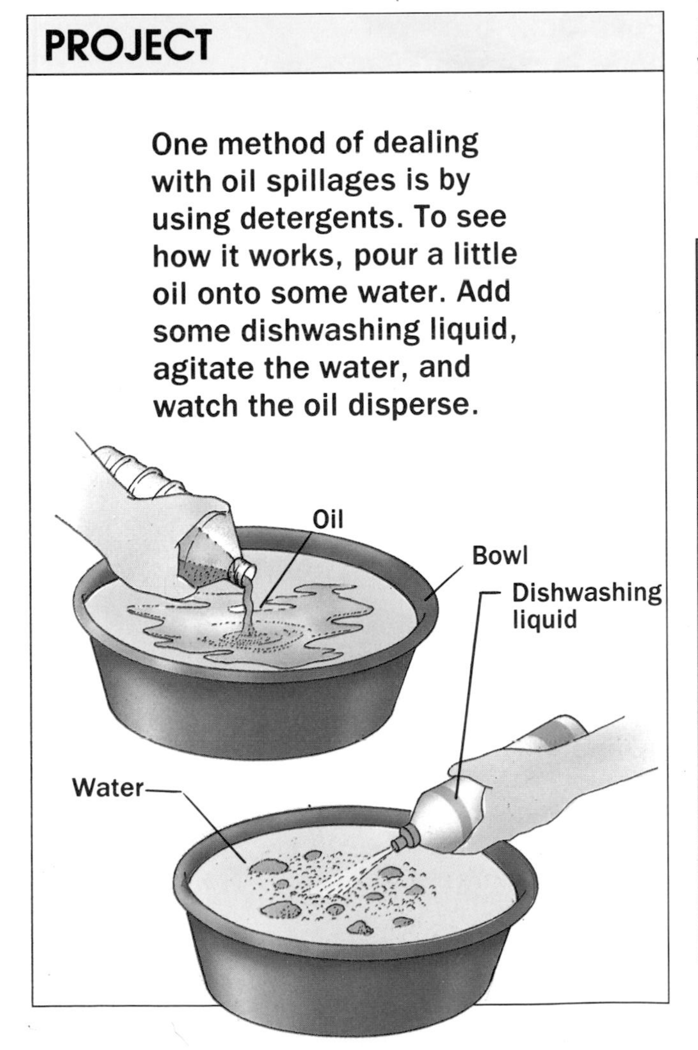

OIL AND CHEMICALS

Crude oil, either spilled accidentally from ships or dumped deliberately from tankers, is a major threat to the oceans. Spilled oil drifts ashore and ends up coating beaches with a black, sticky mess. It gets into the feathers of seabirds, poisoning them as they try to clean their plumage. Scientists have devised various methods to deal with spillages, but the best approach is to prevent them happening in the first place.

Even more dangerous are the toxic chemicals dumped deliberately into the sea, particularly heavy metals such as cadmium, lead, and mercury. During the 1950s and 1960s, Japanese chemical industries dumped 600 tons of mercury compounds into Minamata Bay. The chemicals accumulated in fish which were eaten by the local people. Many people became ill and died, and babies were born deformed. This should serve as a sufficient warning, and bring about an international ban on the dumping of any chemicals in the sea.

Industrial waste being poured into a river

Much remains to be discovered about the oceans. Hundreds of years ago, hardly anything at all was known, and people believed that the earth was a large, flat island in the middle of a sea with no boundaries. People also thought that the sea was home to various kinds of terrible monsters.

An old map, with a flat earth and monsters

One early belief was the existence of a sea serpent, many feet long. It was supposed to attack ships and devour sailors. The giant squid was also a myth, until dead squids were discovered. We now know that giant squids can grow up to 60 feet long, and propel themselves through the water at 30 miles per hour. A giant squid has two long tentacles and eight shorter ones. People think that it was the huge tentacles that gave rise to the sea serpent myth.

A less fearsome myth concerns the mermaid. Half woman and half fish, it resembles several others from Greek mythology. Mermaids were supposed to sing alluring songs and tempt sailors to their deaths by drowning. Again, an actual creature may have given rise to this myth. The dugong, or sea cow, is a large, plant-eating mammal that lives in the shallow waters off the coasts of Africa, Asia, and Australia. It has smooth skin and the females have small breasts, which are thought to resemble those of a woman.

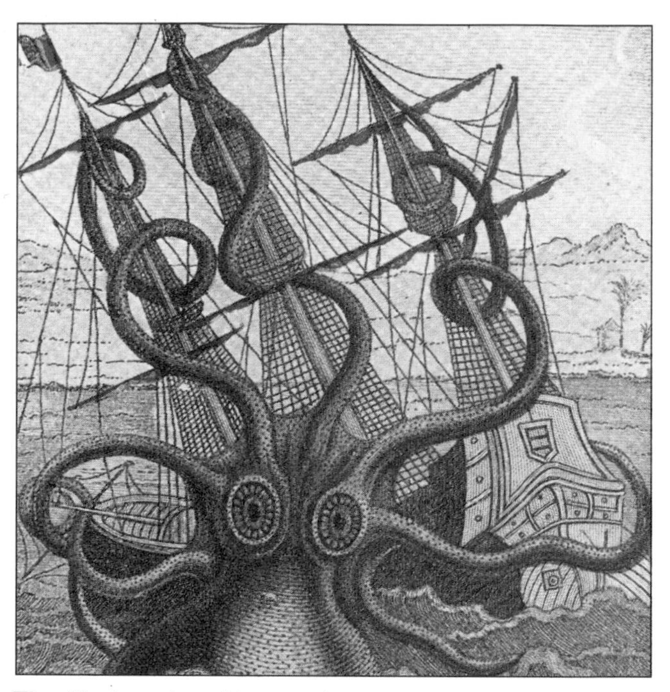

The Kraken is a Norwegian sea monster

In Greek mythology, the monsters of the deep were supposed to be under the control of the god of the sea, called Poseidon, the brother of Zeus. People believed the monsters were offspring of gods and mortals. Poseidon's counterpart in Roman mythology was Neptune, usually depicted holding a trident and keeping company with dolphins. He is sometimes shown with a man's upper body and a fish's tail, rather like a male mermaid. Dolphins were themselves thought to be derived from humans. We now know that after humans, dolphins are the most intelligent mammals.

Mermaids lured sailors to their deaths

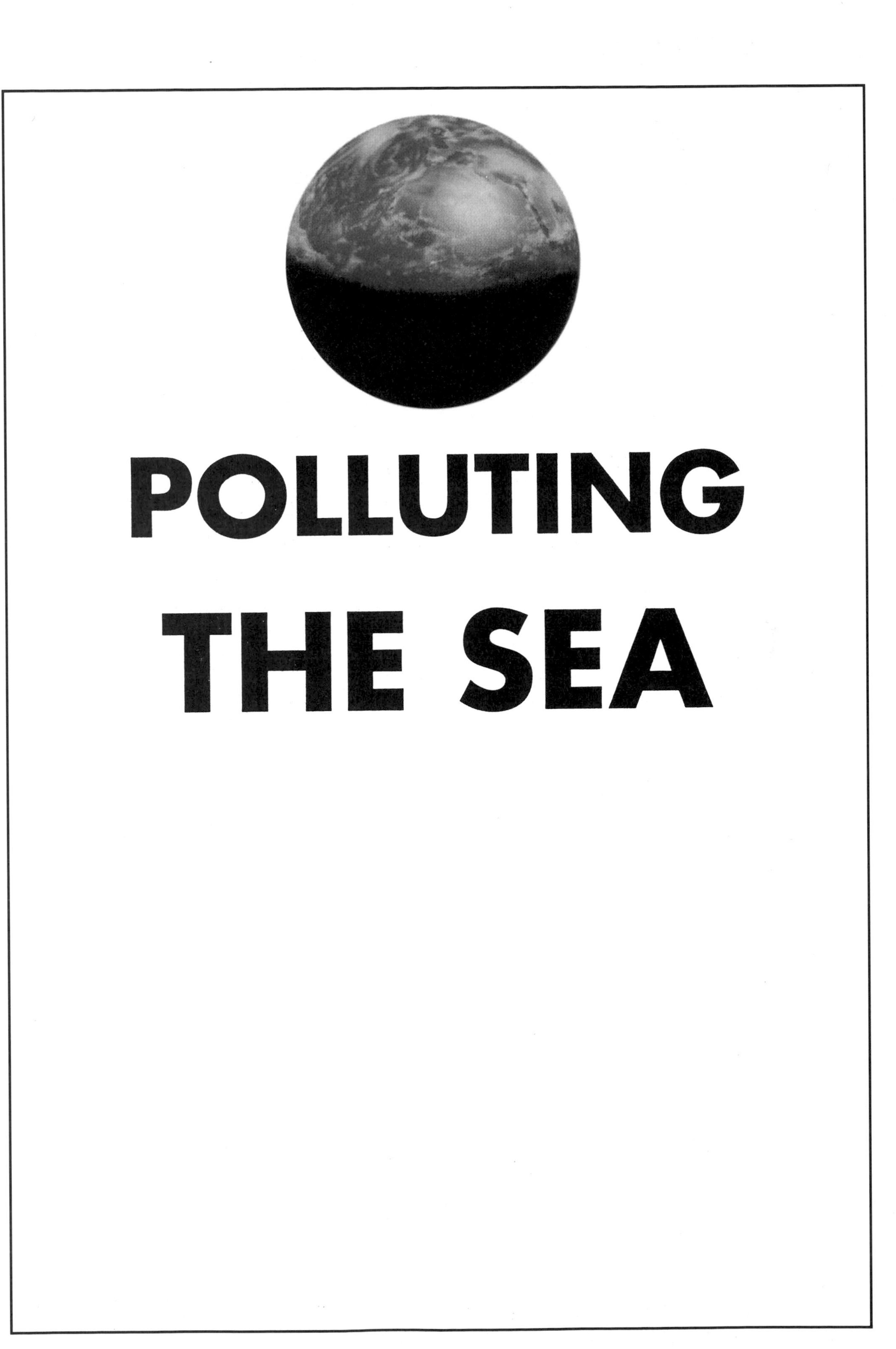

POLLUTING THE SEA

PEOPLE AND THE SEA

More than half the world's population live on or near sea coasts. All around the coastlines of the world there are settlements, from tiny fishing villages to coastal resorts.

The ocean is full of resources. Six million tons of salt are extracted from the sea each year. Energy, in the form of oil and gas, lies beneath the seabed, and thousands of platforms pump out these fossil fuels. Most importantly, the sea provides a huge amount of food. The kinds of seafood we consume vary from great fish like tuna to tiny animals like shrimp. People in some countries, like Japan, eat sea plants. Food from the sea supplies about 23 percent of the world's protein.

If we use the sea sensibly, it will continue to supply food in the future. The growing population will need more and more food from the sea. Fish farming in coastal areas already supplies 10 percent of the world's fish harvest. But by polluting the sea we damage wildlife and we poison, or kill, our own food supply.

► Overfishing, as well as pollution, threatens fish supplies. Traditional fishermen, like these Malaysians (inset right), only take as much fish as they need, leaving plenty behind to breed in order to ensure future stocks. However, modern fishing methods involve taking as much fish as possible. Overfishing has devastated many fisheries, including North Sea herrings and Namibian pilchards.

Many people enjoy traveling on boats. A few compete in the great ocean races, such as the Round the World Race. But the vast majority work on fishing boats or travel on pleasure cruises and ferries as part of their vacations. There is no need for these boats to pollute the sea with garbage or oil, or damage its life, but often they do. Many countries have laws against ships' crews disposing of rubbish over the side of their boats, but these laws often do not apply in deep waters.

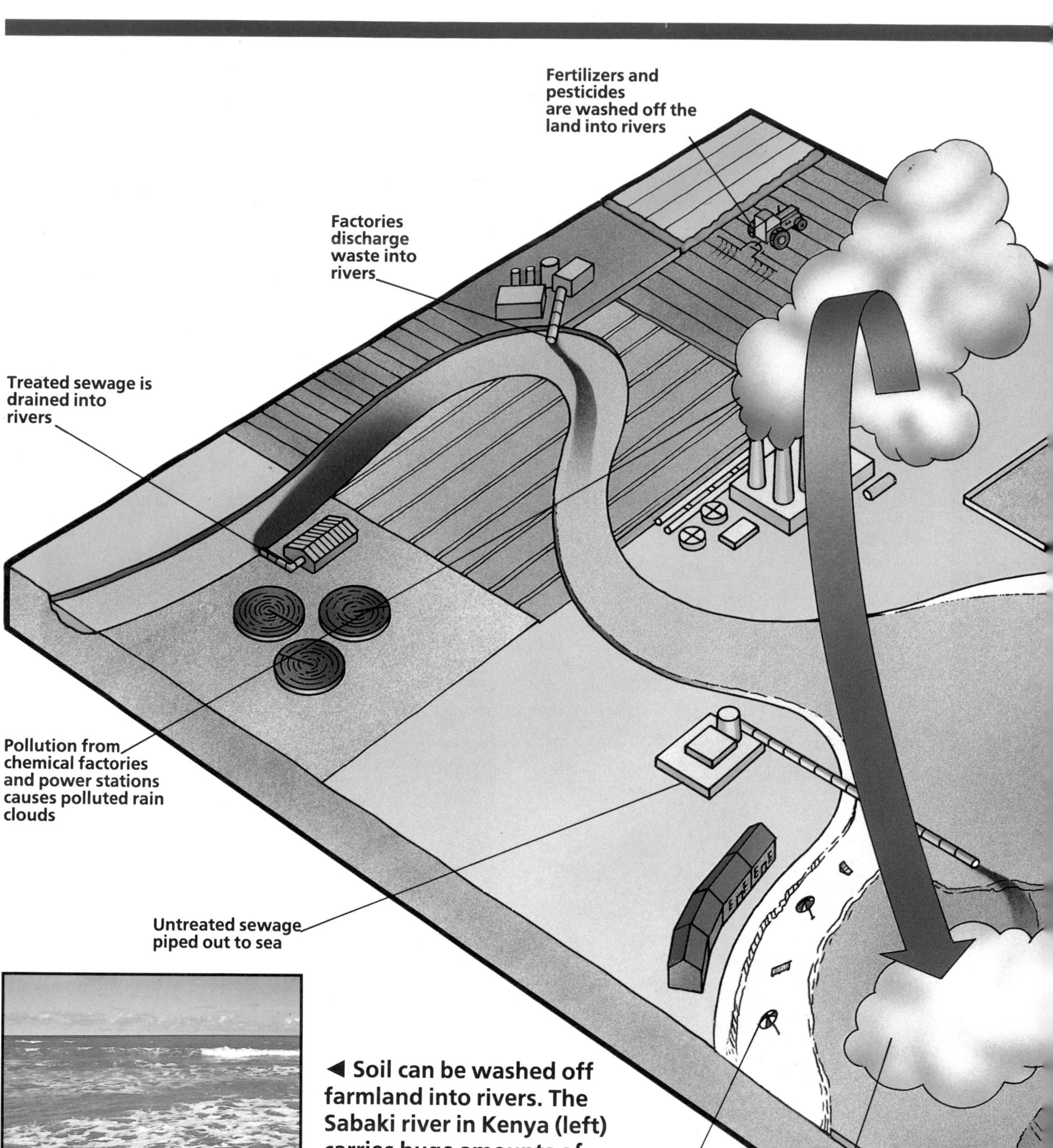

◀ Soil can be washed off farmland into rivers. The Sabaki river in Kenya (left) carries huge amounts of eroded soil to the Indian Ocean. When rivers reach the sea their flow slows and they drop the soil, smothering seaweed and animals. This can turn seabeds into deserts.

HOW THE SEA IS POLLUTED

The sea receives pollution from many sources. Ships dump sewage and other wastes directly into the sea. If ships are wrecked, their cargoes add to the pollution. Rivers carry to the sea chemicals used in farming, like pesticides which kill pests, and fertilizers which help plants grow. Soil from farms also gets washed into rivers and carried to the sea, along with poisonous wastes discharged from riverside factories. Coastal towns add their sewage and wastes from industry and power stations. Litter washes out to sea from the shores of tourist resorts. Regulations exist for some of these sources of pollution, but they are often difficult to enforce.

Nuclear power stations discharge radioactive water into the sea

Dredger dumps sand and gravel on the seabed

Oil leaks from wrecked tankers

Burned chemical particles drift into sea from waste incineration

Sewage sludge dumped at sea by barge

► About 465,000 pounds of sludge are dumped into the ocean from New Jersey every day.

OIL POLLUTION

When oil spills it covers the surface of the ocean in oil slicks which can extend over large areas. Oil can kill marine wildlife. If it washes up on the shore it ruins beaches. Oil is the best-known type of sea pollution because it is usually visible – and very damaging.

A low estimate is that about three million tons of oil a year (one tenth of one percent of the world's annual oil production) end up in the oceans. Wrecked tankers are not the only cause of oil pollution, in fact they account for only about 10 percent of human-created oil pollution. The rest is discharged during production or from oil tankers washing out their tanks. If oily waste from cars and factories is dumped on the ground or into drains, rivers can carry it out to sea. Oil also naturally seeps from oil deposits beneath the ocean.

Oil slowly gets broken down naturally by bacteria. Oil spills can be cleaned up faster by people, but this is expensive. A better solution is to reduce oil pollution by recycling car oil and using better methods to clean out tankers' oil tanks. However, accidents still happen, so oil spills are likely to continue to make news.

▼ Today there are over 3,000 tankers on the seas, transporting half of the world's oil. Over a third of human-created oil pollution comes from transportation, through operations such as tank-washing and from accidents. Risks to shipping are greatest near coasts. So the chances are that when accidents happen, coastlines and their wildlife will be affected.

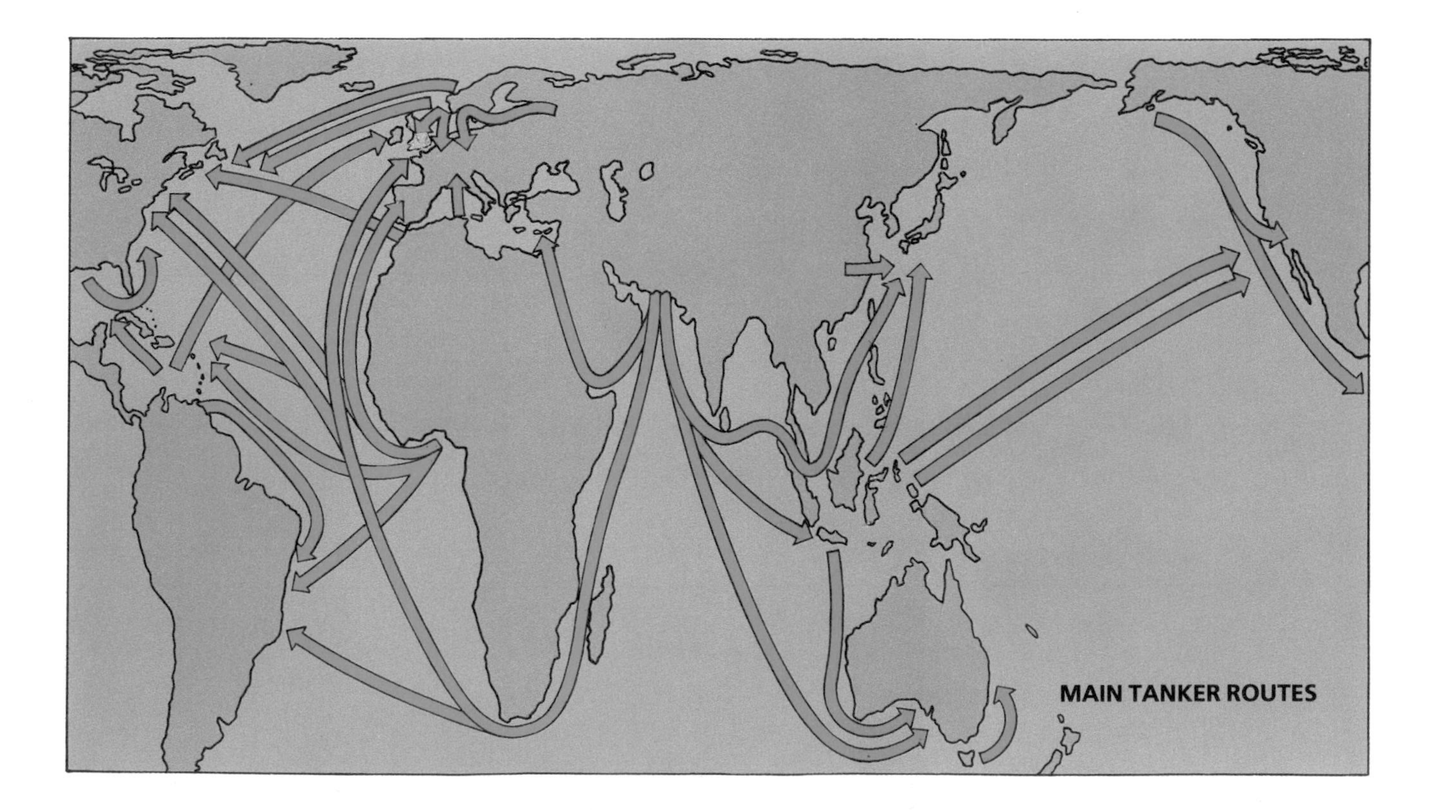

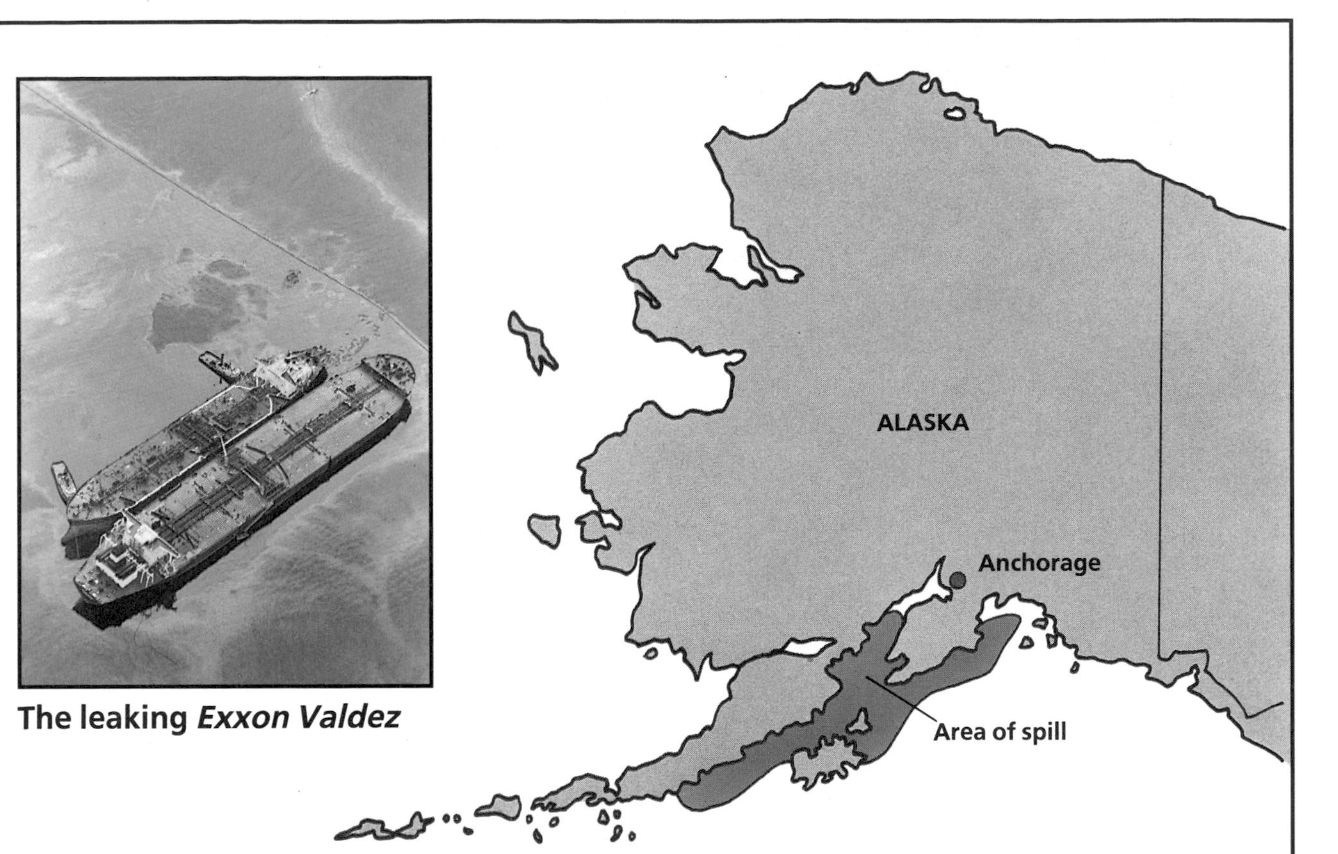

The leaking *Exxon Valdez*

On March 24, 1989 the oil tanker *Exxon Valdez* ran aground in Prince William Sound in Alaska. It spilled over 11 million gallons of crude oil. The effect on the local environment was devastating. Fish, seabirds and sea otters were killed in huge numbers. Otters are poisoned by oil, either by swallowing it as they swim through it or by trying to lick it off their coats. However, the main cause of death is exposure to cold. If oil clogs otters' fur they freeze to death. A few of these sea otters have been successfully rescued and cleaned. But about 3,000, along with 36,000 seabirds and over 100 eagles, are estimated to have died.

◀ This bird got caught in the oil spill from the *Exxon Valdez*. When oil clogs up a bird's feathers or an animal's fur it can no longer float. It also loses its insulation and cannot keep warm. The victims die from drowning, cold or poisoning if they swallow oil while trying to clean themselves.

OCEAN LITTER

Scattered across the surface of the sea and strewn across beaches, ocean litter is a very ugly type of pollution. It appears in many different forms, including plastic packaging, cartons, abandoned fishing nets, ropes, cans and bottles. The main litter culprits are ships' crews. Many of them throw their garbage overboard into the sea. Rivers also carry garbage from towns, and it washes into the sea from beaches.

A lot of ocean litter is made of plastic. It is estimated that 6.5 million tons of plastic are thrown off ships every year. The main problem with many types of plastic is that they decay very slowly. A plastic cup thrown from a ferry may still be in the sea 100 years later.

Ocean litter kills. Every year thousands of seabirds, fish and mammals drown or are wounded by getting tangled up in fishing nets and packaging. Others may suffer after swallowing tiny plastic balls which make them feel full and stop them from feeding properly.

► The metal object trapped on this Canada goose's beak may make feeding difficult. Plastic rings that hold six-pack cans together can also be dangerous or even fatal to marine wildlife which get them caught around their necks and bodies. Some manufacturers are starting to put their cans into cardboard cartons instead of using plastic rings.

▼ Litter such as bottles can often be found on beaches. Glass is dangerous to both humans and wildlife. Bottles get washed ashore after being dumped at sea, and others are left on beaches by tourists.

▲ Lost fishing nets can drown wildlife. This Northern fur seal survived, but the net remains.

◄ This barge is carrying domestic waste to be disposed of on land. One of the problems with litter is that we do not recycle enough of it. It has been estimated that over half the domestic waste that gets thrown away as garbage could be recycled. As recycling becomes more commonplace, the amount of litter tainting both land and sea should decrease. Some 60 countries, including the United States, prohibit the dumping of household garbage in the sea under the London Dumping Convention.

SEWAGE POLLUTION

A huge amount of sewage is drained or dumped into the sea. Around nine million cubic yards each day end up in the North Sea. In Malaysia untreated sewage from Penang is discharged into the sea, raising the bacteria levels 100 times higher than those recommended for bathing beaches in the United States.

Sewage contains substances from human, household and industrial waste which can poison the environment. It also contains bacteria, viruses and parasite eggs which are harmful to human health. The bacteria can give swimmers stomach upsets or infections. In many places sewage is left untreated before it is disposed of. It can be treated to make it safer, but this is expensive. To provide a treatment plant for a city of 200,000 people costs about $50-80 million. Sewage does break down naturally, but in the process it can seriously disrupt the environment. If dumped in large quantities it can cause wildlife to die from lack of oxygen.

▼ Because sewage contains nutrients that sea plants like algae need, they are able to reproduce very quickly when sewage is dumped in the ocean. They cover the surface of the sea with algal blooms, which can clog fishes' gills. When algae colonies die their remains are whipped to foam by the waves. These algal blooms have been washed up on a beach of the North Sea, where they can cause skin and mouth irritations to people.

▼ **Fish and other marine animals need oxygen to live. Bacteria use up oxygen as they break down organic materials like sewage. The sea is normally in balance, with oxygen dissolving into the water from the atmosphere and also being produced by sea plants. But when there is a great increase in the amount of organic materials, the bacteria use up the oxygen faster than it is replaced and oxygen levels plummet. This process is called de-oxygenation. Fish and other animals cannot breathe and may die.**

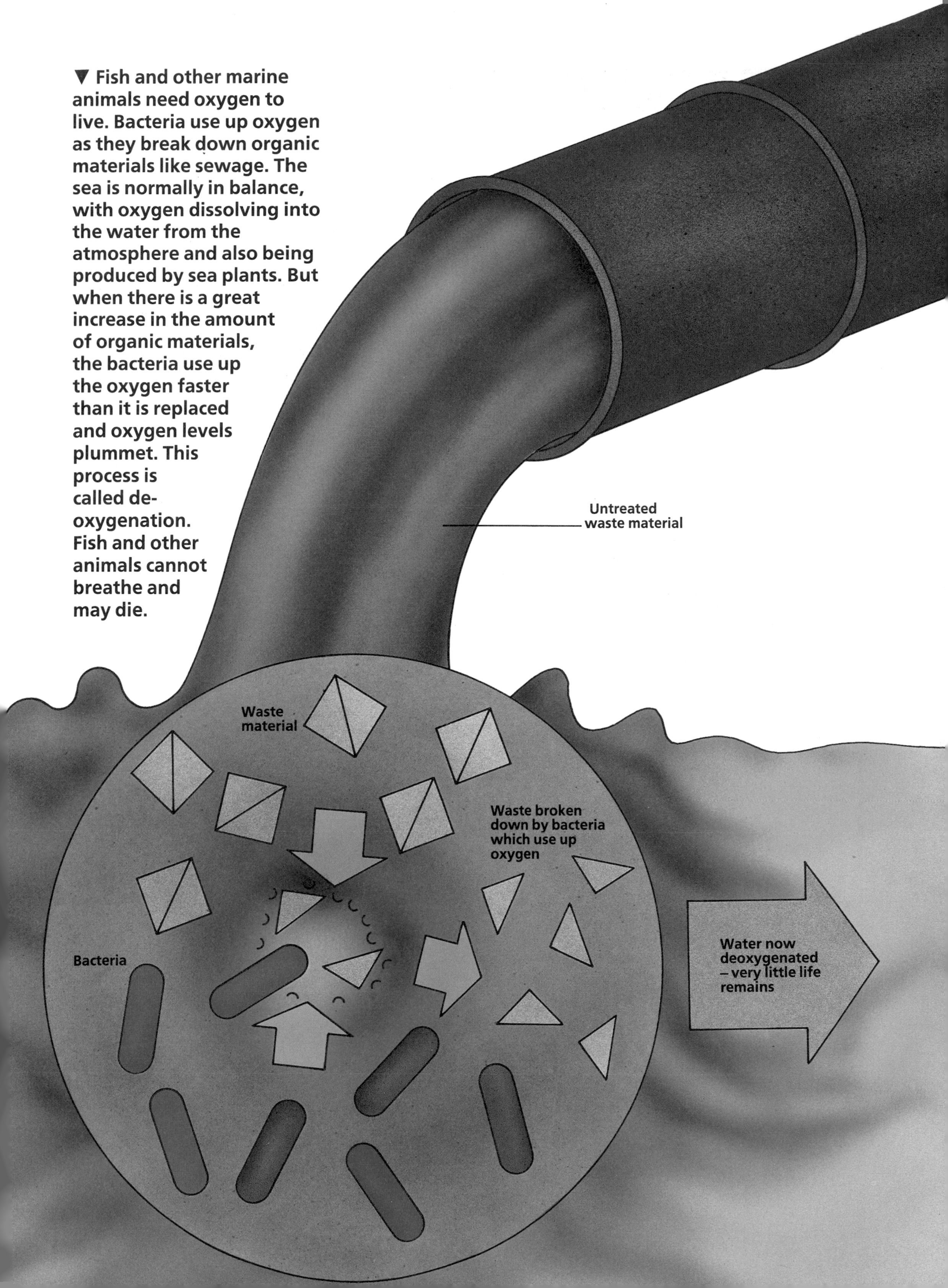

Untreated waste material

Waste material

Waste broken down by bacteria which use up oxygen

Bacteria

Water now deoxygenated – very little life remains

METAL POLLUTION

Metals can be very poisonous pollutants although they occur naturally in the environment; blood, for example, contains iron. Metals get into the sea from volcanoes and forest fires, but also end up there as a result of human activities. Ocean dumping of some metals is illegal. However, along coastal areas with a lot of industry, metal pollution causes serious problems. Some industrial processes release metals into the air and water. Factory waste can carry metals. Chemicals used in farming also contain metals which can be washed into the sea by rivers and rain.

The level of metals in the sea is rising, and some of these metals can be very dangerous in large amounts. Copper, for example, is vital to many small marine animals, but when it was dumped off the Netherlands into the North Sea in 1965, the pollution killed all the plankton and fish in its path as it drifted up the coast. Also, animals retain metal if they consume it, and dangerous levels can build up in the food chain.

▼ The metal tin is used in TBT (tributyltin oxide), which is painted on boats' hulls to keep them free of barnacles. The tin slowly dissolves into the sea and has a serious effect on wildlife. Oysters, for example, suffer reduced growth and dog whelks become unable to breed. TBT is banned on small boats in many countries, but is still used on larger ships.

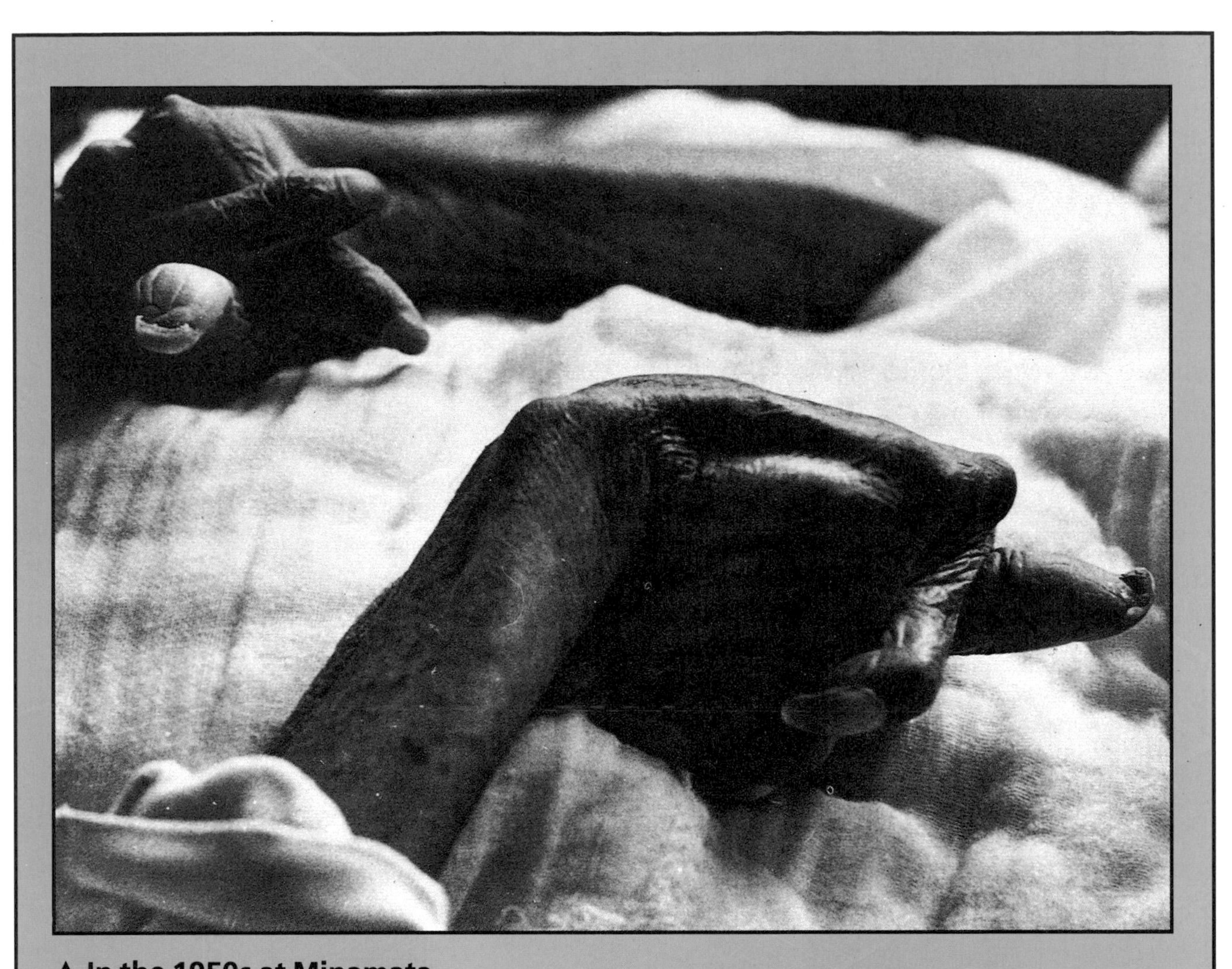

▲ In the 1950s at Minamata in Japan, mercury pollution entered the sea from a factory. The local people then ate the mercury-poisoned fish, with tragic consequences. Around 2,000 people were affected; some became crippled (above). Fishing was banned and eventually the pollution was stopped, but altogether at least 43 people died and 700 were left permanently affected.

► Mercury levels in white-tailed sea eagles, which feed on fish, have increased nine-fold during this century in Sweden and Finland. Mercury poisoning may be a factor in their decline.

CHEMICAL POISONS

A wide range of the artificial chemicals that we manufacture, including pesticides, end up in the sea. Many pesticides do not easily break down in the environment, so their levels are continually rising. Plants and animals may build up high levels of pesticides because they cannot eliminate them from their bodies.

Pesticides poison wildlife. The insecticide DDT can cause the shells of birds' eggs to be so thin that they break before they are ready to hatch. This especially affects fish-hunters, which are at the top of the food chain, when they eat fish that contain high levels of chemicals. DDT can also cause cancer. Its use has been banned in many countries since 1972, but its effects will remain in the environment for many years to come.

Among the huge numbers of other chemicals reaching the sea are detergents, acids and other industrial wastes and chemicals. Even though they are diluted by the sea, they can be harmful.

▼ Chemical pollution in the sea can have a variety of effects. The deaths of sea-birds at the Los Angeles Zoo in 1976 were blamed on the fish the birds were fed, which contained high levels of DDT. Deformities seen in ocean wildlife may be due to chemical pollution like PCBs; chemicals used in the electrical industry. It is believed this cormorant was born deformed as a result of PCB poisoning.

► The Rhine is a severely polluted river. By 1982, most of the species of fish that used to swim up it to breed had gone. Each year the Rhine receives over 300,000 tons of waste from cities that line its banks. The pollution does not just affect wildlife: about 20 million people get their drinking water from the Rhine. Much of the Rhine's pollution ends up in the North Sea.

▲ On November 1, 1986 a fire broke out at the Swiss Sandoz chemical factory on the Rhine. The accident released so much pollution that over 60 miles of the river were left lifeless.

RADIOACTIVITY

Radioactivity consists of rays and particles given off by decaying atoms. It can be harmful to living things. Radioactivity occurs naturally in the sea at low levels, but the amount has increased due to human activity.

The nuclear bombs exploded in tests between the end of World War II and the early 1970s produced large amounts of radioactive dust, called fallout. The dust that was not immediately brought to the ground with rain was blasted high into the atmosphere where it still circles the earth and gradually falls out of the sky, adding to the level of radioactivity.

Nuclear power stations use water for cooling during their normal operations and they discharge radioactive waste water into the ocean. Also, in the past, some radioactive waste was dumped at sea. Although this practice has now stopped, between 1967 and 1983 about 95,000 tons were dumped. Eventually the canisters will corrode and release radioactivity, although the levels are not likely to be high.

▼ Worldwide there are about 600 submarines powered by nuclear energy. Normally they discharge a small amount of radioactivity which is spread throughout the sea so it has little effect. However, there is the risk of an accident which could expose the nuclear reactor which runs the submarine. This could lead to a large release of radioactivity in the area of the accident.

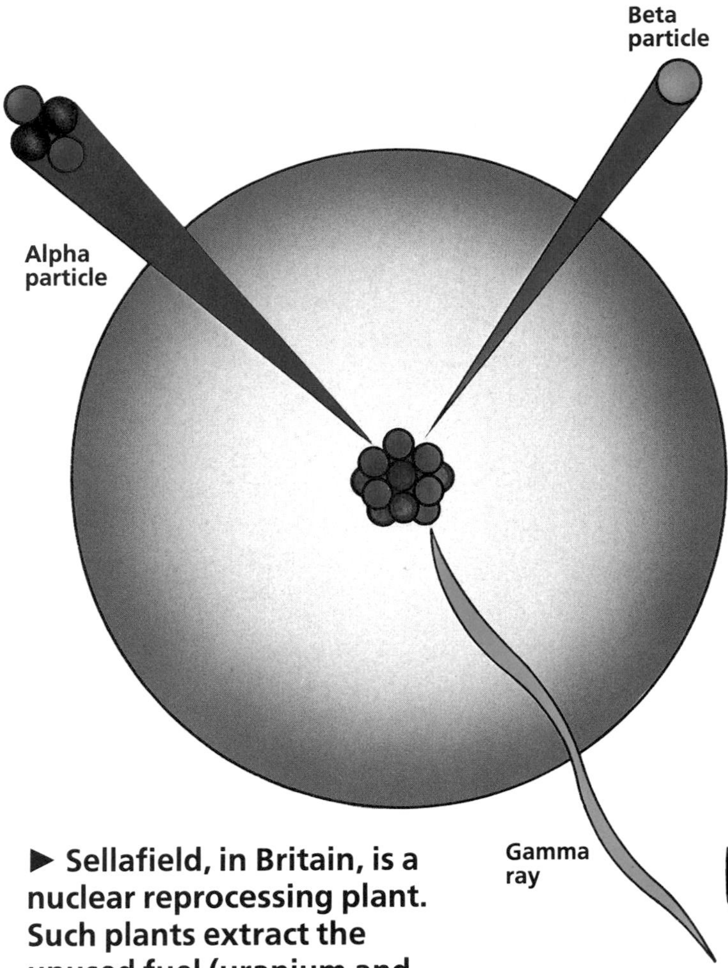

Beta particle

Alpha particle

Gamma ray

◄ Radioactivity is invisible. Some types can pass through solid objects. There are three types of radiation: alpha particles, beta particles and gamma rays. Alpha particles can be stopped by a sheet of paper, beta particles by a thin sheet of metal and gamma rays by a thick sheet of lead. At high levels radiation can cause death, and at lower levels it is believed to cause cancer.

► Sellafield, in Britain, is a nuclear reprocessing plant. Such plants extract the unused fuel (uranium and plutonium) from old fuel rods used to generate energy in nuclear power stations. Reprocessing plants discharge large quantities of waste water with a low amount of radioactivity. Fish in the Irish Sea near Sellafield have to be monitored for radiation pollution since people eat the fish.

◀ **The Mediterranean Sea is almost completely surrounded by land. The time it takes to exchange all its water with the Atlantic is 70 years. The result is that pollution is not efficiently diluted; it is not replaced with clean water. So pollution builds up, mainly from industries like these on the Gibraltar coast.**

The North Sea

Some 31 million people live around the North Sea and millions of visitors go there every summer. Every type of pollution gets into the North Sea. Much of the sewage from coastal towns is pumped untreated into the sea.

The Mediterranean

Tar balls, a type of oil pollution, are very frequent in the Mediterranean. Also, many coastal towns discharge untreated sewage into the sea.

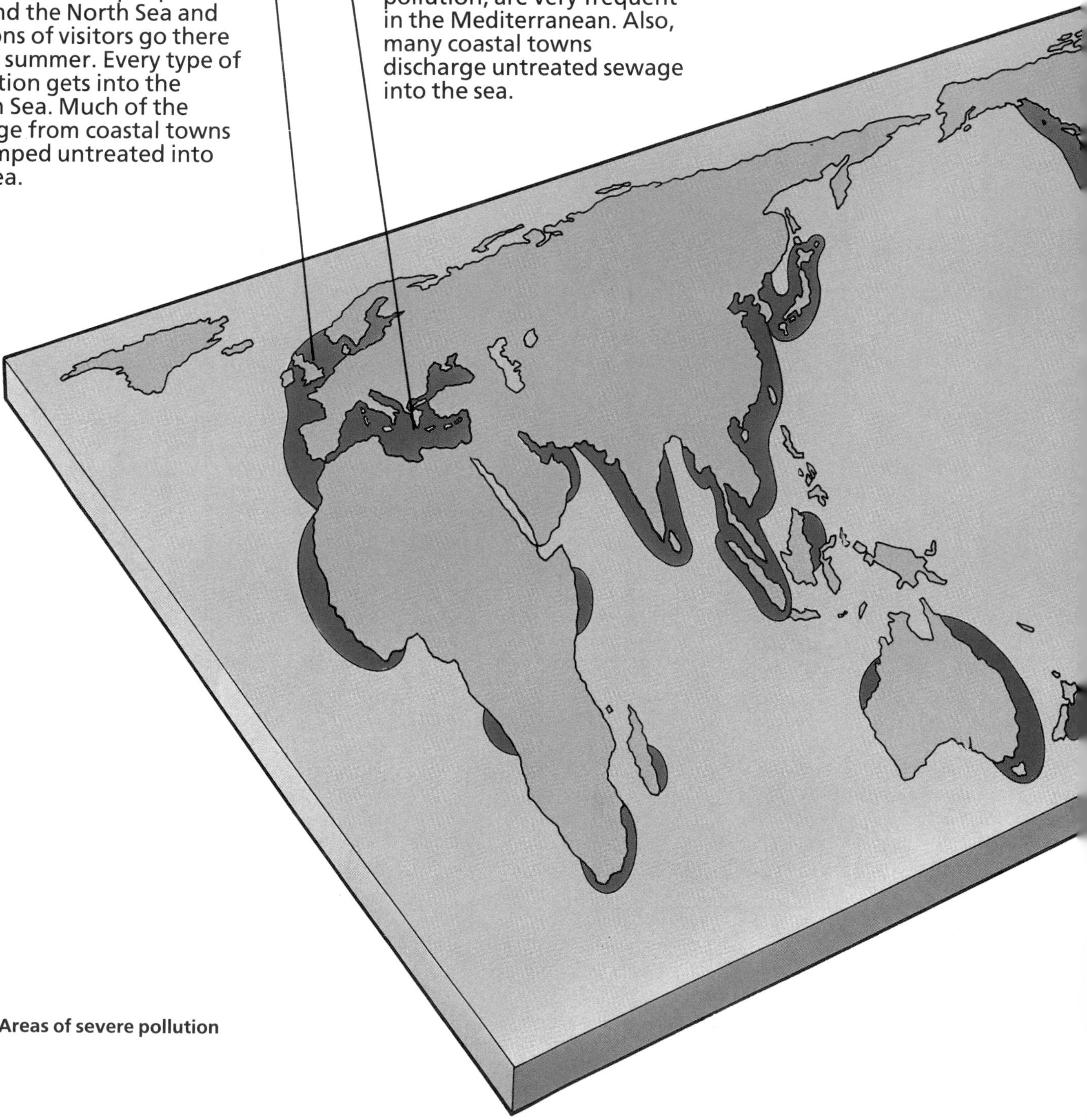

Areas of severe pollution

POLLUTION HOTSPOTS

Seas and oceans worldwide have been affected by pollution, particularly coastal waters. To change this we need increasing awareness among those who daily use the sea, as well as the general public, about the dangers to wildlife and people from sea pollution.

Factories must have rules on what and how much waste they drain into the ocean. This can be enforced by governments agreeing on strong pollution laws and by making polluters pay for the damage they cause. Governments can also ban industries from using pollutants until their effects are fully known. Most importantly, factories and power stations should produce a minimum amount of waste in the first place, use biodegradable products (which break down naturally) and attempt to recycle waste where possible. Sewage can be recycled to make fertilizer, for example. These steps would begin to tackle pollution problems.

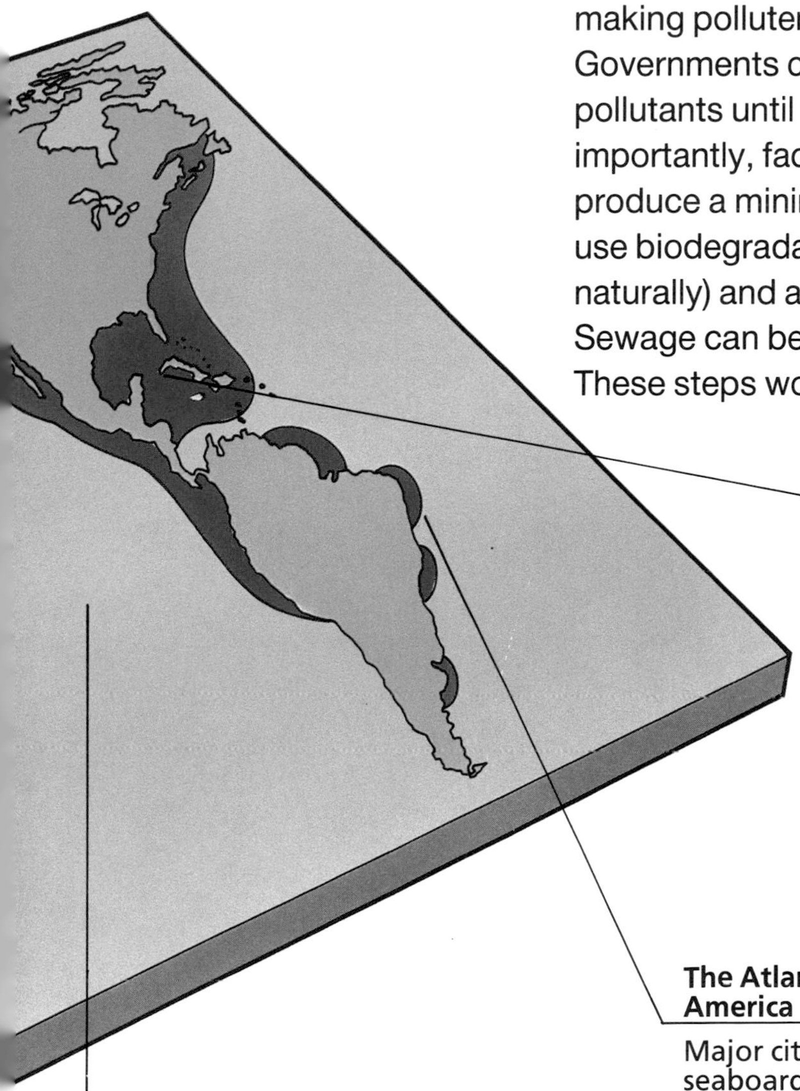

The Caribbean and Gulf of Mexico

There is little coastal industrialization in this area, but pesticides from farming are washed into the Gulf. Also, serious local problems have occurred, including oil pollution at Galveston in Texas, mercury at Cartagena in Colombia and sewage at Port-au-Prince in Haiti.

The Atlantic coast of South America

Major cities along this seaboard include Recife and Rio de Janeiro in Brazil, and Buenos Aires in Argentina. These massive, expanding cities with their large populations and industrial activities are causing pollution problems in the western Atlantic.

The Pacific

The Pacific is the world's largest ocean. Some of its isolated islands have been used for nuclear weapons' testing in the past, and are now so radioactive that they have been declared unsafe for habitation for thousands of years.

FACT FILE 1

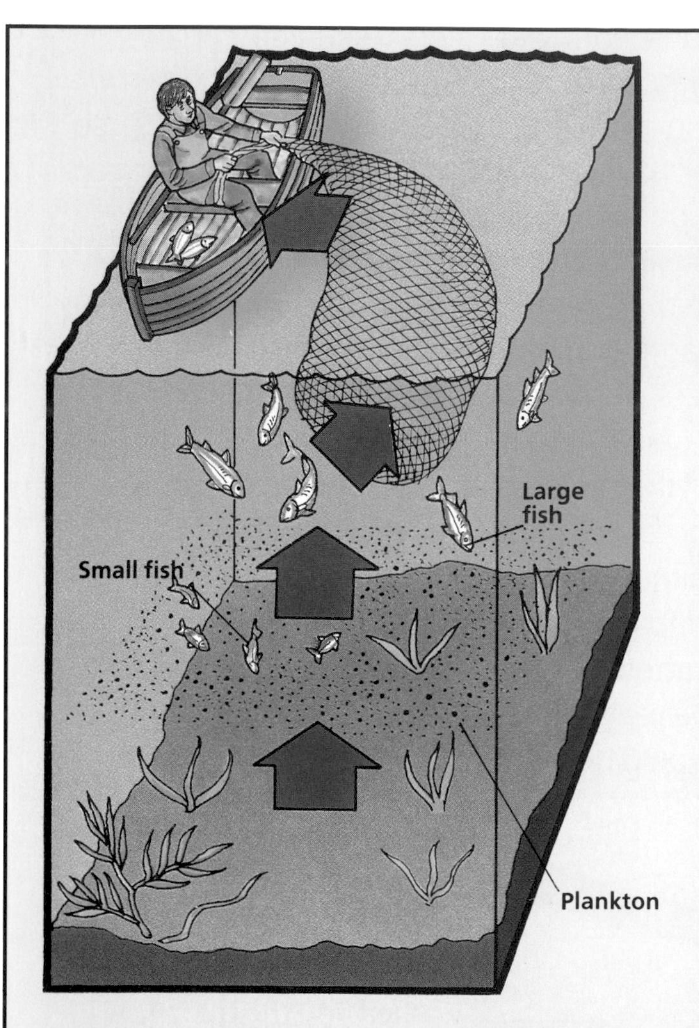

Food chain
The food chain in the sea starts with plant plankton (which live in the surface waters where there is plenty of light), which are eaten by animal plankton. Small fish eat plankton and bigger fish eat the smaller fish. Seabirds and sea mammals feed on all fish. Some pollutants build up in animal and plant tissues. Animals at the top of the food chain eat animals that have pollutants in their bodies and can retain high levels of these pollutants.

Incinerating waste at sea
Waste incineration, burning waste at very high temperatures, has become frequent in recent years. Ocean incineration of PCBs at 2,192°F takes place in the North Sea in ships like the *Vulcanus* (below). Incineration is said to get rid of 99.9999 percent of the PCBs. However, partially-burned chemicals can escape from the incinerator smoke stacks and drift into the sea. These chemicals can be very toxic. Many nations have agreed to cut back or stop some types of ocean incineration in the 1990s.

Natural pollution
Many substances that we introduce to the sea as pollution can also get there naturally. Oil seeps into the sea in many coastal places. Oil is fossilized plant remains made up of chemicals called hydrocarbons. These are usually only harmful in the sea if concentrated in small areas.

Solid waste
Dredgers are ships which scoop up mud from the beds of rivers and seas. Like this one (right) in the Suez Canal, they keep waterways free for shipping. The solid waste they dredge up is often dumped at sea, smothering bottom-dwelling animals.

Politics and pollution
Protecting the seas from pollution depends on countries acting together. Countries around the North Sea and around the Mediterranean have met in recent years to work out ways in which they can clean up the seas which are their responsibility.

Public protests can pressure governments to obey rules decided at international conferences. This Greenpeace demonstration outside the North Sea conference in 1987 protested against ocean dumping of toxic waste.

FACT FILE 2

Beaches
Pollution of all kinds washes up on beaches. Many Mediterranean beaches are affected by oil pollution. One litter collection on a Texas beach found 15,600 six-pack holders in just three hours. One of the most disturbing kinds of ocean litter washed up on beaches is medical waste. In 1988, syringes, blood samples and infectious hospital waste were found on New York and New Jersey beaches (right). They were probably dumped illegally, perhaps by laboratories or health clinics.

Air pollution
Pollution rising into the air from factories and power stations, like those below on the west coast of England, falls to the sea in rain as solid particles or as gases, which dissolve in the surface water of the sea. It is very difficult to determine exactly how much sea pollution comes from the air because oceans are spread out over such a large area. However, scientists believe that the amount is large and contributes to ocean pollution. Around 3,000 tons of mercury a year, for example, are estimated to reach the sea from the burning of fossil fuels, especially coal.

EARTHQUAKES TO VOLCANOES

CHAI

EART

INTRODUCTION

Over a period of a few hundred years, the surface of the earth appears not to change. But during the millions of years of the earth's existence, it has changed many times. Earthquakes and volcanoes alter the face of our planet. But there are also slower, long-term processes at work.

The solid surface of the earth – the crust – consists of gigantic slabs of rock called plates that float on the molten magma beneath. As they move, their edges slowly collide into each other, pushing up mountains and releasing molten rock to form volcanoes. Folding and cracking of the rocks at the surface also change the landscape.

As well as these forces from within the earth, outside factors come into play. Wind, rain and frost erode rocks and break them into fragments, which rivers carry to the sea. The sea itself erodes coastlines as waves pound the shore.

Erosion has worn away soft rocks to leave jagged pinnacles of hard rock.

The earth is a vast globe, 8,000 miles across, spinning on its axis as it orbits around the sun. Seen from space, it looks mostly blue, with patches of white where clouds hide the oceans and land below. But underneath that fairly calm exterior is a boiling hot caldron of molten rock and metal which makes up the inner earth.

FORMATION

The earth was formed about 4.5 billion years ago at the same time as the other planets and the sun. As the earth took shape from spinning masses of gas and dust, the heavier materials sank to the center. Lighter solids, liquid and gas formed a layer around the outside.

Heat from the center of the earth kept the surface a bubbling mass of molten rock for millions of years. Then, about four billion years ago, it began to solidify into a rocky crust dotted with thousands of active volcanoes. Rain poured down while violent thunderstorms raged over the whole planet.

About 1.5 billion years later, blue-green algae began to produce oxygen changing the composition of the atmosphere. The crust settled into enormous plates floating on the fiery material beneath. These are the same moving plates that form the crust today.

▽ A cross-section view of the earth reveals that it is made up of layers, which get thicker toward the solid inner core at its center.

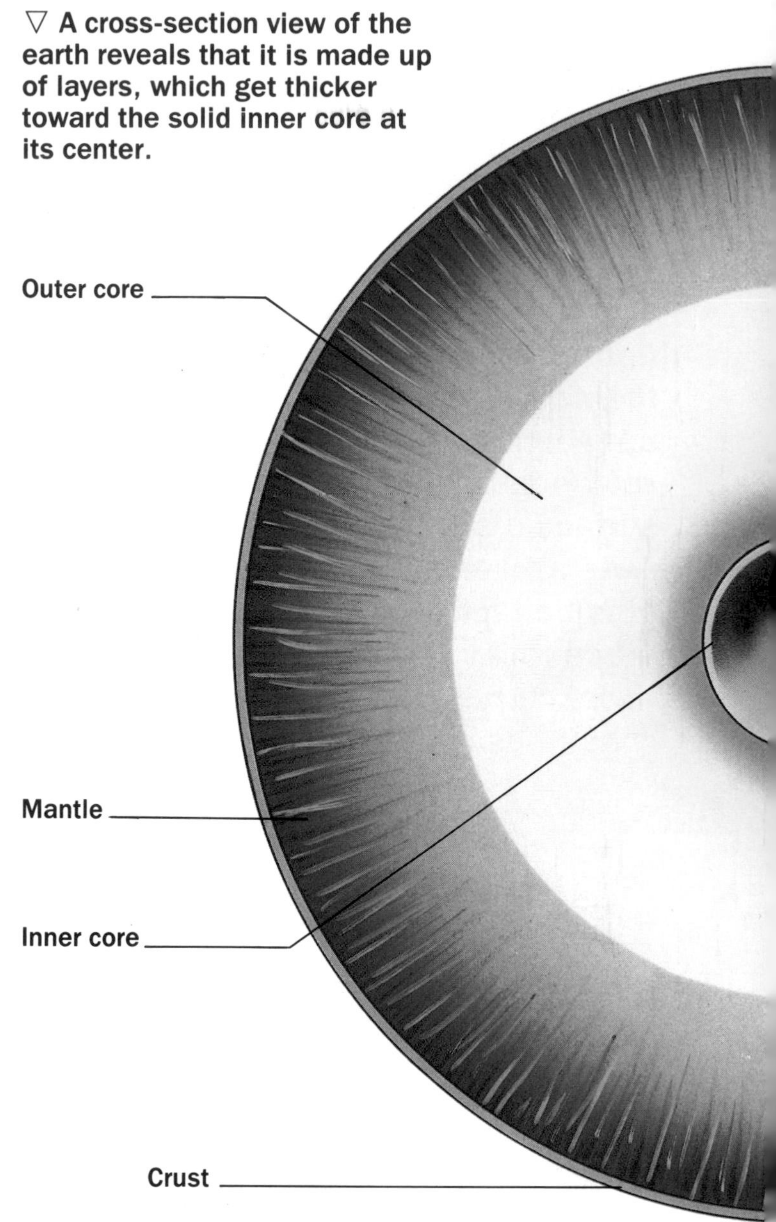

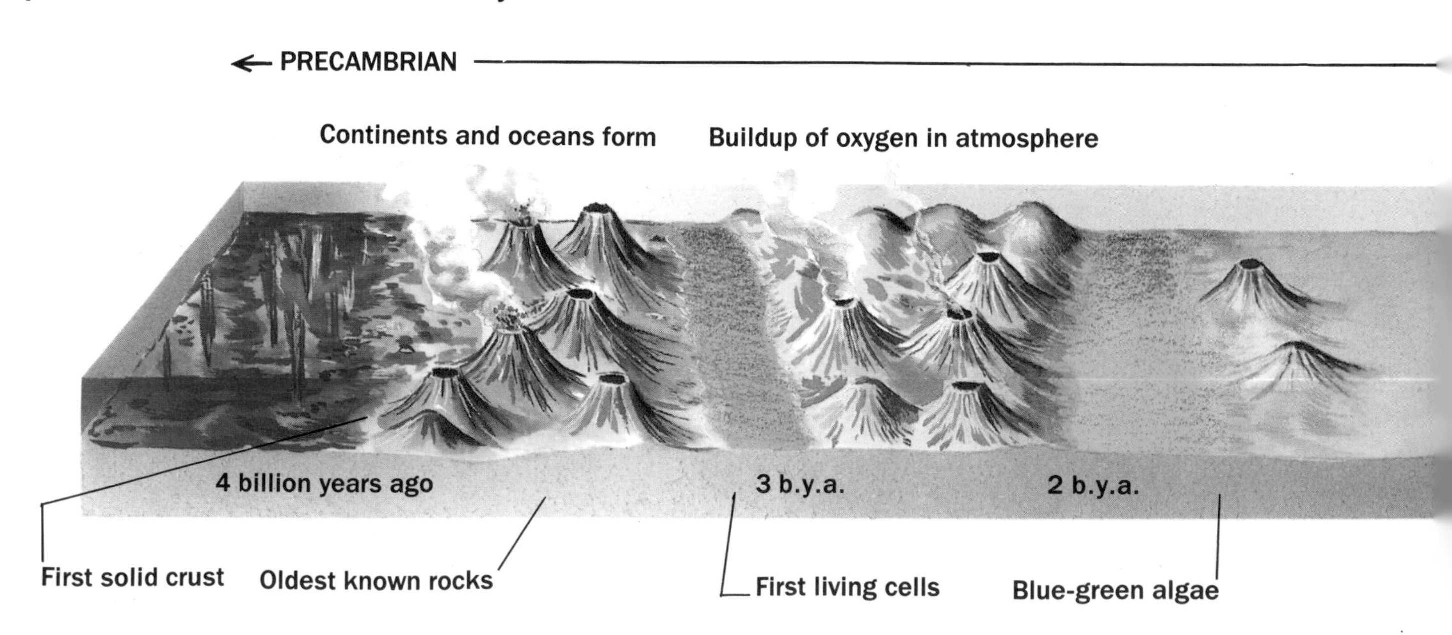

FROM CORE TO SURFACE

The land masses of the earth consist of solid rock. The ocean beds also are made of rock. But the earth is not solid all the way through. The land and the ocean beds form the outer crust, and below this is the solid mantle. Beneath that is a deep liquid layer of molten iron, with a central core of solid iron and nickel.

The earth has a layered structure like an onion, but only the center and the outer crust are hard. About one-third of the crust is dry land. The rest is covered by the oceans. Both on land and on the ocean floors the crust moves. This causes earthquakes and gives rise to volcanoes where liquid magma (molten rock) forces its way to the surface.

△ Much of the earth is covered by water, with the continents resembling giant islands. Above the surface is the atmosphere, which extends upward for over 300 miles before it fades into outer space.

DID YOU KNOW?

The pie chart (below) shows that the most abundant element in the earth's crust is oxygen (46.6 percent by weight). Most of it is combined with the second most abundant element, silicon, in the form of silicate rocks. Aluminum is the most common metal.

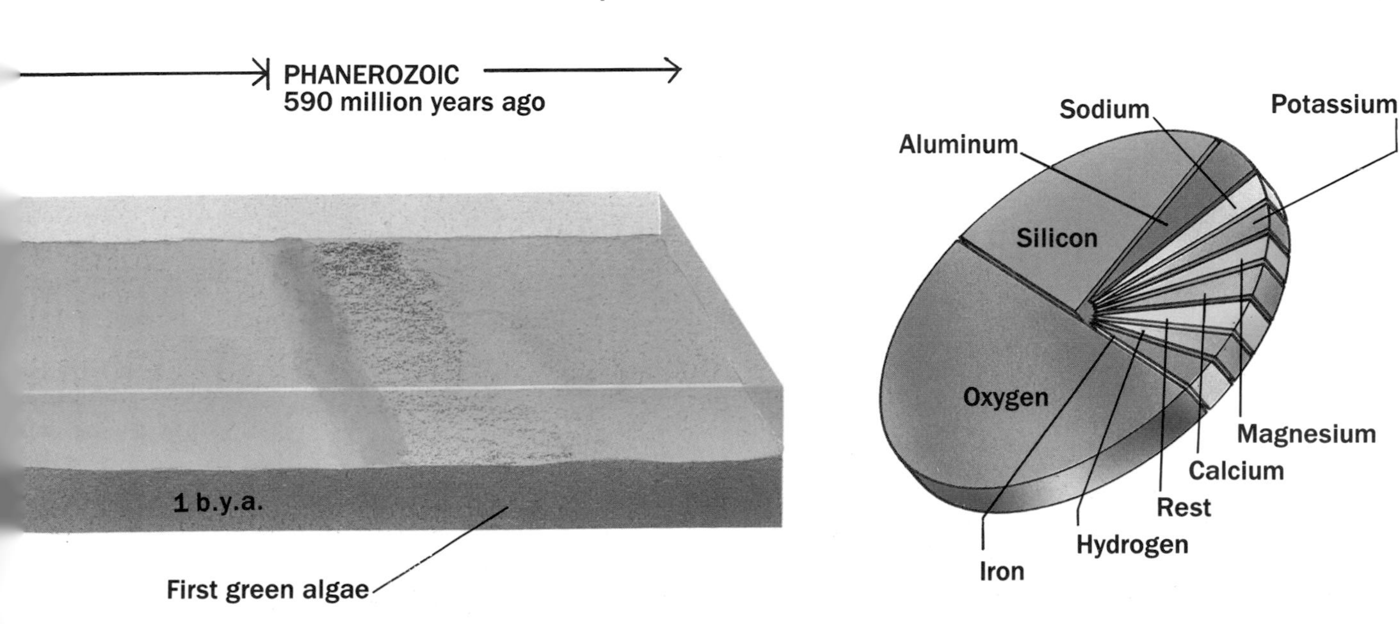

The earth's crust is a rocky skin formed of huge interlocking plates, which are about 25 miles thick in areas occupied by the continents. But beneath the oceans the crust is only about 5 miles thick. The crust is constantly changing, as currents of molten material deep in the earth keep these plates on the move.

DRIFTING CONTINENTS

Each of the continents is anchored to one or more of the earth's crustal plates (see map opposite). The continents have not always been in their present position. About 200 million years ago they were grouped together into a single super-continent called Pangaea. But as molten material from inside the earth forced its way up between the plates, new crust was formed and the plates began to move apart, breaking up Pangaea into the continents we know today.

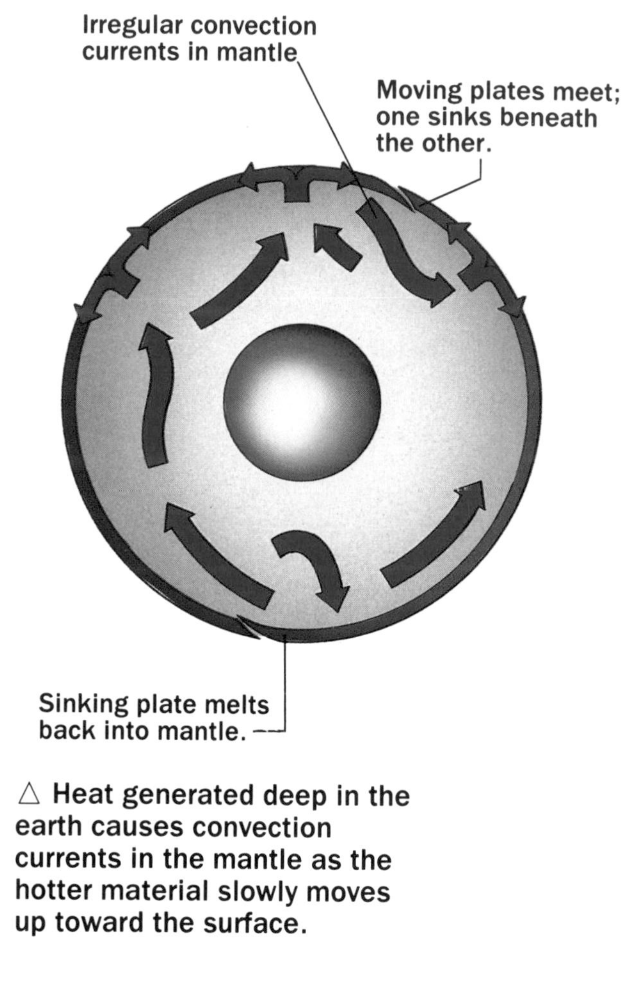

△ Heat generated deep in the earth causes convection currents in the mantle as the hotter material slowly moves up toward the surface.

200 million years ago

100 million years ago

50 million years ago

▷ The continents are still moving today. North America and Europe, for example, are slowly moving apart, so that the Atlantic Ocean is getting wider by about an inch every year.

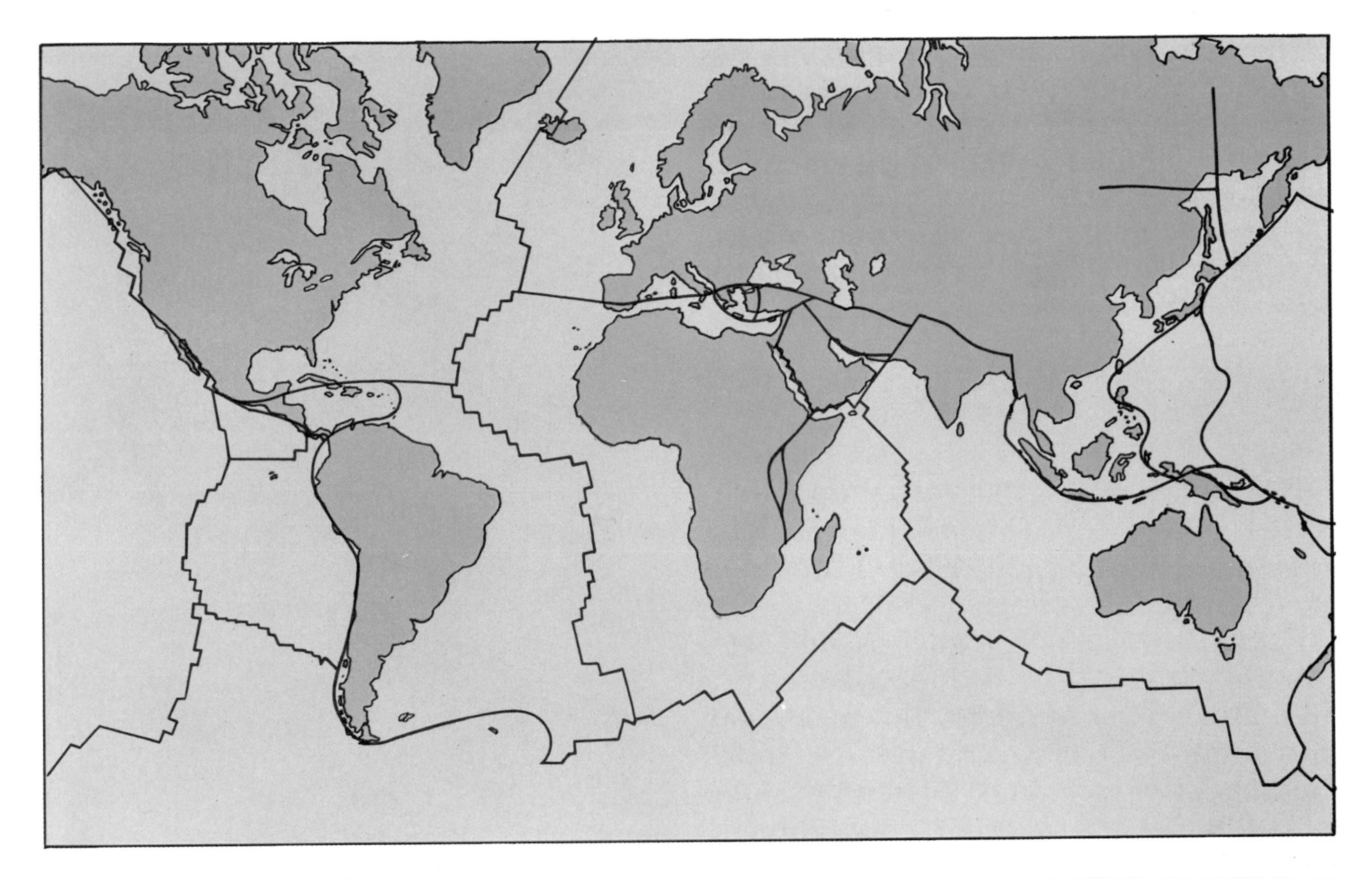

△ The map of the world shows the boundaries between the main crustal plates. Volcanoes, earthquakes and mountain ranges are characteristic features along these boundaries.

PLATES IN MOTION

Sometimes at the edges of moving plates violent and spectacular phenomena occur. Plates push against one another with enough force to throw up great mountain chains. The tremendous pressure in the mantle squeezes molten material upward between the plates to form volcanoes. Plates under great tension may rupture and snap into a new position causing devastating earthquakes.

Present day

DID YOU KNOW?

The rocks that make up the earth's crust are made of crystals. Some, such as quartz and sand, are obviously crystalline. Others only reveal their crystal structure when polished, sliced thinly and viewed with the aid of a powerful microscope (left).

Earthquakes are among the most destructive and terrifying of natural events. They vary in strength from minor tremors to violent vibrations that topple buildings and open up huge cracks in the ground. Fortunately, most take place beneath the sea, although even then they may cause tidal waves that can reach the coastline.

△ Loss of lives, wrecked buildings and cracked roads followed a devastating earthquake in Mexico City in 1985.

WHY THEY HAPPEN

Earthquakes will arise at plate boundaries where two plates are pushing against each other under the pressure of continental drift (see page 8).

Rocks have elastic qualities and they can absorb this pressure for hundreds or even thousands of years. But eventually the strain is too great and the rocks rupture and jerk into a new position releasing all the pent-up energy in the form of an earthquake.

Vibrations spread out from the center or "focus" of the earthquake causing the ground to shudder violently. The point on the surface immediately above the focus is called the epicenter. Here the earthquake is most severe and damaging.

1. Plates try to slide against each other

2. Stress builds in stretching rocks

Epicenter

Vibrations

3. Rock snaps into place, causing earthquake

△ Most earthquakes on land are caused by movements of crustal plates as they become stressed and then suddenly move into a new position.

MEASURING EARTHQUAKES

The strength of an earthquake can be measured by instruments called seismographs. Most have pens that trace wavy lines on a chart as a recording of the event, and these tracings are called seismograms. These instruments have a very heavy weight which, although suspended like a pendulum, tends to stay still while the rest of the device is moved rapidly by earth tremors.

The effects of an earthquake in a particular place are described by the Mercalli scale, which ranges from I to XII. The Richter scale, a logarithmic scale which has a maximum of nine, measures an earthquake's strength at its focus.

△ Earthquake tremors are caused by shock waves traveling rapidly through the ground. A seismograph mirrors these tremors as a series of wavy lines on a chart.

MAKE A MODEL OF AN EARTHQUAKE

To model the sideways movement of rocks that causes most earthquakes, you will need two rectangular blocks of wood and a sheet of paper. Put the blocks side by side and glue the paper to them, being careful not to let glue get in between the blocks. Now stand some thumbtacks upside down on the paper. Finally imitate the forces of plate movement by pushing on the ends of the blocks in opposite directions. At first the paper will resist your pushing, but then it will suddenly tear, splitting apart the blocks and toppling the tacks.

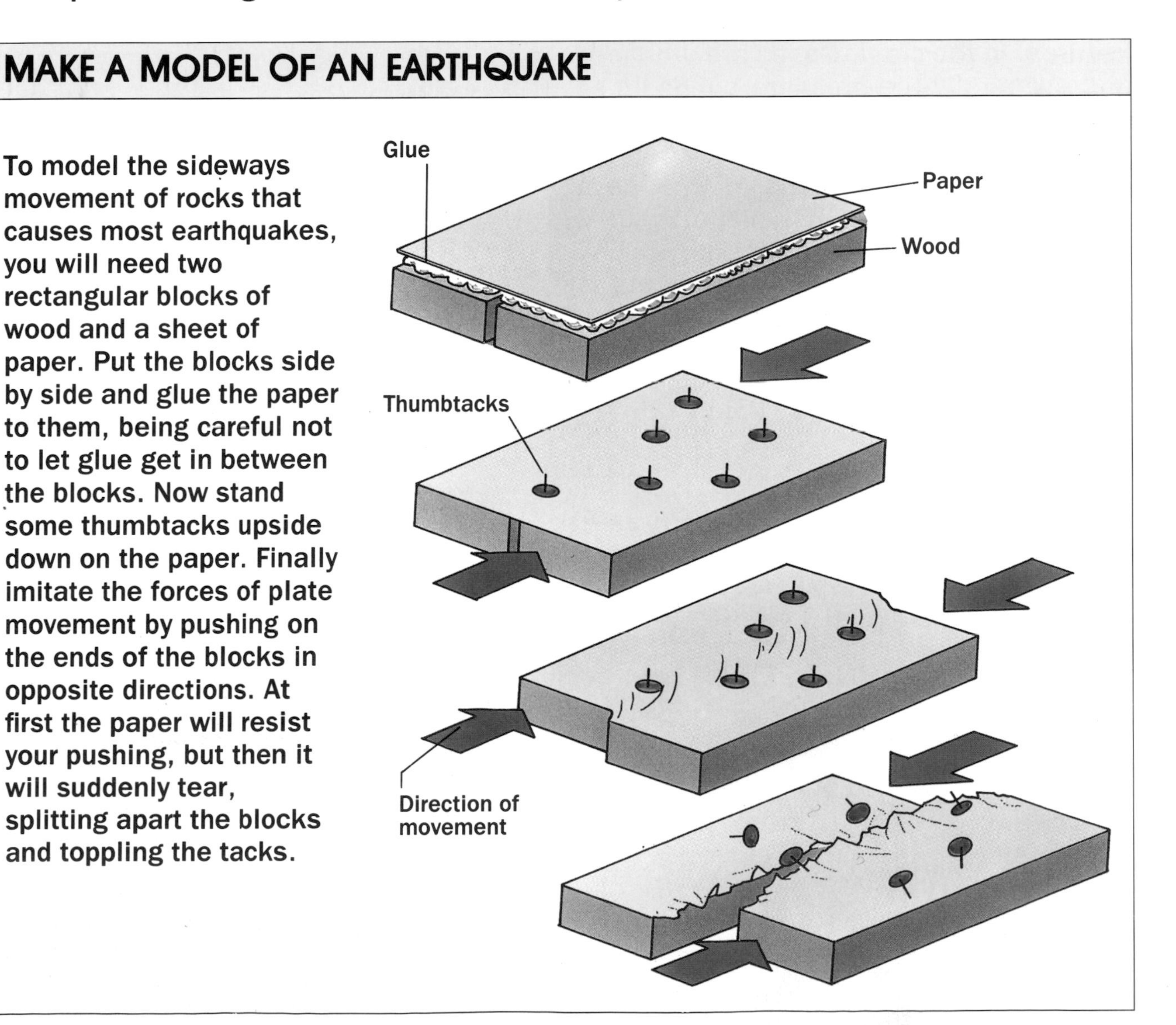

A volcano forms when a hole or crack in the earth's crust lets magma force its way through. On land, ash and smoke may first explode into the air. Then magma, called lava above the surface, oozes out of the volcano. Undersea volcanoes cause great clouds of steam to bubble to the surface.

VOLCANO CREATION

Underneath a volcano there is a cavity of molten rock called a magma chamber within the mantle. It forms below a weak point in the crust, possibly below a midocean ridge where crustal plates are moving apart. The magma is under pressure and less dense than the mantle so it gradually rises, often up cracks, or fissures, in the crust. Gases are produced and eventually the pressure builds up so much that they blast a way to the surface.

At this stage, the volcano belches out gases, dust and fragments of rock. Lava flowing from a crack in a plane forms a lava plateau. Lava that piles up around the opening (called a vent) forms a typical cone-shaped mountain.

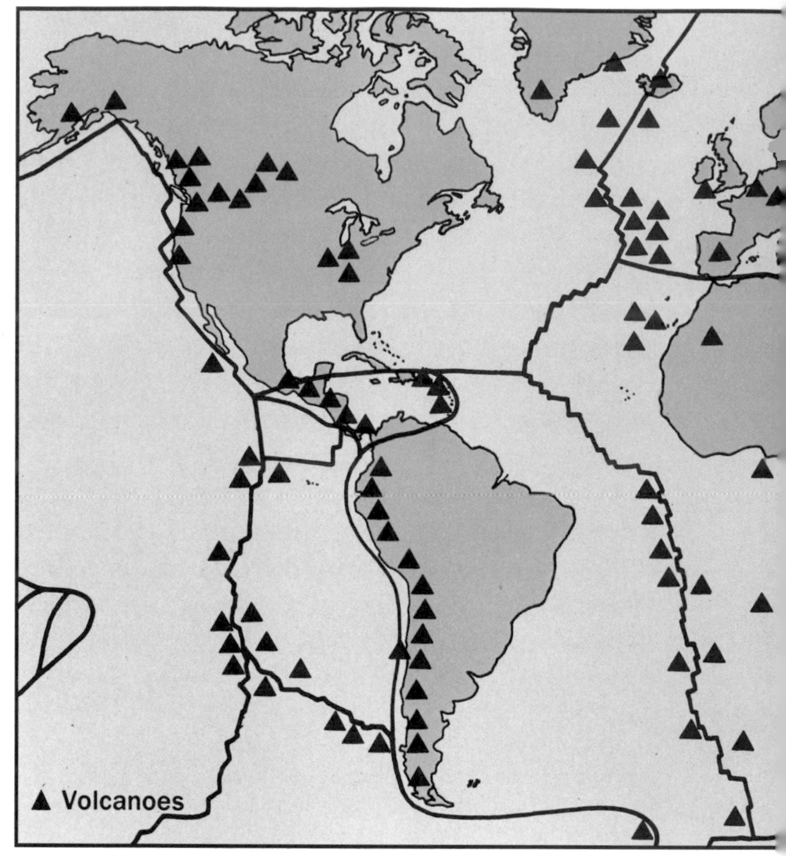

△ There are more than 2,000 volcanoes under the sea. Most land volcanoes are in mountain chains, such as the South American Andes.

▽ Many volcanoes take the form of cone-shaped mountains. If the vent becomes blocked, the volcano may erupt with explosive violence.

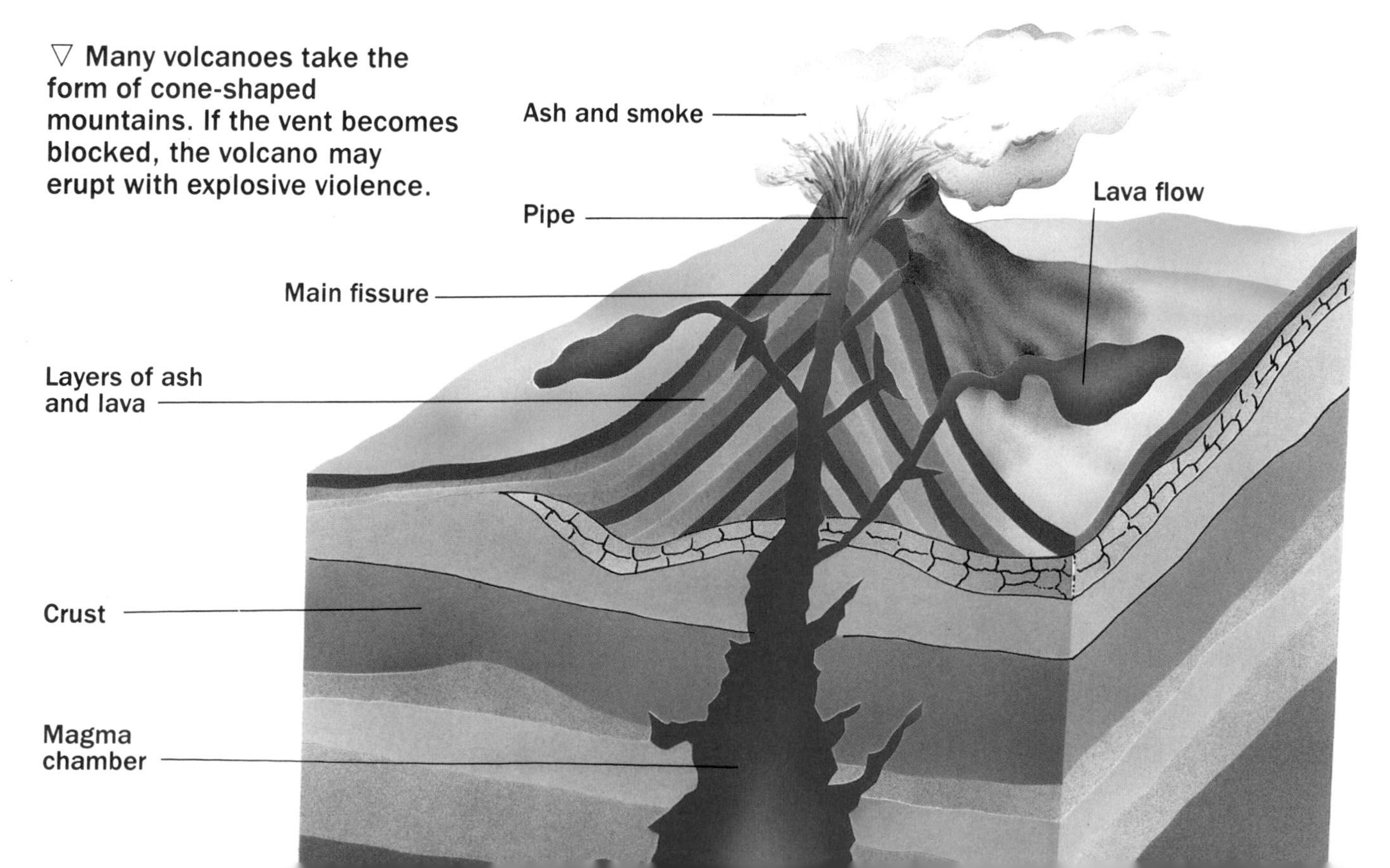

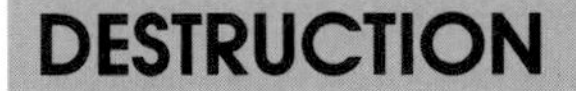

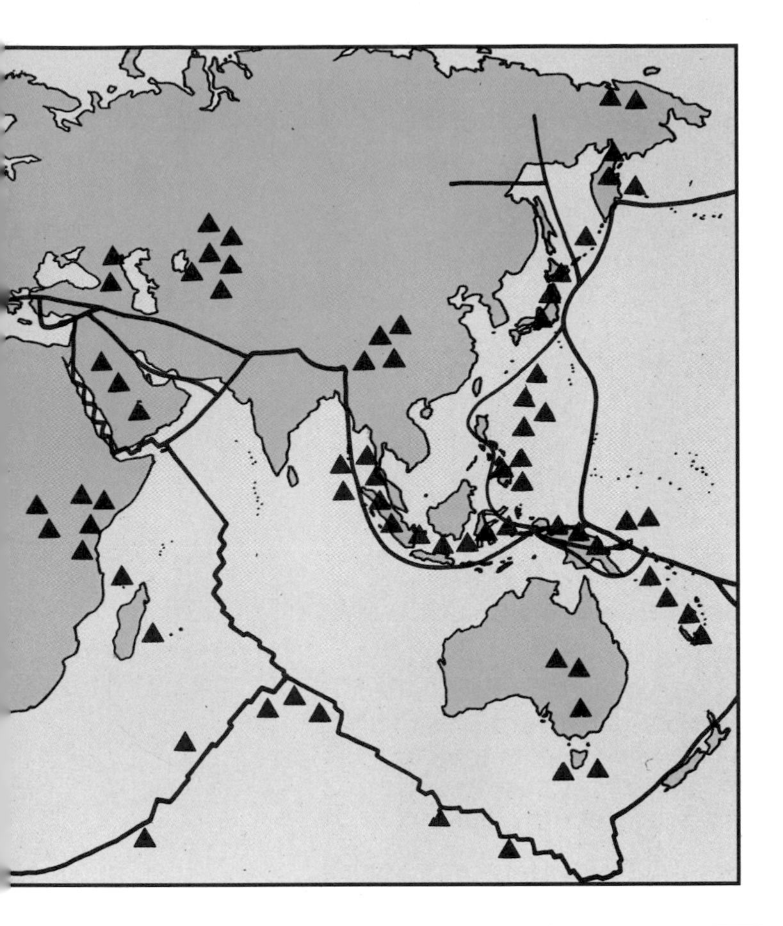

WHERE THEY ARE FOUND

Over half the world's volcanoes arise in a belt around the Pacific Ocean called the Ring of Fire. Here plate edges overlap and are dragged back into the mantle. The old crust melts and immense pressure can force magma back to the surface. Along midocean ridges the crust is thin and weak and magma rises to form a line of volcanoes.

DESTRUCTION

An unexpected, sudden volcanic eruption can shower the surrounding area with burning hot ash and cinders. Such an eruption of Vesuvius in Italy wiped out the Roman city of Pompeii in AD 79. A much more recent disaster occurred on May 18, 1980 when a whole side of Mount St. Helens, a volcano in the state of Washington, was blasted away. A white-hot cloud of gas and powdered magma smothered everything within 5 miles of the mountain. The explosion was estimated to equal the power of 500 atomic bombs. Another danger from volcanoes is fire. This is caused by molten rock hurled into the air or lava flows down hillsides setting fire to things.

▽ Thousands of sparks and lumps of molten rock hurled high in the air create a huge fireworks display as a volcano bursts into life.

▽ Layers of ash welded with solidified lava shape the mouth and sides of the vent.

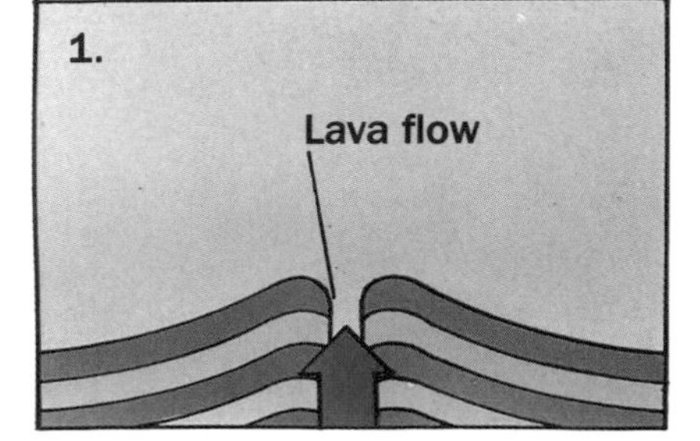

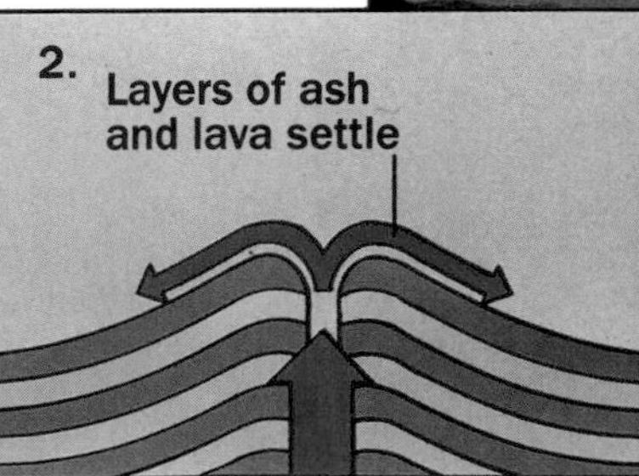

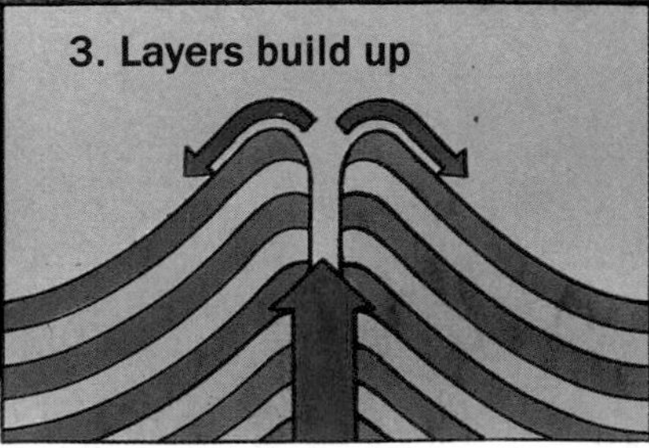

The earth's crust is made of rocks, and the rocks are made up of minerals, which are chemicals formed in the earth. There are three types of rock: igneous rock, metamorphic rock, and sedimentary rock. Each type contains characteristic minerals. Rocks are being created and destroyed all the time in the "rock cycle".

△ These mountains are made of granite, a hard igneous rock formed when molten magma from the earth's mantle cooled to form part of the crust.

IGNEOUS ROCKS

Igneous rocks are formed when molten magma from deep within the earth cools and solidifies to form the crust. When magma is forced through the vent of a volcano as lava, it also solidifies to rock as it rapidly cools. Igneous rock is classified by its silica content. Those rich in silica, such as granite, are light in color and are called "acidic" rocks. "Basic" rocks, low in silica, are dark in color.

Granite tor
(Igneous)

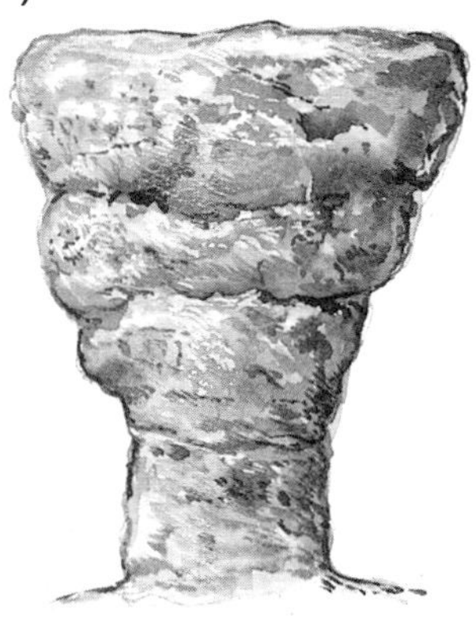

1.
Igneous rock forms as lava is deposited and cools around the volcano.

2.
Rocks are also brought to the surface by the movement of the earth's crust.

3. Metamorphic rock is formed from igneous and sedimentary rocks under heat and pressure deep in the earth's crust.

The rock cycle
▷ Different types of rock are formed from existing ones in a continual process known as the rock cycle.

METAMORPHIC ROCKS

Metamorphic rocks are formed when conditions within or on the surface of the earth change other rocks. Deep underground, heat and pressure can alter minerals in rocks, for example changing the sedimentary rock limestone into its crystalline metamorphic counterpart, marble. Pressure under mountains produces layered rocks such as slate which cleave into thin plates if damaged.

SEDIMENTARY ROCKS

At the earth's surface, wind and rain cause erosion. Rocks are broken down into small grains which are washed away by rivers to form sediments. As layers of sediment build up, those underneath are squeezed and the pressure turns them into sedimentary rocks. Limestone and sandstone are typical sedimentary rocks. Earth movements or erosion may expose them at the surface.

Marble

Claystone, a sedimentary rock, metamorphoses into slate.

4. Sedimentary, metamorphic and igneous rocks are eroded by weather and carried down by river.

Ocean plate descends into mantle and changes to magma.

5. Sedimentary rocks eventually form due to pressure from continuous layers of sediment.

DID YOU KNOW?

The remains of dead animals may be buried in the sediments that later turn to sedimentary rock. When they do, the hard parts (such as bones and shells) may be replaced by rock-forming minerals and become fossils. Leaves, pollen grains, and even dinosaur eggs also form fossils.

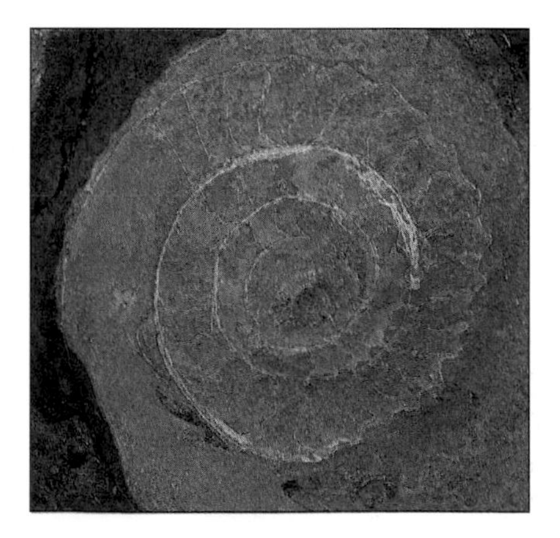

Sedimentary rocks are laid down originally in horizontal layers, or strata. But the pressure of crustal plate movements may push the layers and bend them into folds. Alternatively, the rocks crack under the pressure, and breaks, called faults, appear. The results are hills, mountains, valleys, and gorges.

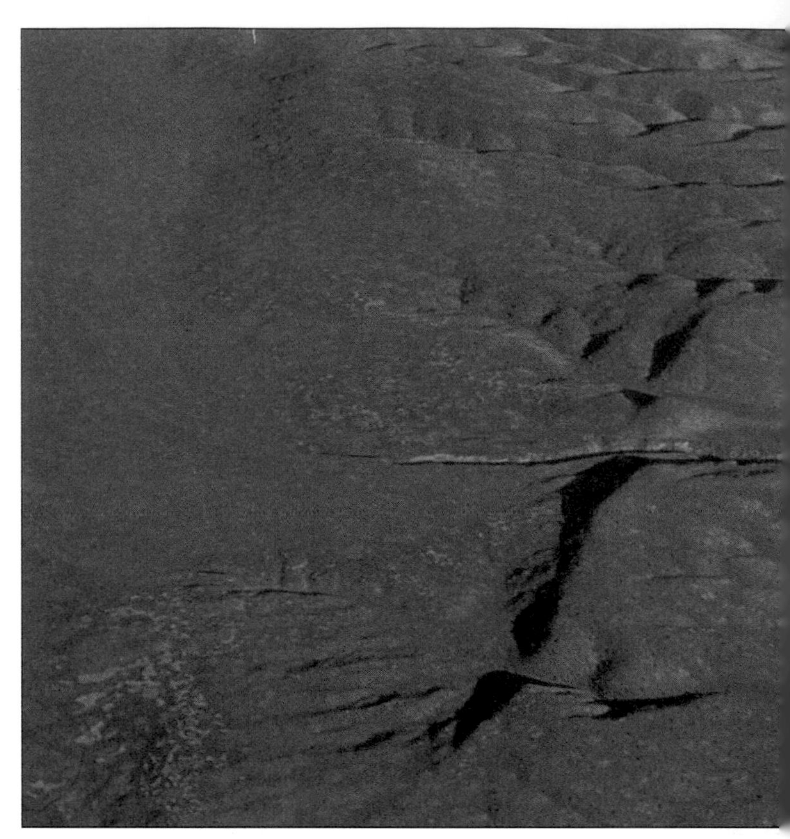

△ The San Andreas Fault in California (ridge running top to bottom in picture) is subject to sideways movements causing earthquakes, like the devastating San Francisco quake in 1989.

COLLIDING PLATES

Most folds are caused by movements of the huge plates that form the earth's crust (see page 211). If the resulting sideways movement is small, a range of gently rolling hills may be formed. Large movements push the strata into loops (called anticlines) and troughs (synclines). These may form high mountains and deep valleys. Then over thousands of years, wind and rain erode the mountains, exposing the tilted strata which appears as bands of rock.

Folding also occurs when a plug of igneous rock or crystalline salt is forced upward from below. The overlying layers of sedimentary rock are pushed up and arched into a dome. Often the strain on the rocks at the roof of the dome cracks them into faults. The plug may even break through at the top of the dome. Salt-plugs are important because they may trap natural gas and oil when they are below impermeable rocks.

▽ When one of the earth's huge plates slides below a continental one (1), the edge of the upper plate folds (2). This is one of the chief ways that mountains are formed.

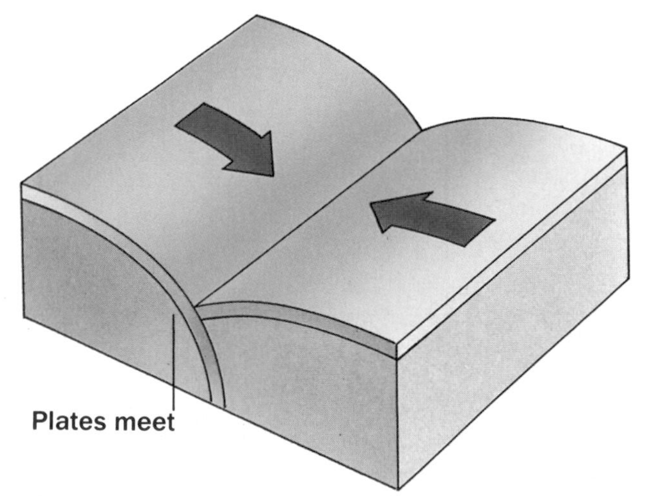

1.

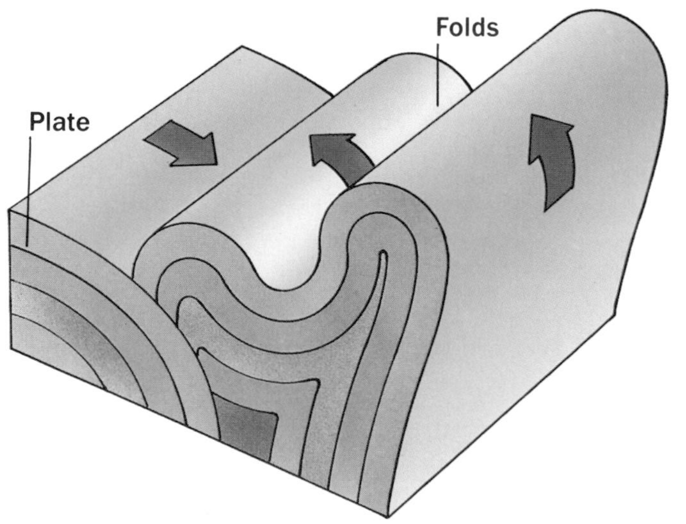

2.

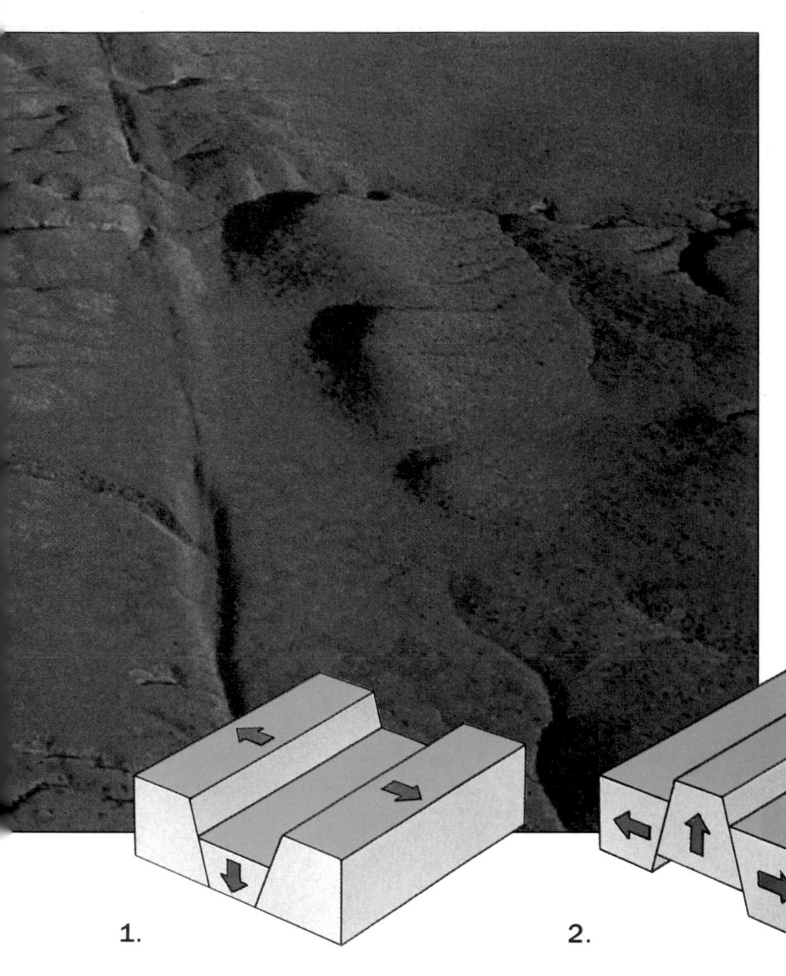

CRACKING ROCKS

When regions of rock are pulled apart or pushed together, a block of rock between them may fall between what are called normal faults. If the angle of the fault is very shallow, one block may rise over the next in a reverse fault.

Sideways movements of large blocks of rock cause a transcurrent fault, which can cause earthquakes (see page 208).

▽ A falling block (1) forms a valley. Rising pressure (2) can form hills. Sideways shifts (3) can cause earthquakes.

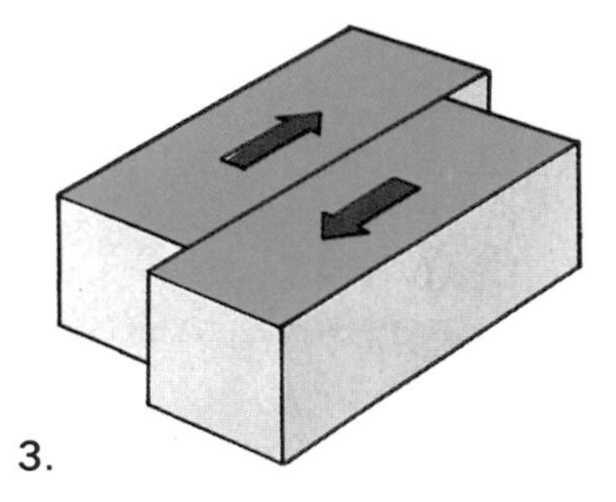

1. 2. 3.

HOW FAULTS WORK

Take three pieces of thick cardboard. Cut two of the pieces at an angle of 45 degrees. Cut the other piece into a flat-topped triangle. You can see the shapes this will make in the drawing. Put the pieces of cardboard onto a flat table. In turn, try the three experiments shown in the diagram, each time pushing the two outer pieces of cardboard toward each other. The outer pieces represent moving crustal plates. You can see what happens when there are different faults arrangements .

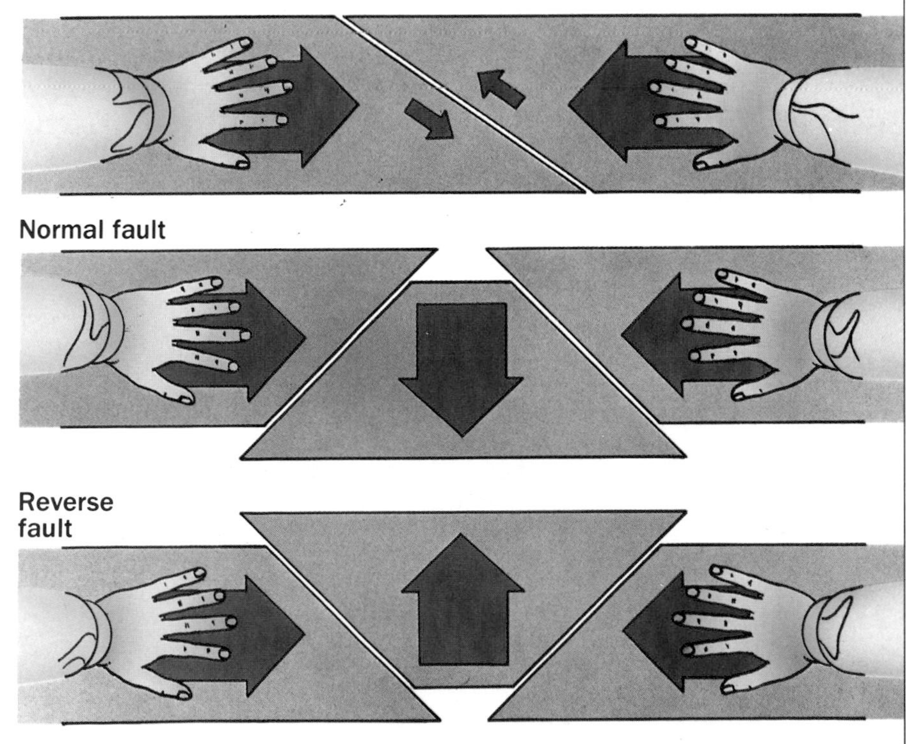

Mountains are chiefly formed by folds and faults (see pages 214-215). The action is particularly violent when two crustal plates collide and the edge of one is crumpled into chains of fold mountains. Faulting can give rise to block mountains, and pressure from rising magma can push up dome mountains.

△ The Himalayas, a range of fold mountains that extend along the northern part of the Indian subcontinent, include Mount Everest (29,029 feet), the world's highest peak.

FOLD MOUNTAINS

At the edge of a continent where two plates meet, the continental plate rises over the denser oceanic plate. The relentless pressure on the plates causes the continental plate to buckle, throwing up a mountain range. It also scrapes off the sediment from the oceanic crust, folding it into more mountains. This process formed the Andes in South America.

When two continental plates collide, one does not rise above the other. The edges continue to push into one another and the tremendous force buckles the two plates and folds them into huge mountain ranges. Examples of this include the Himalayas in Asia and the Alps in Europe. These two mountain ranges are relatively young and continue to rise even today.

Rock becomes folded under pressure

Plate

◁ When fold mountains are first formed, they are usually tall and jagged. Later they may become rounded by erosion.

BLOCK MOUNTAINS

The tallest mountain in Africa is Mount Kilimanjaro. Although it lies close to the Equator, it is so tall (the larger of its twin peaks towers 19,341 feet above the surrounding plane) that its top is permanently covered in snow more than 200 feet deep. It is an extinct volcano, one of a chain of block mountains that form the eastern rim of the Great Rift Valley. They were formed when the block that forms the valley floor sank because of extensive faults.

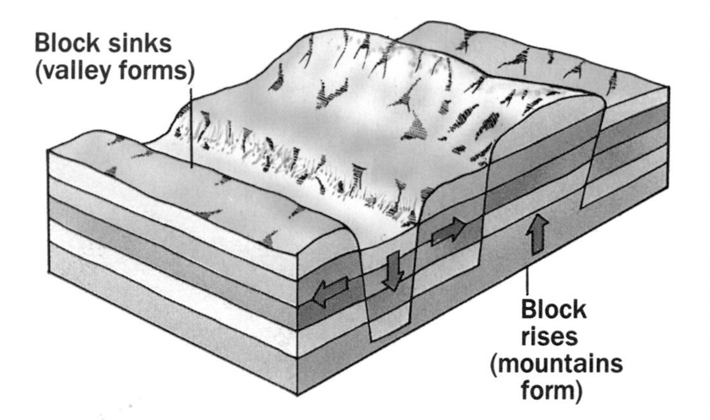

△ Block mountains form alongside a rift valley, and may be pushed higher by the pressure of magma beneath.

△ The Great Rift Valley extends for much of the length of eastern Africa, formed when blocks of rock sank between faults.

DOME MOUNTAINS

Sometimes a great mass of magma beneath the earth's crust gathers to form a magma chamber. As the chamber grows it exerts great pressure on the layers of rock above it. These layers are pushed up into great arcs of rock. The result is one or more dome mountains, such as the Black Hills in South Dakota, United States. The existing Black Hills, up to 3,940 feet tall, are stubs of hard rock that were left when their softer outer layers were eroded away.

▽ Dome mountains, formed by pressure from below, begin as rounded hills, but can be shaped by wind and weather.

Magma pushes up rock

▽ Erosion has stripped away the softer rocks of the Black Hills of Dakota, leaving scores of rounded dome mountains.

Major earth movements give the landscape its basic form. But it is then shaped by various kinds of erosion, mainly the action of wind, water, and ice, and the sea. Wind erosion has its greatest effect in dry regions, particularly deserts, where windblown sand carves rocks into strange shapes.

△ The features of this desert landscape have been caused by the wind as it carries along sand that carves the rocks into fantastic shapes like these mesas (flat-topped hills) and buttes (narrow columns).

DESERT LANDSCAPES

In hot, sandy deserts, a steady wind blows the sand into parallel lines of transverse dunes, which resemble sea waves that have been frozen to show their shape. If the wind is turbulent, it blows the sand into seif dunes and into crescent-shaped barchans as shown below.

The wind also makes coarse grains of sand and particles of soil bounce along within a foot of the ground. When these fast-moving particles hit a pillar of rock, they erode it away near the ground to shape it into a top-heavy feature known as a pedestal.

Small boulders on the ground are worn smooth on the side facing the prevailing wind. If they overbalance a different side is sand-blasted, and then another one, until eventually they form structures known as dreikanters. Larger rock formations are carved into rounded outcrops called inselbergs.

▷ The shapes of sand dunes depend on the direction of the wind and whether it is steady or turbulent. Windblown sand also erodes the rocks into distinctive shapes.

Sand-blasted rocks
Pedestal
Seif dunes
Transverse dunes
Wind direction
Barchan

DID YOU KNOW?

Sandblasting is an industrial process that uses jets of high-pressure air to blow sand for cleaning metal components and buildings. It is similar in action to the natural processes that erode rocks in dry desert lands.

HOW TO FORM A DESERT LANDSCAPE

You can imitate the action of wind erosion and make your own desert land-scape. First take a shallow box or tray and stick in place some pillars made from cylinders of modeling clay (1). Next sprinkle sand into the box until the pillars are covered (2). Then, with the tray on sheets of newspaper, use a hair drier to act as the wind (3). Carefully blow away the sand and watch it form dunes and gradually reveal the buried pillars.

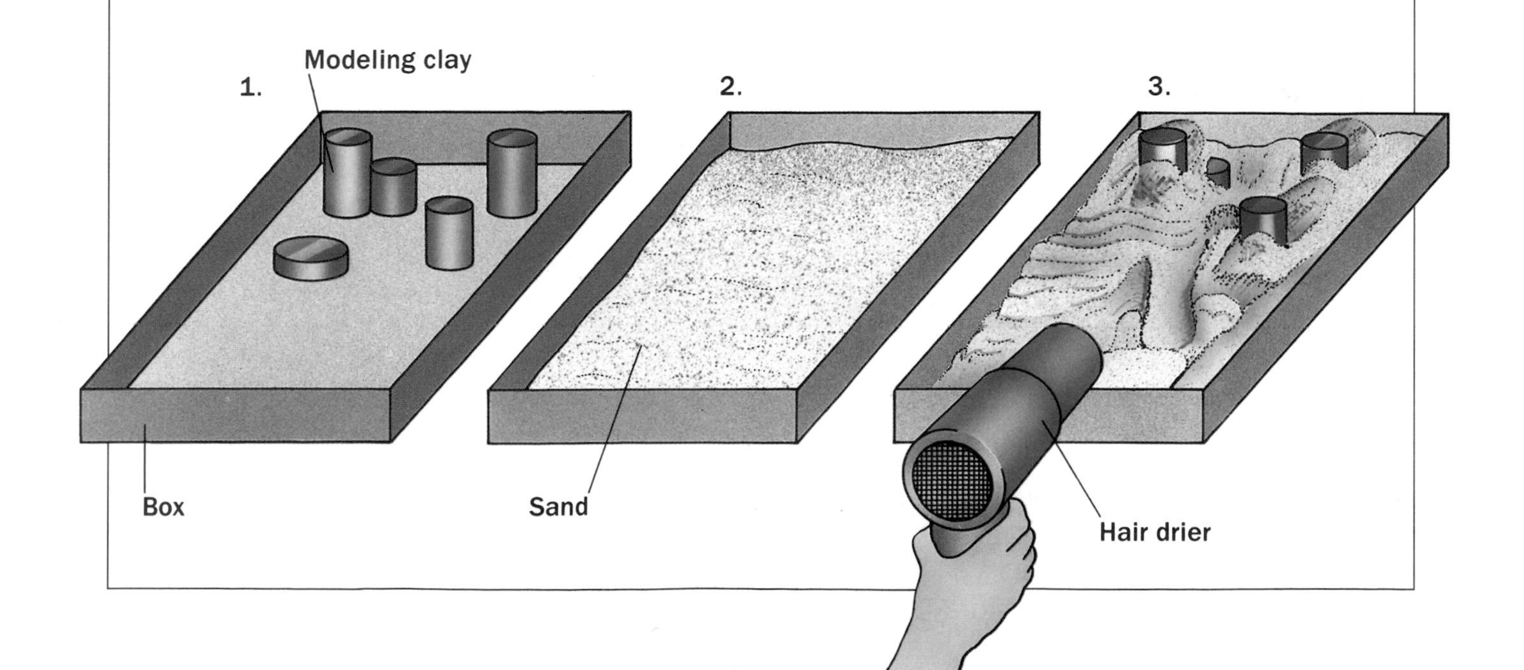

One of the features of a landscape that changes most quickly is the shoreline. Even the hardest rocks cannot withstand the ceaseless pounding of the waves as wind and current drive them onto the shore. Cliffs crumble or become eroded into stacks, caves and caverns. Sandy beaches may be washed away.

△ Waves often erode chalk cliffs into strange shapes. A stack or pillar can be cut off a headland, or an arch formed where a cave is parted from the main cliff.

COASTAL FEATURES

Few coastlines are straight when first formed. Most have inlets and bays separated by headlands that jut out into the sea. But then the waves get to work.

As the wind blows waves toward a headland, they swing around and hit it on the sides. This has the effect of gradually wearing away the headland. Sometimes a stack or an arch of rock is left where the sea breaks through a narrow headland. Often caves are gouged out in the cliffs, particularly if they are made of a soft rock such as chalk.

But even cliffs are not permanent. The pounding of the waves, often carrying rock particles of many sizes in the swirling water, cuts a notch on the waterline at the base of the cliff. Eventually the rock above the notch splits away and tumbles into the sea. Buildings on badly eroded coastal cliffs, may also fall as the cliffs are gradually eaten away. Cliffs might erode by as much as seven feet every year.

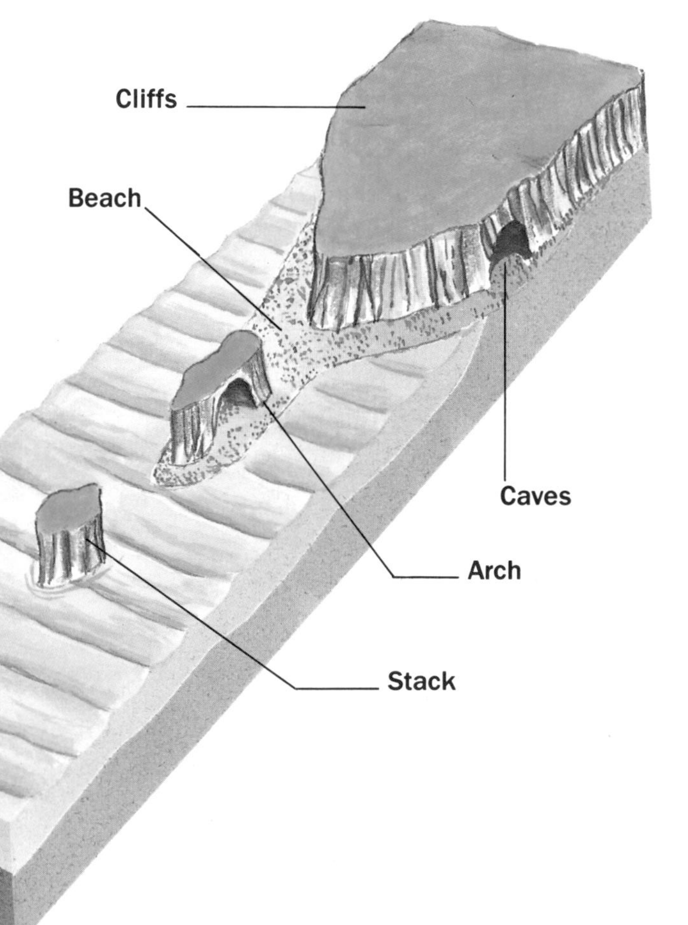

▷ Caves are formed in cliffs where the sea pounds against them. A powerful Atlantic wave exerts a force of about ten tons per square yard and may carry shingle and pebbles that batter the cliff.

DID YOU KNOW?

The relentless pounding of the sea can reduce rocky cliffs into sandy beaches. The waves continually batter the coastline slowly eroding the cliffs. The rocks chip and crumble into the sea where they are constantly hurled against each other and worn down until they become small, smooth pebbles and eventually sand.

MAKE YOUR OWN COASTLINE

Stick some cylindrical blocks of modeling clay in one half of a deep plastic tray, and cover them with sand as in the diagram. Carefully pour water into the other half of the tray. Now use a piece of plastic or stiff cardboard to make waves, and see how your coastline is gradually eroded away.

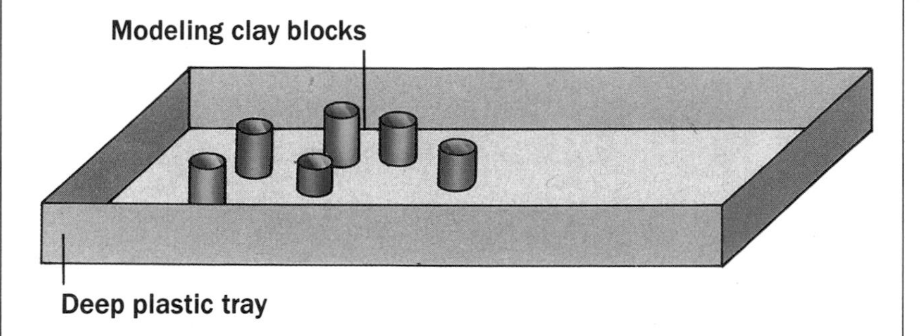

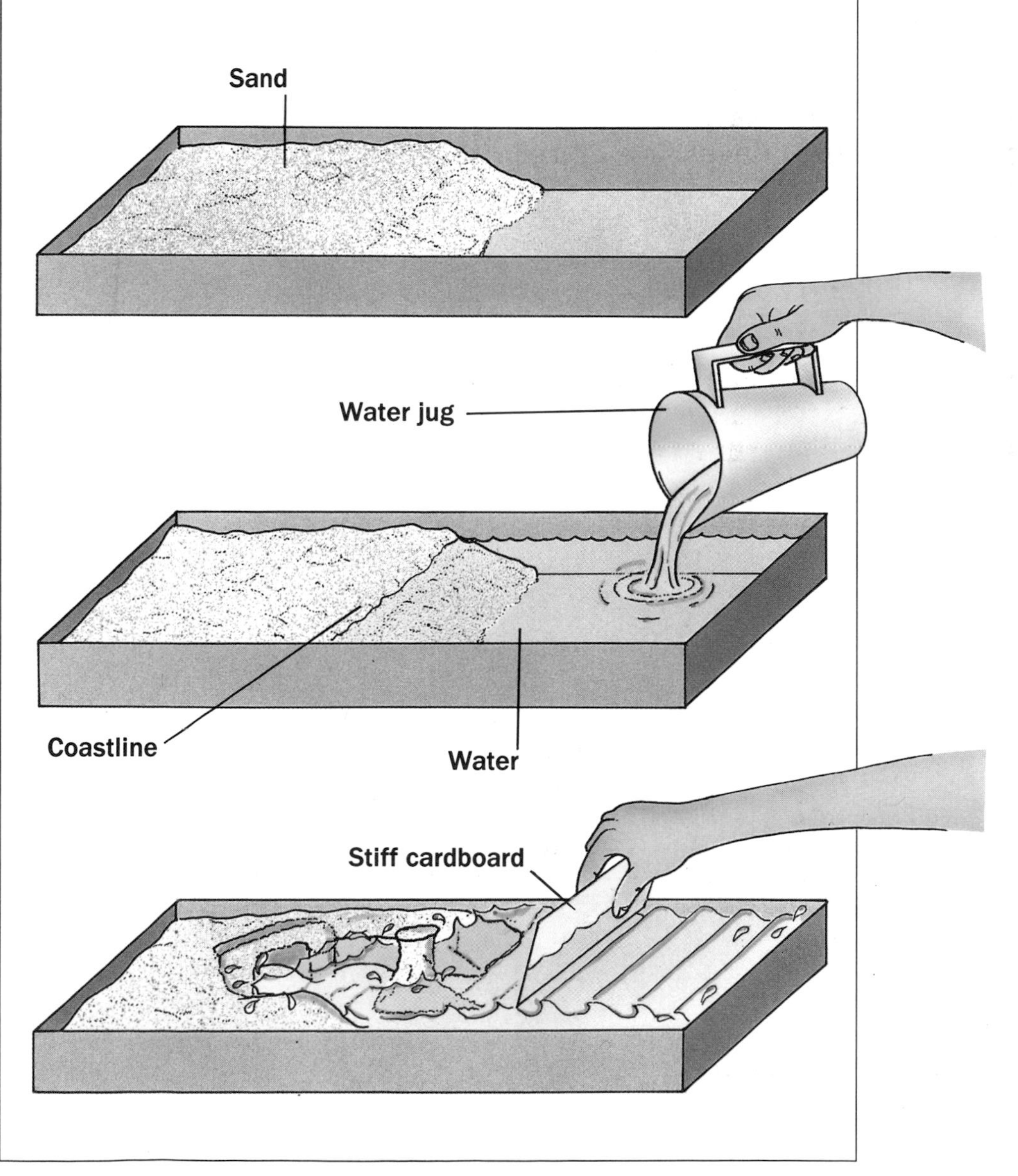

Earth movements and surface erosion are not the only forces that shape the landscape. Some forms of erosion alter regions hidden underground. Occasionally, meteorites from outer space crash onto the earth and form large craters. And human activities such as mining also shape the land.

UNDERGROUND EROSION

When rainwater dissolves carbon dioxide from the air it forms carbonic acid which attacks limestone. It carves out surface gullies and gouges out caves where streams flow through the limestone underground. The process takes thousands of years. Water that seeps through limestone contains dissolved calcium carbonate. As the water drips from the roof of a cave, the calcium carbonate comes out of solution and forms rocky stalactites that hang like icicles from the roof and stalagmites that stand like small spires beneath.

△ The rocky spikes hanging from the cave roof are stalactites. The upward-pointing ones are stalagmites. Both were formed from dripping water containing calcium carbonate.

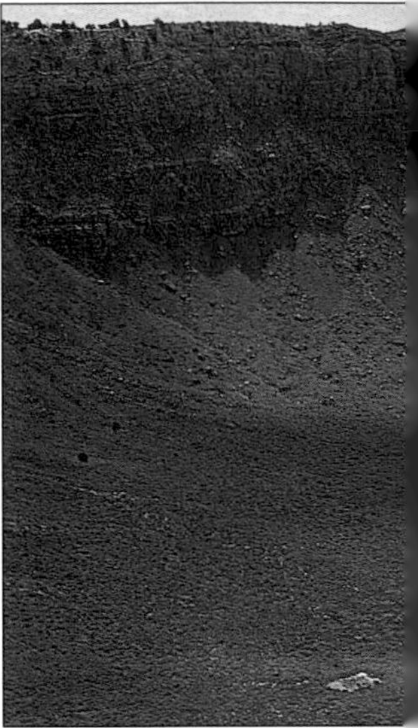

▷ This meteorite crater in Arizona, is about one mile across and more than 558 feet deep.

Stream disappears underground

Eroded gullies in limestone

Stalactite

Stalagmite

Cave carved by earlier stream

Rock impermeable to water

△ Underground streams carve their way through limestone rock forming potholes, caves and sometimes huge caverns.

METEORITE CRATERS

Meteors are collections of rocky or metallic particles often mixed with ice that orbit the sun. If the earth passes through their orbit, they may enter the earth's atmosphere and burn up as shooting stars. Very rarely a large meteor does not burn up completely, but crashes to the ground as a meteorite. The impact can cause a huge explosion and leave a giant crater. In forested areas, it can flatten all the trees for many miles around.

HUMAN INFLUENCE

There are various ways that human activities can change the landscape – usually for the worse. Large strip mines for bauxite, coal and copper can carve away whole mountains. Chopping down rainforests can lead to rapid erosion as the soil is washed away, leaving a rocky wasteland. In dry areas, the removal of shrubs and trees allows winds to blow sand over farmland, thus changing it into a barren desert.

△ Strip mining can permanently alter the shape of the landscape. This enormous hole is a copper mine in Montana, United States.

MAKING A CRATER

This project is messy, so wear old clothes and do it outdoors. First mix some plaster with water to make a very thick paste. Spread it in the lid of a box (1) and drop a stone or a ball of modeling clay into the middle of the wet plaster (2). Carefully remove the "meteorite" (3) and let the plaster set. You will have a good model of a meteorite crater.

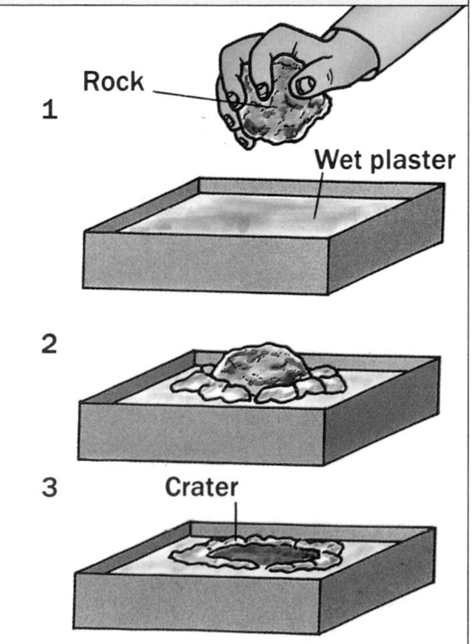

DID YOU KNOW?

Polar regions have rarely had ice caps throughout the history of the earth. Warm ocean currents penetrated into these high latitudes and kept the Arctic Ocean ice-free. But for the past few million years Arctic waters have been almost entirely surrounded by land masses, blocking warm currents. A thin ice sheet consequently formed over the Arctic Ocean creating a unique landscape where there is no solid ground.

In prospecting for oil below the earth's surface, scientists create miniature earthquakes using explosives. By timing the shock waves using microphones set at increasing distances from the explosion, they can work out the rock structure beneath the surface. This helps them determine the likelihood of finding oil.

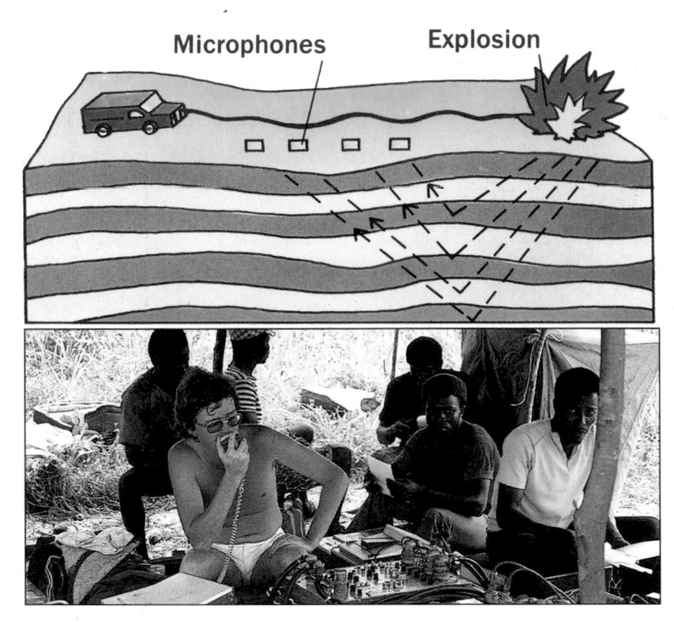

Measuring reflected shock waves

Another way of finding out what is beneath the earth's surface is to take a core sample. A hole is drilled into the earth. Then a special hollow bit (the part of the drill that cuts) is fitted to the drill. This bit cuts a cylinder of rock called a core sample which can then be brought to the surface and studied.

A known earthquake zone in California lies astride the San Andreas Fault. American scientists have placed satellites in stationary orbit immediately over the area. Laser beams at precisely mapped locations on either side of the zone boundary or fault line are reflected off the satellite back to ground receivers. Any ground movement is instantly detected and people warned.

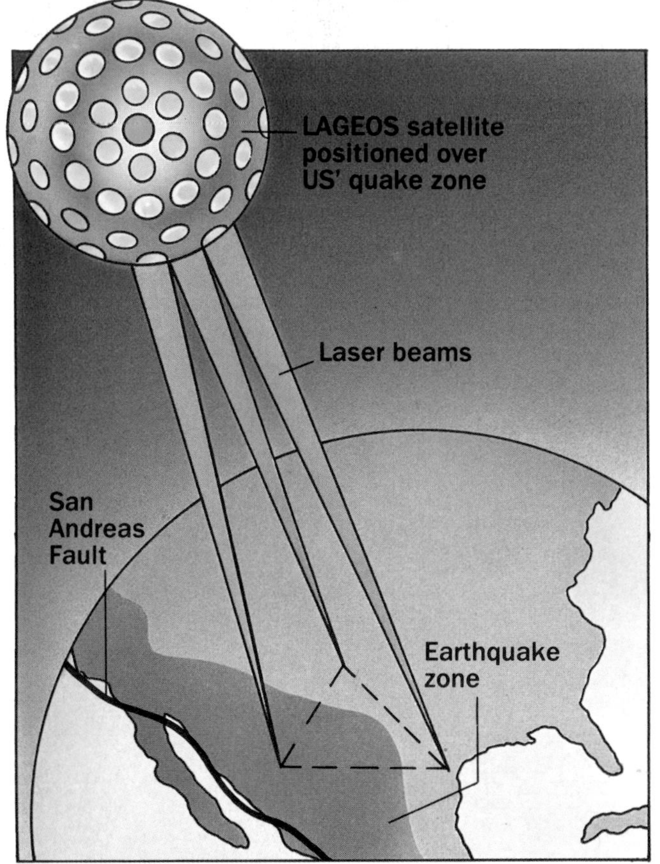

Laser-beam satellite

Drilling for core samples to find minerals

MINING TO MINERALS

CHAPTER SEVEN:

MINING TO MINERALS

HABITAT DESTRUCTION

INTRODUCTION

Minerals are the building blocks from which rocks are made. A mineral itself is inorganic matter consisting of pure elements (the simplest of substances) or, more commonly, compounds of elements. Quartz, for example, is a mixture of silicon and oxygen bound together in a crystal lattice. Ores are naturally occurring compounds rich with substances, such as metals, that can be extracted or mined. Iron ore is a valuable mineral because it is used to make cast iron, which can be converted into steel. Nonmetallic minerals are used extensively in industry, agriculture, and medicine for such things as building bricks, cement, and fertilizers. Gemstones are also highly valued for their rarity and beauty and industrial use. But perhaps most valuable of all at present are the fossil fuels – coal, oil, and gas – which provide most of the world's energy.

A miner digs for opals in Australia.

The earth's crust contains about 3,000 minerals. Igneous rock forms granites and basalts. Erosion breaks these rocks down into sediments which may be compressed to form sedimentary rocks. Heat and pressure within the crust change igneous and sedimentary rocks into metamorphic rocks.

WHERE THEY ARE FOUND

Minerals are found under the ground throughout the world, although certain types are concentrated in particular areas. Major deposits of oil, for example, are found in the southern United States and in the Middle East: the biggest reserves of nickel are in Canada and the Russian Federation.

These mineral concentrations occur due to formidable shifts of the earth's crustal plates, creating ideal conditions for their formation. When molten rock, magma, from the earth's mantle bursts from the mouth of a volcano and eventually cools, rocks like basalt will form. Iron minerals come from water left over when magma cools. Seawater trapped within the earth's crust yields copper minerals. Where land-locked seas have dried up, evaporation results in compounds containing potassium and the sodium used in the chemicals industry.

Coal, oil, and gas, the remains of plants and animals, are buried where layers of sedimentary rock encased them millions of years ago.

Sometimes, because of earth movements or the action of flowing water, minerals are found at or near the surface. Gold nuggets, sulfur and even diamonds are unearthed this way.

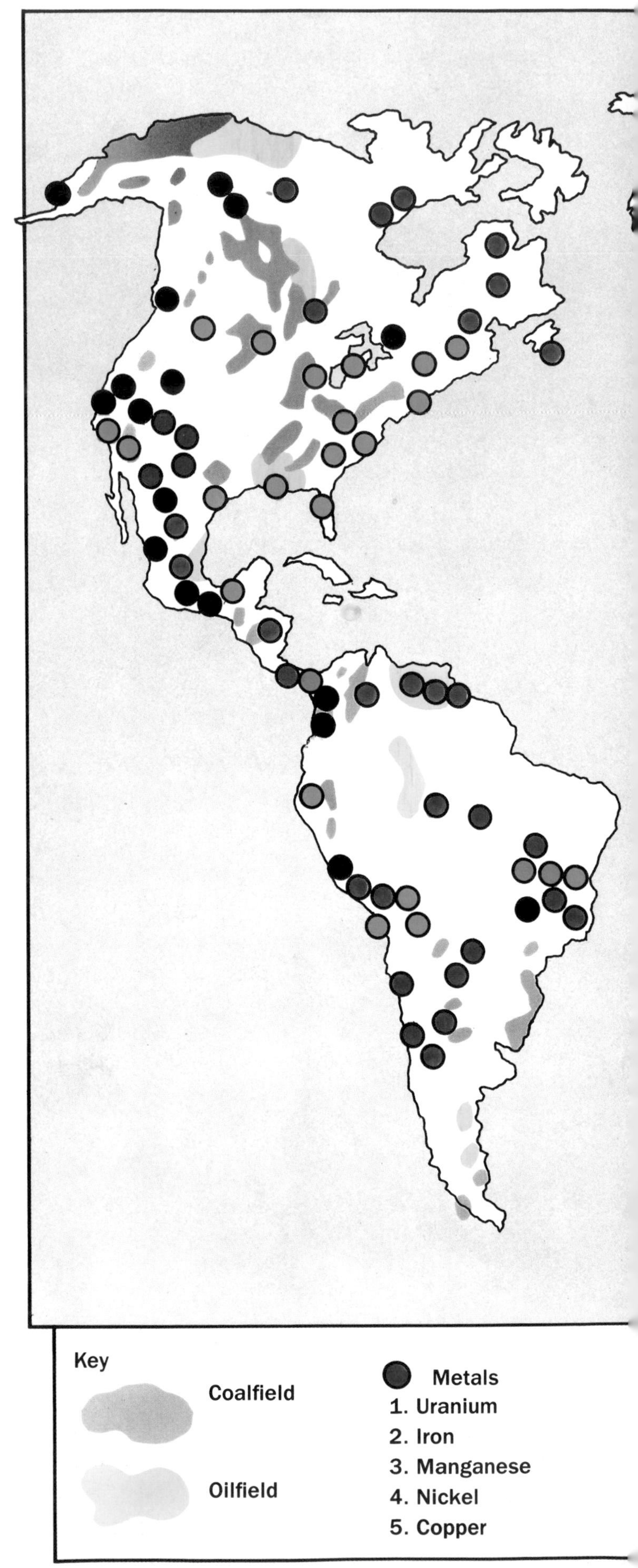

▷ The world map shows the location of the main deposits of metallic and nonmetallic minerals. The seabed and the oceans themselves are also major mineral sources.

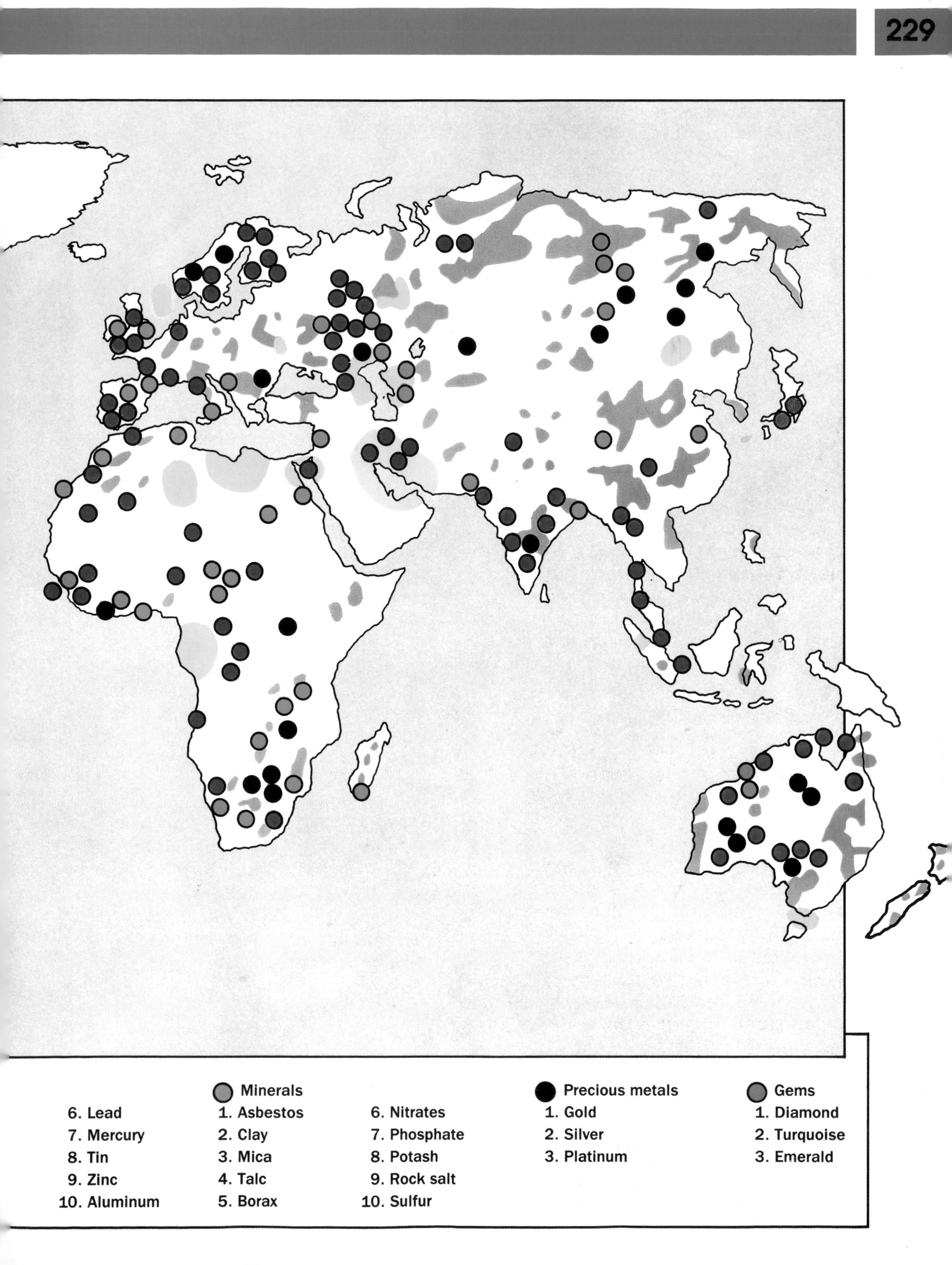

Minerals
1. Asbestos
2. Clay
3. Mica
4. Talc
5. Borax
6. Nitrates
7. Phosphate
8. Potash
9. Rock salt
10. Sulfur
Precious metals
1. Gold
2. Silver
3. Platinum
Gems
1. Diamond
2. Turquoise
3. Emerald
6. Lead
7. Mercury
8. Tin
9. Zinc
10. Aluminum

Engineers use a wide range of methods to extract minerals, depending on their nature and location. Excavating machines scoop up the surface rock and sediment, so that useful minerals can be extracted. Shafts are dug and blasted to extract deeper mineral deposits. Wells are sunk to reach deposits of gas and oil.

△ A large bucket-wheel excavator scoops up coal at extremely high speed at an open-pit mine.

EXCAVATING

Mechanical excavators of all types extract minerals that occur near the surface, such as gravel, sand, and many coal deposits. Digger excavators remove fairly small quantities of minerals at a time but are very maneuverable machines. Dragline excavators scoop up much larger amounts. They have a long derrick, or boom, which drops a large, toothed scoop. Steel cables haul in the scoop to scrape up the soil, rocks, or minerals (see picture, page 252). Most complex of all are the huge bucket-wheel excavators. They have the largest capacity, moving up and down surface deposits very slowly.

△ Oil and natural gas production rigs are familiar sights in the shallow seas off the coasts of western Europe and around North America.

DRILLING

Drilling is used to reach deep deposits of nonmetallic minerals that can rise to the surface as gases or liquids. The underground pressure of natural gas, for instance, is enough to force it to the surface and along pipes to storage tanks. Oil may also rise under its own pressure, or is mechanically pumped to the surface (see pages 236-237). Gas and oil may be located on land, in shallow waters offshore or – using floating rigs – in deep water. Sulfur is extracted by drilling once the deposit is melted with pressurized hot water. It is also a by-product of the purification of natural gas.

Gas rig

Oil rig

Gas

MINING

Minerals extracted by mining include coal, some gemstones, and most metal ores. The principal methods are strip or open-pit mining for pit deposits that lie near the surface, and underground mining for deposits located underground. Underground, engineers use blasting explosives to smash through hard rock to make shafts and tunnels. They also employ tunneling machines with mechanical shearers to extract the minerals. Conveyor belts, railways and elevators shift the mined material to the surface from where it can be transported for refining or immediate use.

△ An automatic shearing machine slowly moves forward as it continuously cuts coal at an underground coalface.

△ A powerful explosion frees tons of rock for building material in this blast at a large quarry.

QUARRYING

Quarrying is employed for surface deposits of hard nonmetallic minerals such as limestone, marble and slate. Instead of excavators, blasting explosives and deep cutting machines shape quarries, which resemble open-pit mines. Sand, clay, and gravel pits may also be regarded as quarries that do employ excavators and dredgers. In a china clay quarry, for example, the mineral is "excavated" using high-pressure jets of water.

▽ Mineral deposits occur in every possible location. The diagram below shows just a few of the methods devised for their extraction.

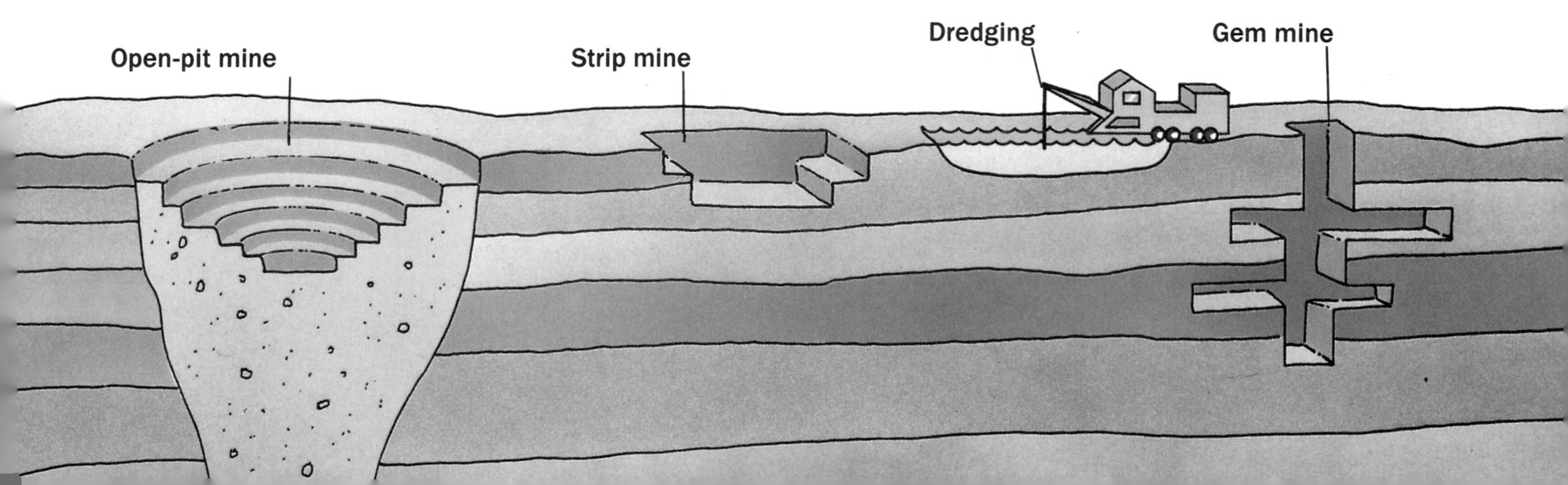

Coal, oil, and natural gas are fossil fuels, so called because they were formed over millions of years from dead plants and animals buried under sediment. Lack of oxygen prevented the material from fully decomposing so that only the carbon or hydrocarbons (compounds of carbon and hydrogen) remained.

△ A fossil of a fern found in a lump of coal indicates that ferns were common plants growing on earth when the raw material for coal was originally laid down.

COAL

Coal, which is made of carbon, hydrogen, and oxygen, consists of the remains of plants that grew about 300 million years ago. When the plants died they sank below the water. Initially plant matter rotted down into a brown, fibrous substance called peat. Mud and silt covered the peat, depriving it of oxygen and preventing further decomposition. Pressure from successive layers of sediment changed the peat into lignite, or brown coal, and then bituminous coal as the compression squeezed out more hydrogen and oxygen. With sufficient heat and pressure, anthracite is formed, which is almost completely carbon.

▽ The formation of coal took place in stages over millions of years as dead plant material became covered in sediments and was gradually changed by heat and pressure. Peat is changed least and anthracite is changed most.

Silt gradually shapes the dead vegetation into hard layers.

Vegetation dies, collapses and sinks. Then it is covered by silt, sealing it from the air.

Silted vegetation

Peat
Lignite
Bituminous coal
Anthracite

Pressure and heat turn the previous vegetation into coal.

OIL AND GAS

Crude oil, also called petroleum, is a dark, sticky mixture of liquid hydrocarbons. Natural gas consists of light, colorless hydrocarbons. Both minerals were formed millions of years ago when dead plankton, the microscopic plants and animals that live at the surface of the sea, sank to the bottom. Covered by clay, silt, and sediment, the plankton remains were deprived of oxygen and did not rot. Further layers on top compressed this organic material, the action of pressure and heat transforming it to oil and gas.

Oil and gas can move through porous rocks and tend to move upward through consecutive porous layers. Eventually, they come to an impervious rock layer named a "cap rock." The oil and gas collect in the porous rock below the cap rock like water in a sponge. This is known as a trap. The oil and gas are extracted by sinking a well down into the trap.

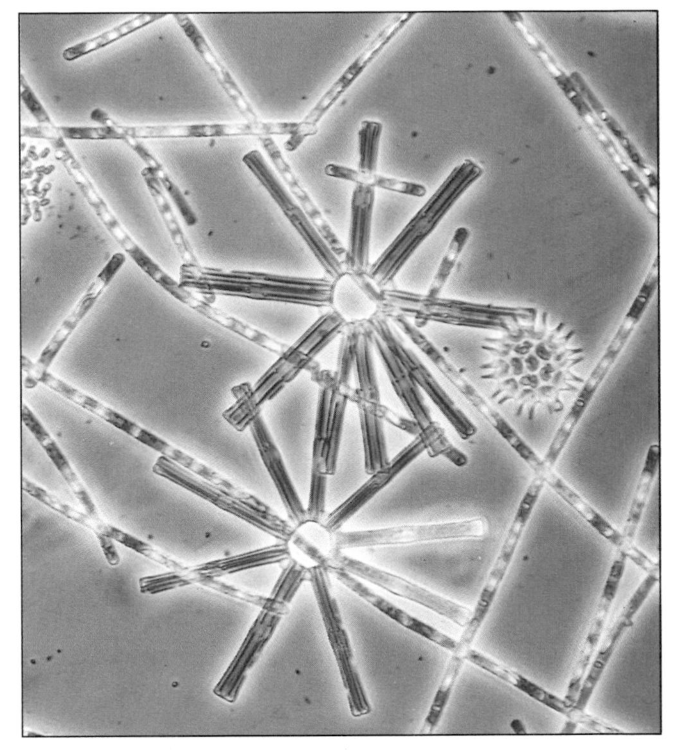

△ Microscopic plants and animals in plankton resemble the creatures whose remains formed natural gas and oil millions of years ago.

▽ Oil was formed in a similar way to coal. But oil is sensitive to heat changes within the earth. Oil will decompose producing gas and carbon if heated above 300°F.

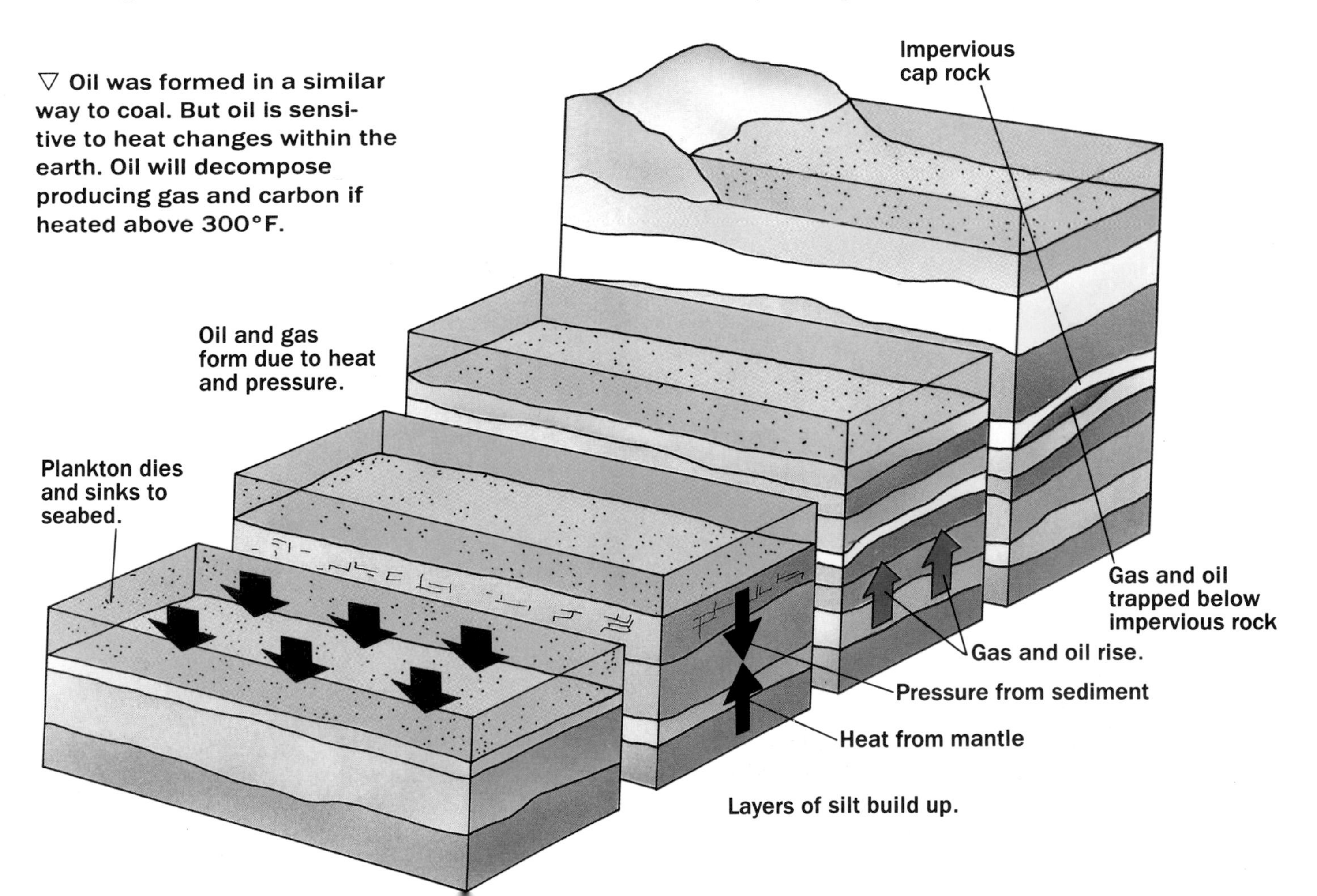

EXTRACTION OF COAL

Coal occurs at various depths in layers called seams. It may be near the surface, under a layer of soil. Or it may lie deep in the ground, under layers of sedimentary rocks such as sandstone and shale. Shallow deposits are obtained by open-pit mining; to reach deep deposits may need tunnels several miles long.

△ The winding gear at the surface is characteristic of coal mines. The gear works an elevator that hauls up trucks of coal and carries miners to and from the coalface.

UNDERGROUND MINING

An underground mine has one or more shafts cut down to the coal seams. From a shaft, miners bore tunnels into the coal seams. Pit props hold up the roofs of the tunnels. In a modern underground mine (below), miners use automatic and semi-automatic coal shearers that slice off layers of coal at a high rate. Hydraulic pit props are moved forward as coal is removed. Conveyor belts and electric trains remove the coal to elevator shafts that bring the coal to the surface. Despite increasing automation, coal mines in China and India still rely heavily on manual work.

▽ A mechanical coal shearer (inset) has rotating picks that chop coal from the coalface and load it onto a conveyor which carries it along a tunnel.

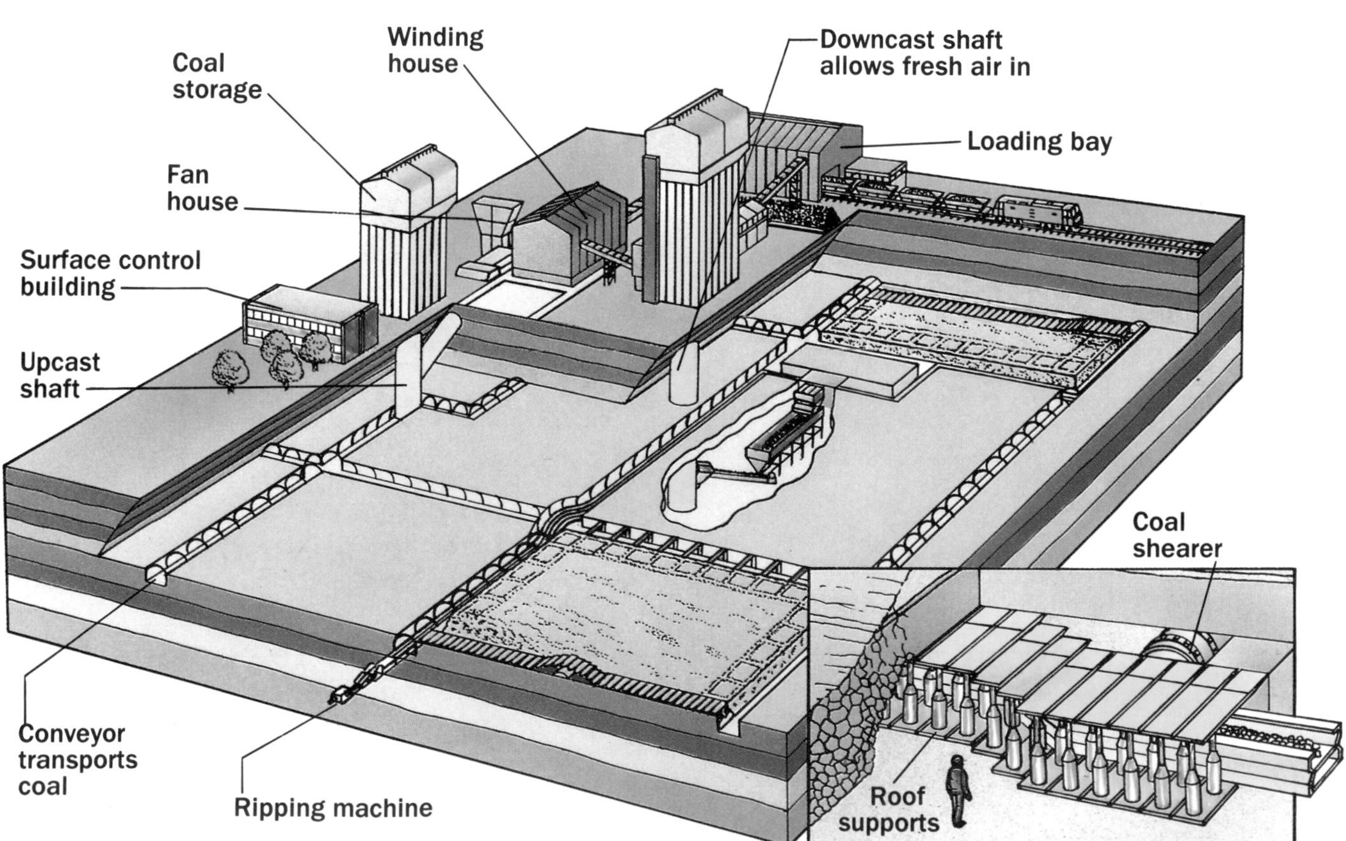

OPEN-PIT MINING

Coal seams that occur at or near the surface can be extracted by open-pit, or strip, mining. Large, earth-moving machines strip away the overlying soil and rock, called the overburden, to reveal the coal seam. Huge excavators use giant grabs to scoop up the coal and load it into dumper trucks for transportation to the preparation plant. Draglines use cables or chains to draw buckets across the coal face. Some excavators, called bucket wheel excavators, have a large wheel rimmed with toothed buckets that dig into the seam as the wheel revolves.

Some countries have laws requiring that farm land is reclaimed after mining. After the coal has been removed, the soil is put back and the land may be returned to agriculture, or turned into parkland.

△ Uncontrolled open-pit mining can ruin agricultural land, so today the overburden is usually replaced and the land reclaimed when mining activities have finished.

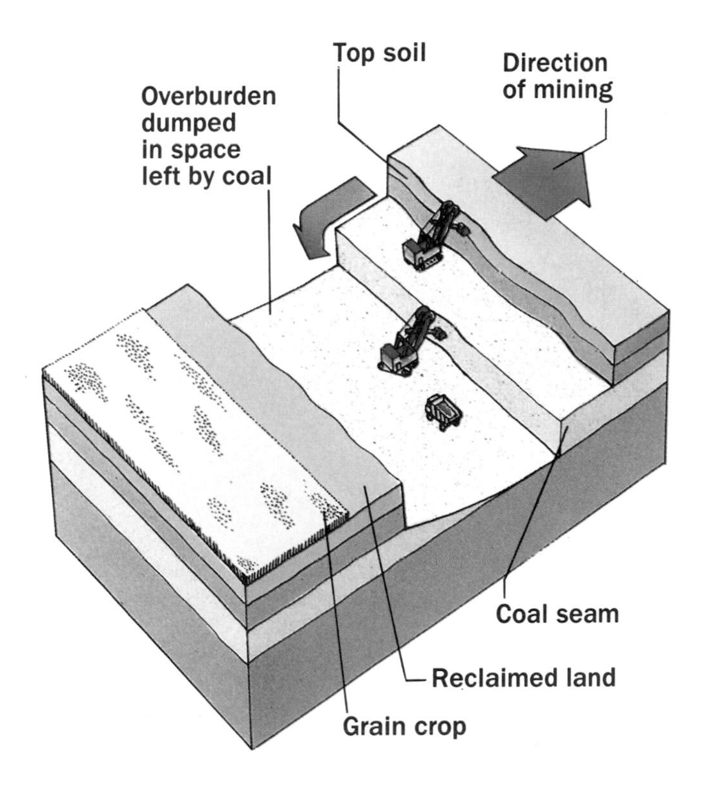

△ An open-pit coal mine employs large dragline excavators to remove overburden, and giant diggers to scoop away the coal.

POWDER AND GAS

Some of the coal that is mined for use in power plants and industry is converted to powder or gas. Powdered coal can be pumped along pipelines like a liquid, and it is easier to burn efficiently. At some mines, the coal is powdered either underground as it is being cut, or at the surface before it is pumped into tanker trucks and carried away.

In an even more advanced process, the coal can be set on fire underground to produce gas. A limited supply of oxygen is pumped down a narrow shaft to keep the fire burning in a controlled way. The fuel gas produced passes up a second pipe to the surface. The solid residue remaining is coke, which is used in iron smelting.

Oil and gas, two of the most valuable natural resources, are used as fuel and in the production of synthetic materials and pharmaceuticals. They are found deep underground in porous rock, which holds them like a sponge, trapped beneath an impervious rock layer which prevents them from rising any further.

EXPLORING FOR OIL AND GAS

The sinking of an oil well is made using a rotary drill bit at the end of joined-up steel pipes called a string. A slurry of drilling fluid, known as mud, is pumped down the center of the drill, and the pressure carries mud and fragments of broken rock back to the surface. There scientists examine the rock fragments and decide on whether to sink a test well. Equipment near the top of the well can seal it off quickly in case there is a sudden blowout of oil or gas.

On land, the drilling equipment is slung from a steel derrick which straddles the hole. For offshore oil and gas wells, the drill is mounted on a rig that floats or stands on long legs that are extended to reach to the sea bottom.

△ Oil drilling rigs are among the largest structures afloat. Some are towed on their sides into position before being swung upright by flooding their buoyancy tanks.

Drill bit and mud system
▽ The diamond-tipped bit used for drilling oil wells is hollow, so that liquid mud can be pumped down its center.

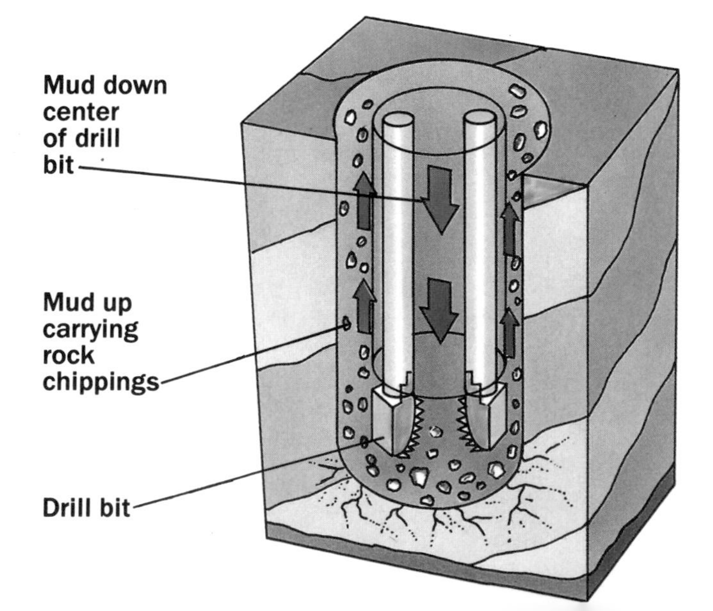

▽ Offshore drilling rigs can reach deposits of gas and oil up to 18,500 feet below the seabed.

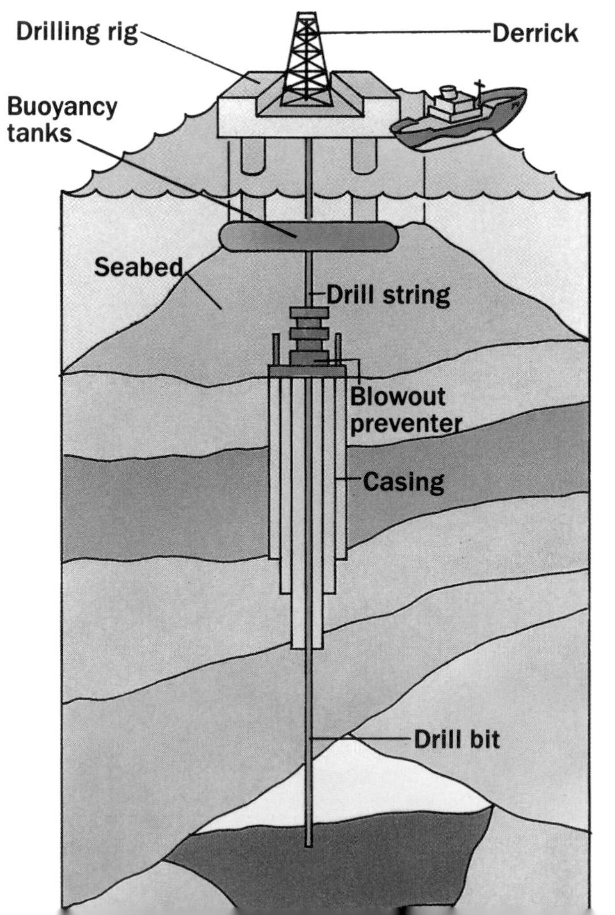

PRODUCTION

Once oil or gas have been discovered in commercial quantity, a production platform is set up. Wells are drilled over the whole field to increase the rate of extraction. A production platform may have up to 50 wells running into the oil field. A tool called a whipstock is used to make the drill change direction. This allows the wells to be bent very gradually up to an angle of 40 degrees. Oil pumped up through the well passes through equipment to separate the gas, water, and other impurities from the oil, which is then piped to refineries.

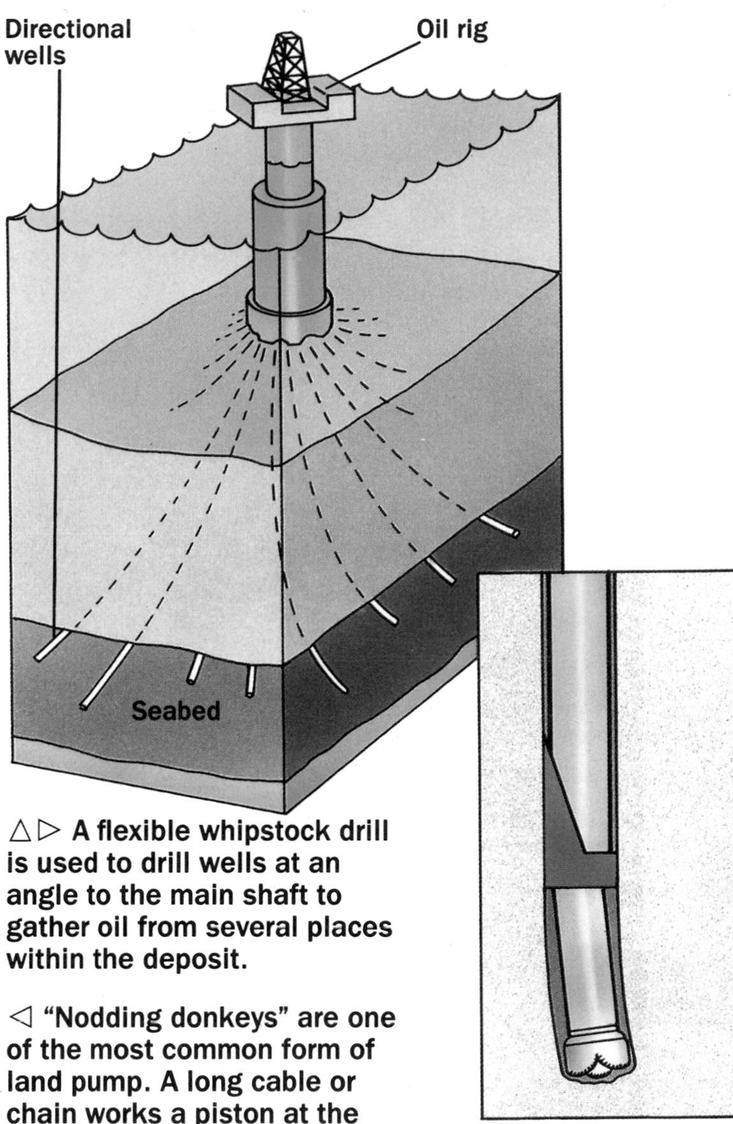

△▷ A flexible whipstock drill is used to drill wells at an angle to the main shaft to gather oil from several places within the deposit.

◁ "Nodding donkeys" are one of the most common form of land pump. A long cable or chain works a piston at the bottom of the shaft.

PRESSURE FOR PUMPING

To see how gas pressure can pump a liquid, cut a piece of plastic sponge to fill a plastic box. Bore two holes in a piece of balsa wood so that they are a tight fit for two drinking straws. Soak the sponge in water. Then fit the wooden lid to the box. Blow down one of the straws and note how water is forced upward out of the other straw.

METAL ORES

Ores are formed within the earth's crust. They are rocks that contain minerals such as metals which can be recovered economically. Gold ores are mined profitably with a low gold-to-rock ratio, because gold commands a high price. Iron, however, which is abundant, has a high iron-to-rock ratio.

△ Iron ore is one of the world's most important minerals because of the widespread use of steel, which is an alloy of iron and carbon.

FORMATION

Mineral deposits containing metal ores are created in different ways in or beneath the earth's crust. Some, like chromium, iron, and nickel, come to the surface in igneous rocks. In some places there are pools of magma which cool and form rocks, leaving a mixture of very hot water and minerals. This may react with nearby rocks and deposit minerals that can crystallize into veins of copper, lead, and zinc (1). Metals are also formed when the hot water and mineral mixture seeps into cracks (2), reacts with rocks such as limestone (3), or seeps through molten lava (4). Water trapped in the rocks may carry mineral deposits to the seabed as springs (5).

Volcano
4
3
Rainwater
1
2
5
Magma
Cooling rock

Some metals, like gold and silver, do not react readily with surrounding rocks and may occur in an almost pure state.

PURE METAL OR ALLOY?

Some metals are used in their pure state. Aluminum in drink cans and copper in electrical wiring are pure metals. Other objects are made from alloys, mixtures of metals with more useful properties than those of the individual components. Gunmetal, a mixture of copper, tin, and zinc, is used on ships for its strength and resistance to corrosion.

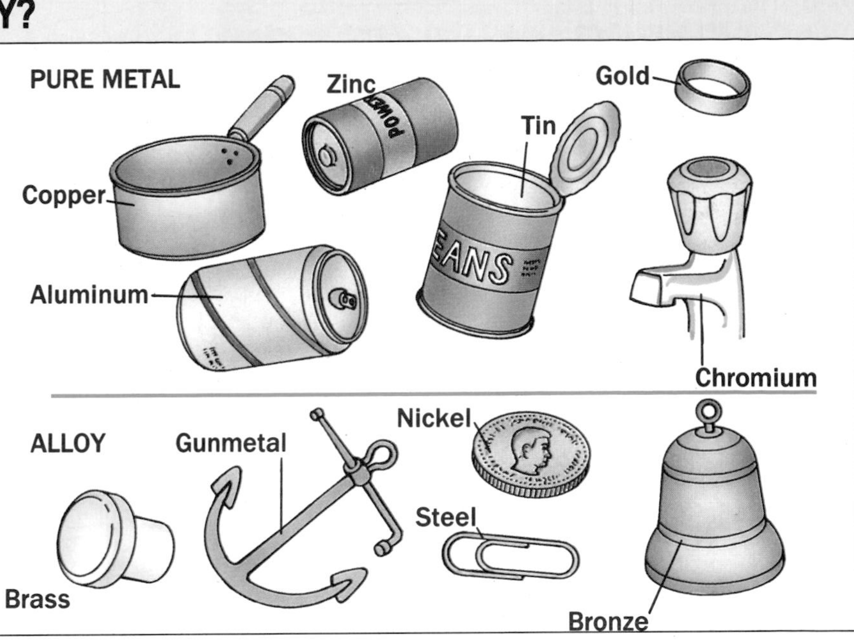

▽ Forced into chambers in the earth's crust, magma cools and releases mineral-rich liquid. Within these mineral "rivers", ores are created.

6

Flowing water may carry minerals and deposit them on the seabed (6).

Seawater

Land surface

Layers of minerals

△ Many minerals are transported by water. They are deposited in rock layers. The diagram shows how the mineral deposits may look after the surrounding rock is removed.

Mining is any method of extracting ores, whether they are deep underground, or very near the surface. Surface mining is cheaper than underground mining, and for this reason underground mining is generally used only for the more valuable ores. But some valuable minerals, such as gold, are also found near the surface.

SURFACE MINING

Ores and metals washed to their locations with sediment are called placer deposits. The sediment is shoveled into a trough. Water flows down the trough, washing the sediment away and leaving the heavy ore behind. Extracting placer deposits by hand is called panning.

If the ore-bearing sediment is thick, the ore is extracted by dredging. An artificial lake is created upon which a dredger is floated. The dredger scoops up gravel and extracts the ore by washing away the sediment with streams of water.

Open-pit mining (see page 233) is also used to mine surface ore deposits in the same way as coal is extracted.

△ Panning for gold is an old method of mining that requires a lot of patience and strong muscles. Gold occurs separately as placer deposits in the gravel of streams.

▽ Copper ores are among the valuable minerals that are extracted by open-pit mining.

UNDERGROUND MINING

Metal ores are often obtained from igneous rock deep underground where they formed due to the action of cooling magma (see page 238).

The techniques for the underground mining of ores are similar to those used for mining coal (see page 234). First miners dig a shaft almost 10,000 feet deep. They then make horizontal tunnels, called levels, into the deposits of ore by drilling or, in very hard rock, by blasting with explosives. conveyor belts or small railway cars carry the ore back to the shaft, where an elevator hauls it to the surface. Apart from being used to obtain the precious metals gold and silver, underground mining is most often used to extract copper, lead, and zinc. In some parts of the world, nickel is also obtained by underground mining.

△ Tin ores that occur as deposits mixed with thick layers of gravel or sand can be extracted by draglines.

PANNING FOR "GOLD"

Half fill a bowl with water, and put in about ten coins and a similar number of small, plastic "pretend" coins. Add two or three cupfuls of sand (1). Then take a saucer or shallow dish and scoop up some of the mlxture of sand and coins. Making sure there is always some water in the saucer, swirl the mixture around in a circular motion (2). The sand and light coins are washed away, leaving behind the heavy coins in the saucer (3).

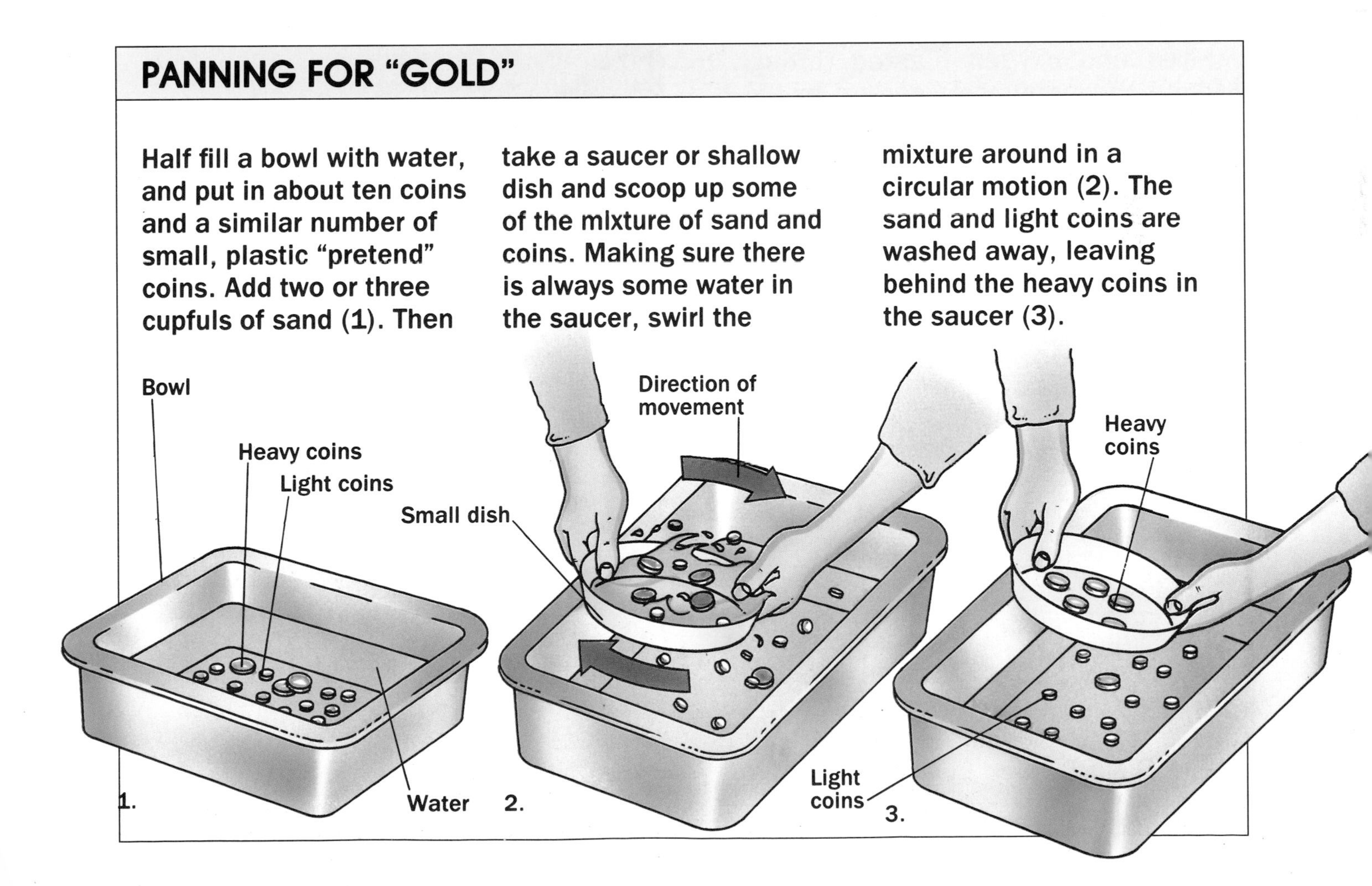

An ore consists of a metal combined chemically with elements such as oxygen or sulfur to produce oxides and sulfides. Refining is the means of extracting the metal from its ore, and includes smelting, which involves heat and often additional substances, and electrolysis, whereby electricity breaks down the ore.

△ Iron is smelted in a blast furnace. The molten metal is tapped off from the bottom of the furnace and run into molds as pig iron.

SMELTING

Some ores, such as an oxide of copper, can be smelted using heat alone. But most need a more complex chemical reaction. Iron ore is smelted by mixing it with lime and coke. The mixture is heated to a high temperature in a blast furnace. Molten iron sinks to the bottom, and impurities, chiefly silicon, combine with the lime to make "slag" which floats to the top.

Iron from a blast furnace, known as "pig iron," is made into steel in a furnace called a converter. Pig iron and lime are melted and oxygen blasted through to reduce the amount of carbon in the pig iron. Lime combines with the remaining impurities to form slag. Steel is poured off and cast into ingots.

▽ Iron from a blast furnace may go straight into steelmaking. In the basic oxygen process, in which lime is added to pig iron, impurities in the metal are oxidized and escape as gases or accumulate as slag.

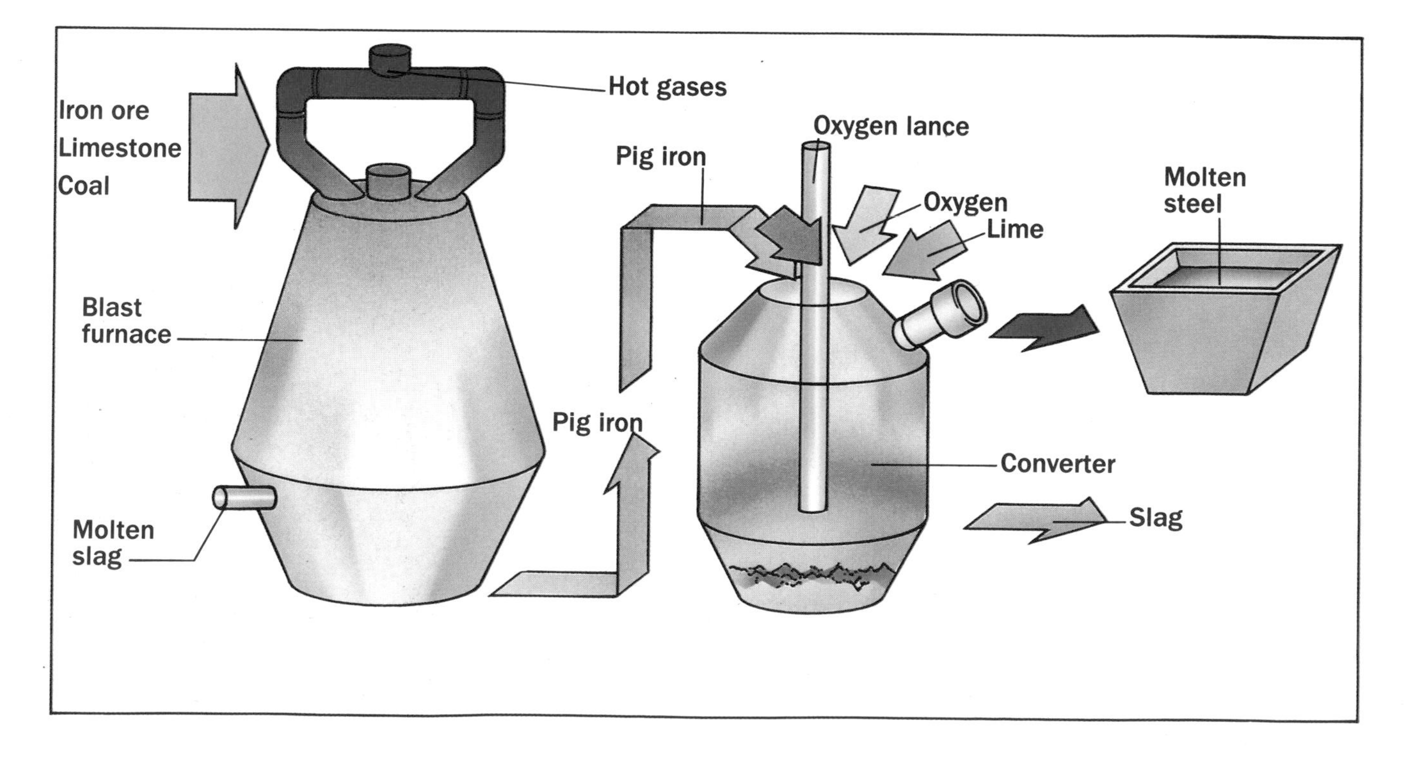

ELECTROLYSIS

Electrolysis is the breaking down and recombining of a substance in its pure form by electricity. Solid compounds are dissolved in water or melted so that molecules are free to move, making mineral extraction possible.

Copper is one such mineral that can be extracted by electrolysis. Crushed copper ore is dissolved in sulfuric acid forming a solution of copper sulfate. A direct current is passed through this solution via conducting plates called electrodes. Attracted to a negative charge, pure copper splits from the rest of the dissolved material and collects on the negative electrode as pure copper.

△ In the electrolytic extraction of aluminum, the bauxite ore (aluminum oxide) is melted with cryolite (an aluminum fluoride).

ELECTROLYSIS EXPERIMENT

Ask your teacher to help you to make a weak solution of copper sulfate in a jar or beaker. Use crocodile clips to join wires to a copper coin and a "silver" coin. Connect the other ends of the wires to a battery – the copper coin (anode) to the positive terminal and the "silver" coin (cathode) to the negative terminal. Pure copper moves from the copper to the "silver" coin.

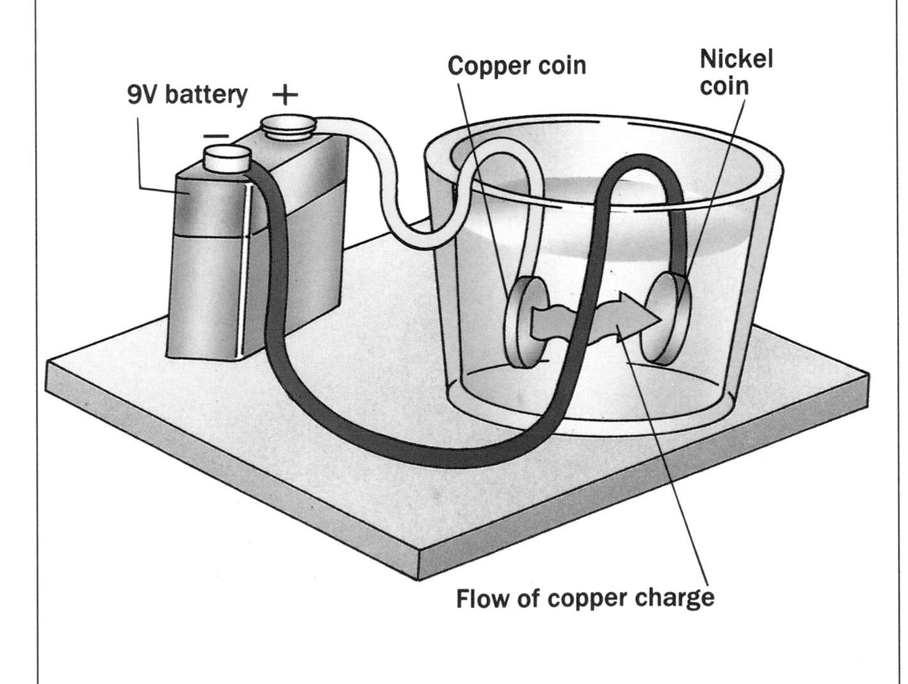

DID YOU KNOW?

Mercury is the only metal that is liquid at room temperature. Its ore (mercury sulfide) is smelted by heating it with a stream of hot air or oxygen. The impure metal is purified using distillation. This process involves heating the impure metal until it forms a vapor, and then cooling the vapor to make it reform pure liquid metal.

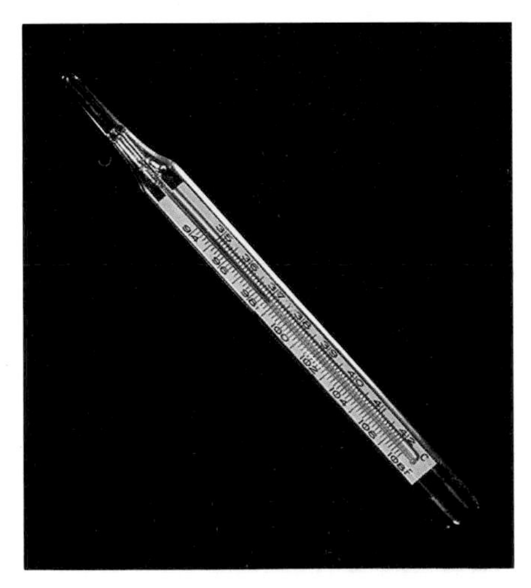

Nonmetallic minerals are among our oldest resources. These include asbestos, mica, and talc. Some occur as salts such as table salt, gypsum and potash. Carbon and sulfur often occur in a pure state. We still rely on nonmetallic minerals today, from crockery to space shuttle ceramic insulating tiles.

△ Sulfur occurs at the surface near volcanic activity, such as in these hot sulfur springs.

FORMATION

Most nonmetallic minerals occur in sedimentary rocks. These are formed when particles of other rocks, broken down by weathering, accumulate as sediments at the bottoms of lakes and seas, and are changed by pressure. Clay and limestone, for instance, are sedimentary rocks that are quarried as minerals. Salt from dried-up lakes and seas is an important nonmetallic mineral also found underground. Evaporation of salt water can also give rise to precipitation deposits of minerals such as anhydrite and gypsum (forms of calcium sulfate) and potash.

Sulfur is a nonmetallic mineral that occurs at the surface near volcanoes, or underground in areas with oil deposits.

▽ Machinery at a quarry (left) crushes rock to make gravel for road-building. The excavator (right) scoops up gypsum for making plaster.

EXTRACTION

Like metallic ores, most nonmetallic minerals are extracted by digging them out of the ground. Near the surface, minerals such as gravel and sand are obtained by quarrying. Open-pit mining can also be used. Salt deposits can be mined, although in hot countries most of it is now produced by the evaporation of seawater from shallow pools.

Sulfur lying deep underground is extracted by a method called the Frasch process. Engineers sink three pipes into the sulfur deposit. Hot water sent down the outer pipe melts the sulfur, which is forced to the surface by air pumped down the central pipe.

△ For centuries people have extracted salt from seawater. The water is trapped in pools called pans, and the salt left to crystallize as the sun's heat makes water evaporate.

MINERAL	HOW EXTRACTED	MINERAL	HOW EXTRACTED
Salt	Salt is mined or extracted from seawater.	Sulfur	Sulfur is mined or extracted from oil and gas.
Quartz	Quartz, a crystalline form of silica, is mined.	Graphite	Graphite is a form of carbon that is mined.
Borax	Borax (for making heat-resistant glass) is mined.	Gypsum	Open-pit gypsum is used for chalk and plaster.

SALT AND EVAPORATION

You can make your own salt-extraction plant. Dissolve as much salt as possible in a glass or jar of hot water and put the glass in a warm place – such as a sunny window sill. The heat causes the water to evaporate while the salt stays behind, appearing as crystals in the glass. The size of the crystals depends on the rate of evaporation.

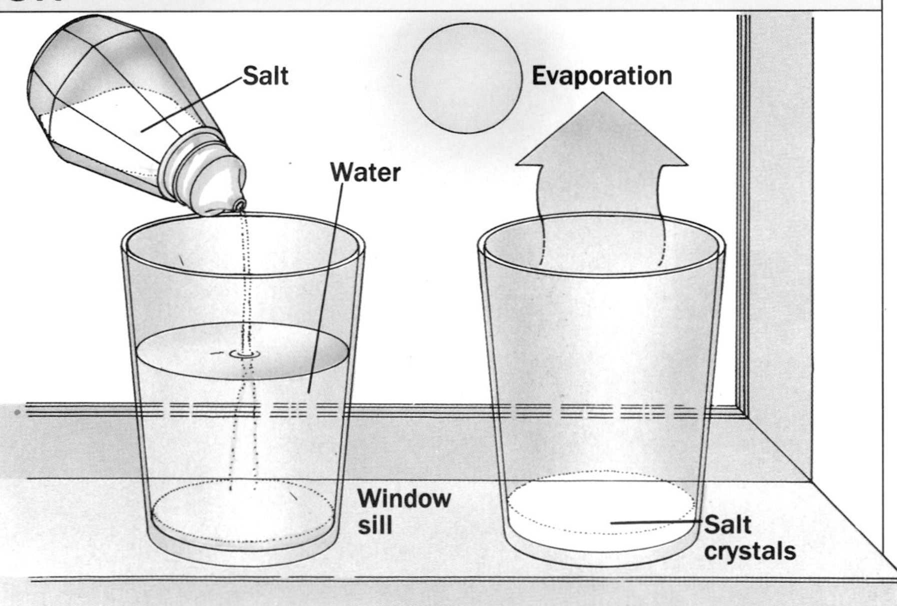

Many minerals occur in the form of crystals. Some, because of their color, beauty and rarity, have been highly valued since ancient times as gems or semiprecious stones. The most valuable are diamond, emerald, ruby, and sapphire. Pearls, formed from nacre inside oysters, are also precious stones.

△ Sapphires glisten among other precious stones in a piece of gem-bearing rock.

HOW GEMS ARE FORMED

When magma from the earth's core pushes toward the crust it solidifies at about 2,012°F, creating igneous rock. If this happens slowly, large mineral crystals will form within the rock. If exposed, surface erosion eats the rock away and these potentially gem-bearing sediments are washed into waterways.

Gems also form where the earth's crust folds into mountains, or magma helps to reforge sedimentary rock into metamorphic rock. When limestone changes into marble, aluminum in the limestone may recrystallize with silica to form rubies or sapphires.

Not all magma is the same and its texture, chemistry, and density determine the type of gemstone it will form, if any are formed at all.

▽ The buckling earth forms mountain peaks from which gem-bearing sediments eventually spill into valleys below. Carried by rainwater the gems end up in distant riverbeds, lakes and oceans.

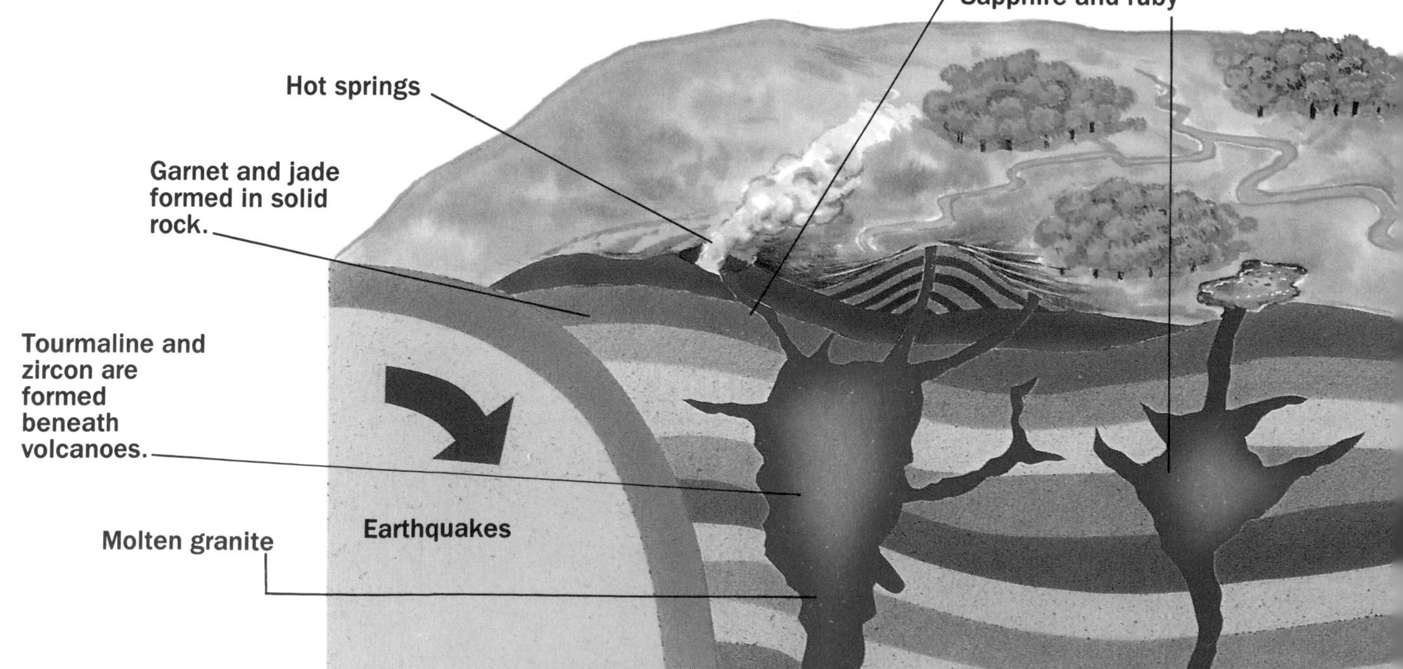

GROW YOUR OWN CRYSTALS

Put some hot (but not boiling) water into a jar or beaker and add soap powder that contains sodium carbonate until no more will dissolve.

Support a button on a length of cotton in it. As the solution evaporates over several days, soda will begin to form a mass of crystals on the button.

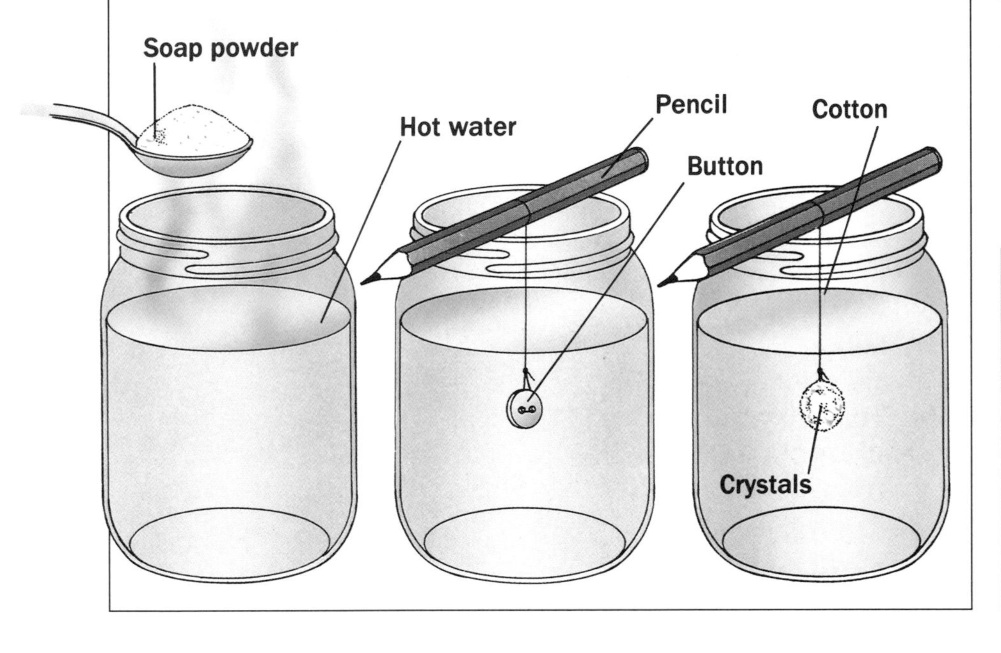

DID YOU KNOW?

Diamond is a form of the element carbon, as are the black substances graphite and charcoal. It is the hardest natural substance in the world. Gem-quality diamonds consist of pure transparent crystals, which are rare. Most diamonds are discolored and used as industrial abrasives. Coal is another mineral that consists mainly of carbon.

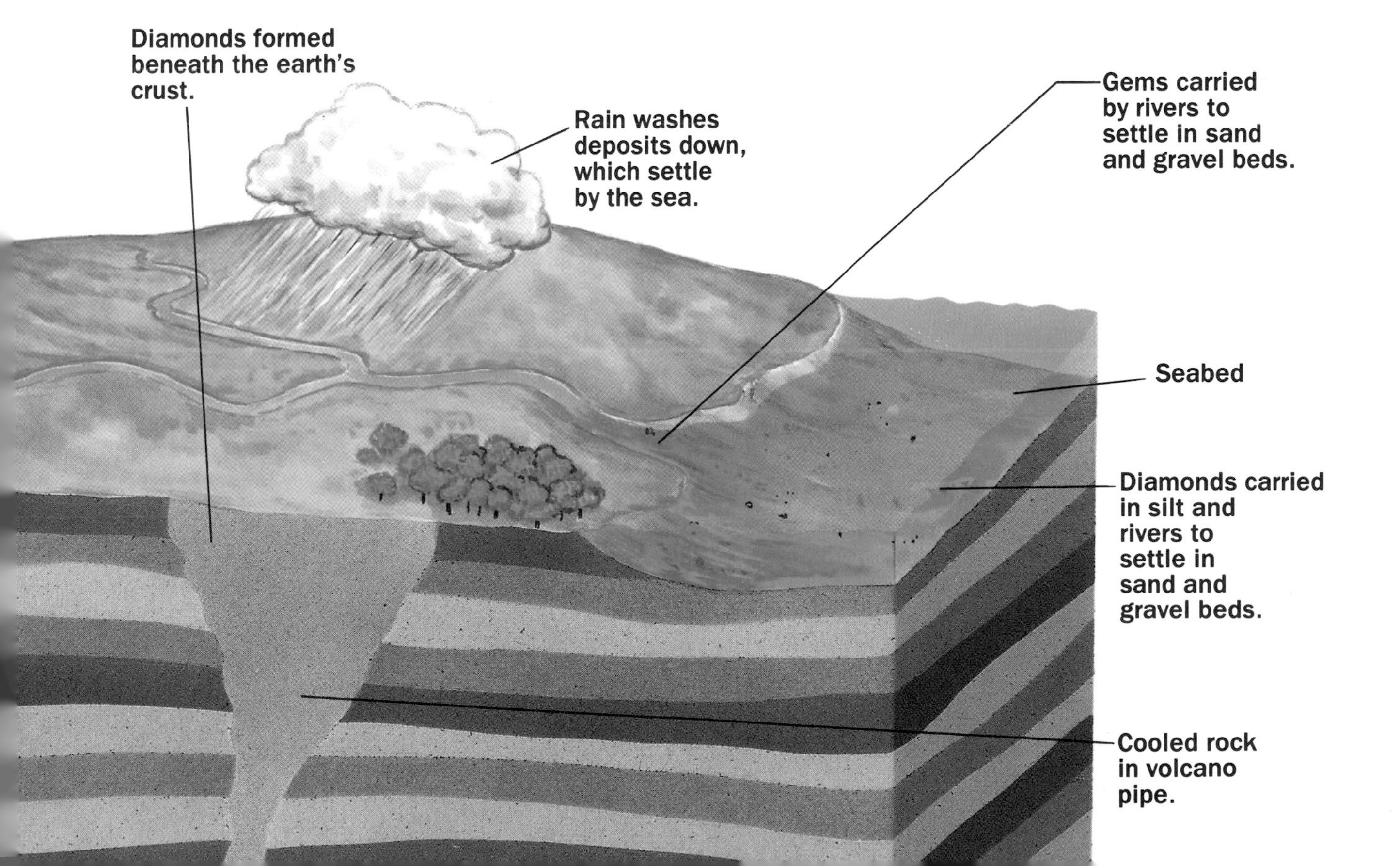

MINING GEMSTONES

Gemstones are mined using most of the methods employed for extracting ores (see pages 240-241). MIning is difficult, however, because gems tend to lie within hard rocks. Also, because gems are rare, many tons of rock have to be dug out, crushed, and sorted to find only a few stones of gem quality.

A LARGE DIAMOND MINE

Large mines are constructed to extract diamonds from the "pipe" of rock, called blue ground, that once formed the vent of a volcano. At first open-pit mining methods can be used, with giant excavators to dig out the blue ground. But as the hole gets deeper and deeper, vertical shafts and horizontal tunnels have to be built. Often the rock is crushed underground before being lifted to the surface for sorting. The crushed rock passes along conveyor belts under strong lights while workers pick out the gems. On average, even in a rich African mine, 14 tons of rock must be dug to produce only one gram of precious diamonds.

IDENTIFYING GEMS

Most gems have characteristic colors: blue aquamarine and sapphire, green emerald and turquoise, yellow – or the rarer blue – topaz, purple amethyst and red ruby. Jade varies in color from white to green, brown orange or, rarely, lilac. Precious opal is iridescent and multicolored.

Rare blue topaz

Diamond

Amethyst

Ruby

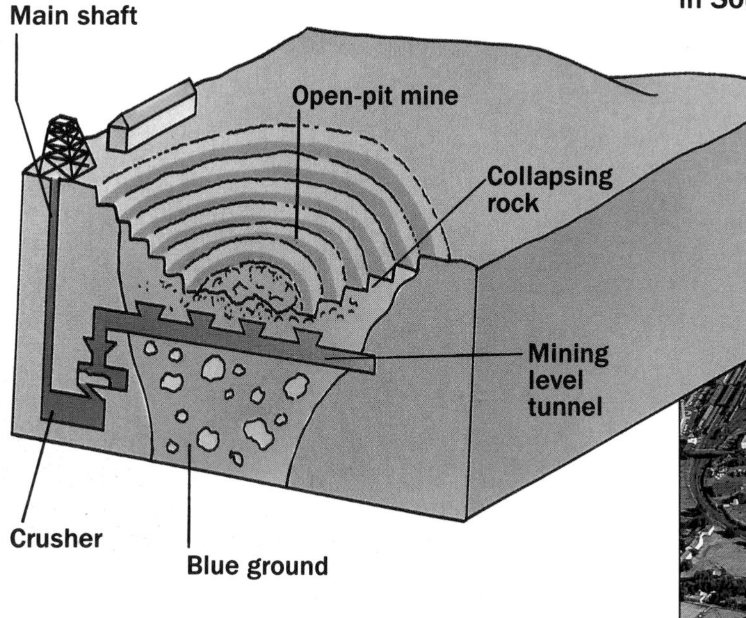

△ Once the diamond-bearing rock is too deep for an open-pit mine, miners dig shafts into the "pipe" of rock, often up to 10,000 feet deep.

▽ Excavators have dug out tons of rock in the search for diamonds at an open-pit mine in Southern Africa.

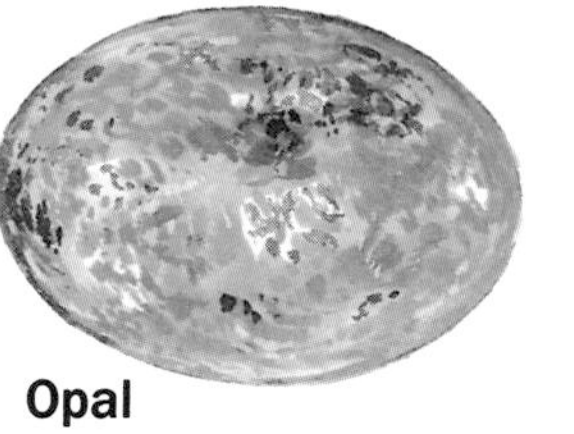

DID YOU KNOW?

Diamonds are weighed in carats (1 ounce equals about 150 carats). The largest raw diamond ever found, the Cullinan, weighed 3,106 carats (21 ounces) before it was cut into smaller stones. One of these, the Star of Africa, weighs more than 530 carats (3.5 ounces).

OPAL MINES

Opals are unusual multicoloured gems consisting mainly of silica (the same mineral that forms sand). They do not form crystals, but are found as irregular lumps in rock cavities. Most come from Australia, where they are obtained from open-pit mines or from underground tunnels that follow the opal seams.

▽ The entrance to an opal mine may be merely a hole in the ground, with a simple crane to lower the miners.

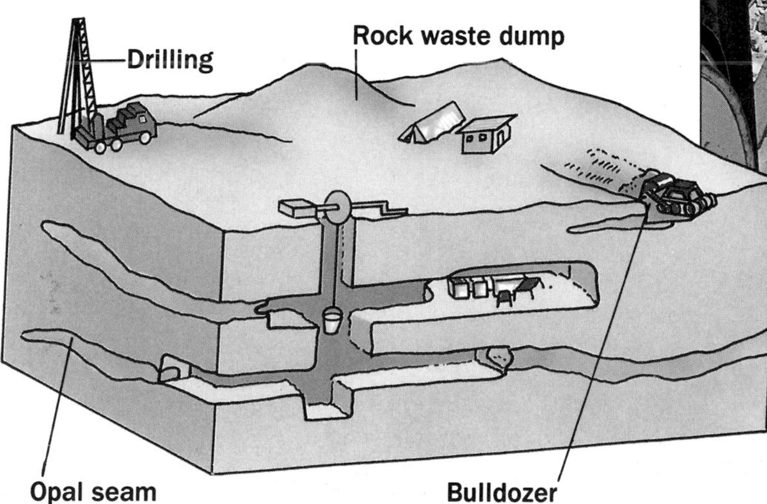

◁ Opals are formed in seams and may be mined at the surface or underground. The most valuable are the black opals that are found in New South Wales, Australia.

Recycling and resource conservation will help us to make the planet's dwindling supply of minerals last. We can also use technology to create substitutes for non-renewable resources. The metals we use can also be recycled. Scientists are looking to develop a synthetic fuel to replace decreasing oil supplies.

△ Glass bottles and jars put into a collection bin can be recycled, thus saving mineral resources and the energy used in making new glass.

RECYCLING

One way everybody can help to conserve mineral resources is by recycling manufactured goods to reuse the materials they are made from. At home, scrap metal (mainly food and beverage cans) and glass bottles can be separated from paper, plastics and food waste. Some have built recycling plants for processing domestic and industrial waste. In addition to saving materials, recycling also saves energy – and therefore fuel – that goes into extracting and refining various minerals. For example, recycling aluminium only uses about five percent of the energy required to separate it from ore in the first place.

◁ Scrapped cars account for millions of tons of waste steel. They can be crushed into blocks of scrap and used in making more steel.

SCRAP METAL

Steel and aluminum are the chief metals used in the world, and the most frequently discarded. But these metals, along with iron, tin, and copper, are also the most easily recycled. Every year millions of cars, each containing a ton of steel, end up in scrap yards. This scrap can be put through a crusher and reused for making new steel.

Food and beverage cans also yield valuable scrap from the billions produced worldwide each year. If collected and recycled, this scrap can be recrafted into new cans, saving both metal and energy.

SYNTHETICS

Some mineral resources can be conserved by using human-made substitutes, which may be cheaper than the natural substances. Artificial diamonds, made by subjecting carbon to tremendous heat and pressure, are employed as abrasives and cutting agents. Imitation diamonds, such as the human-made mineral yttrium iron garnet (YIG), are used in jewelry. Some synthetic materials, such as plastics, consume mineral resources and so should be recycled wherever possible.

△ Artificial diamonds are just as hard as natural ones and are used in industry for making saws, drills, and other kinds of cutting tools.

△ A biogas generator, also called a digester, consumes vegetable wastes to produce a continuous supply of methane for use as a fuel.

ALTERNATIVE GAS

Scientists estimate that supplies of natural gas could run out within the next 100 years. But methane, the principal gas in natural gas, can be tapped from a variety of other sources. Methane is produced when organic matter decays in the absence of air. So it is possible to harvest plants which can be processed for methane. The basic process is fermentation, also used to make alcohol (for fuel) from wood, particularly in Brazil.

REPROCESSING

Reprocessing helps to turn dangerously radioactive spent uranium fuel into material suitable for new fuel rods used in nuclear reactors. The old fuel rods are cooled and dissolved in acid. Unused uranium can then be extracted. To ensure safety, the procedure is carried out by remote control with operators shielded behind thick protective walls. In recovering and reusing uranium, reprocessing reduces hazardous high-level waste.

▽ Waste from a nuclear power plant being moved by rail in crashproof containers, on its way to a reprocessing plant.

In the future, people may seek minerals beyond the boundaries of the earth, mining the moon, asteroids or other planets. Previously inaccessable mineral store-houses on earth may also be exploited as we push the frontiers of technology at home. For instance, ocean beds may one day be tapped economically.

Machine for collecting nodules on the seabed.

Oil shales and tar sands are porous sedimentary rocks that have soaked up thick crude oil, as a sponge might soak up water. Shales can be excavated, or the oil melted and piped to the surface by pumping in superheated steam. But the latter is not yet cost efficient.

Drawing of a proposed mine on a moon of Mars.

Potato-sized nodules of minerals containing the metal manganese have been found in deep water on the bed of the Pacific Ocean. The nodules also contain cobalt and nickel. It may become possible in future for remote-controlled submersible machines to gather the nodules and take them to the surface.

Another future possibility is the use of remote-controlled "platforms" on the seabed to drill for small deposits of gas or oil that cannot be extracted economically from the surface.

A dragline excavator mining tar sands.

HABITAT DESTRUCTION

POPULATION EXPLOSION

The world's human population is growing fast. Every day about 230,000 babies are born, adding to the five billion of us who already inhabit the planet. Since you started reading this page, about 25 people have come into the world. Children are important for the future, but growing populations can damage habitats. More and more undeveloped areas have to be cleared to provide people with food, resources and places to live.

One reason for the population explosion is that advances in medicine in the last 200 years have helped people live longer. Yet in poor countries good medical care is not always available and many infants die. Families in these areas rely on having many members to bring in money or to farm the land. And because survival is uncertain, women have more children in case some die. Families get poorer as they struggle to feed all their children. As their poverty grows, they are forced to clear wild habitats in order to farm.

▼◄ The world population in A.D. 10 stood at around 250 million. It is expected to reach six billion by the year 2000. Nearly half of these people now live in cities. The expansion of urban areas has been particularly rapid in poor countries as people move from the countryside into the city to look for work. Often they cannot find jobs and end up in poverty-stricken shanty-towns which grow up around the edges of cities. In this way urban areas spread into wild land.

YEAR AD14 1000 1500

▼ **Modern farming produces enough food to feed the world, but if the population keeps growing, soon it may not be able to keep up.**

POPULATION IN HUNDREDS OF MILLIONS

40

30

20

10

5

1750 1900 1975 2000

HABITAT DAMAGE

The increase in population leads to a demand for more houses and industries, and the need for food requires more acres of cropland to be cultivated. Finding land for these uses often means the replacement of wild habitats with human-made environments.

Agricultural land covers 9 million square miles of the world's land surface. This area represents nearly all of the land on our planet that is easily cultivated, because ice, mountains and deserts account for a large percentage of the earth's surface. Much of the farmland currently under cultivation is being damaged as farmers try to squeeze more crops out of the soil. This means that the soil may not be fertile in the future, creating the need for new farmland. This is likely to put increasing pressure on the world's remaining wilderness.

Many other types of development demand land. Roads, industry, mines and dams all need land, and their construction often means the disappearance of some habitats and the disruption of others.

▲ Although population growth in the richer countries of the world is low, the people in these countries use far more resources than those in poor countries do. Extracting resources damages habitats. The copper taken from this mine in Utah will go to make wire or pipes, but the mountain will never be the same. Vast amounts of rock are destroyed, disrupting the area's wildlife.

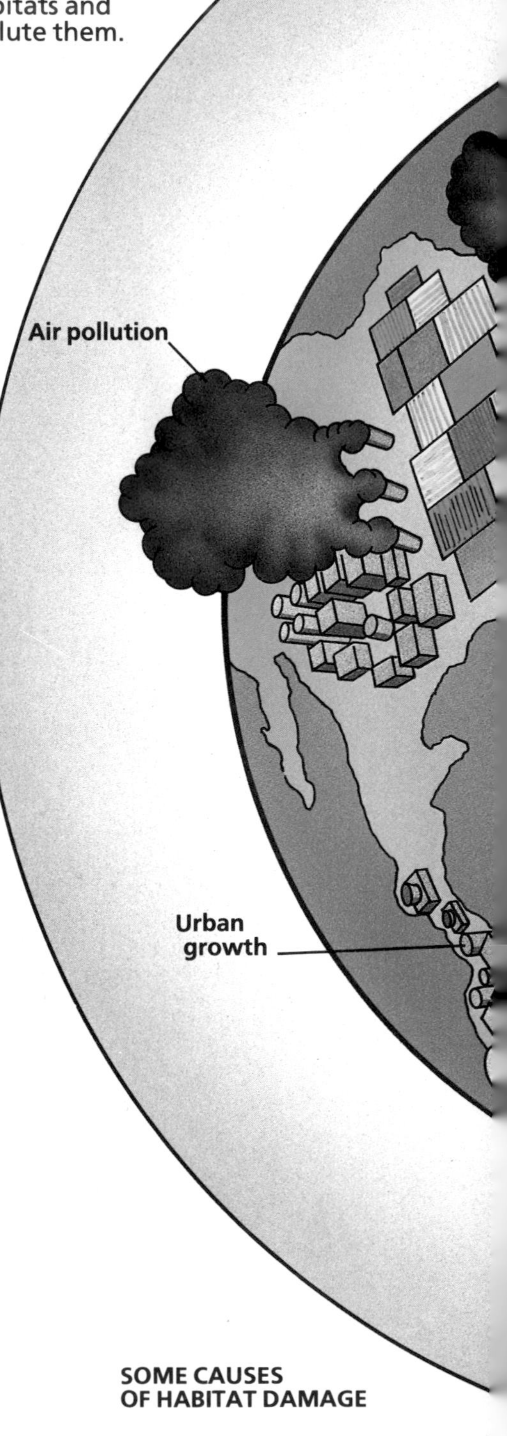

SOME CAUSES OF HABITAT DAMAGE

Cities have factories that dump their wastes into the ground and water. Some of these wastes are very poisonous to living things.

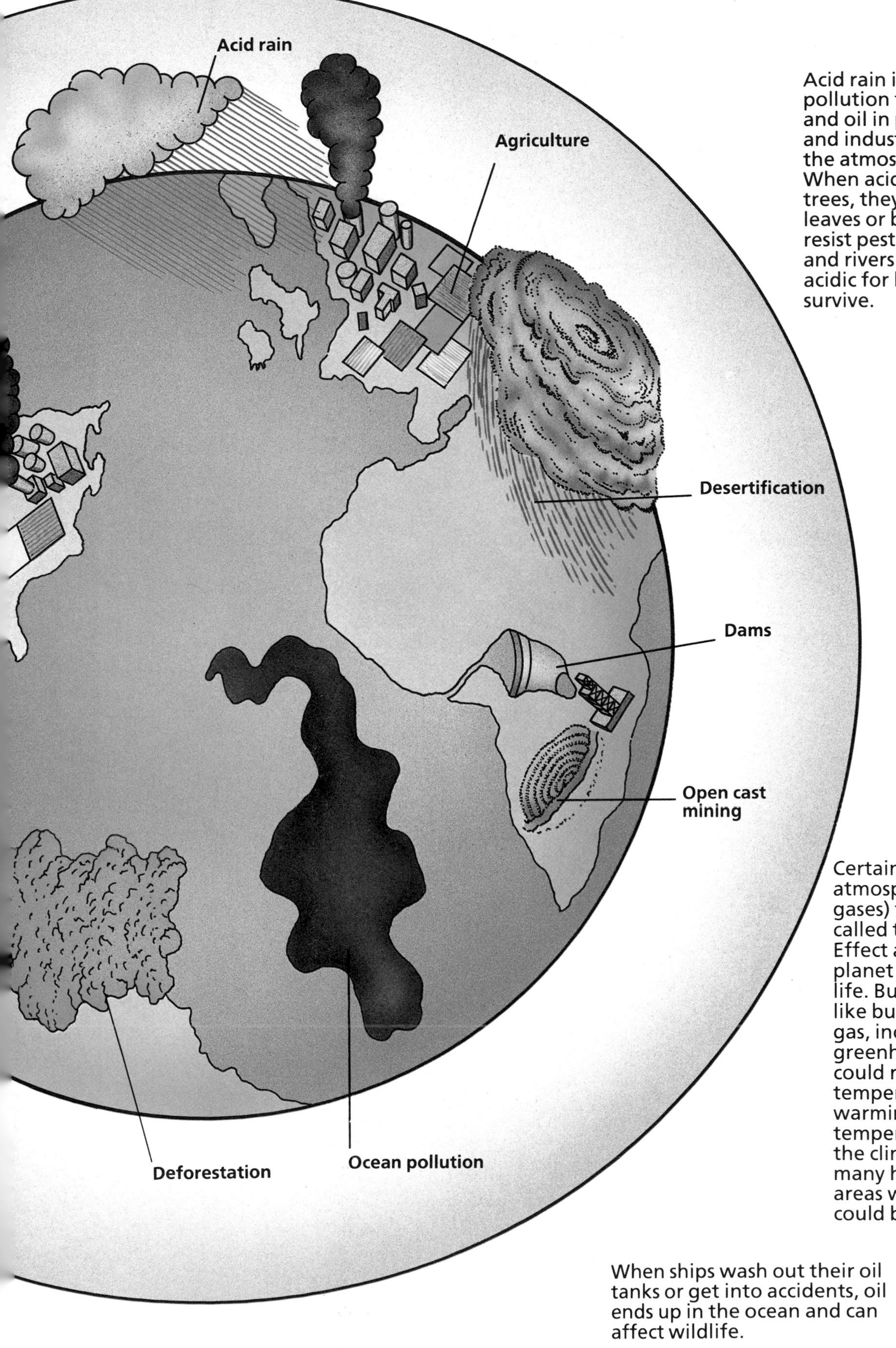

Acid rain is caused when air pollution from burning coal and oil in power stations, cars and industry meets water in the atmosphere, forming acids. When acid rain falls often on trees, they may lose their leaves or become unable to resist pests and diseases. Lakes and rivers can become too acidic for living things to survive.

Certain gases in the atmosphere (greenhouse gases) trap heat. This is called the Greenhouse Effect and it keeps our planet warm enough for life. But human activities, like burning coal, oil and gas, increase the amount of greenhouse gases. This could raise the earth's temperature, causing global warming. Increased temperatures could disrupt the climate and change many habitats. For instance, areas which are already dry could become deserts.

When ships wash out their oil tanks or get into accidents, oil ends up in the ocean and can affect wildlife.

OVEREXPLOITATION

Overexploitation means using a resource until it either runs out or is so damaged that it can no longer be used. This threatens habitats throughout the world. When we overuse habitats it undermines their ability to provide resources into the future.

Grasslands are ideal for wild grazing animals and for raising livestock, like cattle. But if too many animals are grazing, the grass cannot grow quickly enough to keep pace. As the land is stripped of vegetation, the soil becomes exposed and can be blown or washed away. Then no plants can grow back and both wild and domestic animals lose a habitat.

The oceans are also overexploited. They provide us with vital food resources. But in recent years we have been catching more and more fish with equipment like drift nets, which extend for miles. This causes a serious decrease in the numbers of some kinds of fish. All living things in a habitat play an important role, and if species are removed, the whole system can be disrupted.

▼ Cattle have overgrazed the dry grassland south of the Sahara Desert. Plants help to recycle rainfall by giving off moisture from their leaves. When the vegetation is stripped away, the region becomes drier. Millions of people are affected by drought in this part of Africa, and wild animals like cheetah, gazelles and antelope which used to roam here have lost their habitat.

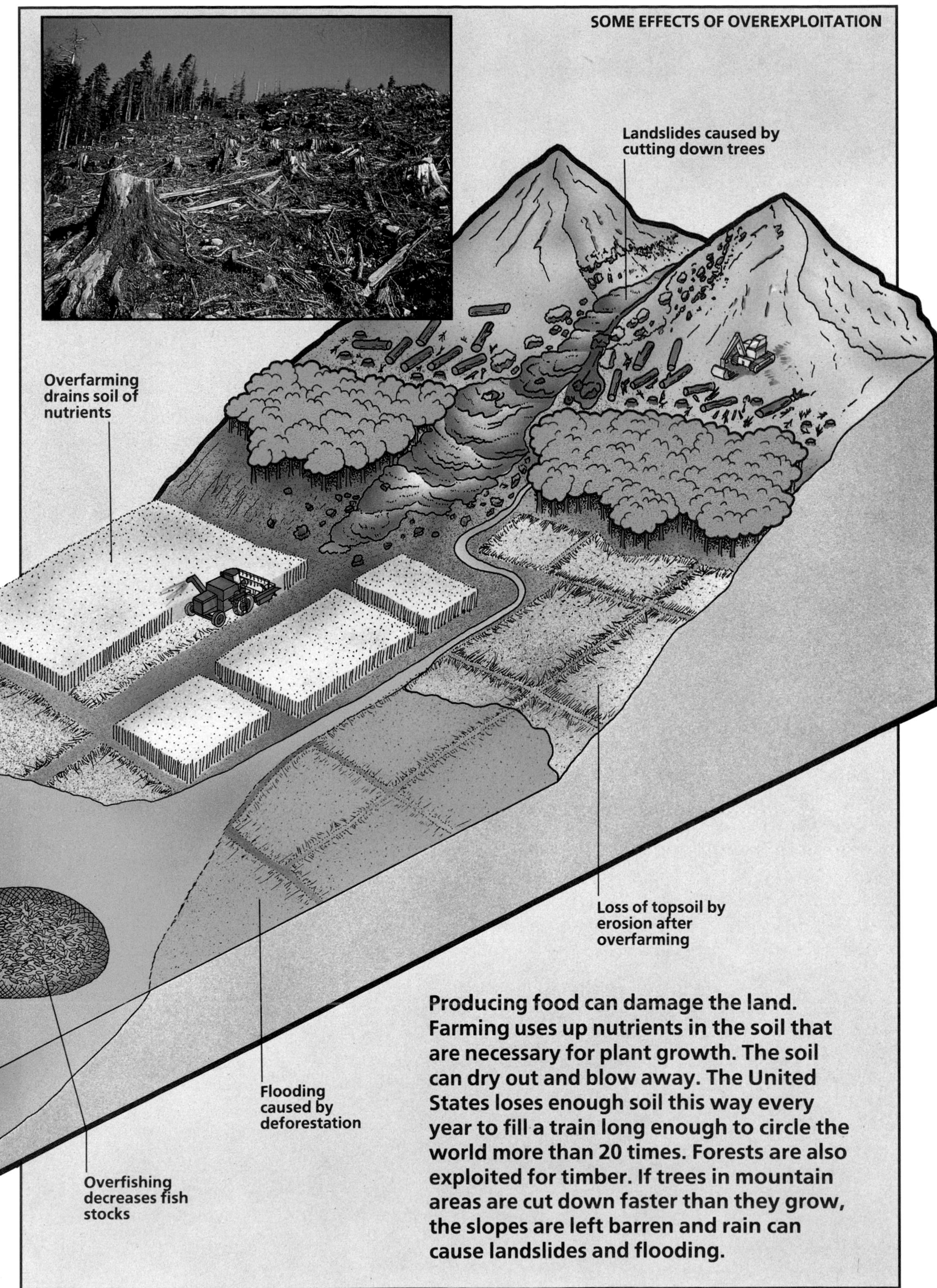

Producing food can damage the land. Farming uses up nutrients in the soil that are necessary for plant growth. The soil can dry out and blow away. The United States loses enough soil this way every year to fill a train long enough to circle the world more than 20 times. Forests are also exploited for timber. If trees in mountain areas are cut down faster than they grow, the slopes are left barren and rain can cause landslides and flooding.

WETLANDS

Wetlands include saltmarshes and mangroves, which are found on coasts, and freshwater swamps and marshes, which occur along rivers and lakes and where the land regularly floods. Wetlands' mixture of water and land and their range of vegetation – from waterweeds to trees – provide homes for thousands of species. Many rare birds depend on wetlands as feeding and breeding areas. In South American marshes, jaguars stalk their prey through the vegetation.

Wetlands are also valuable to people. Two-thirds of the fish we eat depend on coastal wetlands at some stage in their life. Wetlands prevent flooding by taking up water from rivers, and their weeds can filter water by trapping pollution. For example, Hungary uses its peat bogs to filter waste from sewage plants.

Worldwide, wetlands are under great threat. Myanmar, Pakistan, Bangladesh and Malaysia have all lost half of their original wetlands. Many have been drained to create farmland. In Africa, planned irrigation programs and other projects like dams will destroy vital wetlands.

▼ One of the major threats to wetlands is that they can be turned into very good farmland when drained. Channels are dug so that water drains from the land. The dry land can then be used to grow crops. This method has been used in Florida's Everglades for 100 years. However, the price is the loss of fish breeding grounds and bird habitats. Some people believe that one way to manage wetlands is to use them in their natural state: for fish farming, for example. If done carefully this could provide food and make money while maintaining a healthy habitat for wildlife.

► The Okavango delta in Botswana is home to many birds, which nest in its marshy grasses. Part of the Okavango is endangered by a plan to reroute the river which feeds the marshes in order to provide water for villages.

▼ Skunk cabbage thrives in waterlogged conditions, along with many varieties of reeds. The crocodile is a wetland predator found in tropical regions. Hidden below the water except for its eyes and nostrils, the crocodile will approach its prey unseen. Crocodiles feed mainly on fish.

GRASSLANDS

The world's grasslands range from the savannas of Africa to the steppes of Asia and the prairies of North America. They are places where dry summers, cold winters, natural fires and heavy grazing stop trees from taking over. The vast African savannas support some of the world's best-known wildlife, such as lions, giraffes, zebra and elephants. Grasslands also support cattle and goats, but if there are large numbers of them, they eat the grass faster than it can grow. With the ground bare, rain and wind carry away the soil which is necessary for plants to grow. The land then turns to desert.

▼ Desertification threatens the livelihoods of a fifth of the people in the world. On the edges of deserts, wind can blow sand over deforested and eroded land. Both China and India have planted tree "walls" to provide a barrier to stop advancing sand dunes. Overgrazing and overfarming are the main causes of desertification.

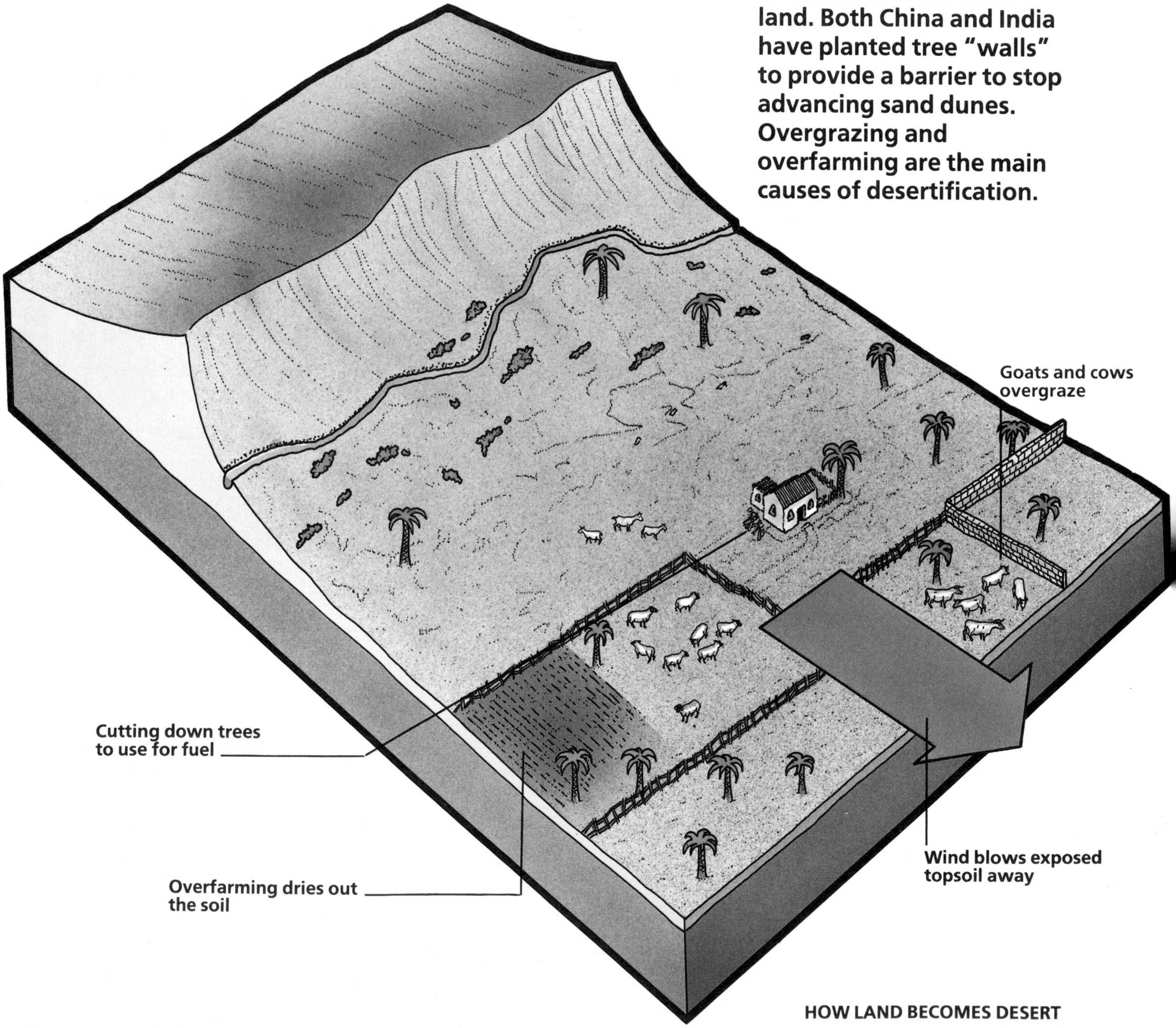

HOW LAND BECOMES DESERT

This process, called desertification, particularly occurs on the edges of deserts and in dry regions. Overgrazing is not the only cause. Grasslands are often converted to farmland, for crops like wheat and cotton. The crops use up all the goodness in the soil, which becomes too dry to support any vegetation at all. In Africa, desertification is made worse as many people rely on firewood for cooking and heating. Trees protect the soil from erosion. When they are cut down, the soil is left exposed to the sun and wind. Up to 30 percent of the world's land surface may be on the verge of becoming desert.

◀▼ Wildlife thrives in a wild grassland like a South American pampas, a North American prairie or a European meadow (above left). Flowers are abundant and they supply insects with food. Grazing animals like deer feed on the plants. But when wild grasslands are replaced by crops, such as fields of wheat, or fast-growing pasture grasses for grazing, such as ryegrass (below), the native wildlife disappears. Pesticides kill off the insects and reduce the food supply of birds and small mammals. Deer are shot if they graze in croplands. Prairie dogs were nearly exterminated by farmers as the North American grasslands were replaced by pastures and farms.

FRESH WATERS

Fresh water makes up less than one percent of the water in the world. However, all forms of life depend on water. Human life would be impossible without it. We drink it, use it to water gardens and crops and use it in industry.

Many freshwater habitats have been altered by people. Rivers have been dammed, flooding the land around them which wildlife like beavers depend on. Dams also block the passage of salmon which swim upstream to breed. Some rivers are deepened to allow ships to pass through, disrupting the living things on the riverbed.

Lakes and rivers are also used to dump our wastes. Sewage from cities and chemicals from factories are discharged into waters around the world, poisoning wildlife. The Ganges River in India is dangerously polluted with human and animal sewage. The water from the Vistula River in Poland is so polluted with chemicals that it cannot even be used for industry. Fertilizers washed off farmland are a major pollutant in North American and European fresh waters.

▼ Remote mountain lakes, like this one in Canada, look pure and untouched. But even they can be affected by pollution. Acid rain falls everywhere, and it has a particularly bad effect on freshwater lakes and streams. In southern Norway, four out of five rivers and lakes are too acidic for fish to survive.

▲ Fresh waters are home to many living things. If the water is contaminated with wastes, wildlife can die.
► Water held in rocks below the earth's surface is known as groundwater. Half the United States' drinking water is taken from groundwater. The top level of groundwater is known as the water table. Streams often begin where the water table meets the surface of the ground. By drilling a well into the rocks, water can be extracted. But as water is pumped out, the level of the water table falls, leaving the stream habitat dry between the old and the new water tables.

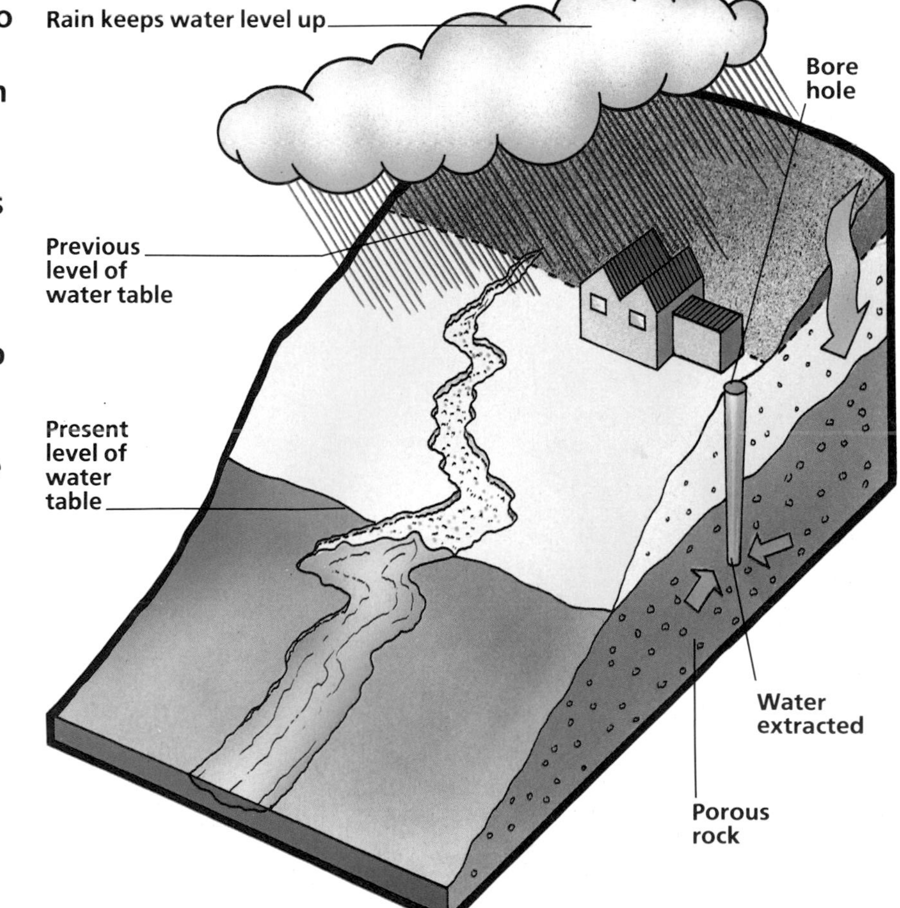

MOUNTAINS

The peaks of high mountains are too cold and windy for much to survive. But many well-adapted plants and animals live farther down the mountainsides. Mountain goats and sheep have superb balance, enabling them to reach high ledges. Plants grow close to the ground, which protects them from the drying, chilling wind.

People of mountain regions often shape the slopes into flat terraces to grow crops. Mountains are important to people who live at their bases as well. The forests which cover mountains absorb rainfall and release the water gradually to fill the streams and rivers below. Removing these forests leaves the steep slopes barren, which has disastrous effects. Half of the trees on the Himalayan mountains in Nepal have been cut down, leading to landslides which have buried whole villages. Flooding also occurs during periods of heavy rain. Recently, Nepal has tried to reverse this process by paying villagers to replant trees to stop erosion.

▼ The Alps are Europe's best-known mountains. Ibex (shown below), which once faced extinction, are now protected and roam the mountainsides in larger numbers. However, the forests are suffering from air pollution caused partly by vehicle traffic on roads through the mountains. Added to this is the pressure from tourists. The European countries through which the Alps extend are becoming increasingly concerned to protect them.

Global warming
Plants and animals suited to high, cold mountain habitats could find their environment changing if global warming raises temperatures. They may not be able to adapt.

Building
Tourist developments are built in mountain habitats for hikers and other visitors. Switzerland has thousands of hotels covering the equivalent of 15,000 football fields.

Acid rain
Rain and snow carried from industrial areas is acidic. Acid rain damages trees' leaves and can also harm the soil, making it difficult for plants to thrive.

Recreation
Millions of people visit mountains to sightsee and explore on foot or by ski, car or bicycle. These activities can wear away soil and vegetation.

Overgrazing
Meadows and mountain grasslands are ideal for grazing animals, but large numbers of them will strip the area of plants. This could lead to erosion.

Reforestation
Tree planting has been seen as one solution to rapid deforestation. However, forest planting can also lead to habitat loss. Timber plantations are often made up of just one type of tree and provide a very limited environment for wildlife.

SAVING HABITATS

Worldwide, concern to protect the environment has been growing. Many people are calling for undisturbed wild places to be made into nature reserves where habitats and wildlife are protected. About three percent of the world's land is now covered by nature reserves.

These reserves have many benefits. They help to safeguard many species from extinction. However, conservation of habitats cannot succeed without the cooperation of the local people. Many countries have recently set up reserves which benefit local communities. New Guinea, for example, has protected its wetlands, but allows local people to continue their traditional way of life as long as they do not do any damage to the reserve. As poverty is one of the main causes of habitat destruction, conservation programs that provide some income for those who live in the area will be most successful. Tackling poverty will reduce the need for people to have many children, thus decreasing another cause of habitat loss: population growth.

▼ Both wild and human-made habitats can be managed in a sustainable way. This means using the resources they offer without destroying the area. Rainforests are one example. They provide products such as rubber and cocoa pods, which these boys are harvesting without cutting down trees or damaging vegetation. In 1990, Brazil created four reserves for sustainable harvesting in the Amazon rainforest.

If human-made habitats are planned thoughtfully there is often room for wildlife. Many farms provide ideal conditions for birds, which can help the farmer by eating insect pests. But some animals need truly wild habitats away from people. In India, where the growing population takes up a lot of land, the tiger has benefited from large nature reserves where it is protected. National parks, like this one in Kenya (below), can earn money from tourists, as well as protect many species in their native habitat.

FACT FILE 1

Habitat neglect

Some habitats are lost through neglect. Europe's lowland heaths are an example of this. Heaths are typically dominated by heather, which covers the land with sheets of beautiful purple flowers in summer. Heath wildlife includes dragonflies, snakes and lizards. Heathlands are also home to some unusual birds, such as the nightjar, which catches insects while flying at night, and the hobby, a small but powerful falcon. Heaths originally came into being when people cleared trees from sandy and gravelly ground in order to graze their livestock. Grazing animals and fires (deliberately started to get rid of old heather and encourage new growth) kept trees from coming back. But during this century, grazing has been abandoned on many heaths. Most sheep now graze on modern human-made pastures. When they are abandoned, heaths are quickly invaded; shrubs and ferns come first, then birch and then oak trees. In the end there is a wood with its own wildlife, but with no place for the specially adapted plants and animals of the heath.

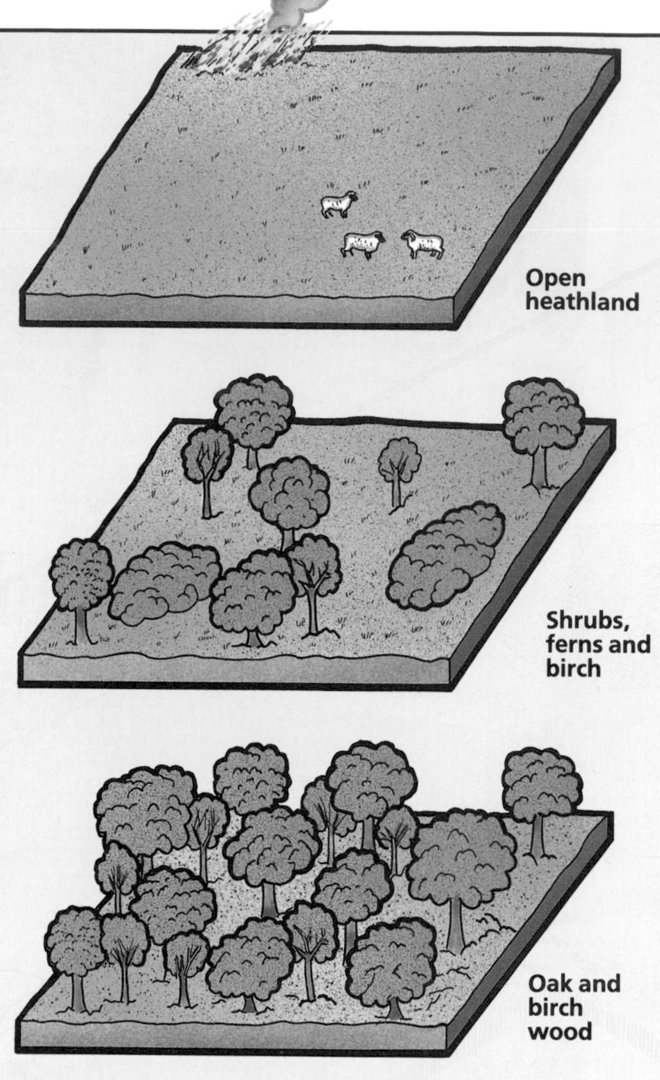

The debt factor

Over the years, wealthy regions like Europe, Japan and the United States have loaned money to poorer ones. But as these countries, mainly in Africa, Asia and Latin America, fall deeper into debt, they get poorer. In search of money they are forced to further exploit their natural resources, damaging habitats.

Wildlife tourism

If wild habitats bring no income to local people, the residents of the area may be forced to replace them with crops. Wildlife tourism can help the economy and protect habitats. In Rwanda, tourists pay to see mountain gorillas in the wild.

Greening the desert

Desertification is a major problem for millions of people around the world. Planting trees in the desert can help stop erosion and can protect croplands from the wind. This method has been adopted in some dry regions of the Middle East, like on the Arabian peninsula (right). In addition, researchers are attempting to bring rain to deserts. Several North African countries are planning to use artificial trees to generate rainfall. The trees are made of plastic, and during the night they absorb moisture from the air. During the day they slowly release this moisture, cooling the air around them. It is hoped that the cooling effect from the trees will cause moisture from the air to create rain clouds. Libya is planning to plant up to 40,000 plastic trees with the hope of creating a new river in the dry area of the south.

The disappearing seas

The need for water for irrigation, industry and drinking has led to the destruction of many water habitats. The Aral Sea in Uzbekistan has lost at least half of its water since the 1960s. Its area has shrunk by a third. The water has been diverted from the rivers that feed the Aral in order to irrigate cotton and rice crops. As the sea has shrunk, 324,000 acres of wetlands around its edges have dried up, and former fishing communities are now far from the water. The once flourishing fishing industry is dead, and abandoned fishing boats litter the ground. The dry seabed stretches for miles.

FACT FILE 2

Organic farming and gardening
Although farms have replaced many wild areas, they can still be managed in ways that help the environment. Organic farmers use natural methods to protect their crops instead of chemical fertilizers and pesticides. For example, they keep hedges and ponds which provide homes for wildlife like birds and frogs that eat insect pests.

Antarctica
Antarctica is the planet's last great wilderness. It covers 10 percent of the earth's land surface, and together with its waters, it supports a variety of sea life, including penguins, seals, whales and seabirds. It also holds huge reserves of coal and other minerals, which make it vulnerable to exploitation. However, there are increasing calls for it to be protected.

MEASURING AND MAPS

CHAPTER EIGHT: MEASURING AND MAPS

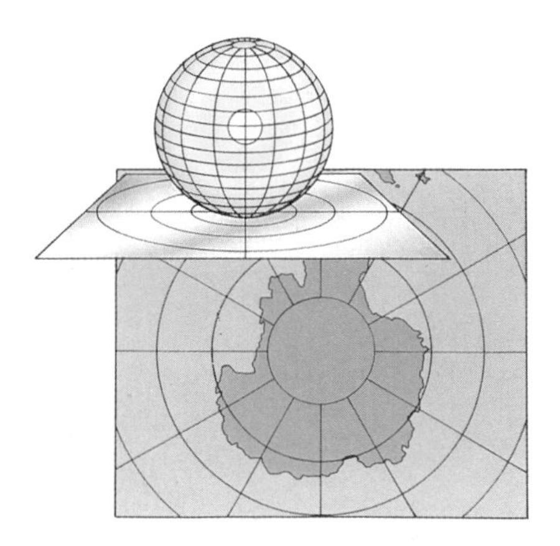

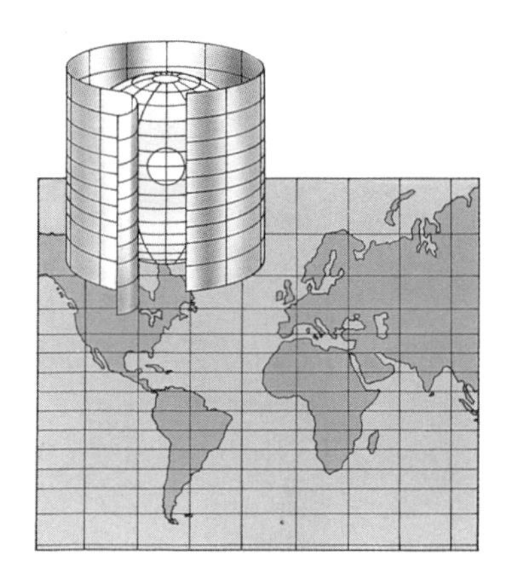

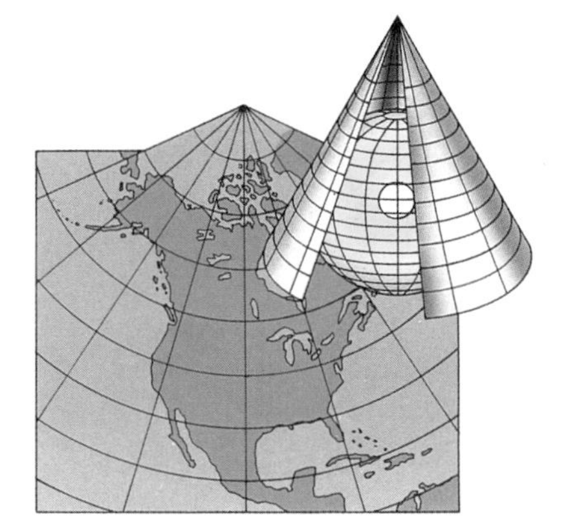

INTRODUCTION

Maps are ways of portraying the earth, or a part of it, on a flat surface – usually a sheet of paper. Maps are similar to photographs taken from aircraft or spacecraft. But photographs give far less information than maps do. For example, map-makers use colors, symbols, words and numbers to show hills and valleys, the heights of mountains, and the names of places and land features. There are none of these things on air photographs.

General reference maps give information about a whole continent, a single country or a particular region. They show two main kinds of feature. First, they indicate such natural features as rivers, forests and the height of land. Second, they show things made by people, such as cities, roads and boundaries. Special maps concentrate on one feature, such as rainfall or rail routes. Books of maps are called atlases.

Models of the ground hanging above a huge aerial photograph.

Space photographs show that the earth is shaped like a ball and that its surface is curved. The curvature limits the distance you can see toward the horizon – the line where the earth and the sky seem to meet. At sea level, the horizon is about 2.5 miles away, although a person on the top of a mountain can see farther.

▷ The diagram shows the equator (0° latitude), the Tropic of Cancer (about 23.5° North), the Tropic of Capricorn (about 23.5° South) and the prime meridian (0° longitude).

Longitude

Latitude

GLOBES

Because maps are flat and the earth's surface is curved, the only true way of showing the world is a globe. Globes are hollow spheres made of cardboard, metal or plastic. Land features may be printed on strips of paper, which are pasted onto the surface of the globe.

Globes show the true shapes, areas and positions of continents and the oceans. But such features are often distorted on flat maps. For example, the shortest distance between two places on a world map seems to be the straight line joining them. But if you use a piece of string to join the same two places on a globe, you will find that the shortest path is a curved line that follows a different route. This curved line is part of a great circle – a line that goes right around the earth, dividing it into two equal parts. For example, the equator, an imaginary line that lies halfway between the North and South Poles, is a great circle. Even so, globes have disadvantages. Their size and shape make them difficult to carry around, whereas a map can be folded and carried in a pocket.

▷ Some globes are fixed and cannot be moved. Others are mounted on stands so that you can turn them around on their axes, which are usually tilted by 23.5°. This is the same tilt as the earth's axis (the line that joins the North Pole, the center of the earth, and the South Pole). By rotating the globe you get a series of views of the earth.

LINES ON THE GLOBE

Lines of latitude (or parallels) are lines on globes that run parallel to the equator. Running at right angles to the parallels are lines of longitude, or meridians. Lines of latitude and longitude are measured in degrees. For example, the North Pole has a latitude of 90° North, the equator is latitude 0°, and the South Pole is 90° South. Meridians are measured 180° East and West of the prime meridian, which runs through Greenwich, London.

◁ A network of lines of latitude and longitude cover the globe. Map-makers use this grid, or graticule, to draw maps. Every place on earth has its own latitude and longitude.

DID YOU KNOW?

The earth is slightly flattened at the poles and it bulges near the equator. The distance through the earth from the North to South Poles is 7,900 miles. The diameter of the earth at the equator is slightly larger: 7,926 miles. This shape is described as an oblate spheroid.

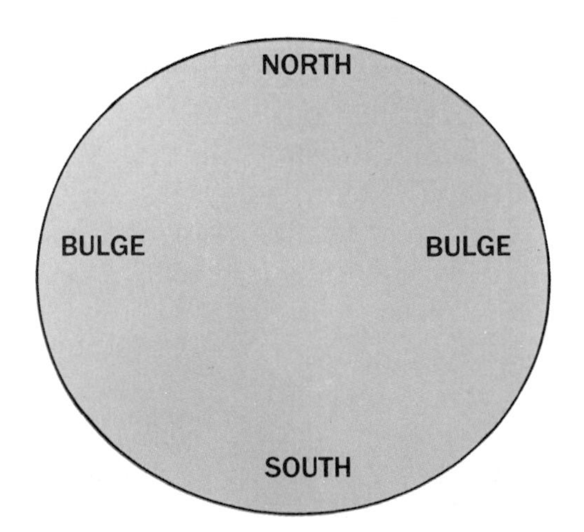

MAP SCALES

Scales on maps are sometimes shown as ratios or fractions, such as 1:50,000. This means that 1 centimeter on the map represents 50,000 centimeters (0.5 kilometers) on the ground. Some maps have scales in words and figures, such as 1 centimeter = 15 kilometers. Others have scale bars showing distances.

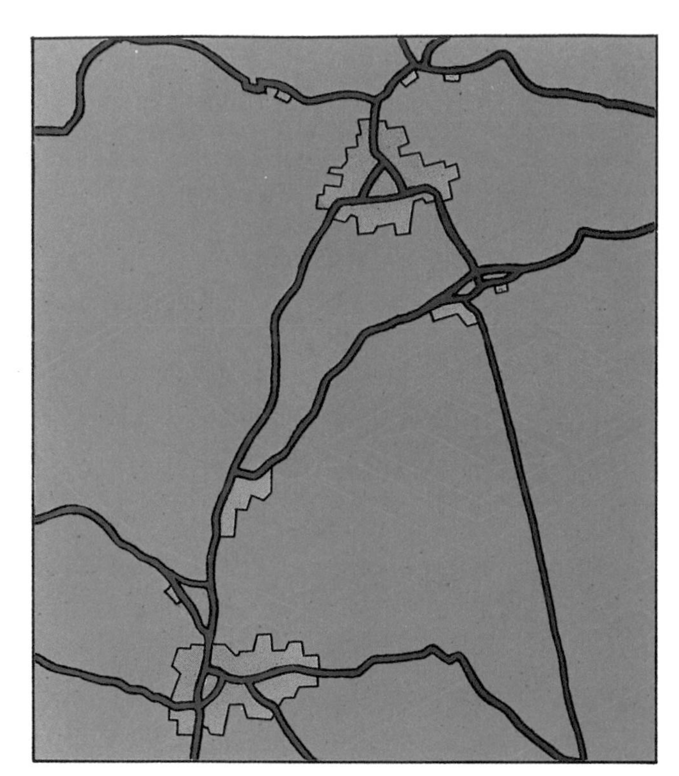

△ This madeup small-scale map shows only main roads, cities, towns, and villages. It shows a very large area.

LARGE SCALES

Maps drawn to a large scale cover only a small area. Some large-scale maps are called plans. For example, a large-scale map might show a street, with each house marked on it. An even larger scale might show gardens and even individual trees. A garden measuring 20 meters long and 10 meters wide might be drawn on a plan at a scale of 1 centimeter = 1 meter (making it 20 centimeters by 10 centimeters on the plan). Expressed as a ratio, this scale would be 1:100.

SMALL SCALES

Small scales are used for maps that cover large areas. For example, a one-page map of North America in an atlas might be drawn at the small scale of 1:35,000,000, or 1 centimeter = 350 kilometers. This map would show the countries, states, counties or provinces, and the positions of major cities. But if you want to learn more about California, you must look at the map of just this state, which might be drawn at a larger scale of 1:2,500,000, or 1 centimeter = 25 kilometers. If you want information about the city of Los Angeles, you must turn to the city map, which might have an even larger scale of 1:30,000.

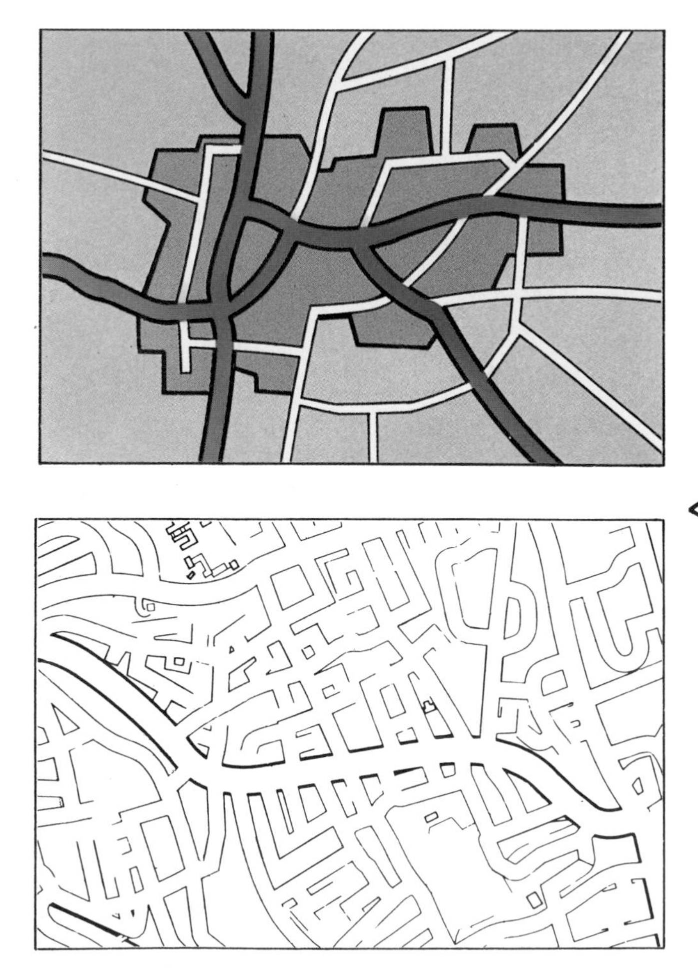

▷ The middle map is at a larger scale than the top map. It shows more detail, such as minor roads. The bottom map is at a large scale. It shows every street.

MAPS WITHOUT SCALES

Some special maps are not drawn to scale and deliberately distort directions and the positions of places. For example, some cities produce maps of this kind showing the routes on their complex underground railway systems. An accurate map showing the precise positions of all stations would confuse travelers. Instead, map-makers simplify the maps, making most of the railway lines appear to be straight, and making the distances between stations appear the same. Such simplified maps are easy to use.

LRT Registered User No. 91/1366

△ London's underground railway system can be shown on an easy-to-use map which is not drawn to scale.

SCALE MAP OF A LOT

A lot 150 paces long and 100 paces wide appears on the plan, at a scale of 1:10, as a rectangle 15 centimeters long and 10 centimeters wide. To show the position of a tree, pace out the distance along one side of the lot until you are facing the tree at right angles. Pace the distance from the side to the tree and mark the distances on the plan at the correct scale.

Pace out the area of a lot or park, taking notes.

Pace distances to features such as trees etc.

Flower bed

Tree

Fence

Use graph paper; one square can equal one pace.

Why did the explorer Christopher Columbus call the people of America Indians? When he sailed west from Spain, he used a map drawn at the wrong scale, making the world seem smaller than it is. He thought he had reached India, but in fact, he had reached the West Indies.

If you want to walk across country between two places, you can find out the distance from an accurate map. Before you set out, you also need to know the direction in which you should travel. All maps show directions. On most maps, north is at the top. On atlas maps, lines of latitude and longitude show directions.

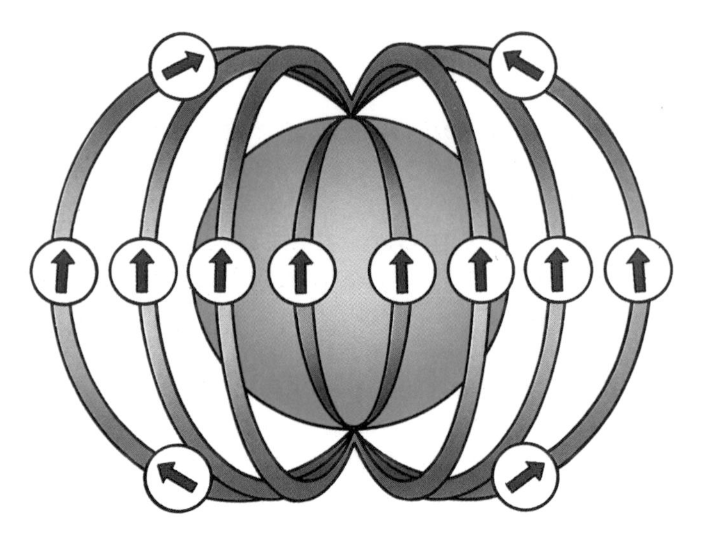

△ A compass always points north along the lines of earth's magnetic field.

COMPASS POINTS

The eight main points (or directions) of the compass are north, northeast, east, southeast, south, southwest, west, and northwest. Many compasses show 16 or even 32 points.

A small magnetic compass, which fits in your pocket, is a simple way of finding directions. The needle of a compass points to the magnetic North Pole, which is near the geographic (or true) North Pole. The difference in direction between the two poles is often shown (in degrees) in the margin of maps. If you stand facing due north, you know that south is directly behind you. West is at right angles on your left, and east is on your right.

▽ When you have found north with a magnetic compass, you can line up, or orientate, the map. This helps you to find out where you are.

FOLLOW A STAR

On a clear night in the Northern Hemisphere, you can find out where north is located by facing Polaris, which is also called the Pole Star or the North Star.

Polaris is the brightest star in the constellation of Ursa Minor, which is also known as the Little Bear or the Little Dipper. Polaris is located almost directly above the North Pole and it appears to remain almost stationary, while the other stars gradually turn around in the sky. For several thousand years, navigators have used Polaris to find their way across seas and oceans at night.

▷ The constellation Ursa Major (or the Great Bear) resembles a saucepan. The line joining the two stars at the front of the pan points to Polaris.

MAPPING DIRECTIONS

The diagram shows the directions that a person must take to walk from home to school. The compass shows the direction of north. Coming out of the house, the person would have to turn east, which is at right angles to north. The road then turns northeast and then east before reaching a crossroads. Beyond the crossroads, the person has to follow roads running south, southeast and east. The final part of the journey leads the walker north, northeast and north.

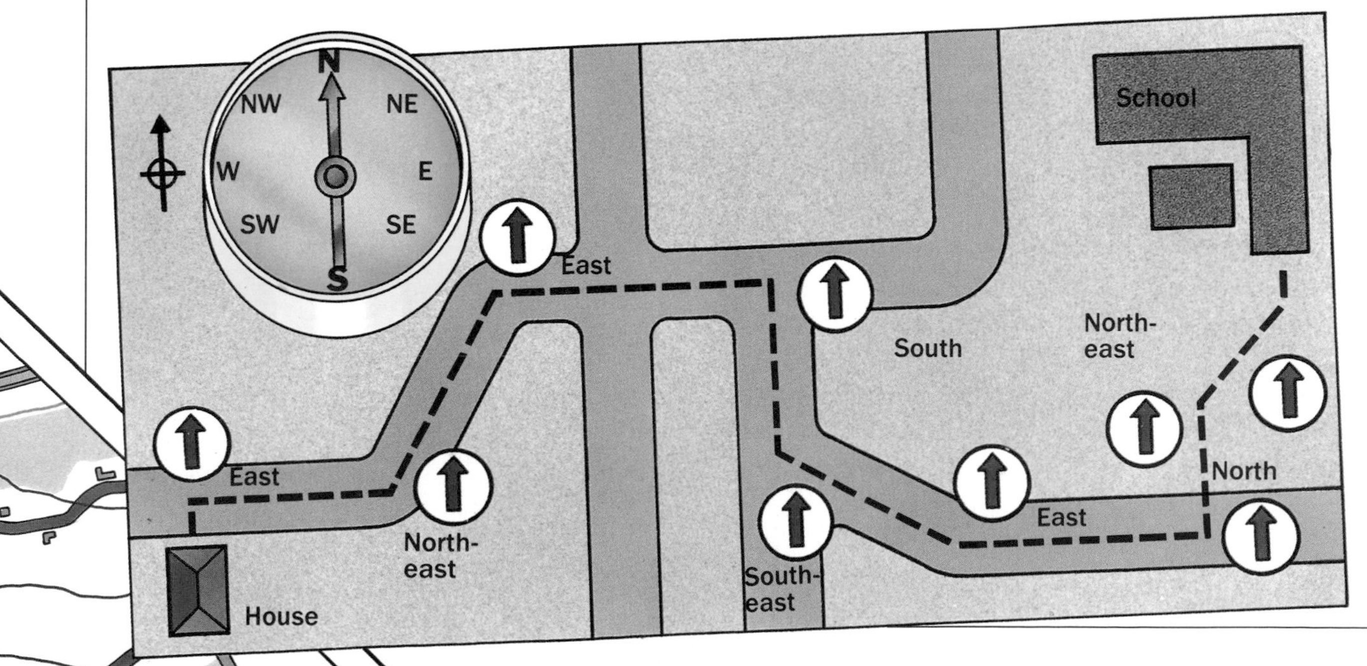

MAP SYMBOLS

To pack as much information as possible on a map, map-makers use a kind of shorthand. For example, a blue line indicates a river and a blue area a lake or sea. A red line may indicate a main road, and a group of tiny drawings of trees indicates a forest. These are all types of map symbol.

SYMBOLS AND SCALES

The amount of information on a map depends on the scale. The finest line that can be drawn on a map is 0.005 centimeters thick. On a map with a scale of 1:1,000,000, this width represents 50 meters. As a result, a main road can be shown only as a thin red line. But on a scale of 1:50,000, which is used on many topographic maps, a road can be made more prominent and shown as a red line between two black ones. Scale also limits information about such features as cities. On an atlas map, a large city may be indicated by a black square or circle. On a large-scale map, the shape of the city can be shown.

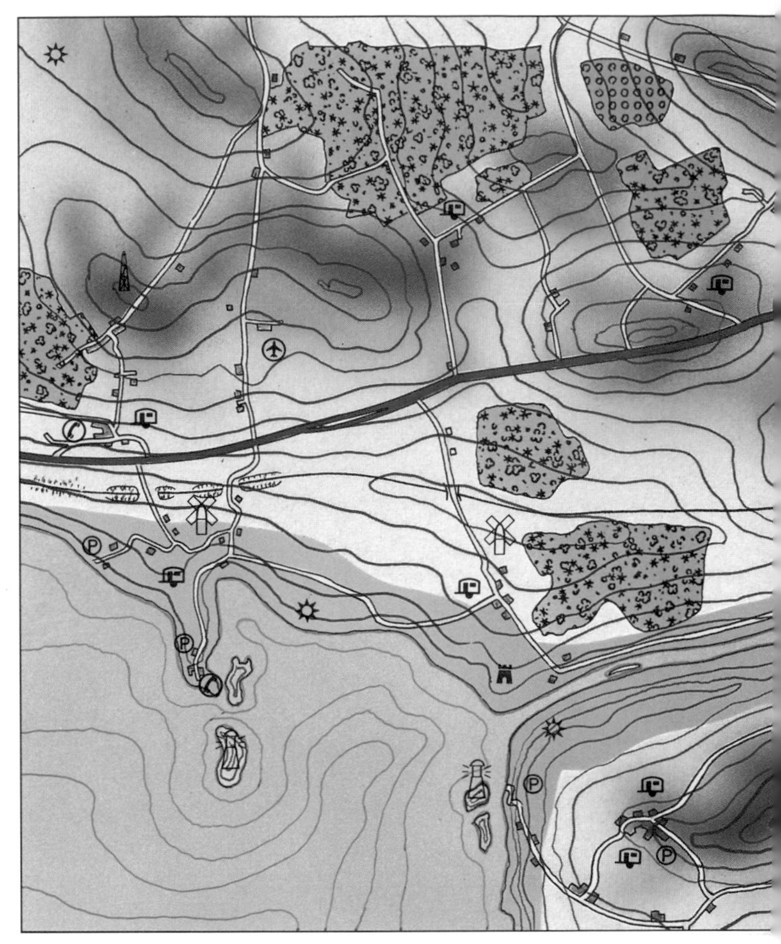

▽ The ups and downs of the land can be shown by hill shading. Another method uses contours, which join together points of equal height.

UPS AND DOWNS

Map-makers use several methods to show relief (differences in height on the earth's surface). High mountain peaks appear as spot heights, which give the precise height of a mountain.

Other methods are needed to show the ups and downs of the land. This can be done by using contours – lines that join places with the same height. Shading is sometimes used for rocky areas to create a three-dimensional effect. Atlas-makers often use layer tints (a series of colors) to show various levels. Sometimes, layer tinting and hill shading are combined. Colored models of the land are lit so that the hills cast shadows. The model is photographed and the picture used to create the effect of relief on the map.

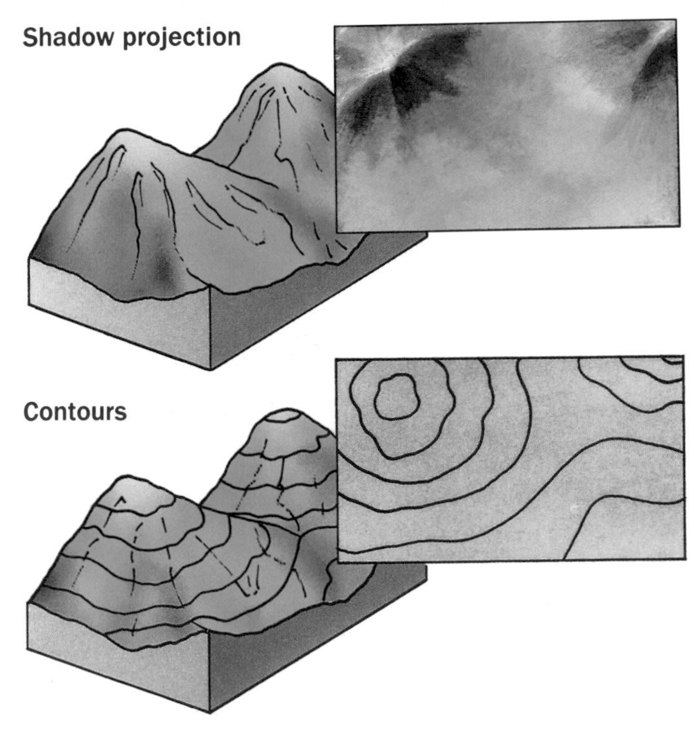

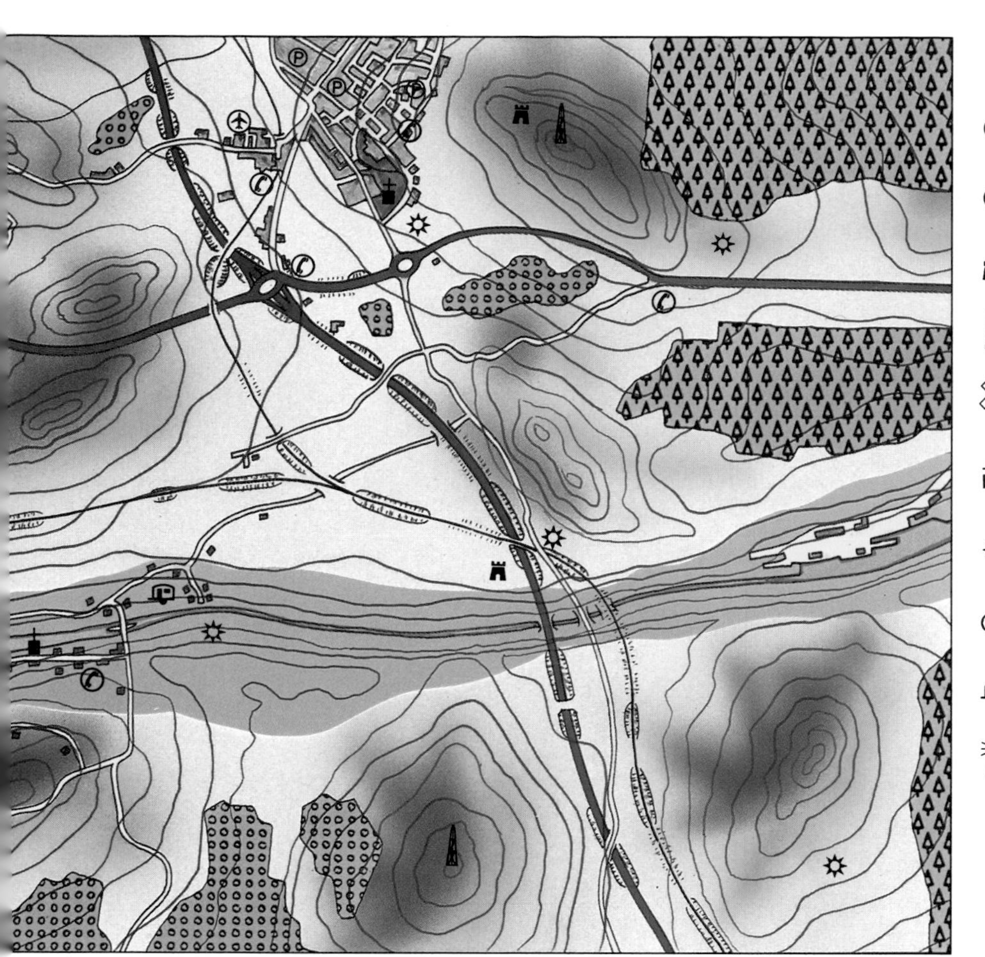

KEY

- Airport
- Telephone
- Castle
- TV or radio mast
- Windmill
- Church
- Ancient site
- Parking lot
- Trailer park
- Lighthouse

◁ Topographic maps use symbols which are shown in legends (keys). Some examples of symbols are shown above.

MAKE YOUR OWN MAP SYMBOLS

Draw a rough map of the area around your home. You will find many features, such as streetlights, mailboxes, public telephones and traffic lights, to put on your map as symbols. When making symbols, remember that they should be simple and easy to draw, but they should also give an impression of the feature concerned.

Draw a simple map

Some possible symbols

Streetlight

Mailbox

Drain

Tree

Phone

Traffic lights

The amount of information map-makers can show about an area is limited by the scale and the space available. Special maps give information about one aspect of an area. Almost anything can be shown on special, or thematic, maps such as physical maps, political maps, population maps and vegetation maps.

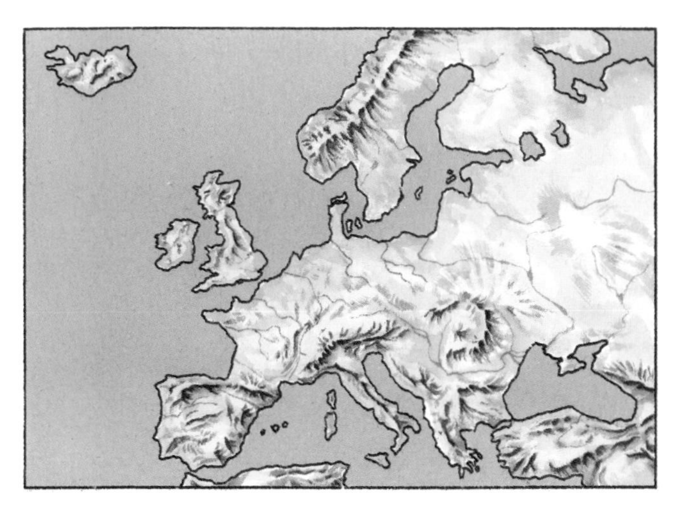

△ Physical maps show land features, such as mountains.

PHYSICAL AND POLITICAL

Physical, or relief, maps show the physical features of the land, including mountains, plains, rivers and lakes. Physical maps in atlases often use green and yellow tints to indicate low-lying areas. Browns, reds and purples are used for high areas, and the highest peaks are often colored white. The names on these maps identify the main physical features, natural regions, islands and the seas and oceans.

Physical maps do not show cultural (human) features, which appear on political maps. The boundaries of countries and smaller divisions, such as states, provinces, counties and other areas, together with political capitals, are shown on political maps. Colors help to distinguish political divisions.

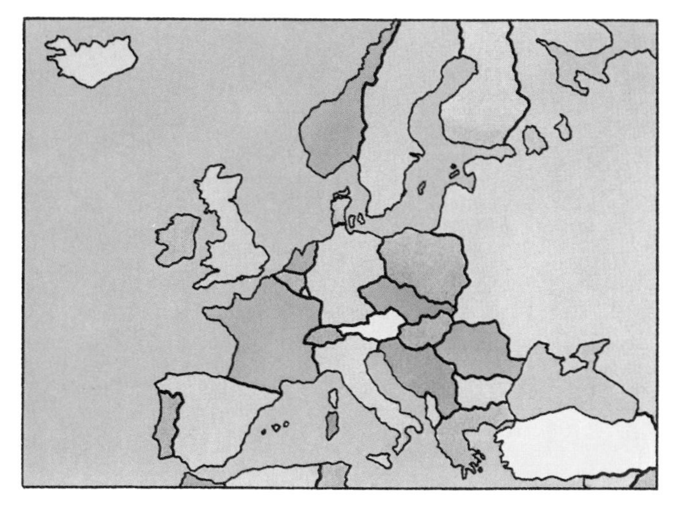

△ Political maps show human features, such as countries.

UNDER THE SEA

Water covers about seven-tenths of the earth's surface. Until recently, little was known about the ocean bed. Most people assumed that it was a vast, featureless plain.

But in the 1920s, instruments called echo sounders came into use. These instruments enabled ships to measure the depth of the water as they sailed along. Since the 1940s, echo sounders have been used to map most of the ocean floor (see page 291). The maps show that the physical features on the ocean floor are as varied as those on land. They have also shed light on the earth sciences.

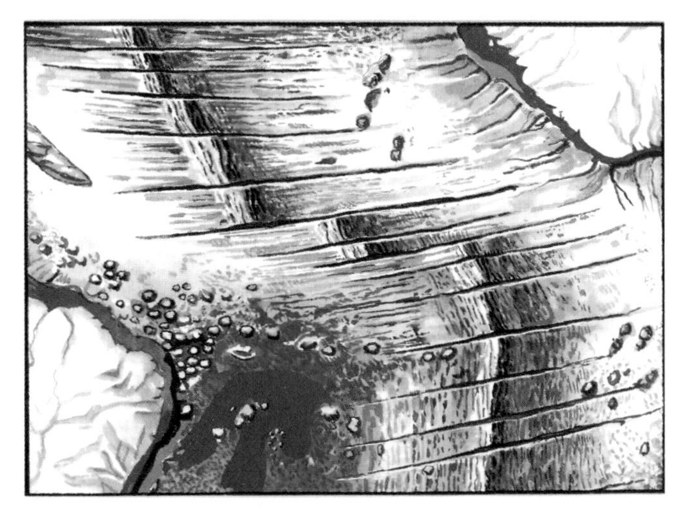

△ Recent maps of the ocean floor show that it contains mountain ranges, volcanic peaks (some forming islands), trenches and broad plains.

RAINFALL MAPS

Some special maps show the amount of rain that falls in different parts of a region each year. They usually use darker shades for areas with heavy rainfall and lighter shades for areas that have little rain. Comparing rainfall maps to physical maps shows how physical features affect the weather. For example, it often rains more on hills and mountains.

▽ The rainfall map of Europe shows a lot of rain on the coasts of the ocean and on high areas. It also shows little rainfall where it is very hot or very cold.

VEGETATION MAPS

Some maps show the plants that grow in various regions. Some vegetation maps use tints to distinguish between vegetation regions. Others contain tiny drawings, or pictograms, to show the main plant types. Comparing these maps to physical and rainfall maps, you can find out the conditions that produce various kinds of plant life.

▽ The vegetation map of Europe shows how the plant life varies between the cold regions in the north and on mountains, and the much warmer lands in the south.

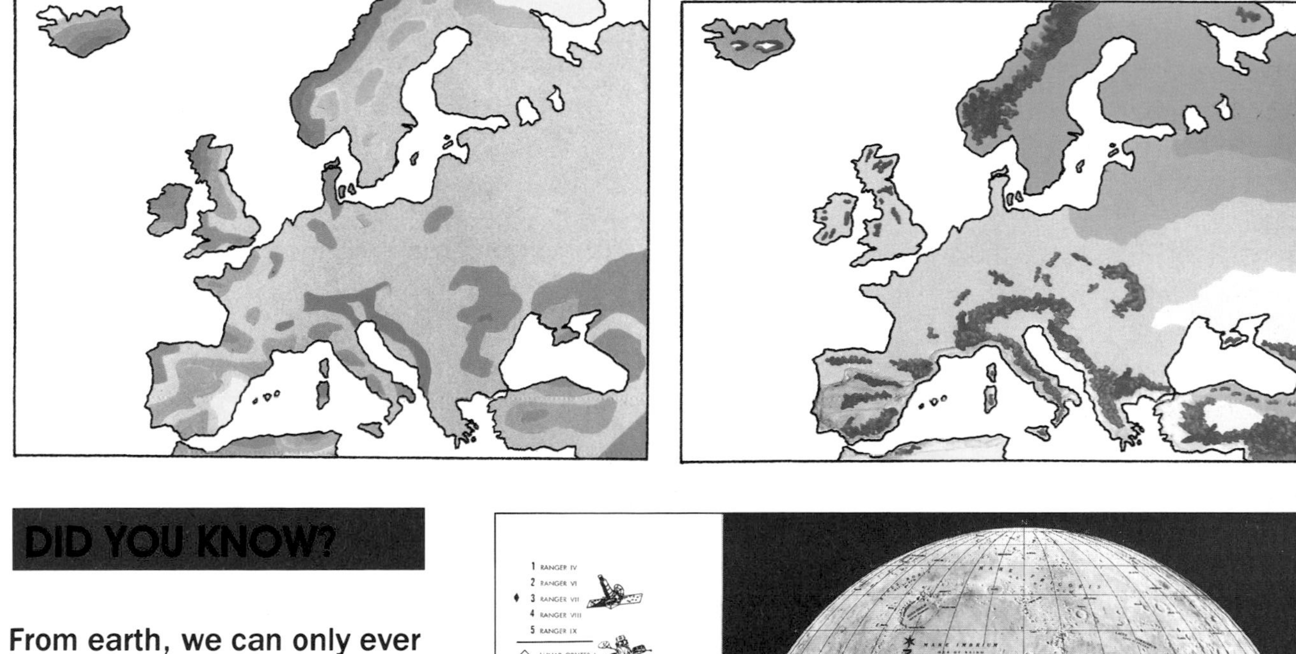

DID YOU KNOW?

From earth, we can only ever see one side of the moon. The features on the far side were unknown until the space age. Between 1966 and 1967, five Orbiter spacecraft took photographs of almost the entire surface of the moon, thus revealing the landscape of the far side of the moon. This map (on the right) includes details of the spacecraft that have landed there.

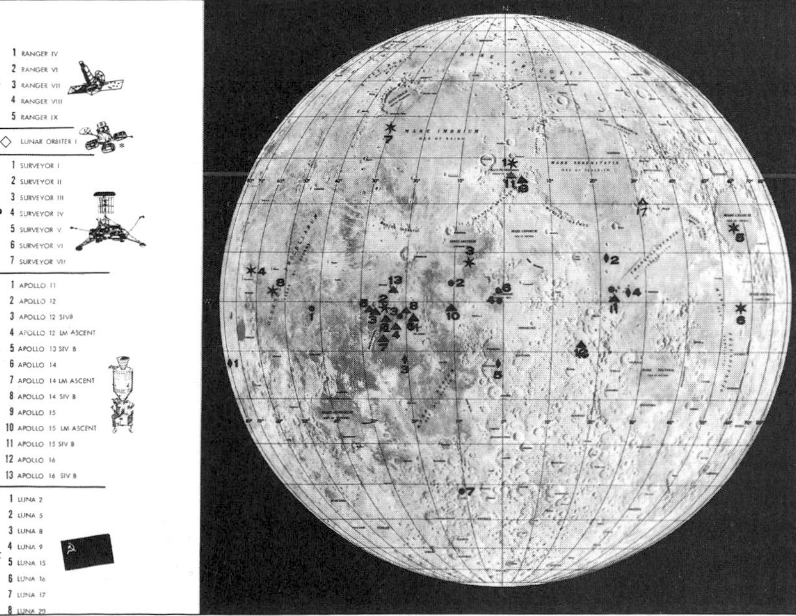

General reference maps have many uses. They are essential tools for travelers, navigators, members of the armed forces, town planners, and so on. The amount of information you can get from a map depends on your ability to read the map. First, you must be able to find places and discover where you are.

△ Members of the armed forces frequently use maps.

FINDING PLACES

Most atlases contain indexes, which list the names of places. Next to each name is a map page number and the latitude and longitude of the place. By knowing the latitude and longitude, map-users can pinpoint the place exactly.

Some maps are divided into squares which are labeled either in numbers, as on many topographic maps, or in letters and numbers. For example, the key to the map may say that a town is in square B4. The system of letters and numbers is used in city street atlases.

▽ Map grids (networks of squares) locate places. Finding a grid reference is like "zooming in" on an area.

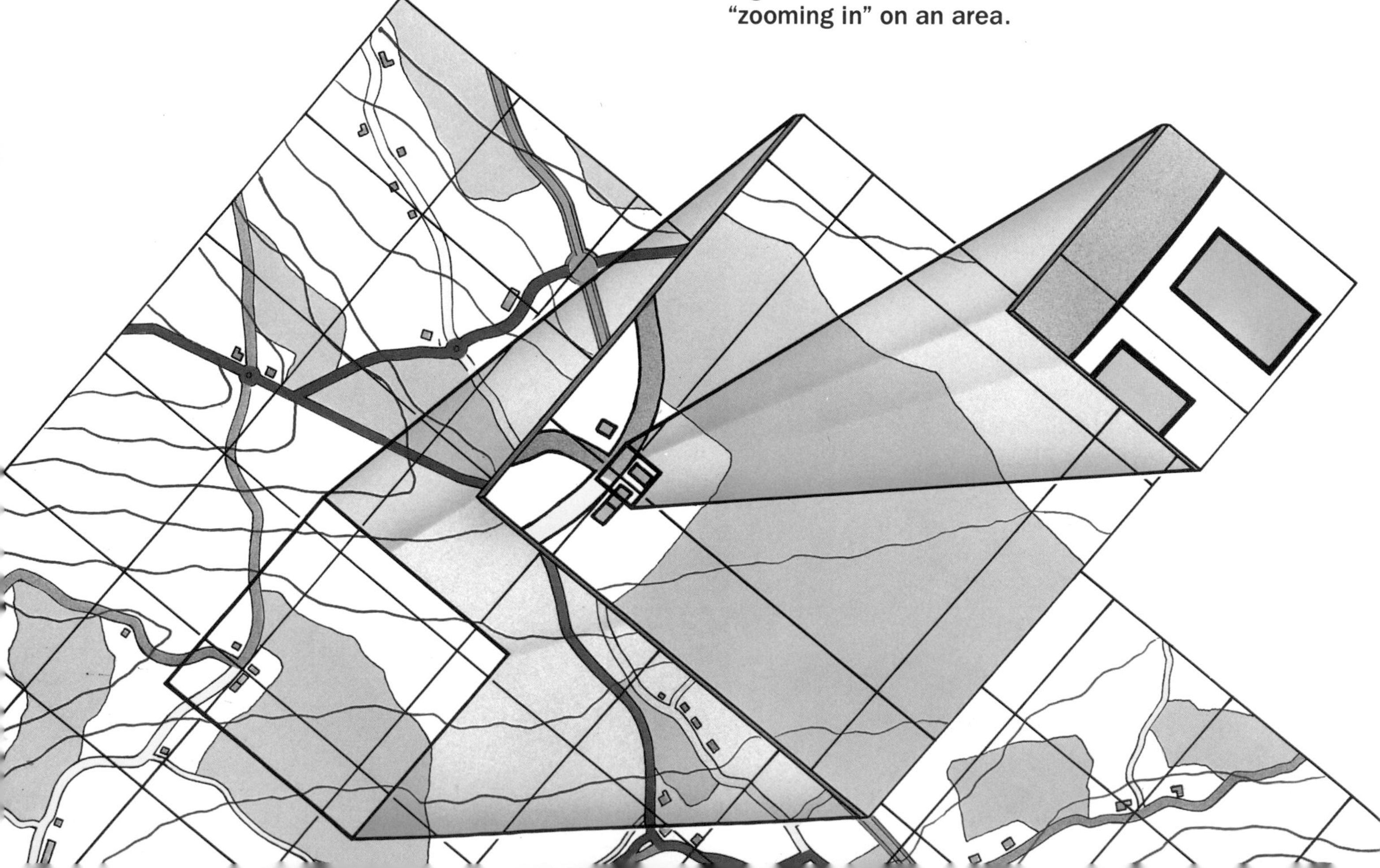

WHERE ARE YOU?

Hikers often use maps to find their way around. They learn how to pick out land features and identify the symbols that portray these features on their map. By taking bearings from the features with a magnetic compass, they can work out their position on the map. They can also find their position fairly accurately without a compass, simply by judging the distance to the features.

▷ A walker identifies land features, such as villages and bridges. By finding these on a map, the walker can judge where he or she is standing.

HUNTING FOR TREASURE

Pirates once hid their booty on tropical islands. They drew rough maps, showing prominent features that would help them to find the spot again years later. You can make a treasure map in a local park. First, make a rough map of the park and draw on an arrow to indicate north. Now plan a route to the spot where the treasure is buried. You must give instructions on where to start the search. Then note down the directions and distances involved in reaching the spot. See whether your friends can find the "treasure" using your map.

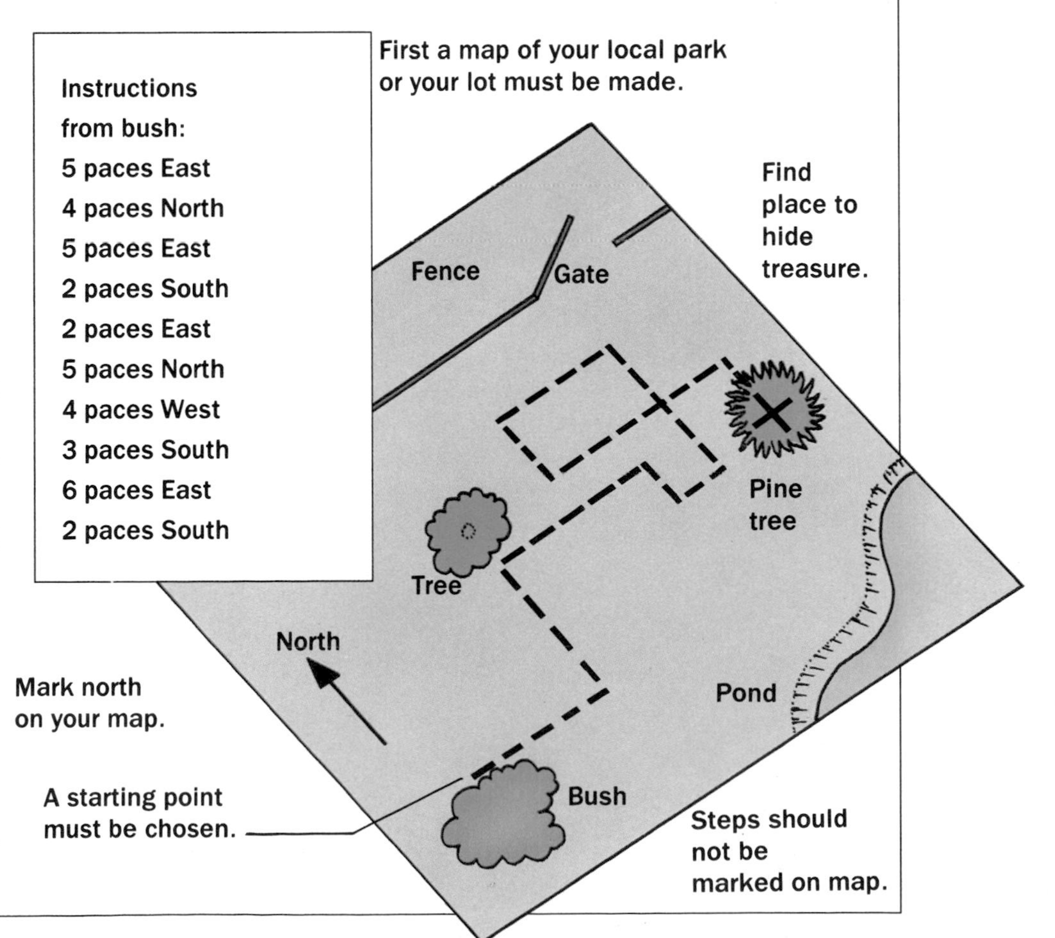

People who measure the land are called land surveyors. The mapping of an area begins by creating a network of points and measuring the distances and angles between them. The second stage is to map all the details of the land, such as rivers, roads, and so on, between the accurately fixed points in the network.

TRIANGULATION

The first step in a survey is to measure the distance between two points, several kilometers apart. This distance is called the baseline. Traditionally, measuring a baseline is done using metal tapes.

Next, the surveyor measures the angles between the two points at the end of the baseline and a third point, using a telescopic instrument, called a theodolite. The three points form a triangle and, if you know the length of one side of a triangle and all three angles, you can calculate the length of the other two sides. The surveyor then continues to fix the positions of other points in a network of triangles by angular measurements alone. This method of surveying is called triangulation.

△ Surveyors use plane tables to measure details of the land.

▽ To map an area, surveyors measure a baseline (B-C) and fix a third point (A) by angular measurements. Other points (F, E, D, and so on) are fixed by measuring angles.

Known fixed points are plotted on paper at a chosen scale, and measured height and depressions are drawn in.

B

F

E

D

DETAILED MAPPING

Until the 1950s, the main method of measuring the details of the land between the fixed points was plane table surveying. Today this has been replaced by mapping from air photographs.

The plane table is a flat board covered by paper, with the points fixed by triangulation plotted accurately on the surface. The board is mounted on a tripod at a known (fixed) "station". The surveyor then uses a sighting instrument, called an alidade, to measure the directions to points, such as the corners of fields. Pencil lines are drawn to these points. When the work at one station is complete, the surveyor moves on to new stations and sights the positions of points around those stations. When three sightings to the same point intersect, the point is then fixed. Gradually, the spaces between the fixed points are filled in.

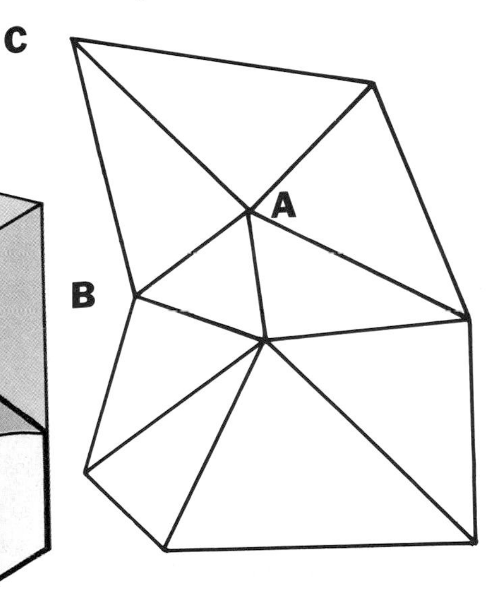

DID YOU KNOW?

Measuring a baseline with metal tapes is a slow job. Surveyors can now measure distances quickly with electronic instruments that record how long it takes light or radio waves to travel between two points.

Besides measuring the details of the land, surveyors must also find out the heights of many points in the area they are mapping. From a large number of these points, they can draw in the contours that show the relief of the land. The heights are measured above mean sea level – the average level of the sea.

FIXING HEIGHTS

Accurate measurements of height are made with a surveyor's level (a telescopic instrument containing a highly sensitive spirit level). The surveyor sets up the level on a tripod over a point whose height is known. By taking a reading on a marked stick placed on a second point, the surveyor can find the height difference between the two points. Accurately fixed points are called bench marks and are cut into walls or rocks.

Surveyors also use theodolites to measure the vertical angles between two points, because if you know the distance and the vertical angle between two points, you can calculate the difference in height. This method is less accurate than leveling. When it is hazy, angular measurements can be distorted.

△ Land surveyors use accurate telescopic instruments called theodolites to measure horizontal and vertical angles.

▽ Surveyors measure the vertical angle between two points to work out the height difference between them. They must allow for the height of their theodolites.

SOUNDING THE DEPTHS

Contours are used on some maps to show the depth of water along coasts. The main instrument used to find the depth of water is an echo sounder. Echo sounders transmit sound waves and record the echo of the wave that bounces back from the ocean floor. The speed of sound is known, and so the depth of the water can be worked out. The depths are recorded as the ship sails along.

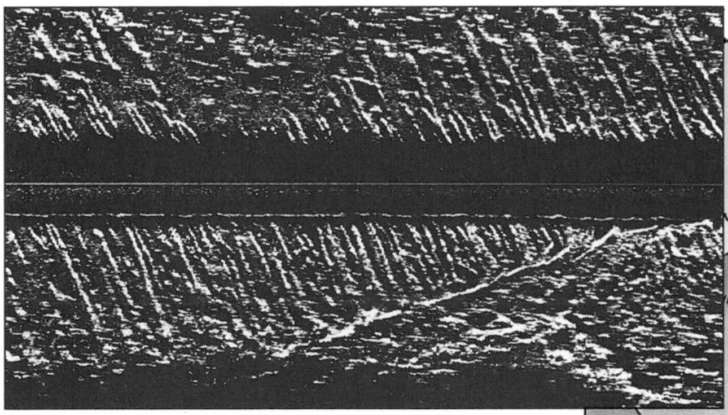

△ An instrument called GLORIA bounces sound waves off the ocean bed, giving "pictures" of a strip of ocean floor.

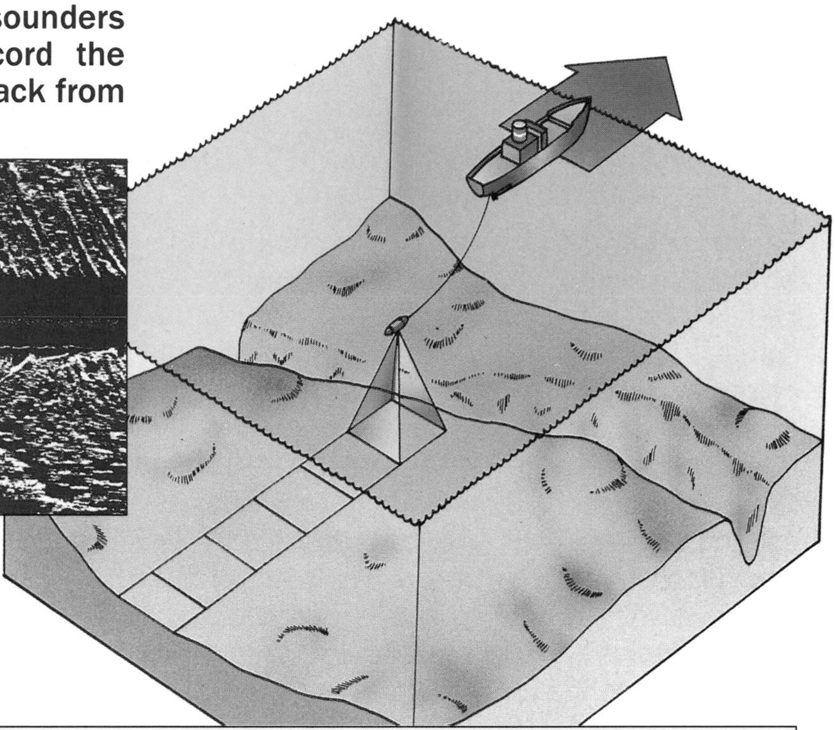

MAP YOUR OWN MOUNTAIN

Build a model of a mountain with clay or modeling clay on a board. Use the point of a pencil to mark rows of dots around the mountain. The dots in each row should all be at the same height. Use a ruler held vertically to make sure of this. Also, the rows should all be the same height apart – say, 3 centimeters. Now join up each row of dots with a piece of string. If you look straight down on your mountain you will see a contour map of the mountain. You could then draw a contour map on paper.

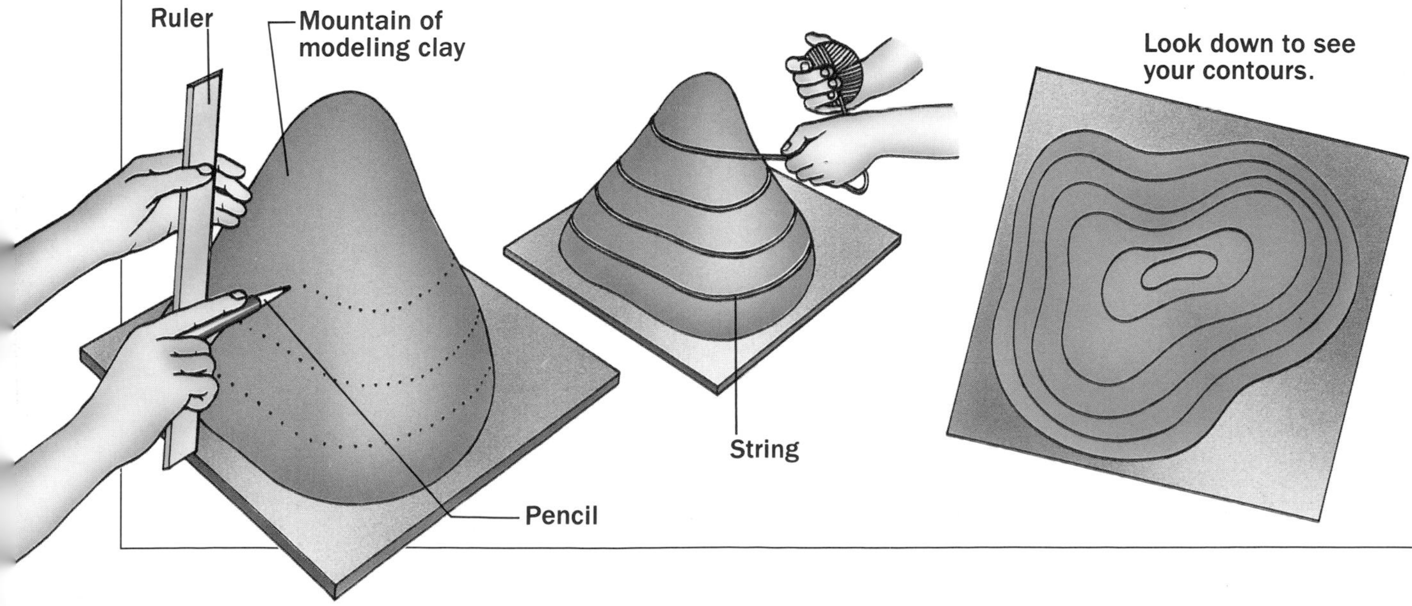

Ruler

Mountain of modeling clay

Pencil

String

Look down to see your contours.

MAPPING FROM THE AIR

Aerial photographs first proved useful in World Wars I and II, because they provided information about the enemy. Since World War II, they have been used for large-scale mapping and a new science called photogrammetry (making measurements from photographs) has developed.

▽ Aircraft photograph the land in long strips. Points whose positions are known are identified on the photographs. They serve as control points when maps are made from the photographs.

Control point

AERIAL PHOTOGRAPHS

Aerial photographs are taken by aircraft that fly along carefully planned flight paths. They fly at a constant level and speed, taking vertical photographs – that is, pictures of the land looking directly downward.

The cameras are specially designed to take pictures automatically at regular intervals, so that each photograph in every strip overlaps the next by about 60 percent. When one strip of land has been photographed, the aircraft turns and photographs the next strip alongside, and overlapping, the first. Many photographs may be taken to cover a large area.

▽ A lot of time may be spent planning a series of aerial photographs. Old maps of the area are studied (if they exist) in order to decide on the best route for the camera-carrying aircraft.

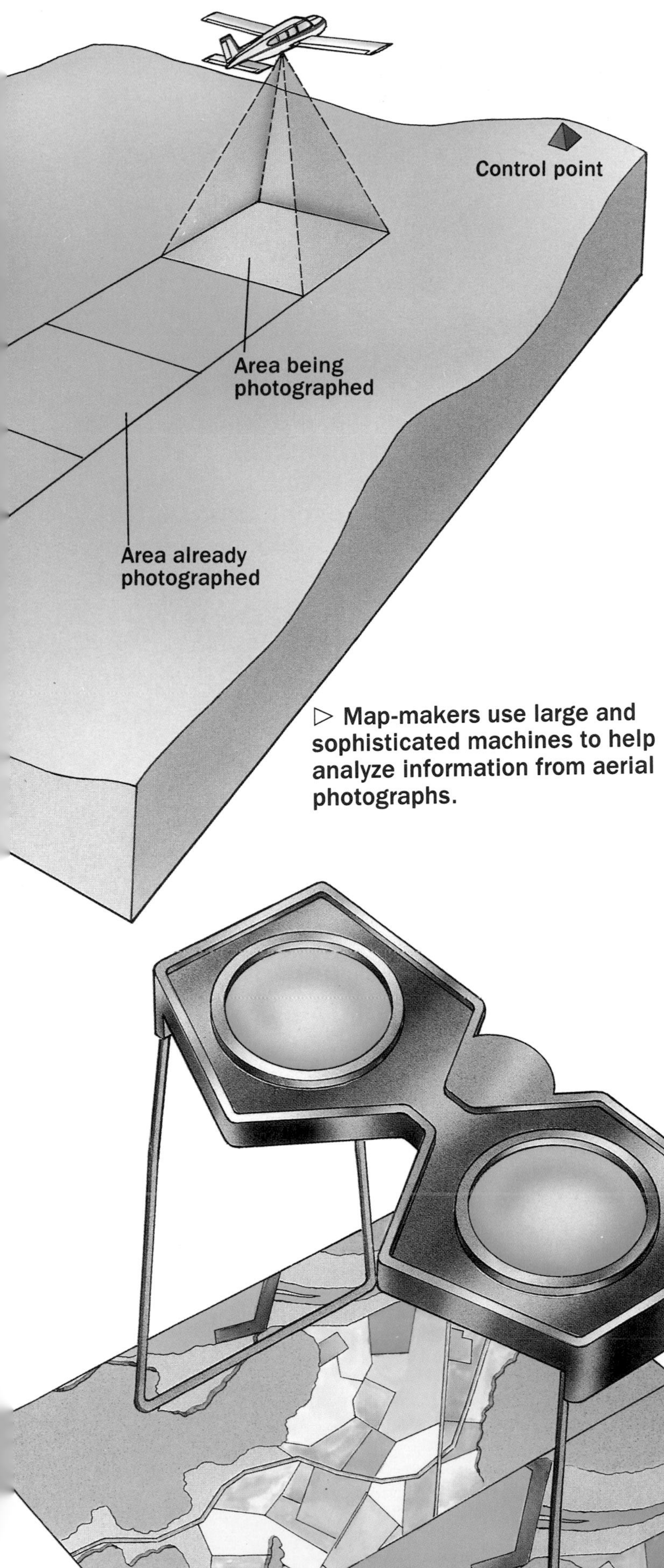

CORRECTING DISTORTIONS

Before aerial photographs are taken, land surveyors measure the positions and heights of a network of points. They mark the spots on the ground so that the points can be seen on the photographs. For example, they may dig a small cross around the point. Aerial photographs are distorted. By using control points, whose positions and heights are known, map-makers can correct the distortions.

▷ Map-makers use large and sophisticated machines to help analyze information from aerial photographs.

3-D EFFECT

If you place two overlapping photographs side by side and view the overlap through a stereoscope, you will see a three-dimensional image of the land. Because of this three-dimensional effect, stereo-plotters can draw contours and show the relief of the land, as well as land features. The use of air photographs has greatly speeded up detailed mapping.

◁ Stereoscopes make pairs of aerial photographs show the land in three dimensions.

In recent years, map-makers have been making increasing use of new technology, including the use of computers, especially to speed up the compilation of maps, and the use of artificial satellites to collect data for maps. Satellite photographs cover large areas. These areas can be viewed at regular intervals.

SATELLITE PHOTOGRAPHS

Measurements from satellite photographs have advanced the study of the weather and the making of maps from which weather forecasts are prepared. Satellites also employ remote sensing devices that create images of parts of the earth to supply particular kinds of information, such as the rocks that lie on the surface. Such photographs are useful in the search for minerals. Some satellites are able to monitor conditions in the atmosphere or in the oceans.

MEASURING POINTS

Satellites greatly help geodesists (scientists who study the size and shape of the earth). The study of the curvature of the earth is important to map-makers who are mapping large areas.

In the last 30 years, geodesists have set up a network of points around the world whose positions are known to within one meter. They do this by a system of triangulation. Geodesists at two stations can make simultaneous measurements of the angle of a satellite. If the positions of the satellite and one station are known, they can calculate the position of the second station.

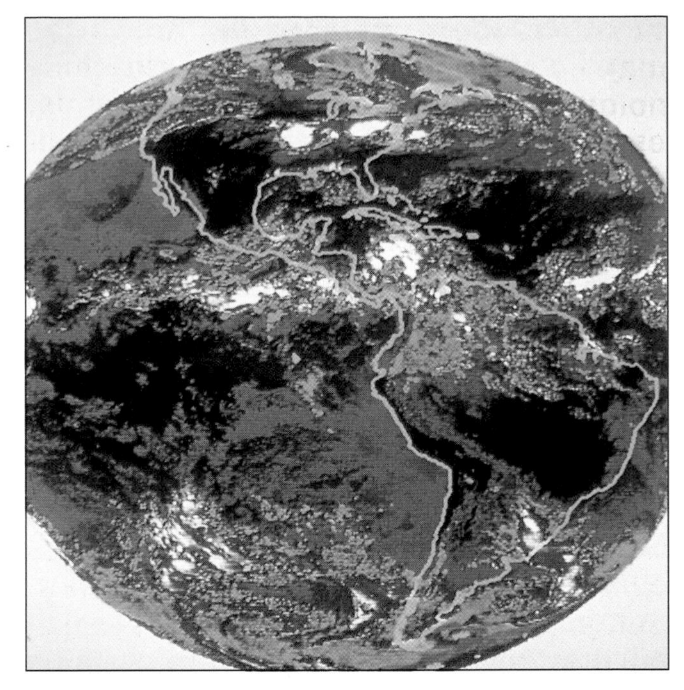

△ Satellite photographs are used to track weather formations. Regular photographs taken from space help weather forecasters to work out how the weather is behaving.

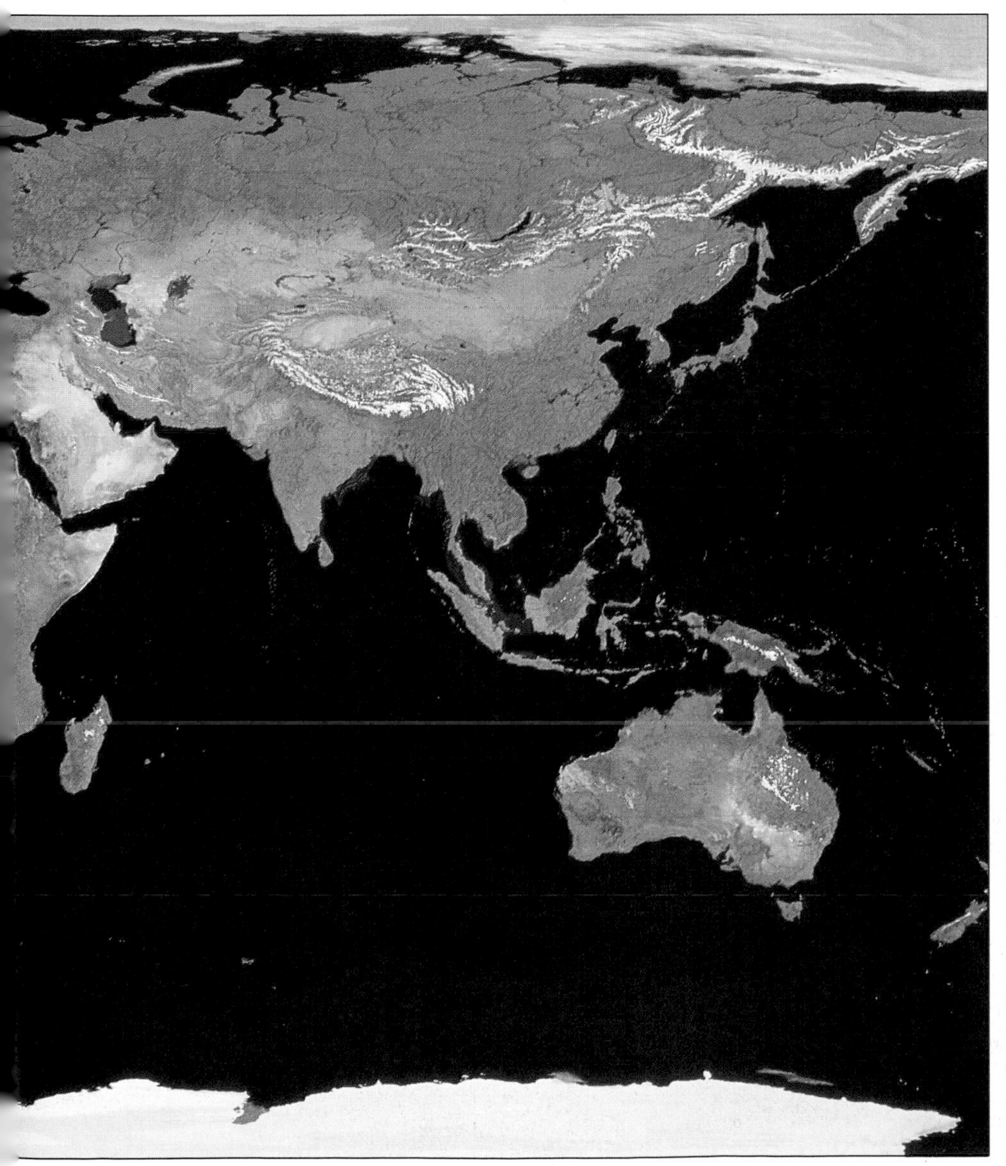

◁ Recently, a series of many photographs covering the whole of the earth's surface has been taken by satellites. Using sophisticated modern techniques, it has been possible to join these photographs together to make one complete picture of the whole of the earth.

DID YOU KNOW?

By the year 2000, you may be able to find your exact position within seconds. This system is based on a computer-receiver which receives signals from four satellites. The computer converts the time taken by the signals into distances and instantly works out its position.

PROJECTING A ROUND WORLD

Small areas are mapped as though the earth is flat. But when measuring long distances, map-makers must allow for the earth's curvature, which makes it impossible for map-makers to draw a totally accurate map of the world. This explains why the appearance of world maps varies from one atlas to another.

ORANGE PEEL

If you peel an orange, there is no way in which you can flatten the peel without breaking it. The same applies to the curved surface of the earth. As a result, map-makers use map projections which ensure that some map features, such as areas or distances, are true. But no world map can show all features accurately.

Most projections are worked out by mathematics. But they can be understood if you imagine that the globe is made of glass, with a light at its center.

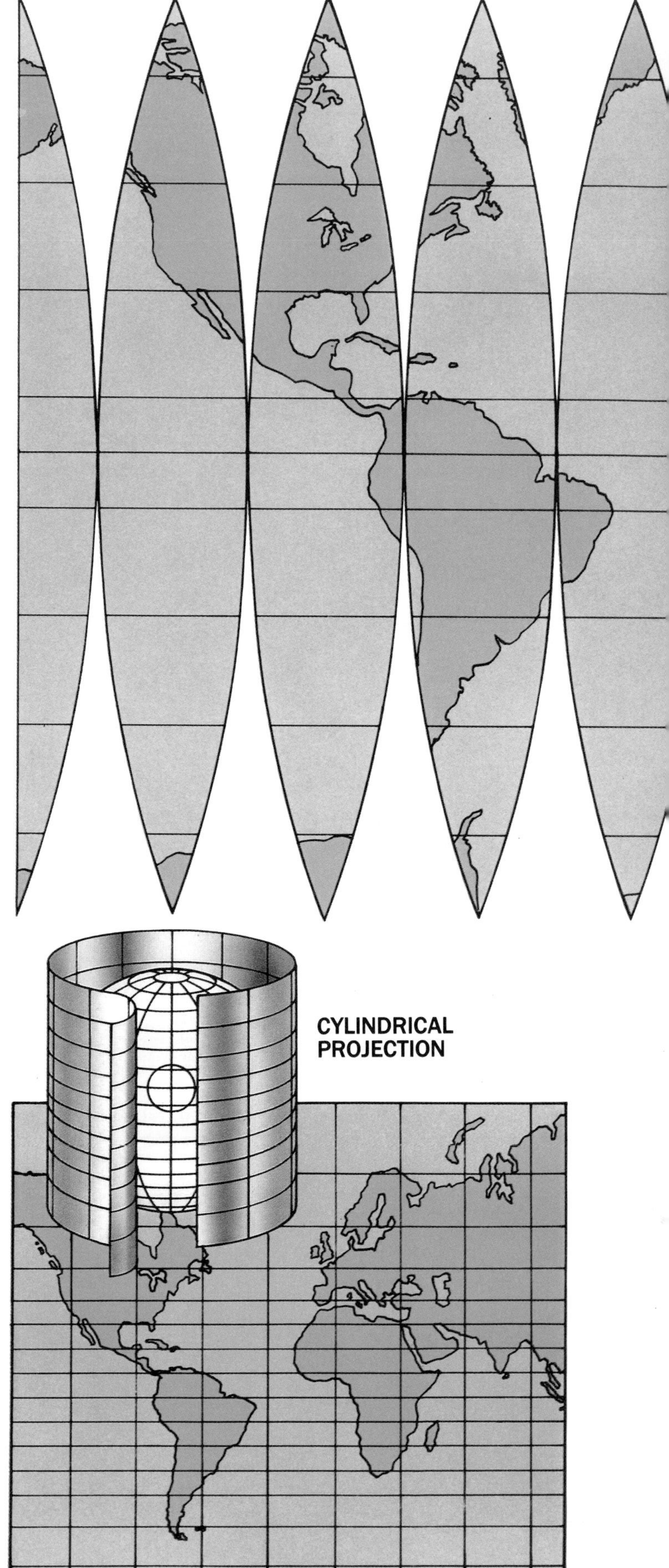

▷ An interrupted projection shows strips of the earth's surface, like those that globe-makers use. But as a world map, it is not very useful.

PROJECTIONS

A cylindrical projection is formed by wrapping a piece of paper around a globe, touching it along the equator. The light casts shadows of the graticule onto the paper. The length of the equator is the same on the cylinder as it is on the globe. But other lines of latitude are longer than those on the globe. The poles do not appear on this projection.

For azimuthal projections, imagine that the globe is resting on a piece of paper, touching it at one point. Away from this point, the projection becomes increasingly distorted. A third, conical, projection contains lines of latitude and longitude cast on a cone. Here the distortion increases away from the line of contact.

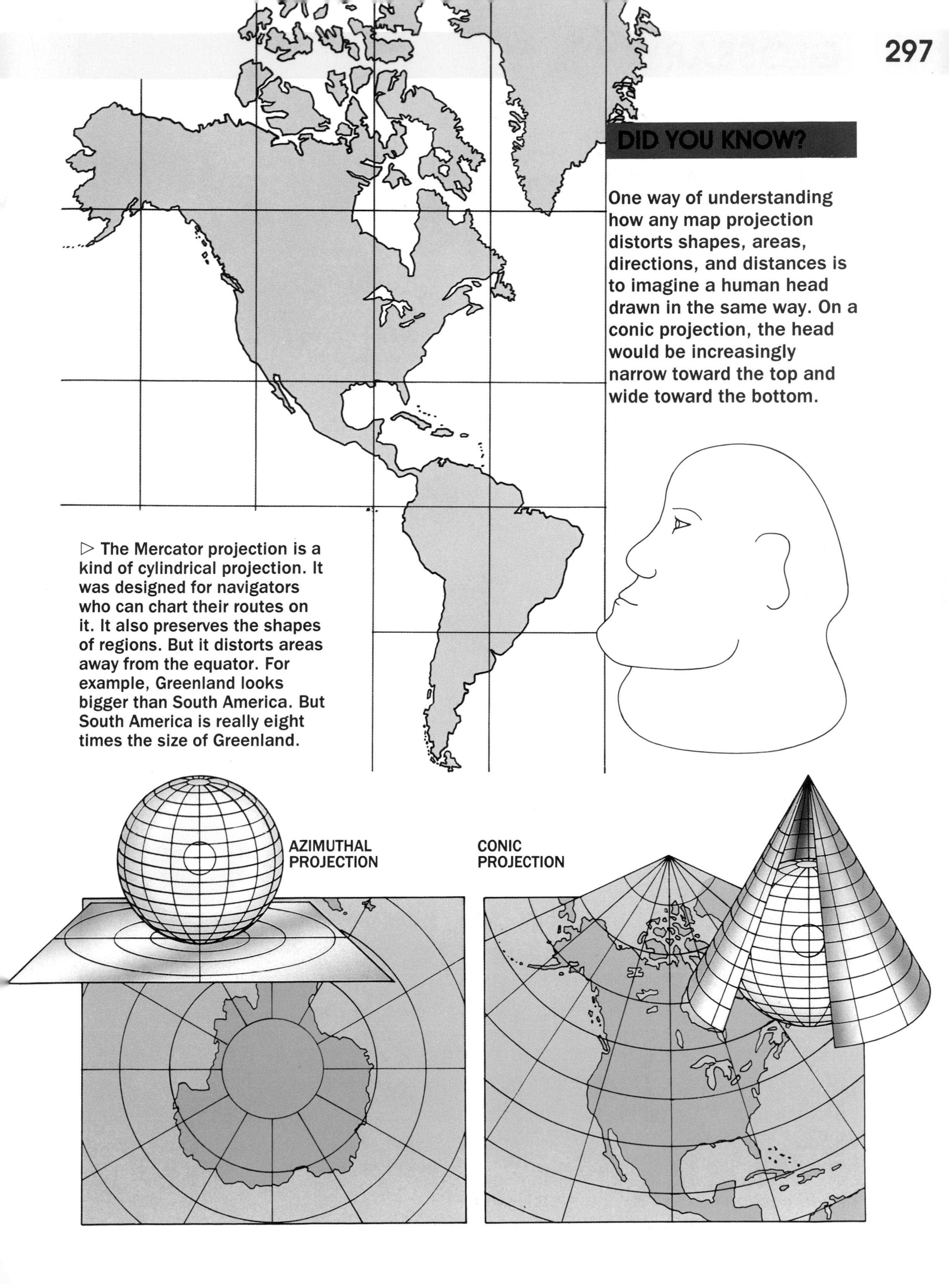

DID YOU KNOW?

One way of understanding how any map projection distorts shapes, areas, directions, and distances is to imagine a human head drawn in the same way. On a conic projection, the head would be increasingly narrow toward the top and wide toward the bottom.

▷ The Mercator projection is a kind of cylindrical projection. It was designed for navigators who can chart their routes on it. It also preserves the shapes of regions. But it distorts areas away from the equator. For example, Greenland looks bigger than South America. But South America is really eight times the size of Greenland.

Acid rain
Rain that is acidic because it contains dissolved sulphur dioxide and other substances. It causes damage to trees and buildings.

Air mass
A volume of warm, cold moist or dry air in the atmosphere.

Air pressure
The weight of the earth's atmosphere pressing down on the earth's surface (or any other surface).

Anticline
The type of fold in which layers of rock are domed upwards.

Anticyclone
An area of high pressure in the earth's atmosphere.

Barometer
An instrument that is used for measuring air pressure.

Bathyscape
A pressurized steel ball in which a person is lowered into the deep ocean.

Boreal forest
Northern forest zone consisting almost entirely of coniferous trees.

Canopy
The dense layers of leaves above the floor of a tropical rainforest.

CFCs
Organic gases (chlorofluorocarbons) used in refrigerators and aerosol sprays. These are released into the atmosphere where they can damage the ozone layer.

Cirque
Hollow in which a glacier forms.

Climate
The average weather in a particular place on earth.

Cloud forest
Mountain forest that occurs under a permanent layer of low cloud.

Condensation
The process in which water vapor turns into tiny drops of water as it cools below the dew point.

Conifers
Trees with thin needle shaped leaves, which produce seeds in cones.

Contour
A line on a map that joins places of equal height.

Convection
The process by which light, hot air rises, cools and then sinks before being heated again, creating a circular current.

Core
The central part of the earth. The inner core is solid metal; the outer core consists of molten iron.

Crude oil
A major fossil fuel mineral consisting of a sticky liquid mixture of hydrocarbons, also known as petroleum.

Crust
The outermost layer of the earth, consisting of the rocks that form the land and the ocean floors.

Cyclone
A region of low pressure in the atmosphere with winds that spiral inwards.

Deciduous
Describes trees that lose their leaves annually in the fall, and regrow them in spring.

Depression
An area of low pressure in the earth's atmosphere.

Dew point
The temperature at which water vapor in the air condenses into droplets.

Drumlins
Rounded hills formed by a deposition from a glacier.

Electrolysis
A chemical reaction brought about by an electrical current. Typically a salt, either insolution cr in its molten state, is decomposed into its component elements.

Emergent
Tall tropical tree that reaches up to 65ft above the forest canopy.

Epiphyte
A plant that physically grows on another, but without harming its host.

Erratic
Rock fragment or boulder transported far from its source.

Fossil fuel
Any mineral, based on carbon, that is extracted for use as a fuel. Examples of this include coal, oil or natural gas.

Graticule
A network of lines of latitude and longitude on a map or globe.

Greenhouse effect
Overheating of the earth's atmosphere caused by a build-up of gases such as carbon dioxide (which prevents heat from escaping into outer space).

Grid
A framework of squares on a map which helps map-users to find the places they want on the map.

Guyot
A flat-topped underwater mountain, formed when a volcano "sinks".

Humidity
The amount of moisture in the air.

Hydrocarbon
A chemical compound of hydrogen and carbon; oil (petroleum) and natural gas are hydrocarbons.

Igneous rock
The type of rock that forms when magma becomes solid.

Isobars
Lines on a weather map that join places with the same air pressure.

Laterite
Infertile tropical dust stained red by the presence of iron oxide.

Latitude
On maps, the equator and other lines parallel to it are lines of latitude, or parallels. They are stated in degrees from the centre of the earth, from 0 degrees at the equator to 90 degrees North at the North Pole and 90 degrees South at the South Pole.

Loess
Sand and soil that has been deposited by the wind.

Longitude
Lines of longitude, or meridians, run at right angles to lines of latitude. Lines of longitude are measured 180 degrees East and West of the prime meridian (0 degrees longitude).

Mangroves
Trees that grow in coastal subtropical swamps.

Mantle
The layer of the earth between the crust and the outer core.

Metamorphic rock
The type of rock that forms when temperature, pressure or other forces change other rock types in form or in chemical composition.

Meteorology
The science of studying the weather.

Moraine
A concentration of rock fragments transported by a glacier.

Neap tide
A low tide that occurs when the moon and sun are at right angles to each other, and their combined gravity pulls ocean waters.

Nodule
A rounded lump of matter. A few metalic minerals occur as nodules on the seabed.

Ore
A mineral that contains enough metal (usually as one of its chemical compounds) to be worth mining.

Photosynthesis
The process by which plants use sunlight to convert water and air into food.

Pingo
Crater formed by ice block erupting onto surface.

Plate tectonics
The theory that crustal plates move causing continental drift, earthquakes, and volcanoes, and result in the formation of mountains.

Prime meridian
The line of longitude (0 degrees) that runs from the North Pole, through Greenwich, London, to the South Pole.

Rainforest
Lush forest with a high rainfall. The term is often used to refer to tropical rainforest.

Recycling
A method of saving resources by reusing the materials in discarded goods.

Refining
The extraction of metals from their ores, or of purifying metals after smelting.

Relief
Differences in the height of the land.

Sedimentary rock
The type of rock that forms when sediments (of particles such as soil and sand) form layers under water and are squeezed by pressure to form rock. Some sedimentary rocks are formed from deposits of chemicals.

Spring tide
A particular high tide that occurs when the moon and sun are in line, and their gravitational pull acts on the waters in the oceans.

Stratosphere
The layer of the atmosphere between 9 and 31 miles above the earth.

Thermal
A rising current of warm air.

Triangulation
The method of measuring the land based on the principle that if you know the length of one side of a triangle and all three angles, then you can calculate the lengths of the other sides. It is often used in map-making.

Tundra
Windswept zone with little vegetation. It stretches between the polar regions and the temperate zones.

INDEX

Photographic credits:
Aerad Customer Services, Ancient Art and Architecture Collection, Ardea, Aviation Picture Library, British Nuclear Fuels Ltd, Bruce Coleman Ltd, Christie Dodwell, Dan Brooks, David A.Hardy, The Environmental Picture Library, Eye Ubiquitous, Frank Lane Picture Agency, Frank Spooner Pictures, Greenpeace, Harper Collins Publishers Ltd, The Hulton Picture Company, The Hutchison Library, J. Allan Cash Photo Library, The London Transport Museum, Magnum Photos, Mary Evans Picture Library, NASA, National Maritime Museum Picture Library, National Meteorological Library, NHPA, Oxford Scientific Films, Panos Pictures, Paul Nightingale, Planet Earth Pictures, Rex Features, Robert Harding Picture Library, Roger Vlitos, Science Photo Library, Spectrum Colour Library, Topham Picture Source, Zefa.